TO THE READER

This is a work of non-fiction. All the characters and events depicted in this book are real.

The material is derived from my three-plus years investigation of a death penalty case, which includes the reading of a voluminous trial and post-conviction record, estimated at over 156,000 pages. It also stems from the relationship I developed with Joseph O'Dell's post-conviction law firm, as both an investigator and consultant. Other sources of information include interviews with witnesses and jurors, and information obtained through personal knowledge and discussions with Joseph O'Dell and the lawyers. Referenced in this book are materials that I offer you on my web site, www.loristjohn.com, where I share a variety of never before seen documents and numerous media related materials including TV, radio, video and print articles depicting the wide and international coverage this story received.

Lori St John

ADVANCE UNCORRECTED PROOFS
Please do not quote for publication
without checking against the finished book.

Tentative On-Sale Date: June 26, 2013
Tentative Publication Date: June 28, 2013
Tentative Price: $28.99
Publicity Contact: Suzy Ginsburg,
Global Communication Works,
Tel: 713-721-4774 or email suzy@gcomworks.com

Please note that books will not be available
in stores until the above on-sale date.
All reviews should be scheduled to run after that date.

Please call 303-906-8656 closer to publication date for details.
www.loristjohn.com

Printed in the United States of America

Library of Congress Cataloging-in-Publication Data
Creative Production Services, Inc.

The Corruption of Innocence, a Journey for Justice / Creative Production Services, Inc.

ISBN 978-0-9890401-0-5 (hardcover)

Editing by Ann Fisher
Proofreading by Hilary Westwood
Cover Design by Marc J Cohen
Text Design and composition by Marc J Cohen

To place orders
Email:info@loristjohn.com or visit www.loristjohn.com

Book Discounts for bulk sales are available.

Visit www.loristjohn.com for comprehensive material related to The Corruption of Innocence, including photographs, documents and media related articles, TV, radio and YouTube videos

First Edition

For my darling daughter Jennifer,

and to the memory of her father, Dr. Walter Urs

Contents

Foreword

A powerful and compelling true story. *The Corruption of Innocence* takes the reader on an insider's journey—a rare telescopic view—of an egregious miscarriage of justice. Lori St John's intense commitment to shine a light on a compromised legal system portrays a Herculean effort to discover and share the truth in the death penalty case of a man, Joseph O'Dell, whom she believes to be innocent. And after you descend into the labyrinth of injustices that happen to this man in court after court, I'm willing to wager you'll think him innocent, too.

The story reads like a thriller—a race against the clock. But time is not on Lori's side. The setbacks and constant sabotaging of her efforts keeps narrowing the window of time that is needed to prove O'Dell's innocence. The suspense never lets up, and because there are so many twists and turns, it continues to keep the reader riveted to the unfolding story.

I was privileged to work with Lori and to witness her dedication as she led a fearless fight for justice. It is an in inspiring and remarkable story of the power of one person's ability to make a difference and a tragic indictment of a flawed and callous court system.

— Sister Helen Prejean, csj
Author of the book *Dead Man Walking*

Cast of Characters

Joseph (Joe) O'Dell	Death row inmate
Lori Urs	Advocate for Joseph O'Dell
Jennifer (Jen) Urs	Daughter of Lori Urs
Dr. Walter Urs	Husband of Lori Urs
Helen Schartner	The victim
Sister Helen Prejean	Anti-death penalty advocate and Joe O'Dell's spiritual advisor
Albert Alberi	Trial prosecutor
Stephen Test	Trial prosecutor
Paul Ray	Joe O'Dell's trial lawyer (co-counsel)
Richard Reyna	Investigator who worked with Lori Urs
Robert (Bob) Smith	Joe O'Dell's post-conviction attorney
Joseph Moore	The drunk who found Helen Schartner's body
Jacqueline Emrich	Prosecution's scientific expert

Diane Lavett	Joe O'Dell's scientific expert
Timothy Bougades (Tim Carmello or "Bud")	Witness to Joe O'Dell's alibi (the fight
Judge Spain	Trial judge
Judge Spencer	District Court Judge
Steven (Steve) Watson	The jailhouse snitch
Connie Craig	Joe O'Dell's lover and the Commonwealth's main witness at trial
Floyd (Ike) Wright	Helen Schartner's boyfriend
Dr. Joseph Guth	Joe O'Dell's scientific expert
William Honbarger	Insurance investigator for the County Line Executive Inn
Joe Jackson	Reporter for the Virginian-Pilot newspaper
George Allen	Governor of Virginia
Vito Piraino	Italian Consulate in Virginia
Luciano Neri	Leader of the Italian Parliament campaign to save Joseph O'Dell
Franco Danieli	Member of the Italian Parliament
Senator Mario Occhipinti	Member of the Italian Parliament
Calogero (Rino) Piscitello	Member of the Italian Parliament
Monsignor Gabriele Caccia	Assistant to the Secretary of State at the Vatican
Rosa Jervolino Russo	Member of the Italian Parliament

Mayor Leoluca Orlando	Member of the Italian and European Parliaments
Georgio Morelli	Italian newspaper reporter
Clive Stafford Smith	Joe O'Dell's post-conviction attorney
Dr. Michael Baden	Scientific expert who offered opinion during post-conviction investigation
Warden J.D. Netherland	Warden at Mecklenburg Correctional Center
John Nutter	Joe O'Dell's alibi (man he fought with)
Barry Scheck	DNA expert

Prologue

As the daughter of a state Attorney General and wife of a prominent orthopedic surgeon, I would have been aghast at the suggestion
that one day I would marry a death row inmate on the day of his execution. But here I am in the death house standing in a circle holding
hands with a nun, a minister and Joseph Roger O'Dell III. On the
other side of the world, gathered in the town square of Palermo, Italy,
parliamentarians watch by satellite broadcast, surrounded by Secret
Service men with dark visors shielding the sun from their eyes, while
mine have been seared by the horror of what has led to this day. I am
here—I know because cameras are everywhere and the marriage is being broadcast around the world, yet I am numb, almost paralyzed from
having witnessed and participated in the ceremonial preparation for
his death.

Joseph O'Dell was sentenced to die for raping and murdering a
Virginia Beach secretary. But if the Commonwealth of Virginia hadn't
denied his request for DNA testing, would it have proven him innocent? He had strongly proclaimed his innocence from the day of his
arrest, throughout his trial, and for twelve years on death row, up to
and including today, the day they plan to stick a needle in his already
prepared veins to ensure his uncomplicated death.

My eyes are still transfixed on the execution chamber in the room directly beside me. I can hear myself breathe as I watch the phone that sits on a nearby table, waiting for it to ring. Any minute now. Sister Helen Prejean by my side, millions of our supporters, including the Pope and Mother Teresa, are attending via satellite TV. After a pause to observe the clock on the wall, I reach for the ring that has dropped to the cement floor, my feet unsteady as I rise to join in the ceremony. I am being watched, scrutinized by the press and people from all around the world, so I will not cry. Tears would simply release all that's bottled up inside after so many years. I am not ready for that. Not yet. I still have so much to do.

The Corruption of Innocence

Chapter 1

~ Destiny ~

September, 1993. A cool, autumn day. I'm sitting in a yuppie cafe called Rosas, sipping a cup of tea while casually reading the Princeton Packet. I'm at one of those well-known crossroads in life, searching for a new purpose, not realizing it would stare me in the face on page three. Since the death of my mother in 1987 my life had drastically changed. My father passed away just two years earlier at the age of 65. This was followed by my separation from an incredibly successful and drop-dead gorgeous husband. I longed for a new and different life, seeking something other than tennis, lunch dates, hospital balls and shopping. Little did I know that I would soon move from a comfortable, sheltered world to a world of prisons, death and corrupt politics.

As I watch the morning crowd, I recall a recent interview in Trenton for a job at a children's home. I wanted to help those less fortunate and thought it was a great opportunity to work with homeless kids. But I soon realized that working with children, in that setting, was not for me. I wanted to give back in a personal way, not monetarily, as was suggested when the interviewer first met me. I suppose my current lifestyle revealed itself all too well. Gold jewelry, manicured nails and carefully selected outfit with matching shoes. The interview was short and I left unsatisfied. I needed, wanted desperately, to feel passionate about something.

The cafe was busy. It was 8:00 a.m. and I had just dropped my daughter Jennifer off at the elite Princeton Day School. Then something in the paper I was reading caught my eye. "Princeton Organization Frees Wrongly Convicted Persons." I read about this seemingly misplaced organization, situated right here in the middle of Princeton, New Jersey. "Wrongly convicted, spending life in prison or facing a death sentence." I thought, how could this be? *The system doesn't work?* Before this morning I had no reason to believe the system didn't work, nor did I care. Like the vast majority of people I was more concerned with getting ahead and making the right impression.

"That's it!" I said aloud, oblivious to those seated near me sipping coffee or tea with their croissants and pastry. I knew I needed to find out more about this organization called Centurion Ministries. What could be worse than being locked up in prison for something you didn't do? The article mentioned volunteers did most of the work so I had a way in. "This is what I want," I shouted, as if anyone around me cared. I felt invigorated, already planning on marching into the organization for an interview, along with a new focus in life.

I park across the street from Princeton University. The majestic college buildings fit in beautifully with the ambience of the streets of Princeton. Inside a gray building on Nassau Street I take the narrow elevator to the third floor. As I enter the small, simple room of Centurion Ministries I am immediately comfortable. It's an unpretentious atmosphere, and oh what a change from my 15-year career as a certified public accountant. The greatest excitement came back when I took the grueling CPA exam, my unborn child furiously kicking away in my belly, challenging my ability to remain focused. Even though there were many times when I enjoyed my career and had started my own practice, I was still unsatisfied. Something was missing.

A smiling, friendly woman greets me at the front desk which is adjacent to another room where three volunteers are eagerly reading through letters from inmates. Their desks are cluttered with legal papers and correspondence, giving hope to those who are so desperate for freedom. I have a few minutes to wait for the boss, Jim McCloskey, so I browse the room, scanning the newspaper articles on the walls, framed for their importance and indication of success. The first article I read is of a man wrongly convicted of rape, freed after spending ten years in prison. I move on. Another man, charged with murder, freed after a long investigation revealed he was innocent. One after the next, just begging my attention and intriguing my thirst for excitement, passion and a sense of purpose.

The interview goes well, and they say they will call me next week. But the very next day Kate, the office manager, telephones. "Come on in and we'll put you to work. We could use your help." She points to a desk and gives me some simple instructions. "Read the letters that pour in from hundreds of inmates around the country and make a preliminary determination whether they fit our guidelines for help. The inmate must be facing a life sentence, or death, and have exhausted all of their appeals," she says matter of factly. *Nothing like desperation,* I thought. I read the letters with intense interest, creating index cards for my inmates and sending standardized forms back to those that seemingly fit our criteria, while rejecting others.

In one letter the words "rape" and "innocent" jump out at me. Having grown up in the suburbs of West Hartford, Connecticut, I am ill-prepared for the rude awakening I instantly receive. During my lifetime, the only encounter I ever had with crime was through TV and the newspapers. An occasional bus ride into Hartford for clothes shopping was the closest I came to seeing the city and its less privileged population.

****

My father was an assistant Attorney General for the State of Connecticut, my mother a costume designer for the Hartford Ballet Company. She taught evening tailoring classes at the local high school. I remember watching my father leave the house dressed for court. He was an impeccable dresser. Always wore a bow tie, a handkerchief in his suit pocket and a stylish hat. A graduate from Yale University, UConn law school and president of the Hartford chess club, he set a fine example. We were one of few Catholic families (my dad was Catholic, my mom was Jewish) living in a Jewish neighborhood. I remember feeling like I a minority during my teenage years, thinking the world was mostly Jewish, until I got to college.

I grew up resenting the gold and diamonds dripping off the socialites in town and the snobby cliquish girls I went to school with. It was sweet revenge when I showed up at a high school reunion, more successful, thinner, more attractive and happier than most of my classmates. Even more important was the realization, after being fortunate enough to be financially in the top 1 percent of the people in our country, that money was not the answer to a happy life.

My father was diagnosed with multiple sclerosis when I was only 14 years old and I remember our family being devastated by the news. I often questioned why God would do this to such a wonderful, good man. At the age of 14 I was angry. I felt a sense of injustice had been laid upon my family. I believe it led to my desire to take up for the underdog and challenge authority. I even earned the nickname "Annie Oakley" from my mom. "Get your gun," she used to say to me when I would become outraged about something or other.

I recall the day I walked onto the soccer fields in East Brunswick, New Jersey. I was the new mom in town. My husband, Walter and I had just built a 10,000-square-foot, million-dollar mansion on two acres of land. It was a Country French chateau with huge African mahogany front doors leading to a grand entranceway. There was a formal dining room with parquet wood flooring, adjacent to a living room adorned with a decorative fireplace. A handcrafted mantel draped over the top of the wood-burning conversation piece. Carefully patterned with Italian marble, the rooms were defined by beautiful wood columns. Eight separate French doors led out to the veranda where two ceiling fans hung above the decorative table and chairs, sprawled out to take advantage of the view to the pool. Majestic arched hallways led to the kitchen and grand family room, which had a full wall fireplace crafted out of stone. On the other side of the house was the master suite with its own fireplace, and two walk-in closets filled with the finest clothes. I remember watching as the contractor took three weeks to carefully lay the marble in the bathroom which, amazingly, could fit ten people in it. The house was wired with an extraordinary sound system and alarms were everywhere. Upstairs from the master bedroom were three other bedrooms, all with private baths. The crown molding throughout the house was so massive and beautiful it could have decorated my home without furniture. And so, we lived in luxury and socialized with many of the elite families in town.

Nevertheless, I walked onto the soccer field with holes in my jeans wearing a hundred-dollar pair of shoes. I mean the jeans had holes *everywhere*, and I paid dearly for them that way. The women all turned and stared at me as if I were from another planet. I smiled and knew that not a single one of them was better than me. They were all striving to live the life I was so fortunate to be living. My new wealth and status in the community did not make me feel better than others. Instead, it gave me a new sense of freedom. Spiritual freedom. This spiritual freedom would grow profound as I became increasingly aware of myself through my work as an investigator and death row advisor.

****

He was innocent, he said. Yeah, that's what they all say.

Joseph Roger O'Dell III. Born September 20, 1941. Charged with the capital murder, rape and sodomy of a Virginia Beach secretary. Arrested on February 8, 1985. Sentenced to die on November 11, 1986. A death row inmate. I was assigned his case. I had seen his name on the "board" as a potentially innocent man wrongly accused and facing death. On the wall outside of Kate's office was the board. If you were lucky enough to be listed on it, you were among the few fortunate men or women whose cases we would take on. Joe's name would become internationally known, but for now he was just a death row con.

It was on February 6, 1985, at 8:30 p.m. on a cold rainy night, when Helen Schartner met up with friends and a cousin at a country western bar, the County Line Lounge, in Virginia Beach. It was "ladies' night" and packed with city-slick cowboys. Helen sat at a table with four women, Dana Wade, Linda Bunton, Janice Bailey and her daughter Jennifer Hunt. They drank and danced until approximately 11:15 p.m., when Helen's boyfriend, Ike Wright, walked through the saloon door. He slow danced with Helen, and after a brief bathroom visit she returned only to find his arms in a similar embrace around another woman. Visibly upset, Helen left at approximately 11:25 p.m., and no later than 11:30 p.m. She was carrying a black umbrella, her car keys and pocketbook.

Joseph O'Dell was at the same bar that night. He was seen by the victim's cousin on the other side of the nightclub. It was established there was no contact between Joe and the victim that night, or any other time, nor did they know one another. Testimony at trial from an employee revealed that Joe O'Dell was still at the bar at midnight. When questioned how he remembered the time, he replied, "That's when we stop collecting the cover charge. I was counting the money when I looked up and saw Joe O'Dell by the bathroom area."[1]

Unchallenged by the defense was the prosecution's claim that Joe waited outside for the victim. As she approached her car he slid a gun to her side, forcing her into his car where he began a violent sexual as-

---

[1] Trial Transcript, Vol. 21, Tab 57, page 37 (paraphrased).

sault, strangling her before dumping her body in a muddy field across the street, behind the parking lot of the After Midnight Club. She was found the next day by a passerby, who never testified at trial. She had been beaten in the head, her clothes soaked with blood. The prosecution claimed O'Dell then went across town, showed up in the parking lot of another bar, covered with the victim's blood, and walked into to a 7-Eleven convenience store before returning to his girlfriend Connie's house. Having no explanation for O'Dell's lack of concern—having just committed a murder and showing up in a public parking lot of a bar he is known to frequent—the prosecution claimed he was "high" from the murder.

My job was to find out the truth. Was Joseph O'Dell a rapist and murderer, or was he facing the death penalty for a crime he knew nothing about? Either way, strangely enough, I have no fear of him.

The case is a huge undertaking so to encourage me along I am told by Centurion staffers that they are impressed with my intelligence and dedication (they probably just love the endless hours I'm putting in). After given the task of reading the trial transcript and summarizing Joe's case, I am instructed to contact a major New York law firm to obtain the entire record.

My first phone call is to an associate lawyer at Paul, Weiss, Rifkind, Wharton & Garrison, a prominent law firm with offices all over the world. Jeff Eilender was assigned the *pro bono* case. He speaks to me with reserved kindness. After informing him of our investigation into Joe's claim of innocence I could hear the skepticism in his voice, the reluctance to *share* his client with anyone. His hesitation gives me the impression he thinks we are radicals ready to free even the guilty from prison.

A week later we receive four huge boxes filled with 31 volumes of trial transcripts. The boxes contain pre-trial motions, the trial record, and post-trial motions. My task is to read the transcript, summarize it and make a list of witnesses from the record for our investigation. As

I read the file I begin to create a summary of the transcript by volume number, including a list of the witnesses and the location of their testimony in the transcript. The list would ultimately include their address, mother's name, girlfriends, anything that will help identify and later find them in the investigation. In the meantime, I read scores of legal documentation. From privileged interviews with Joe O'Dell, to psychiatric evaluations, his prison record and court documentation spread from 1985 through 1993. I was creating what would later become my "bible"—a summarized source of information at my fingertips that will give me the knowledge and power to fight on his behalf, like no other advocate in the world. At the moment, I was just doing my job.

The volunteers' desks are side-by-side forming a square in the middle of the room. They are all down-to-earth, good people, and I love working with them. Often I arrive earlier than anyone and am the last to turn off the lights. The task of reading the material is actually fun for me. I relish the idea of pulling it all together, like an old Dick Tracy mystery. I soon realize this work is for me—it's either in your blood or not.

Reading the transcript is like watching a play. The characters are unfolding right before my eyes. I am getting a good sense of the witnesses, the prosecutor, the defense, the judge and the defendant. It's the only way to really understand what happens at trial. No wonder many appellate lawyers struggle with the record—no one practicing law has enough time to read the voluminous material I was assigned to summarize. I, too, will never be able to devote so many hours, days, months and years to a single case. For now, it is starting to become my daily work routine.

Meanwhile, something else was happening in my life. The reading of this case inspired me to pursue an interest in justice that occasionally accompanies new law students. I eagerly take the Kaplan course to prepare for the law school admission test (LSAT) exam. This exam is designed to test your ability to be successful in law school. It was a night course, and I religiously make the drive to and from the classroom and study hard in preparation for the exam in February 1994. My determination was compromised only two months prior to the test.

Christmas Eve, 1993. I was returning from a lavish dinner party at the home of a close friend in Pennsylvania. With a drift of snow on the ground I travel the bleak highway home. Unaware of the conditions beneath the road I hit black ice at 50 mph. The Mercedes Benz started spinning out of control, heading straight for another car that had met with the same fate just minutes before. In the split seconds before the crash I thought silently to myself "I am going to die." Amazingly, I am not afraid. While the car sustains major damage, I survive. The accident leaves me with neck and back problems which interfere with my studying ability, but nonetheless, does not deter me.

In the middle of a blizzard, during the freezing month of February, I drove to the Kaplan office to use the tapes while preparing for the LSAT exam. My neck and back were killing me. But as Walter always said, "It's only pain." He was a football player at the University of Connecticut—a typical jock, extremely bright and ambitious. Tall, dark, curly hair with a mustache framing his mouth, he was every woman's dream. Mine too. We met in his first year of medical school. He went on to become an orthopedic surgeon, one of the best on the east coast. Women always fawned all over my husband. Fortunately, Walter always ignored it, until we separated. Even then he was loyal and faithful, until time took its toll on us both. As I was in search of some meaning in my life, he was finding his own.

It was the day of the exam. I woke up that morning with painful neck spasms. I made an emergency appointment with my therapist and prayed for relief. It didn't work. The spasms and pain only got worse. I went to the exam with six Advil in my stomach and a back brace wrapped around my sore body. My score did not reflect my ability to perform well in school. I knew this. I felt I had a natural gift to succeed in law school. I enjoyed my work far too much for failure. I decided to take the test again. I continued to study and exercise and took the exam for the second time in May 1994. The results would come out in June, too late for admittance into law school that year. As a result I was placed on waiting lists. So I waited. I reapplied several months later, in December of 1994.

As it turned out this was a blessing in disguise. My future was unfolding almost in a predestined fashion, surprisingly without my awareness or permission. I was unaware of the incredible experience I would gain during the next year of my life, an experience that no law school could offer me. By the time I entered law school in 1995, I was well on my way to learning how the system really worked, not how ideally it should function. Was there a difference between the two?

I was accepted into several schools. Opening the first letter of acceptance was sweet. Like a teenage girl I ran around the house, arms flailing in the air, thrilled that my future was now unfolding. As other acceptances arrived I made my choice. It would be New England School of Law. It was a small school with an excellent reputation, located in downtown Boston, and close to my summer house on Cape Cod. I planned on using the place as a weekend getaway, but would soon later find out that the first year of law school is so demanding there is no such thing as spare time. Except to go to the food market for sustenance, or one of three trips to the mall that year. Having now been accepted into law school, I continued to delve into Joe O'Dell's case.

The reading of the trial record taught me legal terminology which helped considerably in law school the following year. I had *Black's Law Dictionary* by my side and enthusiastically looked up each and every word that appeared foreign to me. There were *many* of them. As time progressed the word "exculpatory" would have significant meaning to the O'Dell case. It meant "Evidence tending to establish a criminal defendant's innocence."[2] It also could be applied to any "favorable evidence for the defense," such as evidence tending to show that a witness was lying or that mitigation evidence could help reduce one's culpability. I was beginning to learn a new language.

As I steadfastly read the pre-trial motions, I become aware of some inconsistencies in the testimony. In the middle of reading at my Centurion desk I mumble to myself, not so softly, "Those liars, I can't believe it! On page two you said something completely different." My colleagues seem amused at my display of emotion. When I later left Centurion they told me they missed my outbursts as I read through the voluminous transcript. My passion was steadily growing. With each passing day I acquired new and useful information for the investigation of this death row case. Information that would challenge the death penalty verdict handed down by twelve very confident, but inexperienced jurors.

I created a list of inconsistencies and areas to investigate. In my mind I sized up the prosecutor and detectives and was able to evaluate whether a witness was credible or not. This is much easier to do when you read a script already laid out in front of you. I imagine it would have been much harder had I been sitting in the courtroom, even with the opportunity to observe the witness's demeanor.

~The Arrest~

As I dissected the 15,000-page transcript I quickly became aware that there were few main characters in this play. Connie Craig was Joseph's landlord and lover. In her sixties, she was 20 years his senior, still wearing pink hot pants and high heels. I envisioned her to be an old country-style lady, trying to hold on to her faded youth by dating a young "stud", as Joe was often referred to by her. Joe later claimed he

---

[2] *Black's Law Dictionary* 475 (8th ed. 2005).

was using her for a steady address for parole, plus the material and sexual favors he could obtain from her. He also said he loved her. Later, he would tell me it was in a maternal sort of way. Theirs was a fractious relationship. He was always out, gone days at a time. She begged to hold him down, jealous of his encounters with other women, especially the younger ones.

I am reading this murder mystery line by line, but I know it is not a mystery so I pay careful attention to the details. The morning after the murder, Joseph O'Dell had gone to Connie's house to crash. He knocked on the door and after being let in sometime later, told her he had vomited blood on his clothes and asked her if she would wash them for him. He placed them in the garage. He would later explain that he didn't tell her about a fight he'd been in the previous evening for fear she would call his parole officer and send him back to prison for being in an area he was forbidden to visit—a clear parole violation. So he stuck with his bleeding ulcer story of vomiting blood on his clothes.

The next morning, Joe threw on some jeans, a clean shirt, and grabbed a cup of coffee before letting the screen door slap his butt on the way out. He was off to his job as an engineering machinist at the General Foam Plastics Corp. in Norfolk. Joe was an exceptional worker who was very good with his hands. At home, startling news from the day before was beginning to unfold. Splashed on every television station and the front page of the local paper, was the sensational story of the rape and murder of a 42-year-old woman named Helen Schartner. Connie would later testify it was "intuition" that told her Joseph had committed the crime. He was out the night before and she was angry and jealous over his womanizing. She had, once before, called the police to inform them that she felt Joe had murdered a girl. This turned out to be untrue. The judge would later characterize Connie: "She was after your case, no doubt about it. It was obvious there was no love lost between you."[3] For now, she could provide me with valuable information about Joe's habits, routine and history with women.

Unsuspecting of the fact that he would soon be on trial for a vicious rape and murder, Joe went about his day like any other. On his way home he stopped to see his parole officer. Eleven years earlier he had been arrested in Florida for the robbery and kidnapping of a convenience store clerk. He spent seven years in prison on a 99-year sentence. It was a mystery to everyone how he had gotten out so early. Later in the investigation he would tell me the reason behind his early release. He had always been secretive, claiming he didn't want me involved, or hurt in any way. The truth was, he said, he had been involved with Mafia drug dealers in prison. When he got caught smuggling drugs in the Florida prisons, he made a deal with the Feds to testify against the dealers. He claimed to participate in setting them up. It was heavy stuff I thought. Was this true, or an embellished war story? I would read about this in great detail at the end of the investigation when I read his biography. He would later disclaim the biography as fiction, due to its incriminating contents. No inmate wants to be labeled a snitch. On death row it was suicide.

Connie ran to the garage after reading about the murder in the paper. "The clothes were soaked in blood," she would later testify. Hysterical and not knowing what to do she placed a call to Joe's younger sister, Sheila Knox. "Sheila, there's blood all over Joe's clothes. I think he murdered that woman at the County Line Lounge. What should I do? Should I call the police?"

Sheila would, many years later, regret her answer. They set a plan in motion. Connie would call the police and lure Joseph home, acting like nothing was wrong. She would leave a note for Sheila behind a picture frame, just in case anything happened to her. Since there were no witnesses to the crime and no connection between the victim and

---

[3] *Commonwealth v. Joseph O'Dell*, Petition for Executive Clemency, page 38, footnote 9.

Joseph O'Dell, Connie would become the Commonwealth's main witness.

Joseph arrived home at around 7:00 p.m. As usual Connie prepared dinner, fearful that a change in routine would alert him that something was amiss. After they ate, Joe reached into the laundry basket for a clean towel and went straight for the shower. While soaping the grease off his body he yelled to Connie, "Can you get me some clean clothes?" Quickly, Connie ran to the garage to fetch some. She reached through the pile of clothes she had thrown out on the front porch days earlier, searching for a pair of pants and a shirt. She prayed he didn't notice the missing bloodied clothes from the night before, her heart pounding as she handed him trousers and a long-sleeved shirt through the open bathroom door. The police had already been to the house to pick up the bloodstained clothing. They instructed Connie to keep him at home until they ran some tests.

Bingo! Type O—the same as the victim. The police called Connie to tell her they were on their way. Within minutes the SWAT team had surrounded the house. At midnight there was a knock on the front door. Unsuspecting, Joe asked, "Who's that at this hour?" He was lying in bed, totally naked. With a facade of bewilderment Connie walked through the living room and reached with sweaty palms for the antique knob on the door. Instantly, several cops rush through the house and into the bedroom, guns pointed at Joe's head. "Get dressed O'Dell, you're coming with us. You have the right to remain silent. Anything you say can and will be used against you in a court of law..." Joe knew the routine.

Chapter 2

~The Trial Transcript~

From January through June, 1994 I steadfastly read through the transcript, outlining and preparing my notes. During these six months I devote at least 20 hours a week to reading the record. Some weeks I devote more than 40, as I've been informed that the initial stage of the investigation is crucial for acquiring knowledge. By June I had read 26 volumes of transcripts and had five volumes left. I estimate the number of pages to be 15,470. It would cost somewhere between $5,000 and $7,000 to obtain a copy of the trial transcript, but we got it free, courtesy of Paul, Weiss, Rifkind, Wharton & Garrison.

In February, 1985 Joe O'Dell was assigned a public defender named Peter Leigler. Peter would later ask to be relieved of his services due to a "conflict of interest." Another of his clients, an inmate named David Pruett, had *confessed* to killing Helen Schartner! David apparently confessed to several inmates and a guard. It was a jail chaplain who went to the police with this information, but they didn't want to know about it, they already had their man.

A second public defender was assigned Joe's case. He, too, suddenly quit. William Burnside was a zealous advocate for Joe, so when he left, Joe was at a real loss. During Burnside's initial investigation he asked the prosecution if the soil samples taken from the muddy field of the crime scene matched the soil on O'Dell's pants. This was a critical point as it would have either sealed Joe's fate, or offered exculpatory evidence. As my investigation continued it became more apparent just how important this was. I would later learn, in notes from Joe's subsequent public defender, that Burnside wrote "no," the mud on Joe's clothes was *not* consistent with the crime scene. I began to wonder, since the record indicated the police had collected soil samples for testing, did they actually test them? Or were the results unfavorable, leading them to ignore the devastating evidence to the Commonwealth. To a layperson, me, this makes no sense at all. During pre-trial hearings the prosecution fought hard against Burnside. He was a strong and focused attorney who fought back, zealously defending Joe O'Dell. The record is void of any logical explanation for Burnside's removal from the case. It was a loss that an indigent defendant could not afford.

Soon thereafter, Joe was assigned a third attorney named Paul Ray. Ray was anything but a zealous advocate for him. Joe begged for another lawyer. The court refused his numerous requests. Even Ray wanted out. He was under tremendous pressure to "hand Joe over". The record read as though Joe were fighting by himself. Paul Ray seemed to be either totally incapable of defending a capital case, seemingly indifferent to Joe's plight, or helping the prosecution. I couldn't figure out which, but I had to find out. As I perused the record, my opinion of him grew more and more suspicious and disturbing. In fact, he seemed to be working *against* Joe O'Dell. Joe was taunted by the prosecution and at the same time fighting with his own co-counsel. At one point during the trial the judge admonished Prosecutor Alberi. "I have had it with you. You have done everything to bait the defendant...If you continue with this behavior, I will find you in contempt of court."

Further into the transcript it became apparent that Joe didn't feel he had the kind of representation he expected from a criminal defense attorney. He continued to file motion after motion for new counsel, despite the judge's orders were stamped *denied* each and every time. As a result, he reluctantly decided to defend himself. The court, however, insisted that Paul Ray act as co-counsel. He, too, reluctantly agreed. I pondered this for a moment and thought what wonderful news this was for the Commonwealth. Two trained prosecutors, Albert Alberi and Stephen Test, against a convict. A sure conviction. Joe had little knowledge of the law or courtroom procedure. I was amazed at his decision, yet understood his frustration. His tools consisted of a pad of paper, a pencil and an occasional law book which he fought daily to obtain from the jail library. It was an insurmountable task. Yet, for 19 months he would defend himself in the longest, most expensive and publicized murder case, at the time, in the history of Virginia.

On August 11, 1986, the courtroom was filled with spectators. It was the first day of trial. The press began to fill the remaining seats over the next five weeks until the foreman finally handed the verdict to the judge on September 10, 1986. I was impressed the process lasted as long as it did with a *pro se* defendant, i.e. an uneducated street man. Joe filed more pre-trial motions than most skilled attorneys, reported at more than 179 handwritten motions. He was articulate, clever and had a grasp of the law that was just plain unbelievable. David up against Goliath. He was as strong as many attorneys in the courtroom. In fact, he was damn good. But being damn good and being your own attorney never work together. It's a recipe for failure in any courtroom. Let alone a highly publicized capital case. My job was to investigate this case. For now, I was simply reading about the brutal rape and murder of a Virginia Beach woman, carefully and painfully laid out in the next few pages before me, in great detail.

The body of a young secretary, Helen Schartner, was found in a muddy field across the street from the Executive Inn, the last place she was seen alive. Her skirt was lifted above her knees, her panty hose pulled down to her ankles, a white jacket covered her face. Fingernail marks were apparent on her neck from the tightly gripped fingers that drew the last breath from her body. She had sustained eight wounds to her head and had bruises on her hands from her thwarted attempts to block her killer's attack. Her clothes were stained with her own blood. Although the prosecution claimed she was raped and sodomized, the medical examiner testified that he saw no tears or rips in her vagina or anal area. Could it have been consensual sex turned murderous in a rage of anger?

A wino by the name of Joseph Moore was walking through the muddy field at 3:30 p.m. on February 7, 1985. He discovered Helen's twisted and battered body. The prosecutor allowed detective Steven Dunn to testify he had found the body. This seemed odd to me. It was misleading to the jury and I wondered, is this allowed? In an interview, Moore said he thought it was a mannequin when he first noticed the still body laying in the field in the dead of winter. Joseph O'Dell fought hard to find and interview this man, but after the preliminary hearing he disappeared. Joseph Moore was an important witness. Still early in my investigation, I note this as one of the things to follow up on. One thing I knew for sure was that the Commonwealth did not want his testimony beyond the preliminary hearing, thus Mr. Moore never testified at trial. Nor was his name, or the fact that he discovered the body and walked around the crime scene, ever mentioned to the jurors. At the preliminary hearing he attempted to tell the judge that the position he found the victim in was *not* the position she was photographed. He never did get his point across. Because O'Dell did not know how to cross-examine him correctly, nor had any knowledge as to the significance of his testimony, the judge quickly dismissed him. What did this mean? Was Helen's body moved? Why? And by whom? Moore was an important witness. Why didn't the prosecution use him?

Helen's body was found approximately ten feet from a barbed wire fence adjacent to a small public parking lot just outside the After Midnight Club which was across the street from the bar where Helen spent the night with her friends. This seemed peculiar, not a quiet spot accommodating a vicious attack. I wondered why this was not brought out at trial. The detective testified that it seemed as though the body had been dumped, however, the prosecution claimed she was attacked and raped in the open field. It was now my job to find out what really happened that night. I hoped these seemingly insignificant inconsistencies would somehow be the missing pieces to an unfamiliar puzzle in the prosecution of a death row case.

There were no eyewitnesses, fingerprints or other evidence directly linking Joseph O'Dell to the crime scene. The case was entirely circumstantial. The evidence consisted of a cigarette butt found near the victim's body, a tire track in the parking lot near the fence where the body was found, a footprint, semen, hair, a jailhouse snitch and blood evidence. As requested, I dutifully outlined the evidence as follows:

- The prosecution presented a Marlboro soft-pack cigarette butt to the jury and attempted to link it to Mr. O'Dell. Testimony from Connie Craig, his lover, confirmed he smoked Winstons. I wondered how this helped their case. Out of the 14 cigarette butts the police took from his car *14 to 16* months after Joe's arrest, *not one* was from a Marlboro soft-pack.[4] The state failed to perform saliva or fingerprint testing on the butt, though this could have clearly identified the killer. *Why I thought would they fail to do such a conclusive test? A crime lab would never miss the opportunity to directly link evidence to a suspect. What didn't I know about this cigarette butt that caused them to make this decision?* I had to find out.

- The police found a limited impression of a tire track near the fence at the edge of the field where Helen Schartner was dumped. An impression was cast and said to have been "similar" to the tires on O'Dell's car. When asked, "Would you stake your professional reputation on the fact that that tire cast is identical and came from these tires" the Commonwealth's expert replied, "No."[5] Yet he offered lengthy testimony giving the jury the impression that it *was* O'Dell's tire tracks.

---

[4] Trial Transcript, Vol. 19, Tab 53B, page 180.
[5] Trial Transcript, Vol. 18, Tab 52B, page 95.

- A footprint was found in the muddy field next to the victim. An impression was made by casting it for identification purposes. The casting of the killer's footprint was withheld from the defense for several months. Detective Dunn would finally testify that the footprint did *not* match Joe O'Dell's footprint.[6] Nor was it the footprint of Joseph Moore, the man who discovered the body.[7] This also appeared to be out of line with the strong evidence I kept reading about, as the Commonwealth tried to make their case against O'Dell. Although the police did testify that the footprint did not match Joe O'Dell's footprint, the Commonwealth ignored this and downplayed its significance. At the same time, O'Dell did not play up its extreme importance.

- Serology testing, the testing of various enzymes in our blood, was used to link Joe O'Dell with the biological evidence. The prosecution presented semen evidence suggesting a rape and sodomy had occurred. The expert witness testified that the semen had an enzyme marker of PGM 2-1. Since Joe O'Dell's marker was PGM 1, she testified that it was *her own* "theory" (not scientifically supported and therefore legally not reliable and typically not allowed at trial) that the victim's marker overrode Joe's marker and resulted in a PGM 2-1 reading.[8] Another of the prosecution's witnesses testified that "one could not make a determination who the donor was" and corroborated the other expert who testified that the donor of the sperm could be a PGM type of 1, 2 or 2-1. This testimony was insufficient to identify O'Dell as the perpetrator, yet the jury, once again, was emphatically led to believe that it was Joe's sperm. The autopsy report reveals the sperm secretions were PGM 2-1.[9] Nowhere did the results implicate Joe O'Dell.

---

[6] Trial Transcript, Vol. 18, Tab 51B, pages 37-38.
[7] Trial Transcript, Vol. 18, Tab 51, page 56.
[8] Trial Transcript, Vol. 21, Tab 56B, pages 2-142.
[9] See Autopsy report, February 13, 1985. Frank Presswalla (on file with author).

- The state removed several hairs from O'Dell's car. The trial record is clear that the large majority of hairs found in O'Dell's car were neither O'Dell's or Schartner's. The prosecution introduced three hairs to the jury; two head hairs and one pubic hair. The expert testified that they were "*consistent*" with the victim's hair. Yet, the trial testimony of the *prosecution's* witness was that hair could *not* be attributed to a particular person. On cross-examination the defense asked: "As far as hair is concerned, you can't say that hair is the same as another person, isn't that true?" The expert answered, "That's correct." When asked by the defense, "You can't really say that pubic hair is from the decedent, is that true?" The state's witness responded, "Right." The trial record is clear that the Commonwealth's own expert agreed that the hair samples may be "consistent" with members of the jury or people in the courtroom. Yet the prosecution led the jury to believe it *was* the victim's hair.

- The transcript reveals there were no fingerprints of the victim in Joe O'Dell's car, although the Commonwealth suggested Schartner struggled with him in his car before she was murdered. The victim's fingerprints, hair or fiber evidence were not found on O'Dell's clothing. Nor were there fingerprints, hair or fiber evidence found on her body or clothing that could be linked to O'Dell. There was a blue-green fiber found on the victim's clothing, but no attempt was made to compare it to anything.[10]

- The prosecution brought in a "surprise" witness at the *end* of the trial. The judge called it "dirty pool," but "legal."[11] This surprise witness was a jailhouse informant who offered testimony that O'Dell confessed to the killing while in jail. Jailhouse snitches are notorious for surfacing at criminal trials, especially during that pe-

---

[10] Autopsy report, February 13, 1985. Frank Presswalla (on file with author).

[11] Trial Transcript, Vol. 22, page 45. Quoting, "The expression trail by ambush is not a bad descriptive term as to the procedures that have been used, but it's legal. It may fit into the category of dirty pool, but it's legal." Judge Spain.

riod of time in Virginia Beach. At the time of O'Dell's trial, several jailhouse snitches in other murder cases testified to confessions by other inmates.[12] Although the prosecutor knew that all witnesses testified that O'Dell did not talk to, dance with or otherwise engage with the victim, the snitch testified that he bought drinks for and engaged in conversation with the victim.[13] *This, too, appeared strange to me, almost unethical. A prosecutor allowing a witness to testify in contradiction to his other witnesses?* I add this to my list of inconsistencies.

- The main evidence at trial was blood evidence. Since DNA technology was not readily used in 1985, the Commonwealth tested the blood using the serological method. The Commonwealth used a novice by the name of Jacqueline Emrich as their expert witness. Since reading the transcript is like watching a play, I listen to her describe her credentials to the court, keeping in mind Joe O'Dell was arrested in February, 1985:

    Question:
    "How long have you been employed as a forensic scientist?"
    Answer:
    "Since February, 1984," she replied.

I carefully move through the lines on the page as Emrich describes that she had ten months of training with the Commonwealth of Virginia Division of Consolidated Laboratories, and that this training was part of her full time employment. In other words, she finished her training at the lab just two months prior to testing the blood in this case. During cross-examination it was elicited that she neither took a final exam nor was she required to write a thesis to obtain her masters degree in the area in which she was about to testify. Instead of focusing

---

[12] See Joe Jackson and June Arney, *Virginian-Pilot*, June 26, 1994, at A1.

[13] Trial Transcript, Vol. 20, Tab 55.

on her limited experience, Joe's co-counsel went into a lengthy question and answer dissertation about her classes and grades, which did nothing to discredit her.

The prosecution claimed that blood found in O'Dell's car and on his clothes belonged to the victim. They theorized that Joseph O'Dell abducted Helen at her car and forced her into his bucket seated Camaro sports car, where he began the sexual assault. He then dragged her to the field where he finished the assault, eventually strangling her. It was in the field that he held Helen Schartner's head between his knees and beat her with a gun. Yet a gun was never found or proven to be purchased by O'Dell. However, Connie Craig did testify that Joe had purchased a BB gun at a local Kmart store. The prosecution's expert testified that the wounds on her head looked like glancing blows from a blunt object, the victim facing her assailant and somewhat lower than him. I imagined instead they were standing and her killer was swinging an object at her as she attempted to defend herself with her hands. This would account for the defensive wounds discovered on her hands and forearms by the medical examiner. But what did I know, I'm no cop. Nor am I a prosecutor looking to support my conviction.

Emrich testified that the blood on O'Dell's clothing was type O, the same as the victim's. At the time of the trial, approximately 40 to 45 percent of the population was noted to be type O.[14] She also conducted enzyme testing of the blood. Out of approximately 15 noted enzymes recognized in the scientific community, the state tested ten and found them "consistent" with the victim. Joe O'Dell and the victim shared five of the same enzyme markers and at least half were known to be common to the majority of the population.[15] The blood found in his car, on the seat, and on the floor, tested inconclusive. With the exception of one stain, which yielded conclusive results and revealed

[14] Trial Transcript, Vol. 21, Tab 56B, page 115.

[15] Trial Transcript, Vol. 21, Tab 56B, page 131.

it was *not* the victim's blood. Yet the expert testified the blood in the car was "consistent" with the victim's blood. There was no attempt to explain this disparity. The trial transcript revealed that no item tested in O'Dell's car had complete testing results. In fact, 8 out of 11 tests identified less than *one half* of the ten markers (See Exhibit I). The sample with the highest number of identifiable enzyme markers was his shirt. With respect to the other samples, the state's expert defined "consistent" very broadly to include samples which had only *one* of the same enzymes as the victim and then confirmed the fact that O'Dell and Schartner shared at least half of the same markers. How on earth this identified O'Dell as the killer was beyond me. I attempted to educate myself about this now antiquated method called serology blood testing. One could see how the web of deception was spun to the jury as the Commonwealth continually used the word "consistent" and the defense failed to properly challenge the already weak results, in part due to the limitation the court placed on the defense witnesses, and the constraint placed on the number of them. Any criminal defense attorney could have raised reasonable doubt here, but O'Dell was too close to it. And besides, he left the examination of expert witnesses to Paul Ray. When it came time for summation it was never properly challenged. It was lost in the array of things the Commonwealth called "overwhelming" evidence. I found it fascinating that Joseph O'Dell appeared quite intelligent in the manner in which he attempted to challenge the scientific evidence. He was fighting hard. He challenged its reliability but the judge wouldn't have it. On July 29, 1986 Joe filed a *pro se* motion for a continuance:

COMES NOW the Defendant, Joseph Roger O'Dell, and moves the Court to grant a continuance in the trial date of August 11, 1986 in the above-styled criminal case and as grounds for this motion states the following:

1. The prosecution has made an inadequate pre-trial disclosure of possible material exculpatory evidence. Such evidence includes but is not limited to the debris from the victim's automobile which was recently turned over to the defendant's expert for forensic evaluation. In all likelihood this evaluation will not be completed by the trial date or available to the defendant in adequate time to use in the preparation of his defense.

2. The defendant requires a continuance in his trial to secure the presence of a new and unavailable witness, Dr. Benjamin W. Grunbaum. The defendant has exercised due diligence to obtain the attendance of this witness, that substantial favorable evidence would be tendered by this witness, that the witness is available and willing to testify, and that the denial of a continuance would materially prejudice the defendant. See United States v. Darby, 744 F. 2d 1508, 1521 n.6 (11th Cir. 1984); United States v. Bourne, 743 F. 2d 1026, 1030 (4th Cir. 1984).

3. According to Dr. Grunbaum, the physiological stain identification and testing done by the State Tidewater Laboratory in the above-styled criminal case and purportedly linking the defendant to the crime is deficient and probably inadmissible at the defendant's trial. See attached Dr. Grunbaum's letter dated July 25, 1986, Curriculum Vitae, People v. Brown, Sp.Ct. Calif. (December 5, 1985), Amicus Brief, People v. Brown, supra. [sic]

4. Another forensic scientist cast serious doubts on the laboratory results of the state forensic experts. The issue of the reliability and accuracy of the state laboratory results goes to the heart of the defense, particularly where the stain evidence has been destroyed by agents of the state. This destruction prevents any defense expert from retesting such stain evidence and determining the correct results. However, and fortunately, Dr. Grunbaum questions the accuracy of these results. His testimony is crucial to the defense of this case.

WHEREFORE, the Defendant respectfully requests a continuance of his trial.

Defendant Joseph O'Dell

Not one, but two experts, opined in a letter, or affidavit, about the lack of reliability of the scientific evidence. They were also highly critical of the methodology used in achieving its results.[16] I found

[16] In a letter dated July 25, 1986, Dr. Grunbaum, an expert in forensic science, stated his opinion of the Certificate of Analysis, along with handwritten notes, offered by the Commonwealth's expert, Jacqueline Emrich. In summary he noted that the results were unacceptable because 1. Results were reported although the genetic marker patterns in the photographs are highly questionable. 2. The electrophoretograms and laboratory data have not been reviewed by a second analyst. 3. There are many unexplained erasures and corrections in the record. 4. Record keeping is inadequate. 5. Unvalidated techniques were used. 6. Techniques were used that are known to compromise the results. 7. The analyst further compromised the procedures by innovations of her own. His letter further notes that "I can be of assistance to you only if you are willing and have the time to familiarize yourself with the problems and limitations of physiological stain evidence and the shortcomings in this particular case. I realize that the trial date has been set for August 11. However, since the defense was unable to get the laboratory records until recently, it appears that you do not have sufficient time to prepare for effective cross-examination. I am heavily committed and...suggest you ask for a continuance until some time in October." In a separate affidavit offered by another scientific expert, Diane Lavett, having obtained a PhD in genetics and cell biology at Yale University, she offered her preliminary opinion as to the results obtained by the Commonwealth: "Deficient in various regards...Standard scientific procedure demands that any interpretation of results be independently conducted by at least two individuals. For these reasons alone, the report submitted by Ms. Emrich does not meet scientific criteria...For most of the tests employed, no known standards were utilized against which the unknown results could be compared. This is a serious violation of the scientific method and invalidates all results from which known standards were not used. For the majority of the tests run, the report reflects no control testing. By this I mean that Ms. Emrich ought to have taken unstained portions of the fabrics bearing the suspected blood samples, treated them with known samples of liquid blood, allowed them to dry for a period of time and in an atmosphere as closely replicative of the crime scene as possible, and then performed similar testing. This deficiency is inconsistent with the most fundamental rules of scientific testing, and only this type of testing can give reliable presumptive results. The report does not indicate any replicate testing of any specimen...Indeed, in serological testing, it is very often an absolute precondition to reliance on results that each test be done in triplicate. See, e.g., Deault, Takimoto, Kwan and Pallos, *Detectibility of Selected Genetic Markers in Dried Blood Upon Aging*, Law Enforcement Assistance Administration (1980)...The report does not reflect which tests were conducted, which methods were utilized and the dates of the testing...Finally, it is very disturbing to see scratching out of results and interpretations. There is no indication as to why this occurred, or who obliterated the results. Quite apart from being contrary to all scientific method, it raises questions of the *bona fides* of the entire report. *Overall, then, the report submitted by Ms. Emrich falls woefully below the minimum standards required of a responsible professional. Reliance upon her results in a court of law would be totally unacceptable"* (emphasis added). The balance of her eleven-page detailed affidavit outlines, in excruciating detail, her analysis of the PGM findings by Emrich and offers scientific basis for their complete absurdity and a finding that either the results are invalid, exonerate O'Dell or include another donor.

their statements unsettling. The judge denied O'Dell's motion, yet remarked immediately thereafter, "Assuming there is a conviction in this case and it goes up on appeal, I think it will be a classic in criminal law."[17]

I mark the page as important and move on. I am now reading about dead people's clothes on mannequins. In a highly unusual move the prosecution dressed two mannequins, one in the clothing of the victim, the other Joseph O'Dell. Although highly prejudicial and not with probative value, the mannequins remained in front of the jury box for most of the day. Blood was evident on Joe's shirt, pants and jacket. The victim's clothes were stained with her own blood. The mannequins were effective in turning the stomachs of the courtroom spectators. The prosecution had won this round. They would use every legal maneuver possible to win their case. As the blood-drenched clothes stood before the jury, the prosecution outlined how they tested blood in three different spots on Joe's shirt, and one spot on the pants and jacket. The Commonwealth's expert testified that all the blood was the same and was "consistent" with the victim's blood. The significance of this would not become evident until years later. The Commonwealth's testing of the blood on the evidence collected was incomplete and yielded results from just one to ten of the 15 genetic enzyme markers in the human blood, yet the word "consistent" was used over and over again to ensure the jury believed the blood belonged to the victim. The Commonwealth would stop at nothing to prove their case. The deeper I got into the record the more evident this became. The stage was set and the theatre included Joseph O'Dell, the prosecutors, witnesses, and the Commonwealth of Virginia. The press filled the audience. Everyone was watching. They *had* to win this one.

---

[17] Trial Transcript. Appendix C. C-5. Remark referenced at page 106, Line 2, Sept 2, 1986 testimony of Jacqueline Emrich.

~Attorney–Client Confidential Information~

The trial transcript revealed the evidence as depicted above, but what it didn't reveal was evidence that never made it into the courtroom. I placed a phone call to Joe's attorneys for his files. In January 1994 I received several boxes of legal materials from Paul, Weiss, Rifkind, Wharton & Garrison. It was my responsibility to read and summarize it all. It was all confidential information, but as a member of his legal team I was now privileged to read each and every bit of it. There were psychiatric evaluation reports, legal memorandums from and to Joseph, Joseph's personal story, legal briefs and judge's opinions from all of his appellate proceedings to date. It was a voluminous record, but I read with interest and enthusiasm.

On January 25, 1994, about four months after I started work at Centurion Ministries, I wrote my first letter to Joe O'Dell. I explained where I was in my review of his case.

"I am on Volume 8 now. I am reading them all thoroughly, even the "boring" parts which you refer to, for I can assess the personalities of the people involved. I also received a ton of paperwork from your attorneys in New York, which I have separated and read through most of at this point. Boy, I must tell you that I was amazed at the arrogance and sexism displayed in the letter from Alberi to Diane Lavett. I can see how he must have bashed her in the courtroom, but I am reserving further opinions until I see it in the transcripts. I also saw the inconsistencies with Watson's story (*the jailhouse snitch*)...Tuesdays would be the best time to call me, between the hours of 8:30 a.m. and 2:20 p.m... By the way I told Kate I wanted to someday meet the man who I spend most of my free time and work time reading about. P.S. On the contrary I was very impressed by your courtroom capabilities, but I can also see how it has so far put you at a disadvantage...Goodbye for now. Sincerely yours, Lori Urs".

Alberi's letter to Diane Lavett was one of the first strong indicators I got of the overzealous character of the prosecutors in Joe's case. Diane Lavett was Joseph O'Dell's only expert witness. She testified that the methodology used by the prosecution's witness during the testing of the blood was inaccurate, incomplete and unreliable. Unfortunately, she could not do any testing of her own since the prosecution refused to preserve the evidence, despite the fact that O'Dell filed a motion to preserve it for testing by his own experts. Virginia law did not make it mandatory to preserve evidence and the prosecution did not want to take any chances that testing by experts other than their own may compromise their case. More importantly, as legal mail, such correspondence is protected by the attorney–client relationship under confidentiality. If the Commonwealth opened and read the expert's letter to O'Dell while in jail, it would have been a breach of such a highly protected privilege. Joe would inform us that this kind of violation occurred often, during both trial and post-conviction communications with his lawyers. At first I could hardly believe this, but as time went on I found this to be amazingly true. *One* day after Joe was convicted Alberi wrote the following letter to Diane Lavett:

> On Thursday, September 11, 1986, the jury fixed sentence for Joseph Roger O'Dell at death in the electric chair...Your role in this case deserves some comment. In my opinion, the letter which you wrote to Joseph Roger O'Dell constitutes an actionable libel of Mrs. Emrich. I am recommending to Mrs. Emrich that she consult a competent tort lawyer for full review of a potential lawsuit against you. **For your sake I hope you are as poverty stricken as you claim, because, if you are not, you may well be at the conclusion of all the civil litigation. Please feel free to come to the City of Virginia Beach in the near future. Steve Test and I both look forward to "spanking" you as thoroughly as we did in this case. You were worth every penny you were paid!** (emphasis added).

> Sincerely yours

> Albert D. Alberi, Assistant Commonwealth's Attorney.

It was not unusual for an expert to be solicited *pro bono*, which means they offer their services to the indigent free of charge. What *is* unusual is the unleashing of raw emotion and vindictiveness displayed by a member of the prosecution. It was O'Dell who brought this to the attention of the judge, who admonished Alberi in the courtroom, "I find the writing of that letter prior to your sentencing to be utterly outrageous and completely uncalled for. If you keep this up, someone's liable to end up behind bars."[18] Joe told me Diane Lavett had written to him while he was in jail awaiting trial. She said he was being *framed*. It was such a wild accusation with such strong implications that I had to hold off on believing it. He said it with such casualness, as if it was just one of so many problems in his case, that it caught my attention. I wonder, is this the letter Alberi was referring to in his letter to Lavett? If so, how could he inadvertently admit he even read it? Wasn't that against legal protocol? If there was such a letter, I needed to find it.

I was astonished that a public figure would demonstrate such a lack of integrity, displaying such emotions as spite and revenge. What kind of man is this? He had all the resources of the Commonwealth behind him yet felt it necessary to condemn those who differed in opinion from him, those who dared challenge him. Did he take it personally? Why? Had O'Dell challenged his ability and now he was defending it? All these questions ran through my head as I desperately tried to understand this behavior. Having formulated my opinion of attorneys by my father's character and actions, I was in for a rude awakening. My dad was a true gentleman who carried himself with the utmost of integrity. Alberi sent an altogether different message. I found myself, for the first time in my life, questioning the legal system and the characters who were embedded in its structure.

This wasn't the first time Alberi would threaten someone with a lawsuit. I, along with the media, would later receive threatening phone

---

[18] October 6, 1986 hearing before Judge Calvin Spain, quoting the Honorable Calvin Spain.

calls or letters as he attempted to defend his position and preserve his name. In the meantime, I was unaware of his political strength as I innocently continued my diligent study of the case.

Chapter 3

~DNA and the Courts!~

As a New Jersey winter passed and spring slowly made its way to Princeton, I found myself writing my third letter to Joe O'Dell on April 8, 1994.

> Dear Joe: Hi! How are you? I just had a conference with Jim and he asked me to write to you in order to find out the status of your contact with the new attorney on your case. He would like for you to call as soon as possible. I now work 8:30 a.m. to 3:00 p.m. Monday through Thursday, going through your transcripts. I am on Volume 18 now…It's all starting to come together now that I am into the trial, third day.

On April 14, 1994, Joe wrote back to me:

> Lori, thank you for working so hard on my case…I know very well how difficult your task is. I lived it for two years, and have been living it altogether for 9 years, 2 months and 5 days. All the Best Always, Joe.

I responded to his letter several days later:

> It's always so nice to hear from you when you call. I can put a voice to all of the papers and sounds of the courtroom transcripts. Anyway,

after getting off the phone with you I called Jeff Eilender and had quite a good conversation with him. It was very good for me to make my presence known to him and find out the status of your case…I felt so good knowing your case inside and out, it will be very helpful to our work. Who else would have the time? I enjoy it immensely Joe and hope that I can be instrumental in your release.

Joe responded on April 21, 1994:

I was happy to hear that you touched base with Jeff Eilender, the attorney in my case. By you calling him, it seemed to have put some wind into his sails…thanks Lori…you will be the ONLY one in my case who will KNOW the case in its ENTIRETY. You will be the MOST IMPORTANT part of my legal team. I cannot tell you how happy I am to finally have someone on my team who takes my case seriously, and who is interested in my case and has worked so hard to learn everything in the case. My case is a myriad of complexities.

At this point in my work I thought Joe O'Dell was simply encouraging me. Yet it would come to pass that I was the only member of his team who knew his case inside and out. Indeed, I would be educating his attorneys concerning the facts of his case.

It was now time to further verbal communication with Joseph O'Dell. To meaningfully discuss his case I had to. At first he was hesitant to call and we spoke very briefly. On April 20, he called to say he enjoyed talking with me and said that he couldn't wait to meet me and Kate. He had been conversing with Kate at Centurion Ministries for six or seven years now, but had never met her. It was also the first time he let me in on a prison smiley face. "Those little colons and half-parentheses are my sideways smiley faces," he wrote. He was charming as he spoke about Kate's puppies, and his kittens at the prison. He was very effective at revealing his "softer" side. His last sentence was "God Bless." This served to balance the hardened criminal I was reading about, each and every day now.

My letter to Joe on May 2 read:

> Good morning! It is Monday and I'm at the office ready to start Volume 24. But before I do I just had to write to you with a lot of comments and questions which arose upon my reading of the last two volumes and respond to your two letters dated April 20 and 21, 1994. I must first tell you that Volume 23 leaves me at the point of what appears to be the end of the trial, before the closing statements. I know that this may sound strange to you, but I must tell you that as I read the transcript at one point I actually felt what I perceived as your feeling of defeat and uncertainty, and the sadness in your voice. I almost felt as though I were right there. I realize that this is somewhat after the fact for you, but for me I can get a sense of the reality and the actual scheme of things as I read through the transcripts. You would not believe how many times I talk to myself as I read and curse at some of the things I read, or make comments of disgust in the margins of the pages. Yes, I have a copy of the summary of the transcripts and I do refer to them, but Joe, give me credit, for I am creating my own summary of the transcripts which is in much greater detail. I have gathered quite a list of people required for the investigation. I also have quite a list of inconsistencies and comments. And I have a few questions that need some honest answers. It is true that I, outside of the attorneys and courtroom spectators, know your case inside and out. I have quite the mind for detail so I seem to remember things you would never imagine. Please be candid with me concerning these questions for they are critical to my complete devotion to this case. Anyway, I will be looking forward to your response. Please be as thorough as possible. Thank you.
>
> Sincerely,
>
> Lori Urs

At this point I was feeling his pain. The self-defeat he must have been feeling as he worked day and night to defend himself against an entire Commonwealth, a mass of experts and scores of reporters who were looking for sensationalism to report back to the community.

~Truth Doesn't Matter in the Courts?~

During the course of my reading it became apparent that we needed to contact many witnesses to resolve some of the unanswered questions that arose during my initial investigation of the record. I had also
learned that, in insisting upon his innocence, Joe was relentless in his
search for someone to help prove it. He researched the scientific tools
available to him and without the assistance of a scientific expert he
prodded ahead to find a way. He had heard that DNA testing was being used to convict the guilty. In his desperate attempt to prove his innocence, and with keen insight into the usefulness of DNA to exonerate the innocent, he told me he wanted to do DNA testing long before
his lawyers got involved. "My lawyers wouldn't pay for it, nor would
they file a motion to ask for it." I found that hard to believe. I ultimately stumbled upon his *pro se* request to Judge Spain. It was a bold
move, one that was on the cusp of the new era of DNA testing which
was in its infancy. At the time, it was unheard of. There had never been
an inmate released based upon DNA tests.[19] As DNA testing started to
emerge as the most scientific tool to convict the guilty, Joe wanted to
use it to prove his innocence. It was a brilliant idea. Could it be used
to free the innocent? Joe was on the threshold of entering a completely
new field in the practice of criminal law. His insight intrigued me. His
persistence caught my attention. Less than two years after his conviction, and on August 16, 1988, ignoring the advice of his attorneys, he
wrote a letter to the trial judge.

Dear Judge Spain:

I have been in contact with Dr. Robert Schaler of Lifecodes Laboratories in Valhalla, New York, getting pertinent information concern-

---

[19] In 1993, Kirk Bloodsworth was one the first people to be released from death row based upon
DNA testing. He went on to become a national spokesperson against the death penalty and for
the use of DNA tests to exonerate the innocent. Death Penalty Information Center website.

ing DNA Fingerprinting and the prerequisites of having evidence sent to his laboratory for testing the above-referenced case.

The first step is obviously making a request for the evidence to be released to Lifecodes and a "Chain of Custody" to be established. I would like to request that all the serological evidence in the above-referenced case be prepared by a person not connected to the Police Department or the Prosecution, and that this person be delegated by this Honorable Court to deliver this evidence to a "Federal Express" Office and have the evidence shipped directly to Doctor Robert Schaler, Lifecodes. Old Saw Mill Road, Valholla, New York 10595.

Lifecodes has an impeccable reputation, and is used by Police Departments and Prosecutors Offices all over America, so I do not anticipate any objections from the Commonwealth concerning their credentials. Further, I do not think the Commonwealth would want to object to the DNA Fingerprint Testing being done in this case... it is in their best interests as well as mine. They do not want an innocent person being executed and this test will prove innocence or guilt to an acceptable "Absolute Certainty." It is so acceptable that VIRGINIA is setting up their own DNA Testing Laboratories and are training personnel to conduct the testing. If I were not innocent of this crime I would have to be insane or non compos mentis to request DNA Fingerprinting. I believe that the Commonwealth of Virginia owes me this chance to prove my innocence, and on the other hand, they owe themselves the opportunity to KNOW that they either have the RIGHT or WRONG man on Death Row. This is no "Self-Serving" request Judge Spain...this request affords me the chance to prove my innocence, and it affords the Commonwealth of Virginia the chance to prove guilt. One of us had to be wrong...we both cannot be right, and I am the one that is adamantly professing my innocence...now I have the chance to prove it. If the Commonwealth of Virginia refused to allow me this chance, then it is going to appear that they are hiding something, and further, it will appear that DNA Fingerprinting is being used to only CONVICT accused persons. This is an opportune time for Law Enforcement to prove that they protect the Innocent as well as prosecute the Guilty.

I ask this Honorable Court, humbly, to consider this request and allow me the chance to prove my innocence.

Respectfully submitted,

Joseph Roger O'Dell, III[20]

In my review of the files I studied the court transcript and noted the judge's comments. It confirmed my suspicions, yet heightened my awareness that even the judge thought the scientific evidence was questionable. Why then did he allow it if someone's life was hanging in the balance? Perhaps this was an opportunity for him to give O'Dell a chance to prove his case, once and for all. Joe's plea was so well-written he made it almost impossible to refuse his request. The judge agreed. He granted Joe O'Dell's request due to "problems he had with the scientific evidence in this case all along."[21] It was the first time in the history of Virginia, and quite possibly the country, that post-conviction DNA testing was ordered to prove innocence. When the judge alerted Joe's lawyers that he was going to allow the testing, they finally joined in the legal process.

The judicial process was set in motion for the lawyers to now file a formal request for DNA testing. One might think to accomplish this would be a matter of weeks, perhaps months. Yet the truth was, someone could enjoy a lustful night and watch as a newborn child develops and joins our society by the miracle of its first breath, quicker than the court could spit out a decision. I was finding out that the wheels of justice turn slowly, very slowly. It would be maddening if I were in Joe's shoes.

The attorneys filed their motions and the Commonwealth opposed them all. While they originally agreed to a DNA test, the Attorney General's office would become Joe's worst nightmare. I read in horror as the court continually reviewed, one by one, a motion to dismiss by the Commonwealth. "It doesn't matter what the DNA test says," they exclaimed. "There is no remedy in the court system for

---

[20] Letter from Joseph O'Dell to Judge Spain. August 16, 1988 (on file with author).

[21] *Joseph Roger O'Dell, III v. Charles E. Thompson, Warden.* Circuit Court of the City of Virginia Beach. CL89-1475. May 2, 1990. page 23. Hearing before the Honorable H. Calvin Spain.

O'Dell, so let's not waste our time." As I read the latter part of the sentence I found myself retracing the cold words, one by one . . ."let's, not, waste, our, time."

What! No remedy? How on earth is that possible? Even in a barbaric society, no one wants the innocent to die. I was now learning about Virginia's 21-day rule, i.e., a defendant has 21 days after his conviction to bring in newly discovered evidence, or else it is *forever* barred. However absurd this sounds, it was the law in Virginia. One could barely recover from a guilty conviction, re-group and obtain new lawyers in that short a time let alone find new evidence. This law was outrageous. As I poured over the court documents I came across the stenographic transcript of a hearing before Judge Spain on August 22, 1989, over one year after Joe requested DNA testing. Before the court was a motion to dismiss by the Attorney General's office.

> Mr. Murphy: "Your Honor, it's our position the results of those tests will not affect the petition of habeas corpus. I think we submitted authority within our response. All of the issues with the exception of two are clearly procedurally barred."

> The Court: "Well, even if there be a DNA finding that is beneficial to him, I'm not sure that's the only remedy. Should the Attorney General's office get a little upset, the petition for executive clemency could become very much a trial issue, not a pardon issue. Somebody's got to order a new trial if that became the question and the governor in fact let him go I would think...I mean, after all, it's an old case. I'm characterizing perhaps, but it appears that the majority of evidence in this case is tied together by circumstantial matters."

> Mr. Murphy: "What I'm saying is that if the evidence was such that it demonstrated his clear innocence—I'm certainly not saying that that's what will happen; but if there were such evidence, the only remedy would be a petition for executive clemency; that the habeas corpus court doesn't have before it the question of guilt or innocence."

The Court: "Assuming it isn't clear-cut, what's the remedy then?"

Mr. Murphy: "There is no remedy."

The Court: "Somewhere along the way I would think that some court is going to say it's going to be admissible for something. Let's put it that way."

Mr. Murphy: "Well...after-discovered evidence does not affect the validity of the underlying judgment."

The Court: "I think they many have to reconsider that position in light of DNA...I'm not sure they have confronted quite this type of issue...I understand where you're coming from, but I'm not sure I'm prepared to dismiss anything on that point until I have the test results and see what I'm dealing with. Somebody's got to bite the bullet first and last and address the issue, and it seems to me that at some point someone's going to have to address the issue of whether a new trial is appropriate depending on the results of that DNA, I don't pretend to know where that intervention is going to occur, but somebody is going to have to be the first and last."

Mr. Murphy: "...21 days have [sic][22] passed after his conviction, the Court has [sic] no authority to vacate the judgment."

The Court: "...They certainly aren't going to summarily walk someone to the electric chair when there is a question. I'm not saying there's going to be a question involved. May very well not be. That remains to be seen. But I don't think even precedent gets that iron-clad and concrete. Always some judicial discretion to accommodate time and evolution of facts in evidence, and this has been a problem that's been bothering me in this hearing is just suppose it does come out. Then what is the remedy? And I appreciate where you're coming from and what the courts traditionally held the case to be, and it is a perplexing problem.[23]

---

[22] 'Sic' added immediately after a quoted word or phrase indicates that the quotation was transcribed exactly as found in the original source, including errors or other incorrect presentation. *Wikipedia*.

[23] Stenographic Transcript, at 38-42, hearing before Judge Spain. August 22, 1989, pages 38-42.

I continued reading, searching for more explicit reasons the judge may have allowed Joe's unprecedented request for DNA testing. I was unprepared for the sharp and outwardly frustrated remarks Judge Spain made during a hearing on Joe's request almost *two years* later, on May 2, 1990, in the Circuit Court of the City of Virginia Beach.

> Judge Spain: "You know without question my thought on the adequacy of the evidence in this case."
>
> Mr. Coffey (Joe's lawyer): "Of what evidence, Your Honor?"
>
> Judge Spain: "The scientific evidence in this case. It's printed throughout the entire transcript what I have to say about it, but that's not the way the law is in the State of Virginia and apparently the United States at the moment as far as the Supreme Court is concerned. So so [*sic*] be it. Perhaps it will be reversed. Perhaps somebody will see the light, something should have been done. Doesn't mean the defendant isn't guilty or wasn't guilty—couldn't have been proven guilty or whatever, but this particular evidence I had problems with; but that's been ruled on; so lets get on with it and put it in proper format and let somebody make a decision upstairs as to whether there needs to be a new statement of the law in this Commonwealth on the subject."
>
> Mr. Coffey: "Your Honor, with regard to subsequent courts, regarding Supreme Court opinions. I'm not optimistic that we'll get another shot…If we don't do it now, the Commonwealth will…prevent any court from allowing Joe the opportunity to present the egregious issues in his case."[24]

Indeed they tried. The record was replete with indications of their relentless effort to prevent any challenge to their conviction. It belonged to them, how dare anyone challenge it.

Joe was fortunate in one regard. Judge Spain was planning to retire and had he not ordered the DNA test Joe might never have had the opportunity. The Commonwealth would take advantage of the new

---

[24] Stenographic Transcript at 23, *O'Dell v. Thompson* (CL89-1475) (May 2, 1990).

judge six months later in a hearing before Judge Owen in October, 1990. Assistant Attorney General Murphy would argue that O'Dell's witness should not be allowed to opine on the unreliable and unacceptable procedures and standards used by Emrich. He would claim it was "cumulative" testimony. Yet Judge Spain ordered DNA testing because of his concern that the serological evidence was highly unreliable. O'Dell needed to show that Emrich's procedures did not follow acceptable standards. He was not allowed to challenge that properly at trial. O'Dell won, but every step of the way Murphy would ask that the petition be dismissed, based on whatever reason he could pull out of his sleeve at that particular moment. It became crystal clear that the Commonwealth did not care if the unreliable tests at trial would kill an innocent man. They fought hard against any challenge to their verdict, whether it was morally justifiable or not. This inflamed me. The system is supposed to represent justice. It's not a chess game of who is the stronger opponent. The purpose is to flush out the truth. I am learning that's the way it's *supposed* to work. The way it *does* work is highly dependent on the players. If one was unethical, unethical results will occur. My game would be straight. I vowed that much.

Chapter 4

~Your Attorney or Your Enemy?~

Though I was becoming more aware of what appeared to be an unfair legal process, I was stunned to learn that O'Dell's standby counsel, Paul Ray, had refused to give Joe's files to his appellate attorneys. To me this was a strong display of betrayal, and a direct attempt to prevent his client from seeking any kind of meaningful appellate review. Alberi and Test had to be behind this. I knew that Paul Ray had aligned himself with the prosecution, but this was beyond any basic ethical and legal standard. It was as low as one could get as a criminal defense attorney. It was as low as a prosecutor could get to assist in any way with such practice. Basically, it was intolerable.

Devouring each document piled in dusty tattered boxes led me to the disheartening truth. In a letter dated March 21, 1989 it became apparent that Ray's refusal to help Joe was real. Joe's court-appointed counsel, Andrew Sebok, had written a letter to the judge and submitted it along with a Motion for Prior Leave of Court to Obtain Discovery and a Motion for Subpoena Duces Tecum and Protective Order. The Commonwealth was not playing fair. In fact they were dirty as hell.

> Dear Judge Spain: …Petitioner seeks discovery of the files of Paul H. Ray, petitioner's standby counsel at trial, which are indispensable and highly relevant to his adequate representation at this post-conviction

state. Mr. Ray has refused to produce these files voluntarily to Mr. O'Dell's present counsel. Production of these documents to us is not barred by any privilege, since it is Mr. O'Dell to whom the attorney–client privilege belongs…and he has consented to have these privilege papers turned over to his present counsel. (See Consent Form attached.)[25]

The balance of the May 2, 1990 court transcript answered my questions and at the same time opened my eyes as to why O'Dell seemed to be blocked every step of the way. The judge was hearing a motion on discovery and the defense attorney's request to amend their petition. They were offering legitimate reasons why they needed this, but the reasons were startling and gave me new insight into O'Dell's insurmountable battle.

> Mr. Coffey (Joe's lawyer): "…As you know, since we filed the petition, we have been clamoring to get discovery; and Mr. Murphy said that he agreed to discovery in August. Well, that's not the case. They signed a discovery order we tendered to them at the time—they signed it in February, and they only did it after he had a hearing in February…If I may. We asked for discovery of Mr. Ray's files, we got them just five weeks ago, Your Honor…We got them, and we're still going through them. There are 4,000 pages of documents."[26]

My non-lawyer mind was troubled by this. Andrew Sebok filed a motion for discovery in March of 1989. Why did the Commonwealth take over a year to comply? This manifestation of injustice got me boiling over the edge of a steaming pot of confusion. And then I read the following:

> Mr. Coffey: "…But with regard to Mr. Ray's files, up to that point in time Your Honor, we came on this case, all we had was the trial transcript; and we had Mr. O'Dell. Mr. Ray wouldn't talk to us. **I be-**

[25] See Letter from Andrew Sebok to Judge Spain (March 21, 1989) (on file with author).

[26] Stenographic Transcript at 16-17, hearing before Judge Owen (May 2, 1990).

lieve the Commonwealth advised him not to talk to us (emphasis added)."[27]

If ever there was a time I wanted to reach into the papers, and grab at someone it was now. I wanted to shake Mr. Murphy by the collar and ask him why he supported such a corrupt prosecutor. How could he put his career or reputation on the line for such a scumbag? Maybe they would all get away with this. I didn't know. The thought of it made me sick.

The rest of the transcript was mildly disturbing. It contained dialogue pertaining to the lack of the Commonwealth's effort to comply with the discovery requirements, the effort by them to dismiss the DNA results, regardless of the outcome, and lots of talk about Virginia's 21-day rule. Mr. Murphy argued that O'Dell's conviction was legal, regardless of what the DNA results were. He urged the judge not to care—it wasn't about guilt or innocence. The dialogue was appalling. Mr. Murphy had the audacity to accuse O'Dell's attorneys of "dragging their heels," even though it came to light that they made Joe's lawyers wait over a year for Paul Ray's files. They wanted his attorneys to read through them in a few weeks. Four thousand pages. He informs the court that the trial transcript is about 8,000 pages (not including the pre-trial or post-trial motions) and that he did it alone. Having been reading the record for the past several months I found Mr. Murphy's assertion a blatant attempt to prevent the attorneys from reading what was in those files.

> Mr. Murphy: "...I just can't imagine what would be in the files that would not have been known by Mr. O'Dell, himself, who sat in the courtroom when he was being tried that would not have been known by him and which could not have been found out by counsel in what I guess is nearly a year's time since the petition has been filed...I feel like the Court ought to go ahead and act as if essentially it never heard what it heard today."[28]

[27] *Id.* at 18.
[28] *Id.* at 29.

The audacity of this pompous moron was beyond comprehension.

Andy Sebok is furious at this point and lectures the judge that there are leads in the files that can't be given by Mr. O'Dell, and certainly not by Mr. Ray because he refuses to talk to them. *Of course that's the case.* It doesn't take a genius to know that your client cannot possibly know all that the attorney has in his files. Especially in this case, where Joe's attorney seemed to be working more for the Commonwealth than his own client! The Commonwealth wants the secrets hidden in those files. They are relentlessly trying to get them through discovery, but the law only allows that if O'Dell intends to use them in his evidentiary hearing on his habeas[29] issues. I needed to find those files. There are things contained in them that are causing officers of the court to engage in highly unethical behavior.

I had learned enough about our justice system for the day. But my reading was far from over. It didn't come in any order. The files were all over the place. I had to put it all together by dates and acquired information.

My eyes are almost squinting as I read portions of the post-trial transcript dated September 9, 1986 as if I could barely believe the context of the words. I had read earlier that Joe let Paul Ray handle the expert witnesses, recognizing his own lack of expertise and its extreme importance. Ray let Joe down in the most critical aspect of his case. Joe was challenging the validity of his conviction. The judge was frustrated—he knew the weaknesses of the case, yet while it appeared he did nothing to help Joe, it now appears he felt his hands were tied. He commented on the trial, specifically about the cross-examination of the Commonwealth's main expert witness, after Joe's attorney, Mr.

---

[29] Appellate stages in a criminal case address errors committed by the trial judge, while habeas reviews constitutional violations of the trial.

Rosenfeld[30], discussed the disastrous courtroom dialogue[31]:

> Mr. Rosenfeld: "That was something Mr. O'Dell felt he was not capable of doing, and it was agreed that would be Mr. Ray's function; but when the state's main expert witness, Dr. Sensabaugh, took the stand, I think the record shows that Mr. Ray was not prepared to cross-examine him and Mr. O'Dell did that. That's one of our—"

> Judge Spain interrupted: "...there were many decisions made by Mr. O'Dell that this Court felt were very foolish and ill-advised. But then attorneys do very foolish, ill-advised things too. He was foolish to have ever opened his mouth in defending himself. He might conceivably have walked out of the court a free man if he had allowed an attorney to represent his interests."

> Mr. Rosenfeld: "You and I agree on that."

> Judge Spain: "You can read the transcript and determine that, but the law is he's entitled to be his own attorney."

Judge Spain's comments were reflective of his frustration during the trial, his decisions overseen by judicial ghosts, lurking over him in the appellate process. Here was the chance Joe O'Dell needed. The unique approach Judge Spain took in ordering DNA tests apparently was deep-seated during the six arduous weeks of trial. Joe had succeeded this round. The question remained, how on earth was he to get the money for testing? If his lawyers refused to file a motion to even ask for it, they certainly weren't going to pay for it, even though it went to the heart of the case and their client was indigent. Even though it could save his life. Joe knew better than to count on them. All along he had been soliciting help from anyone and everyone he could think of.

Meanwhile, months before writing Judge Spain for DNA testing,

---

[30] Coincidentally, the civil rights lawyer subsequently engaged by Joe O'Dell, and who appears later in this story, is Steven D. Rosenfield; he spells his name differently and is unrelated.

[31] Post-trial transcript at 66, *Joseph Roger O'Dell v Thompson* (CL89-1475) (May 1990).

Joe was writing a different kind of letter, to a different kind of person. He had read about a syndicated philanthropist, columnist and millionaire named Percy Ross in Minneapolis. Joe decided to ask for his help. He needed money to conduct the one test that could set him free. "Please take a chance on me by providing this blood testing. I can't begin to tell you how it feels to be awaiting my death when I'm innocent."[32] Joe's persistence paid off. In a stroke of luck Percy had read his letter and was moved by Joe's claim of innocence. He wanted to afford him the opportunity to prove he was an innocent man sitting on Virginia's death row. So, through his column, on August 1, 1988 Percy answered Joe. "Nothing is perfect and that includes our legal system…I do, however, act with reservation, because if the testing proves guilt I'll feel as though I escorted you to the electric chair. Should it prove your innocence, we'll have righted a wrong and justice will have prevailed. I hope freedom rings."[33] In a private letter to Mr. Joseph Roger O'Dell, III, addressed Death Row 1-C-50, Post Office Box 500, Boydton, Virginia 23917, Ross wrote:

> Dear Joe: I'm starting out on a somewhat personal note. The reason being, you've been the topic of discussion in my office ever since I received your letter…which is the very essence of why I'm writing to you. Your letter moved me!…Please stay in touch. I'm most eager to learn of any new developments in your case. And until such time… my very best wishes. Hang in there, pal! Sincerely, Percy Ross.[34]

Ross forwarded a check for $1,200 to Centurion Ministries for the testing.

A newspaper would never miss a chance to inform the general public of such news. The *Richmond Times Dispatch*, on September 6, 1988 ran an article entitled, "Inmate Turns to Unusual Aid Source."

---

[32] See Letter from Joe O'Dell to Percy Ross (July, 1988) (on file with author).
[33] See Letter from Percy Ross to Joe O'Dell (August 1, 1988) (on file with author).
[34] See Private Letter from Percy Ross to Joseph O'Dell (July 7, 1988) (on file with author).

It was a piece picked up by the Associated Press. I read these articles, not for the joy or interest or sensationalism it meant to most people reading an article. My purpose was simply to gather information for my investigation. Who did the paper interview? What did they say? I highlighted the following phrase in the article: "Percy Ross, 71 of Minneapolis, is a philanthropist whose column, "Thanks a Million" appears in 200 newspapers."[35] *Wide distribution*, I thought. Stephen Test spoke on behalf of the prosecution about Joe O'Dell. "He was afforded more resources, probably, than any criminal in the state's history," said Test. "The costs were astronomical. The state paid $35,000, and $50,000 for his attorney, whom O'Dell ran up and down the street for 24 months."[36] *I suppose a capital murder defendant is not supposed to investigate his own case.* Test was proving to be just as arrogant as Alberi. "He had two forensic experts—one of which worked for free, the other billed the state between $15,000 and $20,000—and he had the services of a detective agency."[37] *He forgot to say they intimidated the pro bono expert and that he also intimidated Dr. Guth* (the other scientific expert), I mumbled to myself. Test informed the reporter that "O'Dell filed between 200 and 300 pages of motions weekly from his jail cell in the two years leading up to the trial. He had 70 hearings on those motions. The total cost of the trial and hearings approached $250,000."[38] *Too much for a convict*, I muttered.

Opinions varied depending upon sides of the courtroom. Clive Stafford Smith, an Atlanta attorney who specialized in assisting death row inmates in their appeals, and who assisted O'Dell from time to time, said the trial was a travesty. "In particular, I note that the prosecution did everything in its power to intimidate the defense witnesses. This appeal is less about the legal issues than it is a fundamental ex-

---

[35] Frank Green, Inmate Turns To Unusual Aid Source, *RICHMOND TIMES DISPATCH*, September 6, 1988, at 1.
[36] *Id.*
[37] *Id.*
[38] *Id.*

ample of the possibility of human error."[39] Smith was working on the motion to allow DNA testing. When asked about Joe's alibi and confronted with Test's statement that the blood on Joe's clothing could not have come from the fight with two sailors across town because "the only injury was a cut lip"[40]. Smith "doubts the state's case is that strong."[41] Why didn't they bring the witnesses to trial and refute the fact that Joe was in a fight across town? This could have proven the blood did not come from the parking lot brawl. Would it muddy the waters? Or was it too risky? It may have proven that Joe O'Dell's alibi was solid. Anything can happen on cross-examination—don't take a chance. The people don't deserve the truth. Neither does the family of the victim.

Joe told me he gave the sailor he fought with a bloody lip. If Joe wasn't there, or wasn't in the fight, how did he know there were two sailors and how did he know one had a bloody lip? Not only did a witness testify that he was in a fight, but Joe described the fight to me the same way the sailor described it to the Commonwealth. Except the prosecution left out the part about Joe being in the fight. I imagine that's why they didn't want the sailors at trial. These new pieces of information were beginning to fit a puzzle altogether different from the puzzle designed by the prosecution.

The article also describes how Ross, who made millions manufacturing plastic trash bags, said O'Dell's letter touched him. It also touched readers of Ross's column. He estimated about 400 people wrote in support of giving O'Dell another chance to prove his innocence. "One man sent a check for $3,000 to be forwarded to Centurion Ministries to help in this case,"[42] Ross said. In trying to convince him he made a bad decision, the reporter tells Ross that Joe was con-

---

[39] *Id.*

[40] *Id.*

[41] *Id.*

[42] *Id.*

victed of murder in the late 1960s. Ross responds, "That really doesn't change anything."[43]

A spokesperson for Centurion Ministries responded, "From what we know, we believe the man is innocent."[44] She stated the DNA testing was critical, "It is the next best thing to the victim rising out of the grave and saying Joe didn't do it."[45]

The statement that sent me over the top was Test's final comment. "I suppose if you stretch it, perhaps there is a one-in-a-million chance that someone else could have had exactly the same blood type and enzymes as the victim. That does leave a door open," Test said. "But the jury heard over 20 days of testimony, and took only 2½ hours to reach a decision. The blood was the victim's."[46] *So glad the jury had the scientific knowledge to have made that decision*, I thought. *So glad they knew that over 40 percent of the population has the same blood type as the victim. So glad they never knew that the one DNA test with definitive results proves their enzyme tests were simply wrong. So glad they knew the defense witnesses were scared, intimidated. So glad they had all the evidence put before them by a competent well-trained capital defense attorney. So glad.* I was steaming mad now.

As a result of Ross's generosity, Joe was able to perform DNA testing on his clothing in an attempt to prove that the source of the blood was not from the victim. Instead it came from a fight he was in across town after he left the bar, and about the same time the victim was assaulted. To support his alibi Joe subpoenaed two witnesses. They were reluctant to testify. Joe informed me that one of them had hit his pregnant girlfriend with his car and thought he was not being forthright with his testimony because Joe had him arrested. At first, as usual, I thought, like so many other things in this case, it was highly unlikely.

---

[43] *Id.*

[44] *Id.*

[45] *Id.*

[46] *Id.*

It sounded like a great story. Yet, as I listened to his testimony, like a witness in the courtroom, and through my eyes as each word jumped off the page, I saw that O'Dell was right. Again.

Paul Ray then called John Rosetti to the stand, the security guard at the bar where the fight took place, the Brass Rail. What should have been a rather lengthy direct examination of a crucial witness turned out to be short and not so sweet. Ray wasn't effective at eliciting the type of information that would raise reasonable doubt. Rosetti testified that someone came into the bar and told him that there was a fight outside in the parking lot. He went outside with the manager of the Brass Rail, Timothy Bougades, where he saw two men engaged in a fight—the same two that were inside the bar earlier and, apparently drunk. They had argued over a cigarette.[47] Rosetti saw two Norfolk police officers outside and a man speaking with Tim. Ray never asked the condition of the man with Tim Bougades, or to describe him. Next, Ray called Timothy Bougades. He duplicated the testimony of Rosetti, but added that it was Joe O'Dell in the parking lot when he went outside. He knew Joe personally. He also testified that the individuals who had been fighting had left the parking lot. Joe was still there. He asked Joe if he was alright because "it appeared…like he had just got in a fight."[48] When asked to describe what led him to that conclusion he stated that Joe appeared to have something on his face, like mud. He didn't say it was blood and hesitated at almost every sentence. I sensed he was a reluctant witness and I wondered why. He also stated that Joe had either "got into a fight in the parking lot or broke up a fight in the parking lot and he pointed…pointed away to…to I believe…I believe it was to a car that was driving off. I don't remember what he said, but he pointed to this car like whoever was in the car was the ones that were

[47] Trial Transcript, Vol. 21, Tab 56A, pages 24-29.
[48] Trial Transcript, Vol. 21, Tab 56A, page 37.

fighting or that he fought."[49] Ray got Bougades to establish the time of the fight: between 12:00 and 1:30 a.m.

Ray's direct examination of Bougades was only about four pages. I was troubled by this—there was so much more to ask. Ultimately, it did nothing to instill reasonable doubt. It should have. Test asks for a recess until the next morning to cross-examine Bougades. He wanted more time to investigate in order to prepare his cross. The judge granted his request, much to my astonishment. Test could now dig up whatever dirt he could to stop Bougades from further offering Joe O'Dell a solid alibi.

My head is swimming with thoughts about a timeline that just doesn't make sense. If O'Dell is accused of abducting Helen Schartner at around 11:30 p.m., even though he was seen in the bar at 12:00 a.m., allegedly takes her somewhere for the sexual assault in his car, brings her across the street, leaves her dead body in the field, just ten feet away from the parking lot of the After Midnight Club, runs all the way over to the other side of town, just happens to approach a fight going on in the parking lot, engages in the fight where he is lucky enough to get blood on him from the cut lip of one of the men he fought, casually walks into a 7-Eleven convenience store after just murdering someone a few minutes earlier, is this possible? No timeline, no attempt to lay out for the jury how this makes no sense if he was in the process of raping and murdering a woman across town at the same time. As a future attorney I could see myself just itching to get Bougades on the stand. I would know the outcome of every question. Unlike Paul Ray, who was clearly surprised that Rosetti actually saw the two men fighting in the streets. I would outline to the jury how this could not have happened if Joe O'Dell were the killer. The prosecution laid it out as if it were just a fly in the ointment. Joe O'Dell couldn't help himself. He was his own worst enemy. His own lawyer.

---

[49] Trial Transcript, Vol. 21, Tab 56A, page 38.

It was apparent to me that the blood evidence was indeed the only evidence to directly tie Joe to the murder, besides Watson, who was a known jailhouse snitch. Joe's insistence on testing the evidence was a strong indication of his innocence. The only other explanation I could surmise for his desire to test the blood would be to shorten the time between now and when he stood before his executioner.

Next, I needed to verify Joe's claim that his attorneys sent every item of evidence to Lifecodes lab for DNA testing. The evidence had been sitting in an unlocked storage locker, gathering dust while Joe was fighting to use this very evidence to escape certain death by execution. This was the *only* thing that offered him any hope of freedom.

Lifecodes lab examined all the evidence to determine which pieces would yield DNA results. As a result of the Commonwealth's refusal to preserve the evidence, the blood was degraded and not easy to test. Because of their potential in yielding results, three items were selected by the lab for testing: Joe's jacket, shirt and vaginal swabs. Of extreme importance was the fact that Attorney General Murphy stipulated in court that the three areas that were tested were adjacent to the areas tested by Ms. Emrich using the polymorphic enzyme test.[50] The report seemed self-explanatory, but I knew absolutely nothing about scientific evidence, let alone DNA testing. The results revealed that the blood on Joe's shirt was *not* the victim's blood, nor was it his. The vaginal swab tested inconclusive, not enough genetic material to test. The blood on Joe's jacket was reported as a "3-probe match." *What the hell did this mean?* A match? Of course upon reading this, we, at Centurion were concerned. How could some of the blood prove his innocence and some suggest that he killed her? What we didn't know was that the method used by Lifecodes to obtain the "match" was unreliable. The result was "inconclusive" until the lab technician applied a certain probe in order to "align" the bands and obtain a "match." There are

[50] Stenographic Transcript at 175. *O'Dell v. Thompson*, (CL89-1475) (October 23, 1990).

usually four or five probes used by the FBI in DNA testing. Lifecodes used three. Without the benefit of other court rulings revealing that this method was unreliable, Joe knew, and attempted to explain to us, that this was not as it seemed. I was skeptical, of course, and knew this was one area that needed a full investigation before we could move forward with his case. I had to question everything Joe said and always looked for other support to corroborate his statements. Nothing could be taken on O'Dell's word alone. Not if we were to lend any credence to it. He was a clever man. For a convicted felon without tools of the trade, he was extraordinarily knowledgeable. As a result of my inability to fully understand the report I asked him foolishly why he did not test the vaginal swabs. Days later he would educate me.

I was starting to grasp the fact that Joe O'Dell seemed to know more about his case, the evidence, and DNA testing than his lawyers. I was right. It was his execution, not theirs. As I discovered, he would surprise me over and over again by overcoming the almost impossible task of being correct in the most unlikely of statement of facts. This intrigued me, as I was sure to catch him in a lie. I was humbled time and time again when his statements were proven accurate by outside sources, the record, or new court cases about which even his lawyers were unfamiliar. This all seemed highly unusual. I was dealing with a death row inmate, yet his tenacity, intelligence, insight, determination and sincerity distorted the stereotype of an uneducated death row con.

~Challenging Joe~

May marked the six-month anniversary since I started to investigate his case. I now became more comfortable writing to Joe. I am quite frank with him.

I must tell you that I have kept an objective attitude with reference to your innocence. I must admit that I was somewhat skeptical, even during the reading of your transcripts. The thing that concerned me most was the blood. I was also perplexed as to why all of your witnesses disappeared. After reading the interview you gave at Mecklenburg I must say I was very "impressed" by your past. There is no doubt in my mind that if you had killed that woman you would have disposed of the clothes and everything else. I was satisfied as to your complete openness about this, but nonetheless was upset with you for your continued display of anger and total disregard for the law. I was most disturbed that after you have spent most of your life in jail you would be brazen and foolish enough to pull the stunt you did in Florida concerning your wife's living arrangements [he hid in the trees to scope out his wife's infidelity and wanted to beat the crap out of her lover]. Joe, am I that naïve to think that a man could be so sick of spending his life in jail that he would do anything not to go back? I don't believe from your history that you had changed for any length of time. You have always been in something or another. Boy, if you used that energy elsewhere you could have been very successful. Yes, I am angry with you, after reading that interview. What are you really like now? Do you really think you have the strength to stay "clean" forever? By the way, one last question. In Volume 24 of the trial you mentioned during the sentencing phase that ...

It was at this time that I learned Joe had catalepsy. It ran in his family. It's a condition that causes temporary memory lapses. It explained why at trial he would drop issues in the middle of them, some of which he should have pursued. It was all starting to make sense now.

As usual, Joe responded to my letter in detail. He admitted to and blamed himself for his bad past. He also described what he was up against at trial. "I was a man fighting for his life against the forces that be, and I had the world against me. I was shooting spitballs with rubber bands while they were shooting M-16s at me. My trial was a circus at the least. Lawyers from all over the city would fill the courtroom to see me in action. This would make Test and Alberi mad. They weren't going to let a 'jailhouse lawyer' make them look like monkeys. They were obsessed with putting me in the electric chair. I was no match for two highly experienced, Virginia Beach's best!"

At the end of the letter he casually explained the questions I had about the Lifecodes' DNA report. "Oh by the way, the bad part on the report from Lifecodes came from a DXYS14 probe which is outlawed in Virginia and the FBI, so the report really doesn't have anything bad in it. I'll elaborate the next time I write to you." I thought *sure, outlawed, how convenient.*

Joe's letters began to educate me about prison life. I had suggested he was "mean" in one of my letters and while he admitted he had no excuse for his past behavior he felt it necessary, and I am glad he did, to let me know that life in a prison environment was not quite the same as life on the streets. We were discussing his second degree murder charge[51] for having stabbed a man in prison who was a known homosexual and was attacking Joe with a knife.

> All my life I've had to fight to survive. In prison only the strong survive. I've witnessed literally hundreds of murders and stabbings in prison. I've seen guards stabbed and killed; I've seen guards attacked and raped (male and female guards both). Prison is a sick society, with sick and perverted individuals in it. One must be strong to be able to walk inside the prison without being attacked. Contrary to popular belief, there is no authoritative protection in prison. It's the law of the jungle. A normal society does not speak the language, nor do they understand the language of the prison culture. Values are totally different! What would be an atrocious act in a normal society would make a person a hero in the prison society.

Unfortunately, he was right.

By now we were exchanging letters every week concerning the facts of his case. I came at him hard with questions, always playing the

---

[51] In the attorney's files I located the autopsy report for Lloyd Bess, the victim. It stated he died 19 days after the incident, from complications. The psychiatric records of Joe O'Dell, at the time, revealed that he was terrified of being attacked by others. His fear was substantiated by prison records. He was only 22 years old at the time. Clive Stafford Smith, one of Joe's attorneys, felt confident the conviction would be overturned and recognized for what it was, self-defense.

devil's advocate. I tried to catch him in lies, watch for inconsistencies, or anything that would prove he was manipulating me, simply playing the game of a con. I asked some poignant questions and when I received what I thought was his response with no answers, I told him how disappointed I was with him. He then sent me a copy of a letter in which he had outlined the answers to each and every question I asked. I had even received the original letter he had written. So when I accused him of "dancing around the issues" I had to eat my words. He was gentle in his response: "Anyway, young lady, you did jump the gun on me by assuming I was sloughing off."

At this point, and having already exchanged some confidential information, Joe started to advise me that my letters should be marked "legal mail" on the outside of the envelope. "Otherwise they will be read by the prison officials," he wrote. This was something I should have been doing months earlier.

Chapter 5

~From Cape Cod to Death Row~

As summer approaches my mind wanders to the lazy, small town New England days that lay ahead. Several years earlier I purchased a summer house in Cape Cod. I wanted my daughter Jennifer to enjoy hot sandy days at the beach, and to watch the Chatham A's baseball games with the locals in town. As I had done for the past four years, I anxiously await June. I pen my last letter to Joe before I depart. It was in this letter, and since I was assigned his case over eight months ago, that I first share personal information with him. I was beginning to share my life, just as he began to share his. I told him that my daughter was "graduating" fourth grade, and that she had a strong sense of right and wrong. I also spoke of her traveling soccer team adventures. To date, I have been very cautious about sharing my personal life or any photos with him. When Centurion Ministries sent a photo of the gang, I was excluded. Yet with all the information I knew about Joe, from his childhood through his incarceration, I felt it was harmless to share a little about myself. He responded kindly, telling me how he "appreciated my sharing little personal things with him…it takes away the all business aspect of our relationship, and allows us to relate as human beings to one another," he said. I started to see the change in our letters. The language became more casual, still directed toward his case, but with less intensity. It was also at this point that I asked Jim

McCloskey if I could participate in the actual investigative process if they decided to take the case. Since most volunteers are destined to simply read scores of letters and reply as assigned, I was happy to hear a positive response to my request. My job was intense and required an enormous amount of reading while summarizing a huge record. Above all, we were delving into the life of a man whose destiny was seemingly balanced on the outcome of our decision of whether to take his case, or not.

Centurion Ministries' policy is not only to ensure that an individual is innocent; they want to be confident that he will remain a law-abiding member of society. This was due in part to a recently released innocent man who had gone on to commit a heinous crime. Jim McCloskey did not want his organization to carry such a burden. As such, he quizzed Joe about his goals. Which required that Joe write a letter explaining how he planned on staying clean. I imagined this would be a self-serving exercise. How on earth could anyone ensure that a former convict would be a good citizen upon his release? Joe diligently wrote about his past and future behavior in a seven-page letter designed to convince Jim of his ability to remain straight. To his credit he admitted, "I have the greatest intentions, but no one could predict the future. I would be lying if I said I could." At this time, it was also starting to become apparent that a major factor in Joe's life, influencing his decision to continue fighting for his release, was the death of his mother on July 1, 1985, just five months after his arrest for the murder of Helen Schartner. He admitted having his mom come to him in his thoughts, as if she were talking to him, telling him to fight for his life and not to give up, to show the world that no matter how bad you've been in your life, that you did not do this crime. I knew one thing for sure: someone or something strong was behind Joe O'Dell, for I have never seen someone fight so hard and for so long with such fierce determination. This was an indication to Centurion that his claim of innocence had merit. The guilty usually cannot, and do not, put such intense energy into fighting for their claim of innocence. By comparison, since his arrest and for nine years thereafter, Joe has been fighting hard for his freedom.

By this time Jennifer and I were heading to Cape Cod and I had read 26 volumes of trial testimony and had only five left. I decided to bring them with us to the beach house. I would read in my spare time. When I completed the last five volumes of the trial transcript, I had started to feel empathy for Joe. I wanted to make his life on death row better. I found myself trying to bring beauty into his tiny death row cell by sharing the summer visions I soaked in while at the beach. The beautiful sunrises, sunsets, the breeze from the ocean, or sand in between my toes. I started to share my life just a little more, in hopes of easing the burden of his. I had witnessed Kate at Centurion sharing her life in letters with Joe. I saw no harm in sharing mine. I wanted to do something good for him, ease the pain of his existence. I knew one thing: the evidence was starting to look strong in his favor. I now questioned the veracity of the testimony of the jailhouse snitch, and the novice blood expert provided by the Commonwealth. Outside of this, the prosecution had nothing. Though still, I was not totally convinced. I had a lot of work ahead of me. The gathering of information is only the first step in the investigation.

My conversations with Joe continued to supply me with answers to the many questions that arose during my reading. They also helped provide me with essential legal information that I could not otherwise have understood without explanation from him and his lawyers. I started to learn the coined phrase "procedure over substance" and the enormous impact it had on Joe's case.

~DNA Exclusion~

I began to read the post-trial transcripts concerning the challenge to the serology testing performed at trial. When Joe's motion for DNA testing was granted by the trial judge, his lawyers requested an evidentiary hearing to bring forth all of Joe's legal issues, including the new DNA results which contradicted the serology blood testing of 1985. Judge Spain had retired. The case was now before Judge Austin Owen.[52] Three DNA experts testified that the blood on O'Dell's shirt, which had been argued at trial to be the victim's blood, could not be the blood of the victim. What? I thought. This is really true? The jacket was found to have inconclusive results. When asked if the blood on the jacket is different from the victim's blood, Doctor Spence answered, "I can't reach a straightforward conclusion, a good conclusion regarding these samples because there does seem to be a…I think it's inconclusive in my opinion because there is some suggestion of similarity, but the bands from the jacket are consistently different than those from the victim." When asked to compare the blood on O'Dell's shirt with the victim's blood, Dr. Spence concluded there was a "mismatch, that the band patterns did not match." When asked by the defense, "And did this cause you to change your opinion regarding the electrophoretic results that Ms. Emrich reached (at trial)?" Dr. Spence replied, "Well, I noted immediately that this mismatch was in contradiction to the reported match between the shirt and the victim's blood for the polymorphic protein markers. I think that it validated my concern, which I have communicated to you here today, that these protein markers have limited degrees of informativeness, and therefore, the fact that they match at these protein loci holds little weight as to whether the samples truly are identical or not." Another expert, Dr. Diehl, testified that he found Ms. Emrich's notes to be "incomprehensible." He, too, agreed the blood on O'Dell's shirt did not come from

---

[52] See Stenographic Transcript, *O'Dell v. Thompson* (October, 1989). It revealed the inability, or refusal, of the Judge to recognize that the underlying basis for O'Dell's conviction had been strongly challenged and remained in question. Moreover, there remained no direct evidence linking him to this crime.

the victim and the blood on the jacket was "inconclusive." Finally, the Commonwealth's own expert, Dr. Richard Guerrieri, agreed that the shirt was an "exclusion," meaning the blood on O'Dell's shirt was not the victim's blood. I compared this to the testimony on September 2, 1986 from the Commonwealth's expert, Ms. Emrich, referring to three stains that she tested from O'Dell's shirt: "Consistent with the blood from Helen Schartner and different from the blood of Joseph O'Dell." "Consistent with the blood from Helen Schartner and different from the blood of Joseph O'Dell." "Consistent with the blood from Helen Schartner and different from the blood of Joseph O'Dell." *Three times* they were wrong. I was infuriated at this point as I read through the judge's reasoning behind dismissing Joe's claims that the evidence at trial did not support his conviction. Though this testimony would have certainly brought different results at trial, the judge ruled that he had to abide by the tests that were used in 1985. And while not as sophisticated and accurate as DNA testing, he was bound to rely upon them to determine the validity of the death sentence. The court's opinion read as follows:

> The second basis upon which evidence has been heard today was the petitioner's claim that the reliability of the serological evidence produced at the time of trial has been brought into considerable question. The court has carefully considered all of the evidence adduced with respect to that aspect and is of the opinion that the petition for writ of habeas corpus on this ground likewise be denied on two bases. First, the court is of the opinion and finds that the Supreme Court of Virginia has already ruled that the serological evidence produced at trial was competent and was properly admitted into evidence and considered by the jury. It is not the function of a writ of habeas corpus to undertake to serve as an appellate court over the decision reached by the Supreme Court. Secondly, that aspect of the matter aside, the sole method used to attack the reliability of the serological evidence adduced at trial related to DNA testing,which the evidence indicates was in existence at the time of trial but not in general usage at the time of trial, that the methods used by Doctor Emerich [*sic*]

were those generally in common usage by experts at the time of trial, that the test results reached by Doctor Emerich [*sic*] from the standard test in use at that time were properly arrived at in accordance with the results reflected by those tests; and moreover and perhaps of equal importance, the **conclusion that she reached as a result of those tests was not that there was a match between the shirt and between the victim's blood or between the jacket and the victim's blood, but rather that on the basis of her test results, it could not be excluded that there was in fact a match** (emphasis added).

In other words, there was not a direct opinion that incriminated, but rather a failure to exclude the result that was sought to be offered by the prosecution in that case. The court is of the opinion that the serological evidence produced at trial was not flawed, that it was in accordance with recognized standards in existence at the time; and **while it may be that current testing methods would have produced a different result, that that does not justify the issuance of a writ of habeas corpus** (emphasis added)."[53]

~Three U.S. Supreme Court Justices~

I was learning fast about "procedure over substance." It was beginning to look like a legal circus, ignoring actual innocence claims in favor of following the path of the judicial system, even if it meant sending an innocent man to his death.

The ruling was appealed to the Virginia Supreme Court. It was the only time the lawyers failed to run a draft by Joe. The lawyers filed the appeal using "assignment of errors", when it should have read "appeal from habeas corpus." The Attorney General sat back and let the clock run. They claimed they would not object to a resubmission. They did. Doing what they did best, they filed a motion to dismiss the appeal on the grounds that it was not a correct appeal and that the time limit had expired, therefore procedurally barring O'Dell from fil-

[53] See Stenographic Transcript (CL89-1475) (October 23, 1990)

ing *any* appeal. The Virginia Supreme Court ruled that the appeal had been filed under the wrong caption and thus was an improper appeal, procedurally barring O'Dell on all of his issues. Basically, all Joe had left were the perfunctory appeals that are routinely filed and dismissed.

This was so unusual and presented such a potential "gross miscarriage of justice" that it hit the media and made the national section of the *New York Times* on December 3, 1991. The U.S. Supreme Court received the case on certiorari[54] (a writ or order to review an appeal from a lower court). Justices Sandra Day O'Connor, Blackmun and Stevens did not see it the way the Virginia Supreme Court did. They strongly suggested (meaning directed) the federal court to review O'Dell's claims. In fact, they were so concerned about this case that they urged the federal court to give "careful consideration to the inmate's challenge to the constitutionality of his sentence."

Justice O'Connor, joined by Justice John Paul Stevens, wrote a five-page statement stating there were "serious questions as to whether O'Dell committed the crime or was capable of representing himself— questions rendered all the more serious by the fact that O'Dell's life depends upon their answers."

There also remained questions about whether Joe O'Dell's constitutional rights were violated. The Court typically offers no comments or explanation when it turns down an appeal, but there were indications that the Court had treated this case as something other than routine. As a result of the diminutive error Joe's attorneys made in filing the state habeas appeal, by filing the wrong caption in the petition, the Justices were concerned that precedent would block Joe's case from being heard at all. They were right. The Virginia Supreme Court refused to hear the case and Joe was barred from federal review on *all* of his claims.

Justice Blackmun wrote: "Because of the gross injustice that would

---

[54] Certiorari is the discretionary decision of the court to accept a case for review.

result if an innocent man were sentenced to death, O'Dell's substantial federal claims can, and should, receive careful consideration from the federal court with habeas corpus jurisdiction over the case." Finally, some relief, I thought.

As I struggled to carry the towels and suntan lotion from a beautiful day at the beach, sand between my toes and in the seat of my pants, I entered the house to the sound of the telephone ringing. I dropped everything and fled to the phone. We were all waiting for the decision by the court. Would it heed the urging from the Supreme Court Justices, and if so how would they frame the hearing?

"Lori, this is Jeff Eilender at Paul, Weiss. I have some good news for you. We just received a fax. The Federal District Court will hear Joe's claims."

I asked him to fax a copy over to me. I had to see it for myself. The hearing was scheduled for August 2, 1994. Soon afterwards I got a call from Joe, who wanted to discuss the Judge's order. Joe's lawyers inform Joe and I that the hearing is restricted to the presentation of DNA evidence only. What about his other claims, we wondered. Didn't they matter? It appeared that Joe was granted an evidentiary hearing on the DNA evidence alone. Or was he? The reading of the court order left it open to dispute. I urged the New York lawyers to call Judge Spencer's clerk to find out for sure. After all, it's his only shot—his *last* shot at getting the evidence before a court. For fear of looking bad before the court, the law firm refuses to call. There is nothing we can do, I am told. It appears Joe is barred on all of his issues except DNA evidence. It was early in my legal education, but I would learn that the justice system really wasn't about justice. There is no room for error, not even the use of the wrong caption on a motion. That sole mistake could cost Joseph O'Dell his life.

~First Encounter~

For a death row inmate Joe was incredibly capable of articulating the facts of his case, the rule of law and any procedural bars that affected him. He was also very intelligent, smart enough to be "sweet" , and charming enough to soften the rough edges that often come with communication from a death row inmate. I finished reading his most recent letter before readying myself for the DNA hearing in Virginia. I was tickled by what Joe was describing to me.

> Joe: You might get a kick out of this story. Roy Smith's cat, Taffy, is "Sassy's" mama. (Sassy is my kitten). Taffy and Sassy were under the window at the loading dock next to my window. There's a hole about the size of a quarter in the screen, so me and Roy made up a long aluminum tube out of Pepsi cans and made the tube into a funnel. The kittens were meowing for food so Roy and I took a can of Salmon and rolled it into little balls and were rolling the little balls of salmon out of the window to the ground. Taffy and Sassy were going crazy chasing the balls of salmon and eating them. One time Sassy got in the way of the salmon rolling down the tube and a bunch of it landed on her back. She jumped 2 feet in the air it scared her so bad. The touching part of the story was to see their little tummies start to bulge from the food that we had sent down to them. They were very, very hungry when they came beneath the window.

How could such a tender thought come from a monster? I was beginning to see the softer side of him. Curiosity caused me to wonder—*what is he like in person?*

On my way to attend the evidentiary hearing, seated in the rear of the plane, I anxiously await my first encounter with Joe. Kate, from Centurion Ministries, agreed to meet me at the courthouse. This will be the first time I lay eyes on the man I am devoted to learn about. What will I feel when I see him? What will the hearing be like? How will the lawyers react to our presence? I was excited for Joe, knowing he had waited so long for a chance to be heard in court. As I approach the second row to sit beside Kate I smooth the skirt of my black suit, almost in a nervous gesture. Not long after I am seated a door creaks open. I watch intently as guards lead a tall, large man through the back of the courtroom, chains wrapped around his ankles and wrists. Gray hair fills the edges of his face and around his ears, softening the skin across the top of his head. Steely blue eyes shadow his pasty complexion. A broad smile surrounding faded white teeth takes attention away from his prominent nose. I could see that in younger days he might have been quite the "ladies man." Now, as the walls of death row (its food and sounds of daily living) take their toll, he appears almost broken, only a shell of who he resembled over nine years and five months earlier. He nods at us and takes a seat beside his lawyers. The lawyer sitting adjacent to him asks the security guard to remove the handcuffs. After almost six years of begging, pleading, and working day and night to get his case before a court, Joe O'Dell was finally here. I imagine he must be incredibly nervous. There, at the defense table, are Pat Schwarzschild and Robert Smith.

Pat reaches for Joe's hand under the table to calm his nerves. Such decency, I thought. Moments later, I go to the ladies' room and catch Joe glancing at me through the corner of his eye. In the bathroom I encounter Joe's sister Sheila and his odd cousin Patti. We engage a few pleasantries and then I return to my seat to watch the hearing unfold. This is strictly a hearing limited to the issue of DNA. All other issues related to his innocence are not allowed. Or so we think. I watch as the lawyers examine the witnesses. It is becoming apparent that the DNA results were exculpatory, meaning it points to Joe's innocence. The Commonwealth attorneys are anything but cordial. You can feel their strong desire to win the case, at any cost. The hearing progresses uneventfully until the end, when the Commonwealth attorney stands up and makes several false and misleading statements to the judge. They stand uncorrected. Having studied the record with intense interest, summarizing all the transcripts, court documents, interviews and reports, I knew this record cold. The Commonwealth is misleading the judge! They must know the truth. I sit in awe, listening to this mischaracterization of evidence and just how easy it is for them to spin the truth, using carefully chosen words to whirl a web of deceit. Sitting silently, I have no power to correct the lies. Joe's lawyers let it slide. Did they miss it? Did they not know what just happened? I had flown in from Cape Cod to meet Kate for the hearing, in support of Joe's case. I had done my job. It was time to go home. But something strange happened in the courtroom. Joe and I made a connection that was unsettling. I did not take the time to define it—I just felt its presence.

I returned to my summer vacation and waited, like everyone else, for the court's ruling. The spirit in my style was starting to emerge, instigating me to call the lawyers and insist they correct the record. While I knew nothing about court proceedings, I knew one thing: the Commonwealth had lied about the blood evidence. If left uncorrected, it would become a permanent part of the record. I started making demands of the lawyers, instead of the mild requests they had grown used to.

During these summer months I continue to learn more about Joe's daily life in prison.

> My cell is a tiny structure with a window located at the rear, a solid steel door at the front that slides sideways electronically when it is opened. There is a plexiglass window about 4 inches wide and about 20 inches long in the door, and there is a square hole in the door where food is put through on a tray when we are on lockdown and search. I can take four steps one way and one in the other direction. The cell is about 7 ft wide, 10 ft long and 9 ft high. The sink and toilet are made into one unit out of stainless steel. The bed is too small for me. It is made of a piece of steel that has holes cut into it. The mattress is one-inch thick and has a green vinyl cover on it. My pillow is about 2 inches thick and it has the same green vinyl covering on it. There is a fan, television combo, radio, cassette/recorder, electronic organizer, electronic dictionary and thesaurus, a word proces-

sor, electric clock, electric razor, hair clippers, a footlocker made out of plastic, writing materials, legal materials, 3 sweat suits, one blue, gray and black and a pair of LA Gear tennis shoes, and a beautiful gold nugget Seiko watch my 81 year old Uncle Reggie sent to me for my birthday, that is too pretty and too expensive to wear in death row, so I keep it in my typewriter case.

We are allowed an hour at a time on the phone. The MCI system is sure to get their surcharge from the inmates by cutting off the phone after 15 minutes so that an extra $1.65 gets dumped in the corporate pocket. The day starts at 6:30 a.m. with a voice over the public address system saying, "good morning, it is 6:30 a.m., time to get up. If you need to get on sick call an officer will come by your cell." This is repeated. At 7:00 a.m. a loud whistle blasts the cell block. "Count time, Count time," a gruff voice yells. At 7:15 a.m. the doors open. A stainless steel food cart comes into the hallway. There's a cell block identical to this one across the hall, and the food cart person fixes trays for the men in each cell block. After we finish eating at the stainless steel tables, on stainless steel, un-cushioned seats, we stack our trays in the door slot. At 8:00 a.m. we are locked up again. We stay in our cell until noon, the food cart appears again we are fed and at 1:00 p.m. we are locked in our cells again. At 4:00 p.m. they let us out to eat again. This time we get mail call, sick call, can take showers, play cards, visit each others cells and talk, trade candy, cigarettes and sodas. At 9:00 p.m. we are locked up, this time until the next morning. During the time in the cell we can watch TV, type letters or do whatever we want. Most guys sleep or watch the talk shows. Each morning at 9:00 a.m. 3 guards come around with handcuffs, chains and hammers, the inmates are handcuffed one by one, and a guard comes into the cell and beats on the window to see if we have tried to cut the window out. They also give the cell a perfunctory look-see/search, and then they remove the handcuffs and chains and leave. The inmates are not allowed to be around anyone except each other, without being chained down and handcuffed.
The inmates are allowed to go outside to a wire cage that is like a dog compound to play basketball or jog in a circle. The cage is about 2 ft long and 15 ft wide. They get to go out three times a week for an hr. and a half to two hrs, each day. The reason is I hate the embarrassment of having to take off all of my clothing and hand it through the

hole in the door, and then turn around naked with my back against the steel door while the guard reaches through and puts handcuffs on my wrists. Then the door is opened up and I have to step outside the door naked with my hands handcuffed behind my back. There are female guards with the guards when they do this and these female guards are standing outside our doors. Most of them will turn their heads to help alleviate the obvious embarrassment, but some of them won't. I complained about it one time and told them that they were in violation of my civil rights but the officer said "you don't have nothing I haven't seen before."

The guards all dress in black uniforms. Joe guesses it represents death or something. "But all of the guards aren't bad," he says. "There are some nice ones, both male and female." Having been there so long he is on a first name basis with them.

On the row it's tough enough to simply exist—even harder without some sort of financial assistance from the outside. If they are lucky enough to have support they can usually get by with the things they need to help keep them occupied in their cell. Or fight for their life, however they chose to spend their time. Joe chose to fight, so he needed all the resources he could get his hands on. Having none, he used his trade skills to give him what he needed most: a way to communicate with the outside world.

Having worn out eight typewriters, he was desperately in need of a new one. It was 18 months on the row before he could afford to buy a television set. And while it was the cheapest black and white set on the market, he proudly displayed it in his humble home. His determination to communicate with the outside world was shared with me as he tells the story.

One day I was walking by the trash can and noticed an old beat up typewriter, all torn to pieces. I pulled the typewriter from the trash. It looked impossible to fix. The keys were all bent and broken, the roller was broken off of it and the ball bearings were gone. I took the machine and with the skills I possessed as a machinist, tool and die maker I made parts out of plastic, even the ball bearings. I welded parts together with my cigarette lighter and a tube I formed as a nozzle to control the flame as I welded. When I finished putting the machine together, it was the most unlikely thing you'd ever see in your life. Keys were made of toothpaste tube caps, the return handle was made out of a toothbrush. That typewriter typed perfect, and the type was perfectly aligned. Nobody believed it. Someone named it Lazarus from the Bible, as the man who was resurrected from the dead. To think back to those days and to look down at the beautiful piece of equipment I am now typing on is really mind-boggling.

As our exchange of letters progressed, I learned more about this man. At least the side he wanted me to know about. After the hearing, he wrote about his feelings, sharing the hard work he put into carefully hand crafting a get well card for his "fiancée" Sheryl Murden, a girl who had come to his trial and stood by him over the past several years. In the same letter, he shares his day. "It's 2:30 p.m. and right now I've got my Smokey and the Bandit tape in and I am engaging in three of my major vices, a cup of "John Wayne" coffee, a Marlboro, and I've got Taffy and her kittens on the floor playing with a little mouse I made them out of a sock with stuffing, little ears, a nose and stuff made out of buttons, colored with highlighter pens. :):):) Now tell me, Lori, what more could a man ask for? :):):)"

I had never really believed that a death row inmate could have kittens in his cell. Then, one day, once again, I was proven wrong. "Listen," Joe said. I close my eyes and put the phone up against my ear. To my amazement I hear the distinct sound of meowing in the background. How on earth does a death row inmate get to have a kitten? Joe tells me that the guards are easily bribed. All it takes is a $5 bill and a look the other way. While I still doubted everything Joe said, I was beginning to see that he was honest about everything he shared with me. If he embellished stories, it may have been about his boyhood tales, where I sensed a hint of grandiose recollection of his childhood years. But his case was one area of his life I was starting to know cold, and he knew it.

~The Opinion~

I welcomed the month of September with open arms. The tourists are gone, their children now playing on the school playground instead of white sandy beaches. The air has a cooler, crisper feel to it. Green is now starting to turn shades of red, orange and yellow. On my mind is Joe's fate. We're all anxiously waiting for Judge Spencer's opinion on September 4, 1994. As usual, Joe and I are quick to reach each other by phone. We are stunned. It appears that his hearing was not limited to the presentation of DNA evidence. Instead, it was a full evidentiary hearing, where Joe's attorneys could have presented any and all evidence in support of his case. All along his attorneys had said that they could only present the newly discovered DNA evidence (by this time it was not new since the hearing before Judge Owen was over four years ago). Time and time again Joe complained to me about their apparent indifference to his life and death situation. Indeed, they made an enormous mistake by writing the wrong caption on Joe's appeal, and an even bigger mistake when they relied upon the representation from the Attorney General's office that they would not oppose it. Now, in Joe's only chance to put forth his case, he was being screwed again.

As usual, Joe took things into his own hands and wrote a rather articulate letter concerning the evidence in his case, or lack thereof, and his misunderstanding about the hearing. He wanted his lawyers to file a motion for a rehearing. In his letter to Judge Spencer, he described how he was concerned upon arrest that the prosecution would use a jailhouse snitch against him, as they did in several other capital murder cases. Knowing that in each of these cases in Virginia Beach the prosecutor always brought someone in to say the defendant had "confessed," immediately, upon being placed in a jail (possibly a week or two after his arrest) Joe wrote a letter to the Virginia Supreme Court. He alerted them of his fear that the prosecution would use a snitch to say he had confessed the crime. Richard Townes, another man charged with capital murder, also wrote a letter stating the same thing. Both had jailhouse informants testify that the defendants confessed. Both defendants were convicted and sentenced to death. I wondered how convenient his story was. Could he be telling the truth? It seems to me if he were, how could his attorney miss an opportunity to bring this out at trial? For if one was aware of such things, and made an effort to protect themselves against false incrimination, it seems highly unlikely they would ignore their own concerns and confess to a stranger. I would add this to my list of things that needed corroboration, only to later discover Joe's letter to the Supreme Court among thousands of pages I was now destined to devour.

Joe's letter to Judge Spencer contained strong evidence of his innocence. He was right about a few things. How could the prosecution put a jailhouse snitch on the stand who claims O'Dell talked with and bought drinks for the victim when they were never seen together? How could the Commonwealth fail to conduct soil testing on the numerous soil samples they took from the crime scene to connect O'Dell to the field? More importantly, if O'Dell was in the field, which had elephant grass at least several feet tall, how could there not be botanical debris all over his clothing? Especially if he viciously beat the victim in the field? Wouldn't it be stuck to his pants, his shirt and his jacket? Yet not one trace of this botanical debris was found in Joe's car, his clothes or on his shoes. This seemed impossible, given the circumstances in which the victim died. Also, the Commonwealth had incredible resources. Why not bring in John Nutter, the sailor Joe fought with in the parking lot at the Brass Rail at 1:00 a.m. If the man he fought with was not Joe O'Dell, it seemed easy enough to dispute Joe's alibi with direct testimony from the source. Joe's letter to the judge was strong and well written. It raised serious questions about his innocence. Yet court rules would forbid the judge from engaging in correspondence directly with a defendant. The defendant, Joe O'Dell, was represented by counsel. If I were in Joe's shoes, I would have done the same thing. I would not want to watch the fate of my life rest in the hands of others who "slipped" in the process, causing my chances at proving my case to become more remote with each passing mistake.

Joe knew that when I read Judge Spencer's opinion I would become upset. It contained some factual inaccuracies that were crucial to his case. Left uncorrected these mistakes would climb the ladder to the highest court in our country, never allowing the truth about the evidence to unfold. It was not necessarily the judge's fault. He relied upon the lower court, and then the clerks who knew nothing about the case, to regurgitate the facts as they knew them. I could now see how easy it is for the Commonwealth to spin the truth about the facts, and if left unchallenged, they would become a permanent part of the record. Judge Spencer's opinion contained the following language in his conclusion:

> Based on the evidence at the evidentiary hearing, the blood on the jacket and the blood on the checkered shirt can be excluded as having a common origin. Again, based on the evidence, the DNA comparison on the blood on the checkered shirt and the victim's blood yielded a result that is "inconclusive"[55].

On page 31 of his opinion the reference to the shirt as "inconclusive" is inconsistent with the evidence at the hearing and the dicta in the balance of his opinion. The court further stated that the blood on the shirt was an exclusion and the jacket was inconclusive. This is the correct conclusion, and mirrors that which the experts testified to at the hearing. Judge Spencer's opinion was not entirely clear. In fact, it was downright confusing.

This is significantly important because the blood on the shirt, jack-

---

[55] See *O'Dell v. Thompson*, No. 3:92CV480, slip op. at 31-32. (Sept. 6, 1994).

et and pants were said to have come from the same source, the victim. At trial, the blood was tested using the serology method. If the same blood is tested years later using a more sophisticated, definitive method of testing and it refutes the antiquated serology testing performed back in 1985, it invalidates the basis upon which Joe O'Dell was convicted. *Four* experts, two for the defense and two for the Commonwealth, opined that the blood on Joe's shirt was *not* the victim's blood and the blood on his jacket was *not* a match, it was inconclusive. The judge's finding included the fact that the method used by Lifecodes to correct for band shifting was scientifically unacceptable and outside "match" criteria. This meant the only blood test that yielded results *excludes* O'Dell as the perpetrator of the crime. Judge Spencer relied upon other things to refrain from overturning the conviction. Evidence that O'Dell was told he could not challenge at the evidentiary hearing. Mostly, it involved the testimony of the jailhouse snitch, Steven Watson. After hearing testimony, and knowing that Emrich's antiquated methodology was incapable of pointing the finger at O'Dell, the judge still found "Nor has O'Dell proved that the trial court's acceptance of Emrich's testimony violated his right to fundamental fairness."[56] He also noted that "the Virginia Supreme Court's finding that no plea agreement existed between Watson and the Commonwealth must be presumed correct, and O'Dell's new evidence does not indicate that he could rebut this finding by convincing evidence."[57] In Judge Spencer's factual background he wrote that O'Dell had left the bar sometime between 11:30 p.m. and 11:45 p.m. This is incorrect. Trial testimony from the doorman, Bruce Cooper, has O'Dell still at the bar at 12:00 midnight when he was counting the cover charge money:

> Q. Did you see Mr. O'Dell leave the County Line?
> A. Yes, I did.

---

[56] *Id.* at 32. footnote 16.
[57] *Id.* footnote 17.

Q. And could you tell us the time he left the County Line, sir?
A. Approximately midnight.

Q. And how can you remember that after more than a year
and a half?
A. Well, I remember it because of the incident that happened,
you know, the next day, and it was brought to my attention I
remembered him and because at around midnight we made
deposits. We took the excess cash that was in the cash regis-
ters at the bar and deposit it in the safe so at the end of the
night all the money wasn't out on the floor. And I was in the
process of doing that, and I did that at midnight.

Q. Do you know where exactly he was when [*sic*] the last time
you saw him?
A. He was just out of the entranceway to the lounge near the-
bathrooms.[58]

Not one witness testified O'Dell left prior to that. The prosecution would ignore these facts and make up their own. In their briefs,
they had O'Dell leaving around 11:30 p.m., the same time as the victim. I listed all the factual inaccuracies in the record and made note of
the fact that this needed to be followed up on at some point. However
frustrating this all was, the icing on the cake came when Judge Spencer
stated, "Although O'Dell [*sic*] evidence did establish a 'fair probability'
that, in light of all probative evidence at the time of his federal evidentiary hearing 'the trier of the facts would have entertained a reasonable doubt of his guilt'[59], it wasn't enough. The legal standard was "no
rational trier of fact could (find) proof of guilt beyond a reasonable
doubt."[60]

Upon review it's easy to see how and where the system was failing.
Reading it after the fact made it all the more frustrating. And it must

---

[58] Trial Transcript, Vol. 21, Tab 57, page 37.

[59] See O'Dell v. Thompson, No. 3:92CV480, slip op. at 32. (Sept. 6, 1994). footnote 18.

[60] See Herrera, 113 S. Ct. at 875 (White, J., concurring) (citing Jackson v. Virginia, 443 U.S. 307,
324 (1979).

have been gut-wrenching for Joe. The facts seemed to be more clear in the beginning of the appellate process, but become more misstated, misunderstood, misapplied or just plain wrong, as the case proceeded up the appellate ladder. A fine example of this was the U.S. Supreme Court's memorandum decision dated December 2, 1991. The facts were summarized as follows:

> The Commonwealth's evidence at trial consisted of tire tracks that were "similar" to those left by petitioner's car, blood tests, and testimony by a fellow inmate that O'Dell had confessed to committing the murder. The court refused O'Dell's request for a hearing on the reliability of the blood tests and allowed the technician to opine that the blood samples taken from O'Dell's shirt and jacket were consistent with samples taken from the victim. The court also denied O'Dell's proffer of evidence that the informant had offered to manufacture evidence in other trials as a means of avoiding prison terms. (Footnote 1)

> Footnote 1. Subsequent to O'Dell's trial, the informant was given three years probation on a breaking and entering charge, despite contrary assurances by the prosecution to petitioner's counsel and the court.

By the time this case would reach the Fourth Circuit of Appeals there would be "overwhelming" evidence of O'Dell's guilt and a "match" between the blood on O'Dell's clothing and the victim's blood. There seemed to be no way to stop this snowball of factual errors. The more the Commonwealth came under attack to defend their verdict, the more these errors started to stick in oral arguments, briefs and interviews with the media. It was an innocent person's nightmare. Now I had to find out if O'Dell was dreaming.

~Personal Involvement~

I could see and feel Joe's frustration in some of his writings. Living inside a tiny gray cell on death row, armed with knowledge about his own case that was being misunderstood or mischaracterized. I wanted to scream out for him. I wanted to be his voice, to help get it right. In his nine years on death row Joe had watched 22 men go to their deaths in the electric chair. Two others committed suicide, and two died of medical problems. Death reeked havoc in his life. It was his very existence. I vowed not to let him become another statistic, especially one based upon lies.

Shortly after the opinion came down I read one of the books Joe had contributed to. He was working with a woman who had an obsession with serial killers. I read the book simply to see what Joe had gotten himself into and I was thoroughly disgusted. I chastised him for engaging in such things, even if it were to assist the FBI in understanding such killers. I told him never to associate with them, they would taint his case. This kind of attention was dangerous for him. I was starting to protect Joe. I could see the predators beginning to feed on his situation—believe it or not there were scores of them out there.

Autumn has arrived as I watch the turning of the leaves in New England. It represents the change of not only the seasons, but the cycles of life. My life, in many ways is just beginning. I am now searching for a whole new direction to my own life. For Joe, he is struggling with the end of his.

"My time is running out," he said. "My attorneys spoke of this yesterday. I have a year or less to live if I lose my case. So I have exigent circumstances. Jim has got to let me know something soon."

Joe had been in touch with Centurion Ministries for years prior to my appearance. It was just shy of a year since I started studying his case. At this point he *must* have been getting impatient. He had answered hundreds of questions, offered details of every aspect of his life, his trial and death row existence, and *still* had no idea whether we were taking on his case! Centurion was cautious, but I was beginning to think that they would never move into action, and even if they did, it would be too late to help Joe.

I gave Joe my home telephone number to increase the amount of time we have to strategize and plan the return attack—like a battlefield where shots are fired across enemy lines, each side choosing to either retreat or fight back. I chose to fight back. This was becoming my battle too now. I was becoming too impassioned by what I was learning. I had to dig deeper. I wanted to find out more. In reading the voluminous record, I learned things that no one else knew. They may know bits and pieces of it all, but I was starting to learn it all. I was beginning to gather enough information so that I could advocate for Joe O'Dell.

During the past year I was consumed with professional goals, my daughter's education and interests, and working on Joe's case. Joe and I were becoming friends as well, however that can be defined when the contact between two people remains only verbal, with no physical interaction whatsoever. Joe's letters were sometimes signed, "smiles and blessings" or "smiles and friendship," or "your struggling friend." but now they were also being signed "love and prayers, marantha" (a religious phrase meaning 'Our lord come'). A signature he often wrote to the office manager at Centurion Ministries as well. Now, I too was becoming his friend.

I was becoming a strong source of information and a great resource for him, a man who had no one strong enough to stand up to the strength of his opposition. As I allowed myself to become more personal with Joe, I did not realize that he would soon take it to another level, without my knowledge or permission. It's easy to see that a death row inmate could fall for his rescuer. I was the answer to his desperate attempt to get someone to look at the evidence in his case. For me, I loved being able to make a difference in another person's life. To help someone less fortunate than myself.

In the worst-case scenario, I start to become entangled in one of Joe's creative expressions. One that is well-meaning, but nonetheless calls my objectivity into question and raises more questions than answers for us. In an attempt to have contact visits (a visit which allows us to be in a room together with no glass or walls between us and allows conversations without being monitored over the phone), Joe conjures up a fake Indian union (he has Cherokee blood in him) between us. Except it's not fake to him. He wanted to do something to "unite" us. I would normally never agree to such a seemingly strange thing, but what harm would result if it gave Joe peace of mind in his chaotic world. I *did* care for him, didn't I? In fact, against all I have ever known or believed, and against the norm, I found myself growing fond of him. So I agreed. Even though I was uneasy with it, I agreed.

It's December 1st now and I find out he has submitted this fake document suggesting an "unofficial marriage" to the Department of Corrections (DOC). I am furious. I feel betrayed—he took this unusual and bold step without asking me, knowing I would never have agreed. He knows that I am concerned about remaining credible. The DOC denies his request for a contact visit as being without basis and I was relieved. Little did I know the Attorney General's office would try to use this to discredit me, and the prison would later recognize a fake document as legal. For now, it became fodder for the newspapers. I yelled at Joe, cautioning him that any further action to implicate us in a romantic relationship would jeopardize his case. He didn't seem to care. The truth about his case would come out one day, he said, and aren't we all about truth? Isn't that the way it is? When you know you're innocent, you firmly believe the system will one day reverse the wrong perpetrated against you. It's called faith. I wonder in Joe's case if he will be so lucky.

It was about this time that I felt I needed to either pursue the investigation or drop out of the case. I decided to contact the lead investigator used by Centurion Ministries, Richard Reyna. "Richard, Centurion is dragging their feet and I want to investigate the case. Will you help me?" I ask.

To my surprise he answered quickly and said yes. He, too, thought it strange that Centurion had been "looking" at the case for years without a commitment. With time running out we became a team. Richard is an amazing investigator. He is sought after by some of the best attorneys in the country, especially by those whose clients are on death row. I was about to learn from one of the best how to be effective in getting what you wanted from a witness. I didn't realize my own capabilities would prove helpful in bringing out what others could not in the past ten years of Joe's investigation. The roller coaster was about to climb and I was strapped in for the ride.

Chapter 6

~Prison Visit~

Christmas, 1994. I would spend the holiday at the most unlikely of places—in a prison, dressed for a Christmas feast at a suburban house party. Except this was no party. It is my first visit with Joe and I am understandably nervous. I make my way down to Boydton, Virginia, an isolated, Godforsaken area of the country that is so remote I feel out of place. I fly into Richmond and drive 50 dreary minutes to a small Holiday Inn near the prison. Hotels such as these would have no clientele where I was going. The next morning I find my way to Mecklenburg Correctional Center. I park, gazing at the barbed wire around this maximum security prison. It is my first time entering *any* prison. My velour pants drape nearing the cement. I'm wearing leather boots with two-inch heels and have on a cashmere sweater, diamond stud earrings, beautiful gold rings and a black coat with black rabbit fur covering my neck. I dressed for comfort.

A sergeant greets me from behind a cheap metal desk close to the front door. I am asked to identify myself and sign in.

"Place your belongings in a metal storage unit and lock them up for security, then proceed to the security area where you'll be scanned for contraband," says the male guard. I give him a surprised look. "It's just policy," he says.

At this point I have nothing in my hands other than the key to my locker. After passing through one security entrance, where my body is scanned for metal objects, I'm directed to a private room. A female officer comes in and orders me to stand in the middle of the room where she frisks me with both hands and a wand.

"Take off your shoes," she commands.

She needs to inspect my feet and inside my shoes. I suppose I could have taped some sort of weapon or drugs there. When she is done with me I'm directed through metal doors. I step forward and enter a small enclosed area as a gate electronically closes behind me. I am now standing between two gates in a closed in area about two feet by four feet, steel bars surrounding me. I wait until the gate in front of me opens and then move forward to another closed in area. I feel claustrophobic and frightened as I wait between this closed door and the next one. I guard my fear so no one will know I am terrified. I can see through glass windows what appears to be the visiting area, and an open area outside the building, with walking paths leading from the dungeons surrounding their way out to sanity. Even if sanity is only a visit. I watch as inmates walk in slow motion, chains locked tightly around their ankles, making their way to the visiting area. It is my turn. I am asked to move inside. I pass through another metal door that electronically closes behind me with a loud clang.

Straight ahead is a large, open visiting area, with candy and soda machines to my left. To my right is a "secured" room, long and narrow with eight metal chairs spaced about a foot apart, all in a row. Each chair is bolted to the floor in front of a plexiglass window that divides the room, directly across from a seat on the other side. On the other side of the glass are individual rooms that look like mini cells, with doors behind them leading to a narrow hallway. There is a telephone on either side of the partition. Lowering myself onto the metal stool I suddenly notice a guard escorting someone into the secured room on the other side of the partition. Joe is moving toward me. Chains on his feet and handcuffed wrists slow his gait. The guard directs him right in front of me. Each cubicle is separated from the next. When they open the door for Joe to walk in I can see he is used to the routine. After entering the tiny room the door is locked behind him. He turns around with his back to the guard and through a slot in the door the guard removes the handcuffs. Joe sits down on a metal stool and grabs the phone in his hand. I reach for mine. My heart is racing.

This routine may be familiar to Joe, but it is completely foreign to me. I act nonchalant when I look up at this strange man before me. He's a man I would never have given the time of day to on the street, yet here I am living and breathing his existence. His hair had been cut short since the first and last time I laid eyes on him in Judge Spencer's courtroom. Gray hair covers the sides of his head near the corner of his ears. Age, and death row, had taken its toll on Joe, revealing itself by the shiny spot on top of his head, and wrinkles crossing paths on his face. His eyes appear soft, not steel like, as I imagined a killer's eyes to be. The picture before me is unlike the photograph of Joe when he was arrested over nine years ago. In that picture Joe had a full head of hair, a wide beautiful smile, and eyes with life dancing in them. His demeanor is intimidating only because of his size. Joe is 6' 4". I am not afraid.

With all the security I know we are being monitored. I have to be careful what I say. A guard is at the end of the row seated in a private glass encased room, watching the activity before him. His careful watch, and gun strapped to his waist, make me nervous. Convicts are everywhere. I can't hide my discomfort.

"Hi," Joe says. He, too, is nervous when he makes the first attempt to break the ice. I smile, and as we begin talking over the phone, his voice is soothing and I begin to relax. Ours is a casual conversation. He knows my purpose in town. He also knows we can't talk about it.

"Hello, Joe," I say as I manage to turn a smile. I let the next few hours take its course. I, myself, a prisoner of my surroundings.

These non-contact visits are limited in time by the number of people who show up for a visit. You can get one half hour, or you could be there all day. It's the luck of the draw. The first day I was there from 9:00 a.m. to 1:00 p.m.

Our conversation moves along awkwardly. This is not an attorney–client visit, which means we have no privacy. Everything we say and do is being monitored. When hunger and thirst strikes, the prison is kind enough to have a machine for visitors. Stale candy and soft drinks for substance are in a room adjacent to another visiting area where contact visits take place. Dangerous inmates, and those on death row (I imagine they are the same) are not eligible for contact visits. The only contact visits they get are with their lawyers. I am on the visiting list as an investigator, not officially tied to the defense team. I hadn't earned that privilege yet.

I stayed in Virginia from December 24th to January 2nd. It isn't the Christmas or New Year's I had imagined. Neither is my current life. My first stop was to see Joe. Mission accomplished. After a weekend visit with Joe, I set out Monday morning to visit with his old friend and partner in crime, Bobby Watts. As teenagers, Joe and Bobby had robbed several convenience stores. They had earned the "silk stocking bandits" name because they wore silk stockings over their heads. I recall having read a newspaper article about them that the lawyers had in their files; they had *everything*. One of the victims was not particularly frightened. Instead he appeared to have focused on how scared the boys were, hands shaking, fumbling their way around, certainly not the "experienced" criminal, the victim thought. Bobby was now long retired from a life of crime and owned a small car shop near the beach. I had dinner at his home with his wife Janie. I left around 11:00 p.m. and drove to the County Line Executive Inn establishment, the last place Helen Schartner was seen alive. Afterwards, I make my way directly across the street to the After Midnight Club, where Helen's twisted body was discovered in the back field. Bobby accompanies me, and said that Joe Moore, the drunk who discovered the body, had told an officer that he killed Helen Schartner and that they couldn't do anything about it because of the trial. I wandered if this were true. I didn't think so. The next day Bobby offers me a map and I venture off to check out Bay Vending, Joe Moore's place of employment years ago.

"No," an employee says. "He's not here, but we know where he is."

I wasn't lucky enough to find out where.

"We'll leave him a message."

"Sure. Thanks for your trouble."

I knew they are covering for him; they're not about to give me any information.

The following morning I meet with the investigator for the Virginia law firm that is assisting Joe on his case. Al Brown is a tall, black man, who *looks* like an investigator. The reserved, sneaky-looking kind of guy. My day is spent offering him information and finally, leading him to the crime scene. I am bringing *him* to the crime scene. He had never visited it before. *Must be a new case*, I think, wanting to give him the benefit of the doubt. I was not impressed. He didn't appear to be quick-witted or keen about this case, just casually interested. I have no time to waste educating an investigator. I have an appointment with CBN News. To gain access to the right people I take a two-hour tour and visit with the VP of Operations of the National Legal Foundation, a Christian public interest law firm. I leave a note with the secretary for the producer. It works. The next morning the producer Michael Patrick, and reporter Jennifer Robinson meet with me. They're interested in Joe's story. My goal is to spread the word.

I wanted to share with Joe on a weekend prison visit the results of my first street investigation. He seemed pleased at my accomplishments, yet remained cautiously reserved.

When I get back to Princeton I review the autopsy report again and get Joseph Moore's full name and previous address. I have to find this man.

Jennifer is ten years old now, requiring my attention as well. Juggling my parental responsibilities with my new passion is challenging. Youthful innocence and actual innocence. Two very different things. The innocence of a child and the possible innocence of a man sentenced to die.

On a Monday morning I receive a call from Richard Reyna in El Paso, Texas. He's ecstatic with news about Steven Watson.

"Lori, I located the jailhouse snitch. He lives in West Virginia."

"Oh my God, that's terrific," I am almost shouting back at him. I need to get some money to pay for the investigation. "I will contact you when plans to retain you have been finalized."

I follow up with Kate at Centurion Ministries. They had promised to assist me in the investigation by offering whatever they could in the way of materials. She willingly provides me with Steven Watson's 1989 interview with one of the investigators from Joe's legal team. I call Don Lee at the Virginia Capital Representation Resource Center (VCRRC), the non-profit organization dedicated to assisting inmates such as Joe and ask if we can change investigators from Al Brown to Richard Reyna. I am practically pleading with him. I also speak with Michelle Brace, another lawyer with VCRRC, and suggest we follow through with Joe's New York attorney. Lee agrees to pay Reyna's limited expenses while in West Virginia. I chalk this victory up as a first.

I know I must follow up with CBN News so I put together a package and mail the *1993 Innocence and the Death Penalty Subcommittee Report*,[61] Judge Spain's comments,[62] Alberi's letter to Diane Lavett, three *Virginian-Pilot* articles on Alberi,[63] and a death row series of ar-

---

[61] Due to the escalating number of innocence cases a committee was appointed to investigate and report on Innocence and the Death Penalty.

[62] My investigation reveals several comments by the judge with regard to his discomfort concerning Joseph O'Dell's conviction.

[63] Joe Jackson and June Arney, 'Controversies Trail Alberi in His Quest for Judgeship', *Virginian-Pilot*, March 3, 1996, page A1. The *Virginian-Pilot* ran an article on Albert Alberi and his questionable professional behavior, calling into question his ability to serve as a judge in the

ticles written in June, 1994.[64] I am careful to include Judge Spencer's opinion with a memorandum related to the facts and the attorneys' appellate briefs. This is my first attempt at trying to expose this puzzling death row case.

I then telephoned the Virginia Police Department and learn that the Brass Rail, the bar where Joe was seen in a fight the morning of the murder, had been torn down. "It's a Hardee's now," the cops inform me. Next is my attempt to reach Joseph Moore. The phone rings endlessly, but nobody answers.

Meanwhile, I start assembling additional material for CBN, and try again to reach Moore. Still no answer. I have also tracked down the phone number for Joe's co-counsel at trial, Paul Ray, the defense attorney who refused to turn over his notes to Joe's appellate lawyers. I don't have a good feeling about Ray. The answering machine picks up and, not surprisingly, the sound of his voice makes my skin crawl.

To create a break in my routine I venture out for the evening to join some friends. I hate the bar scene. I feel vulnerable as a single woman, with 26-year-old young guys looking to score a pickup. At age 38 I should feel flattered, but after two hours I am ready to go home and crawl into bed. The night confirms my dislike for the bar crowd. In fact, it was this very type of scene that drew Helen Schartner out that fateful cold February evening, never to return home.

After haggling with the New York attorney, Bob Smith, I decide

---

upcoming nominations. The article depicted questionable behavior regarding three cases, including O'Dell's. A secret subpoena, witness intimidation, and withholding evidence were among a variety of methods noted. "The judges have appeared to be reluctant to discipline some of Mr. Alberi's courtroom shenanigans. The perception in the bar is that he hasn't been dealt with harshly enough," Moody E. Stallings, Jr., a former Democratic state senator was quoted. On March 6, 1996 the *Virginian-Pilot* reported, "Alberi won't seek spot on bench; blames 'politics'".

[64] During 1994 two investigative reporters for the *Virginian-Pilot* newspaper wrote a series of articles about death row in Virginia, noting withheld or omitted evidence, lying witnesses or some form of misconduct that "could have changed the outcome." See Joe Jackson and June Arney, 'Sentenced to Die Without Fair Trials', *Virginian-Pilot*, June 26, 2994, page A1.

to take matters in my own hands and fax a letter to Reyna. Richard consents to a reduced fee if I pay him directly, as opposed to being engaged by the attorneys. I know he is doing me a big favor. The investigation will take five to six days. In an attempt to get the social security number of Watson's wife, I mail a letter to Baltimore to obtain their marriage certificate. And I finally secure $500 from the Capital Resource Center to help pay Richard's bills.

Meanwhile, I start filling out law school applications. It is January 1995 and I'm applying for the fall semester. The more I learn about the system, the more I want to become involved. I prefer to be one of those lawyers who care.

At this point in my life I am also in the middle of a divorce. Walter and I had been married for 14 years but had been living apart for almost five years now. The tremendous demands on Walter's time as a surgical resident and entering a new practice, came at a time when I was experiencing the terrible loss of my mother. Both combined to leave me feeling somewhat lost and extremely lonely—my own needs and desires unmet. And I had become quite unhappy in my life. Jennifer was, understandably, distraught about the divorce, but I tried always to impress upon her that her father and I both loved her very much, and that everything would be okay. She and her father did, and still do have a great relationship. Fortunately, Jennifer was never pitted against one parent or the other, as is so often the case with divorce, nor did she ever feel responsible for what happened. I steered her away from having a "victim" attitude; instead, I instilled strength in her.

Neither Walter nor I felt the need, or urgency to be the "one" to file the papers. I wouldn't do it. I let him bite that bullet. Now, it is finally becoming a reality with papers being served back and forth. Walter and I decide not to let the lawyers come between us. He is, and always will be, a gentleman. He fired his attorney when it became apparent he wanted to turn this into a divorce war. Walter would have none of it. Had I known better I might have halted the process and begged for forgiveness, except I was still in the process of learning much greater lessons in life than to know what was good for me. Or what I thought was good for me.

I finally receive an answer at Joe Moore's residence, except it's not him. It's a woman with a deep southern drawl. Disappointed, I realize I need to go back to square one to locate him. I decide instead to review the legal landscape of court opinions.

The *Schlup* decision has been published with a vote of 5-4.[65] It is one of those precedent setting cases the U.S. Supreme Court hands down during the judge's respective term. The issue in this case is right on point with one of the main issues in Joe's case. It means Joe's conviction could be overturned. It also suggests the possibility of a full evidentiary hearing and is relevant to the issue of the credibility of witnesses. It is critical for us, as Watson was instrumental in tying Joe to the victim. In fact, he was the *only* witness who did. His creditability was untouched in Joe's trial. The judge denied Joe's motion to bring in "prior instances" (a legal challenge in the courts) by Watson, where he wrote letters to other prosecutors in an attempt to exchange testimony for the "get out of jail free" card. The lawyers and I would engage in numerous conversations concerning exactly what this means for Joe, and how likely it was that Joe would get some relief.

On January 24, I am accepted into the New England School of Law which has a reputation for a strong teaching faculty. I wanted a solid first year under my belt. Immediately after I put down the acceptance letter, Richard calls. The New York blue-chip law firm is haggling once again over payment to Richard Reyna for his services, nickel and diming him to death. I promise Richard I'll get more money for him—he deserves it.

Another law school offers me a spot in their class. I welcome having choices. Being one of those "older" students looking to go back

---

[65] See generally *Schlup v. Delo*, 115 S. Ct. 851 (1995).

to school I am more prepared now than I would have been right after college. While in college at the University of Connecticut it occurred to me that I might follow in my father's footsteps so I took, and loved, all the pre-law classes I could find. But I had my future already laid out by the age of 14, when I decided I wanted to become an accountant. I wanted to be self- sufficient as a woman. And I wanted a job that could take me anywhere in the country. I got both. I was 14 years old when the Veterans Administration (VA) Hospital staff informed my family that my father would never walk again. At that moment my entire life changed from that of the privileged daughter of a respected Assistant Attorney General, to a member of a family that struggled to cope with our new existence. Multiple sclerosis is a destructive incurable disease. My family watched helplessly as our father went from a strong, ca-pable man, to walking with a limp, then with the assistance of a cane, then a walker, and finally, a wheelchair. Never letting his declining health deter him, he continued to work. My mom would use a con-traption that allowed you to put a cloth seat under someone's butt in a wheelchair and crank them up high enough to get them into the car. It was a routine that my sister and I shared when we were old enough to drive, taking turns bringing our father home after a long day at the office. We drove across town half an hour each day after school, until the time finally came when we started to find his head resting upon his desk, waiting for us, after struggling to make it through the day. The state allowed him to work probably far longer than he should have, but he never gave up the fight.

For 20 years my mother devoted her life to caring for my father. And for 20 years the stress was always there. They say stress can give you cancer. It was ironic that she would die first—two years before my dad. Her lymphoma wasn't discovered until it was stage four. She never took the same care of herself as she did her husband. By the time they discovered the sore on her hand was not healing, she found herself in a battle to save her own life. My two sisters and I spent our mother's last night huddled around her in a bedside vigil, offering her comfort, even though she couldn't respond. "I don't feel like I am dying," she told me one night as we lay side by side, still at home in her marital bedroom. "No mom, you are not." We never really talked about her impending death except to kid around about who gets what when she's gone. In retrospect, she was never kidding around. I just couldn't bear the thought of losing her, so I played the game, until it was over.

Over the years my brother became an aggressor and fought with everyone in the family, including his own father. I often became my younger sister's protector, as well as my own. He was a troubled son, helping to care for his dad, yet dangling that as a carrot in front of my helpless mother.

While mom catered to my brother, she would often tell me she wanted to run away with me. "Let's go, Annie Oakley, let's just keep on driving." She had always called me Annie Oakley because I became the fighter in the family. I always felt I had to stand up for myself, my sisters, my mom and dad. So the nickname stuck, to this day. If ever I hated anyone in my life, it was my brother, until years later when I learned the laws of the universe and the balance it creates in a family. Though seemingly a dysfunctional family, I learned through a leading human behaviorist expert, Dr. John DeMartini, that it was not. For a long time I didn't understand the family dynamics. I felt it was unfairly dealt to me. Perhaps this is why my own child is, and will always be, the most important person in my life. I vowed never to make the same mistakes I witnessed in my own family. Jennifer has two girlfriends here for a sleepover. I'm baking them cookies and at the same time getting together a package for Richard. Joe and I talk and I'm getting closer to him, in an almost unusual way. With the isolation I feel from my divorce, the lack of parental guidance in my life and no significant other in my life, I'm vulnerable. With both my parents gone now, I feel like an orphan. I *am* an orphan.

Richard Reyna and I set up our first investigative meeting, and in preparation, I call John Reid, the police officer who transported Steven Watson (the jailhouse snitch) to and from the jailhouse during the time Joe was in jail awaiting trial. Richard and I wanted to know what Watson said to him, if anything. His name was one of many on a list of witnesses to interview. For now, I want to focus on Watson. He smelled like a liar and I see his inconsistencies like black and white lines running down a skunk's back.

Having not heard back from Bob Smith, I draft a letter to him, requesting more funds for the investigation. I then stop in at the Tap Room in the Nassau Club in Princeton to rent the establishment for my daughter's upcoming birthday party.

Joe phones me to say that Al Brown is still on the case. I'm furious with the lawyers now. They also want Richard Reyna to report only to them. Joe calls Bob Smith to beg him to relieve Al. I don't want tension to overwhelm the work that needs to be done. To ease the matter, I offer a suggestion, "Joe, Richard and I will work together, forget the attorneys." I want only the best. Reyna is clever, street smart, and just plain good at what he does. And I need all the help I can get.

In anticipation of our move to Boston for my new law school experience, I must find an appropriate private school for Jennifer. While Jen is interviewing I take the time to visit New England School of Law. Before we leave, Jen and I stroll through Harvard Square, leaving the city just before an unexpected, heavy snowstorm. We laugh as we make our way up the steps to our snow-covered home.

Having not heard from the lawyers I send yet another letter to Bob Smith. I am determined to work with Richard. Why investigate a murder if you can't do it right?

The lawyers receive my letter and all hell breaks loose. Pat Scharzschild, the lead attorney from Virginia, threatens to quit after the appeals. Don Lee tries to smooth things out by cajoling her to stay. Bob responds to me, saying his staff did not know Richard was upset with the amount of money they offered. Another fire to put out for another day. My attention returns to Watson. I need to gather more information on this snitch. I leave a message with Richard about Carolyn Watson. Still no social security number on her. I call for copies of the divorce papers in Randolph County. Perhaps I can trace her down from there.

~Breakfast Before Death~

Still juggling divorce aftermath problems and looking for a private school for Jennifer, I get a welcome call from Richard. It's wonderful news. I watch as the fax machine slowly regurgitates a four-page letter outlining his review of the autopsy report. I grab the sheets one by one as they drop from the machine before they hit the floor of my dining room, which has now become a refuge for Joe's paperwork. I begin to read what could be the answer to Joe's freedom.

It starts off in the usual way, describing his assignment and what information he was to review. Then, the next paragraph begins: "...*The victim had to have eaten after she left the County Line bar.*" I am stunned. Richard's sharp mind is already paying off. He will fax the report to the attorneys first thing in the morning. My first question is why, in over ten years of the review of this case, has no one else, including the medical examiner at trial, discovered this or brought it to the attention of the defense? Or had they?

The information concerning the food in Helen Schartner's stomach is vital. It means she was not murdered immediately after she left the bar. She had to have eaten first, suggesting she went to "breakfast." The amount of food retained in her stomach suggests she ate within two hours of her death. There is no indication she ate while at the County Line nightclub that evening after 8:30 p.m. Did she know her killer? It appears, contrary to the prosecution's claim, she could not have been abducted from the bar, assaulted and murdered, without having eaten first. Did the killer offer her a last meal? Or did she willingly have breakfast with someone she knew before she was murdered? The autopsy report reveals traces of food in her stomach, some potato salad-like food. This was never brought up at trial, by the prosecution or defense. It was crucial information. The food contents in her stomach were not discussed in the narrative section of the autopsy report as anything remarkable. How could I have known its significance? Neither did Joe apparently. The experts, however, knew. Or *should have* known. As usual, I had to get this information verified by an expert. I add it to my growing list of things to do.

My attention now turns to Ike Wright, the victim's boyfriend. Ike was a correctional officer at the Powahatan Correctional Center in Virginia. He was dating Helen at the time of her death. Ike met Helen at the bar that night. He arrived around 11:15 p.m., having driven almost three hours to meet her there. He danced with her and sat at her table. I recall that testimony at trial revealed when Helen was in the ladies' room he danced with another woman. Helen was visibly upset when she returned to her seat. They argued and she left between 11:30 and 11:35 p.m.[66] Testimony from Bruce Cooper, the doorman, revealed that he was counting the cover charge monies, which he did at midnight, when he saw Joe O'Dell still in the bar.[67] Conveniently, Ike testified about a 13-hour date he had with Helen, in which they spent time in her car.[68] This would account for any fingerprints or fibers the cops could match to Ike. They never did introduce evidence at trial pertaining to her car, even though Joe pleaded for it, and her car was parked at the motel, the passenger door open while the driver's side door was found locked. There was some discussion about debris

[66] Trial Transcript, Vol. 18, Tab 52B, pages 102-103. Ike Wright testified Helen left "15 to 20 minutes at the most" after he arrived at 11:15 p.m.. On cross Ike testifies she left as early as 11:25 p.m. and as late as 11:40 p.m.. See page 115.

[67] Trial Transcript, Vol. 21, Tab 57, page 37.

[68] Trial Transcript, Vol. 18, Tab 52B, page 107.

in the car, or blood, but I don't recall it going anywhere.

Ike seemed a likely suspect. Why wasn't he a suspect and investigated? Did this have anything to do with the fact that he is one of "them," code of honor and all that among cops. I get Ike's last known address in Virginia and send Richard the crime scene photos and trial testimony of Watson, along with Judge Spencer's comment on Watson, seemingly inferring that it would have made a difference in his opinion had we had proof that Watson was offered a deal in exchange for his testimony. I am more determined than ever.

Saturday afternoons are usually reserved for play dates for my daughter. She is my rock, and her existence alone is a stabilizing force in my life. Thankfully, school is usually a breeze for her—she's always been a great student and has lots of friends. She's been playing soccer since the age of five, on the town traveling team. Center forward or left wing, depending on where they need her. Jen is one of those rare players who can kick with her left foot, as well as her right. When she's on the field, no one wants to anger her because a fierce sense of dedication comes over her and she plays hard. You can literally see it on her face. She's a starter. For years she's remained an incredibly valuable member of her team: Lady Hot Shots, East Brunswick, New Jersey. They would win many games and Jen's room would be filled with trophies. My cup runneth over with pride.

Richard calls to cancel the trip to Virginia due to an evidentiary hearing in Texas. I call the cop to reschedule our interview.

The day turns even more sour when I get word that Al Brown had, unknowingly, proceeded with the investigation and visited with Connie Craig. If someone could have picked the very last person to investigate it would have been her! The trial transcript and other documentation that I reviewed clearly indicate an unusually close relationship between Connie and the prosecution. After trial, both prosecutors, Albert Alberi and Stephen Test, either called or visited Connie at her home to assist her in defending a lawsuit against Joe O'Dell. If one was to begin an investigation, it would not start with Connie. She would certainly run to the prosecution to tip them off. Al blew it and I was infuriated. I call Jeff Eilender and yelled, "How could this happen? I told you Brown was not to do anything more on this case!" I find out that Stephen Test, one of the prosecutors on O'Dell's case, called Al Brown after the visit with Connie and threatened him with criminal trespass, and other charges, if he ever stepped foot on Connie's property again. It occurred to me that this was highly unusual behavior for a prosecutor—to have so much interest and connection with a witness, years after a trial. Connie somehow felt "protected" by the prosecution. She was their star witness at trial; they owed her. Unfortunately, this was not unusual behavior for this prosecuting team. They would intimidate any witness who either disagreed with them or could assist Joseph O'Dell. Trial by ambush, as Judge Spain characterized it on one occasion when the Commonwealth overstepped their bounds.[69]

Al's Brown's report to Jeff Eilender in February 1995 states that Mr. O'Dell requested he discontinue the investigation on February 15. Prior to that he describes his finding:

> Connie Craig:...She said nobody is going to help him (Joe), or talk to me...all anyone knows is his side of it; nobody knew what he had done to her...She did not care about the blood evidence, DNA stuff.

It was apparent Connie didn't care about the truth. She cared about revenge. It was also telling that she knew people wouldn't talk to Al. Had the prosecution assured her of this? Al's report revealed he was successful at tracking down some individuals and that one of the people he interviewed said a police officer by the name of Lisa Baker had arrested Joseph Moore for being publicly intoxicated. Moore told her she may as well let him go for "he had gotten away with murder before and this wasn't nothing." Upon radioing the information in she

[69] Trial Transcript, Vol. 22, page 45.

was instructed by her supervisor to let him go.

What on earth did Moore know?

In the meantime, I started to recruit scientific expert witnesses. Dr. Kris Sperry said he would review the case and will consult if called upon. This was great news. Sperry was affiliated with the Medical Examiner's Office in Atlanta and was Chair of the Council on Forensic Pathology of the American Society of Clinical Pathologists. He would offer his assistance in understanding the serology and PGM enzyme testimony offered by Virginia's novice expert at Joe's trial. I wanted his opinion. This time I choose not to share this information with the NY law firm until the last minute. I don't trust them.

Next, I draft a letter to Al Brown and Bob Smith, copying Don Lee at the Virginia Resource Center, to kindly have Al removed from the case to ensure no further problems.

Briefs are being filed at this point and, as usual, Joe and I review the Commonwealth's brief and offer our comments concerning the evidence. No one can pinpoint the facts about the case, or the evidence, better than myself and Joe. Nor do they care.

It was also time for two more interviews in Boston to finalize our search for the next private school my daughter would attend. The trip offers us a chance to meet friends from Cape Cod. On our way home Joe calls while we are at the airport. I had set up call forwarding to my cell phone in order to talk with him while I'm away. For security reasons, the prison does not allow phone calls directly to a cell phone. But there is always a way around bureaucracy thanks to modern technology.

The next day I call Paul, Weiss, Rifkind, Wharton & Garrison to request a copy of their final brief. We were now appealing to the Fourth Circuit Court of Appeals. The last court before the last resort: the U.S. Supreme Court. Everyone knows the chances of being heard by the highest court in our country are slim to none. I make copies of the brief for Richard and explain the legal issues. I also ask Jeff for the official trial transcripts that are still at Centurion Ministries. A month has passed and Richard's time has eased. "We have to be in Virginia next week," he tells me.

March has crept onto the current calendar faster than I would have liked. Regardless that today is my birthday, melancholy feelings threaten the mood. In the evening, I celebrate quietly with Jen. This year is different. Different because I was used to having extravagant celebrations, even if only the three of us. It was not unusual for Walter to spoil me with a diamond necklace, earrings, take me to dinner *and* give me flowers. It was uncomfortably foreign to be alone, no man by my side, just a death row inmate filling the void in my life.

The following day, after dropping Jen at school, I stop by Centurion Ministries to pick up Joe's 31 volumes of transcripts. I was constantly referring to them; they had become my Bible. I could pinpoint almost anything upon a moment's notice.

Dr. Kris Sperry calls me and I realize he is shaping up to be a great expert witness on PGM. I will follow up with the DNA results and a request for his credentials. I am one-third there. I am also waiting on Richard Reyna for word on the investigation. Next, I receive the final brief for one of Joe's appeals, dated February 1995. I review it and offer my approval, for whatever that was worth. When I finally hear from Richard, he confirms the investigation date of March 31. I fax him the seven aspects of the investigation that I had compiled and also fax the transcripts from Joe's DNA hearing to Kris Sperry. I'm done for the day and looking forward to Jennifer's soccer game tomorrow.

Jen's games are a wonderful distraction for me. They are uplifting, challenging and spirited. I love watching her excel, at anything. I also like to win, as Jen points out to me after a soccer game. "Yes, I do. That's why your grandma used to call me Annie Oakley," I said. "Who?" Jen asks as I laugh. One of the kids joins us as we leave for home—it's time for another sleepover.

In my career as a CPA I had audited the books of Stuart Country Day School in Princeton. It is a highly reputable all-girls Catholic school. I called upon the business manager, Mary, to ask her opinion of Newton Country Day School. It, too, was an all-girls Catholic school. Having confidence in Mary's familiarity with the school, I ultimately select it as the one for my daughter's educational experience. I had already sent the deposit to New England School of Law. Everything was pulling together. Almost everything.

No one ever wants to cause pain to another and I coil when I receive a phone call from Walter. His voice is broken and I can tell he is clearly upset. I know he still loves me, yet I am still naïve and blind to the ultimate devastation a divorce brings, to everyone. I write him a letter which I hand deliver when he drops Jen off. God, if I only knew, I would run back into his arms for the shelter and protection I need but don't know is really there. Somehow it's veiled underneath all of my confusion.

Chapter 7

~The Investigation~

It's Friday, March 31, when Richard Reyna and I meet for the first time in South Hill, Virginia to begin our investigation. Seated at a motel restaurant booth I watch as a hearty down-to-earth looking man fast approaches my booth. Richard Reyna has some of the same characteristics as American Indian and I wonder what his nationality is. It turns out his father is Italian and his mother is Mexican. He's on the stocky side with black hair and an olive-toned, round face, a wide nose and dark brown eyes. Richard offers a warm smile as he reaches his hand toward me. I immediately like him. He will be easy to work with. Our styles are similar yet he offers qualities I do not possess. Experience and ability. Experience at working a death row case, and ability to easily walk among those in prison without looking so out of place.

We agree to narrow the scope of the investigation to the essential aspects. We manage to smile, even joke around to lighten the intensity of our job. I have a feeling that our combined personalities will bring many laughs to an already depressing situation.

The next morning we set out for a suburb in North Carolina to visit with officer John Reid. Reid is well built, tall, with very short hair, and carries a presence that is authoritative. Yet he also appears kind. For almost two hours we interview him. I watch Richard carefully as I sit back and let him take control. He is diligent. Straightforward, but personable. Factual, yet looking for Reid to fill in the gaps. It doesn't take long before I jump into the conversation. Reid remembers Watson and his wife and states that Steve wanted probation in exchange for his testimony against Joe. He had been assigned to pick up Watson at the Virginian Beach City Jail to transport him to Elkins, West Virginia, where Steve was from. While in the back seat of the cruiser, Watson asked if he could fool around with his wife. "One doesn't forget such a request," Reid says. But one more thing was added to this conversation: John Reid was quite upset with the prosecution. "They tried to make me look like a liar," he said. Being a cop, he was used to the respect officers receives from prosecutors, even if it is to obtain a conviction. In the O'Dell case, they tried to discredit him. That was the criminal defense attorney's job. At the end of the conversation Reid says that Joe called him after the trial and thanked him for what he tried to do on his behalf. Reid was surprised, yet pleased by Joe's call. This confirms our suspicions all along. Watson wanted a deal. Did he get one? That's what we need to find out. Richard and I drive back to South Hill and prepare to visit with Joe the next morning. There is a feeling of satisfaction at our first attempt to uncover information that may help Joe. I am smiling, even if only to myself.

Richard and I comb the streets of Virginia Beach trying to find Joseph Moore. We're not having much luck. We visit the courtroom to search the public record for identifiers leading to Moore. Arrest records, civil and criminal records, anything to provide us with a last known address. Court records can be very revealing. Joe Moore was arrested on September 9, 1994 on a charge of public intoxication. Moving from the courthouse to the crime scene, Richard reviews the crime scene photographs before we leave town. Our short visit is unsuccessful in that we never locate Moore. He reportedly still visits with his brother in town, who does his best to avoid him, and also keeps ties at the Bay Vending Company, where his white pickup truck sat idly in the back parking lot. But his buddies covered for him—said he wasn't there. Moore had listed the vending company as a previous place of employment. And in fact, it's right next door to the location where Moore found Helen's body. We also learn that he may be homeless and had recently checked into a Motel 6 on Military Highway, but the clerk told Richard that Moore was gone and no longer welcome there. It appears that the information Joe provided us about Moore was shaping up to be true. Moore was a drunk who may very well know more than the police put in their report. He was very elusive, both then and now.

We're not the only ones looking for him. Richard's report also indicates that in 1994 a law firm in Virginia Beach was actively searching for Mr. Moore. Richard noted the fact that former prosecutor Stephen Test is employed by that firm. Why would they want to keep such close tabs on their witnesses and non-witnesses? Perhaps when Al Brown attempted to interview Connie Craig, Test started to try to locate all the essential witnesses to tell them not to talk to us, yet again. It would fit the pattern. He is turning out to be equally as dangerous as Alberi. What is this vendetta all about? What makes a man act so vehemently to gain and protect a conviction, almost to the extent of an obsession? I wanted to find out. We leave Virginia Beach, knowing we will be back. I return home to Princeton, where I am not dealing with prisons or looking for past drunken witnesses who discovered a dead woman's body. Richard goes to Elkins, West Virginia, where he has located Steven Watson.

I wait patiently to hear from Richard. The ring from the telephone lasts a second before I pick it up.

"Lori, I talked to Watson and I know he is full of shit but he is sticking with his story. He told me O'Dell danced with the victim, sat at her table, bought her drinks and then they left together. No wonder the prosecution called him as one of their last witnesses. His testimony completely contradicts all the other witnesses."

By that he meant Dana Wade, Linda Bunton, Janice Bailey and

Jennifer Hunt, daughter of Janice Bailey. They all sat with Helen that night and not one of them testified that O'Dell was anywhere near her. In fact, Dana Wade recalled seeing O'Dell across the room and testified he never danced with or spoke to Helen. How on earth could the prosecutor allow such lies at trial? Isn't there a rule about suborning perjury? I wonder if that rule is keeping Watson from telling us the truth now.

The reality of my divorce is nearing when Walter and I decide to get together for an early settlement meeting. The expression on our faces fails to hide the pain that has led to this day. After offering each other advice, we hug and kiss goodbye before parting ways. The solitary drive home allows me to release bottled up emotions. For an hour the tears flow. Then, believing that crying is a sign of weakness I quickly recover. There is a much bigger situation that demands my attention.

Later that same day I fax information to Bob Smith to use in a letter to the judge concerning the DNA evidence. In a recent court hearing the Commonwealth misled the judges in a last ditch effort to confuse them about the blood evidence. The Assistant Attorney General stated the blood was a match when in fact it had been litigated and proven in court that it was not. I begged Bob to write a letter to the panel of judges to correct the record, else it remain etched in stone and fodder for further mischaracterization.

To me, an attorney should be fighting hard for his client, doing everything to zealously defend him. This is not the feeling I got from Joe's lawyers. I had to fax additional information to Bob so I take an opportunity to speak candidly with him. He is cool, even-tempered. As we talk, I get him to speak his mind. "Bob, tell me what you think about Joe and his innocence," I ask openly and calmly, trying to elicit an unedited response. He gives me the Commonwealth's theory on the case that I believe is his own. He believes Joe killed *two* people and that one got away! He said the mud on Joe's clothes came from the field and that there was too much blood for it to be a fight. When I ask him if we can just talk to the state he replies, "If I can't convince three judges, how am I going to convince them?" He agrees to go to the governor on a clemency petition. I shake my head. Is this the prosecutor on the phone or is it Joe's lawyer? This confirms my suspicions all along. The New York firm has got to go! How can you represent someone who has adamantly professed his innocence, whose basis for appeal is a case of actual innocence, and believe they are guilty of the crime, and perhaps another yet? If one cannot at least keep an open mind, they will never find an opening for exculpatory evidence. They will instead look at evidence that confirms their preconceived notions. This was a dangerous game. In Joe's case it was deadly.

I had heard of a strong attorney in Virginia Beach who had been known to go up against Albert Alberi, and who happens to dislike him. I was keeping abreast of most of the news in Virginia Beach. This one name popped up more than once. I researched articles and found that David Baugh and Alberi almost engaged in a fistfight in the courtroom. I would have loved to have been there for that one! David Baugh. I look him up and fax him information regarding Joe's case. "Will you help me?" I ask. I had to share with Joe what his attorneys had said. He was understandably upset. Joe had been telling me all along, "My attorneys think I am guilty!" He was right, at least as of this point. That was about to change.

On April 12, 1995, with no apparent indication that O'Dell's lawyers were going to dispute the outrageous lies in the oral argument and contained in the briefs of the Commonwealth, I draft a letter to Bob Smith. My approach with him has softened a little, at least in my letter. I thought perhaps it would assist in getting what I wanted—his cooperation.

> Dear Bob:
> After some discussion with Joseph O'Dell and review of my notes at oral

argument I am in agreement that it is essential to inform the judges of information vital to the understanding of this case. It is apparent by their comments and questions, and the misleading arguments by Murphy, that they need some critical information before them before they are firm on a decision. It is imperative that this letter go now, for any effectiveness. I have faxed to you all I can to support the areas that need to be addressed...Below are the issues that Joseph and I feel are essential to address and request that you include them in your letter.

1. The Lifecodes report-Murphy makes mention of it as if it were a finality. Truth is, two subsequent court decisions, on both a state and federal level, succeeded in proving the shirt stain exculpatory and the jacket stain "inconclusive." It is misleading to the court to refer to the jacket stain as a match. If you need detail in the transcripts, please do not hesitate to call me.

2. Murphy again attacks the information supportive of the source of the blood, which has now been determined NOT to be the victims--the fight. He, once again, misleads the court by actually lying about the fight. Indeed there was testimony as I pointed out and indeed he lied in his previous statement of facts that Bougades said there was "blood splattered" on Joe, Again, the testimony speaks for itself.

3. Judge Luttig needs clarification on the PGM - he said it "matched." Nowhere does it say it matched in the transcripts. Emrich tried to say it was a mixture. But refer to her own testimony, that statement was not a "conclusive statement, only a possibility." Well there is a possibility of a million other things as well—it means nothing. You should note that we intend to prove the PGM means nothing. Please refer to the testimony from the 1994 hearing on the PGM status (see attached).

4. Judge Ervin seemed to be confused about DNA testing. He asked, "What's the difference between the testing 10 years ago and now?" He was unaware that the testing initially done was enzyme testing and that DNA supersedes that in informativeness and reliability. Critical area.

5. Luttig mentions that the petitioner left a few minutes after the victim. Once, again he is misinformed. As indicated in the trial testimony, which was never disputed by the state, Joseph left at least half an hour later. Under the story the prosecutor gave, Joe was allegedly waiting on the victim outside. How ludicrous!

Very truly yours,
Lori Urs, CPA

Emotions couldn't have been running higher. It was becoming more and more apparent that Joe's lawyers were not going to fight for him. They refused to correct the record in the Fourth Circuit, they refused to defend themselves, or Joe, when Judge Luttig threw mud at the Lifecodes report and tried to discredit the lawyers, insinuating, without basis, the possibility of selective testing done. The lawyers refused to even ask Lifecodes what procedure they followed when testing the evidence, offering Joe no opportunity to refute this false allegation. As Joe would say in his letter to his lawyers, "Judge Luttig became an advocate for the Commonwealth by interjecting the intimation that there was selective testing. It is not the function of the Federal Circuit Courts to argue for one party or the other when the other party has not made the challenge."[70] In an act of desperation Joe wrote to Bob and Jeff in April, 1995.

> I have to say this, and I am sorry if it is offensive to you. I cannot believe that nobody could determine what happened at Lifecodes Laboratory concerning the testing of the evidence. This was the reason(s) you gave for not writing the letter to the Judges explaining that there was no selective testing done. The most important part of a death penalty case and nobody on my legal team could determine what happened? I find that to be totally outrageous. Especially outrageous when someone's life depends on competent representation. I lost all of my rights to appeal my issues because of the wrong appeal being filed. Had I not filed, *pro se*, the DNA motion to Judge Spain, I would have been executed two year ago. Then when the evidentiary hearing was granted, I asked you over and over again, through letters, memorandums, telephone calls, and finally at the evidentiary hearing itself, to get the judge to clarify just what we could present and not present. You would not do that. As it turned out, even though his

---

[70] See Letter from Joe O'Dell to Bob Smith and Jeff Eilender (April 19, 1995) (on file with author).

order suggested that the hearing was limited to just DNA, we should have put on the other evidence after asking the judge whether we could or not. This could cost me my life! Then at oral arguments the evidence was misrepresented and mischaracterized by the Commonwealth and Judge Luttig, you said you could not find a justifiable reason to write the letter. Even if the letter would not have done any good, at least an attempt should have been made - but this was not done. The information that you possessed concerning Judge Luttig's father being murdered and that just a few days before he sat in judgment on my case he had traveled to the State of Texas and testified at the murderer's penalty phase, which resulted in the murderer receiving a death sentence, was deliberately kept from me, the client, and you made the decision not to ask for recusal without consulting me.

In the past several years that Paul, Weiss has been handling my case, I have had the following attorneys assigned to my case, and for one reason or another, new attorneys would be assigned: Steve Rosenfeld, Sanford Hausler, Sean Coffey, Sara Mandelbaum, Susan Povich, Paul Indig, David Jaroslaw, then Jeff...In the beginning of my case there were 4 attorneys assigned. Then as time passed and the attorneys left the firm, I would be assigned one attorney. Even if that attorney was assigned nothing but my case it is too much for one attorney to do a competent job...I do not know what the deal is with the firm, and why you believe I am guilty of this crime, because anyone who looks at this case, the evidence, the lies that have been told, the prosecutorial misconduct, and all of the facets of these, can only come to one conclusion—that I DID NOT COMMIT THIS CRIME! All of these crazy and absurd hypothetical's that keep popping up are just that, CRAZY AND ABSURD.

You took the case pro bono, which I am sure the firm is regretting, but the fact is you took the case. If you were not going to give me your best representation, then you should not have taken the case. Now that you have had it for about 7 years, and terrible mistakes have been made, irreconcilable mistakes, and I do not have anyone else to represent me—it puts me, and it puts you, in a very untenable position...I hope you can appreciate my honesty and try to see things in their true light. If I have lied or misrepresented anything said in this letter, please bring it to my attention. If, on the other hand, you see what I have said as being the truth, then please accept it as that, let us reconcile our differences, and get on with this case and fight diligently...Bob, Jeff, tell me, how does one properly and competently represent anyone, but especially a death penalty case if they are not cognizant of all the main points of the case? Presenting any case, it is won or lost on how good the evidence is, but even if the evidence is the best, it is no good if it is not properly presented, and clearly conveyed to the ones who determine the outcome of the case!

Heretofore, everyone has been defensive and have become upset with me because I complain when someone makes a mistake that brings me closer and closer to execution or a LIFE SENTENCE! Would not you be upset if you were told this afternoon that when you walked out of your office this afternoon that a "hit man" was going to kill you, or if you were suddenly told by your doctor that you had an incurable disease that would put you in a bed and hospital for the duration of your life? Of course you would be upset. You are an innocent person, you don't deserve either of those scenarios, but the analogy is neither do I. I have killed nobody, raped nobody, sodomized nobody, and I do not deserve to die or spend the rest of my life in prison!

I will talk with you at your convenience concerning the contents of this letter.

Sincerely,

Joseph R. O'Dell, III[71]

I knew enough about Joe's case to know that each and every statement contained in his letter was painfully accurate. Joe needed strong attorneys, those who were passionate about issues, about right and wrong. They did not need to be anti-death penalty, that wasn't necessary. But they did need to have their heart in this. These lawyers were distant, even cold at times. I was alarmed by their lack of ability, or desire, to stand up for the truth, to right the record. So I made more calls.

I review the facts of the case once again, and decide to call a well-

---

[71] Letter from Joe O'Dell to Bob Smith and Jeff Eilender (April 19, 1995) (on file with author).

known attorney in Virginia and put together a package for his review. While I know the judge cannot acknowledge reading it, I follow Joe's urgent need to get his letter to the judges in the Fourth Circuit in a feeble attempt to get their attention about the factual inaccuracies contained in the record. His lawyer won't do it, so what does he have to lose? They hate letters from inmates, but if it were my life, I would do the same, having already watched countless errors remove the possibilities that I would ever get justice. When I send the letter to the judge I am careful to copy Bob Smith and Assistant Attorney General Eugene Murphy. We play evenhanded while I had to wonder whether they would engage in *ex parte* communication (talking with a judge without opposing counsel present).

Suddenly, I receive a phone call from Jim McCloskey at Centurion. He has discovered that Richard Reyna and I are working together and wants to smooth things over. We hadn't seen eye-to-eye when I left, taking over Joe's case. We agree to put things behind us and he agrees to support Joe in the media.

Now that the media light is green I contact Joe Taylor at the Associated Press, Frank Green at the *Richmond Dispatch* and Joe Jackson at the *Virginian-Pilot*. These were the investigative reporters I needed to reach. I call Don Lee at the Virginia Resource Center and alert him to the fact that he may be contacted by the media. By this time I had gotten the New York lawyers to fund Reyna's investigation with another $3,000. Don agrees to pick up anything above that. I am making progress!

It's at this time that I feel the need for a new venue to discuss the issues and evidence in Joe's case. I am pondering my next move as I slip into my pajamas and climb into bed. Just as I'm about to turn out the light I receive a phone call from Joe. We are both greatly concerned that the Commonwealth is lying about the facts and evidence. A feeling of helplessness was looming over us.

"Joe, I have an idea. Why don't we put your case on the Internet?

It's a way to at least get the evidence to the public, to discuss your case and alert everyone as to what is going on here. People need to know Joe. How about it?"

"That's a great idea, Lori. I just want my story told, the truth about it, not all the lies the Commonwealth is conveying. Let's do it. Can you help me set it up?"

"Consider it done," I said, agreeing to do something I had no idea how to do.

I would learn.

I'm the last person to know what to do with a computer. I'd rather push buttons then to sit down and read a manual, regardless of the outcome. I hated computers, but they were increasingly becoming a part of our life. At the time, the Internet was still a relatively new tool to reach the public, the world! I clearly needed help. To ease my path to success I paid a visit to my old boss at a CPA firm, David Walter. He was a whiz at the computer. He'd tell me how this Internet thing works.

Seated next to David and in front of the computer he walks me through the process of setting up an email address and asks what name I want. I have no idea. He jumps in to offer his advice.

"Since you are advocating for someone, what about advocator?" David asks.

"Sure, let's try it," I agree.

We type it in the screen and it says it's taken. We need to add a number or something to make it unique. He picks "advocator8" and AOL makes it my new official electronic address. I use this address to research the web and find information on how to set up a website for Joe. I start to gather all my material to assist Joe in setting up a page for his case of innocence. The web host designs the page and sets it up. All I have to do is type it all down and forward it to him for placement on a host page. I am now acting as a liaison for this new business relationship that will give Joe a voice. Since I'm learning to use mine to project his, I may as well get it out to the world. The computer was now becoming my ally.

By now I am determined to get Joe new lawyers. I had witnessed firsthand how mistakes had cost Joe dearly in his appeals, and now I know they think he is guilty. I call Kitty Behan at Arnold & Porter, in Washington, D.C. She asks me to send Joe's information for review. To gather what she needs, including the latest briefs and memorandum outlining Joe's innocence, I work the entire day. I also phone the Virginia court to obtain Watson's criminal record.

As I gather the necessary materials, I note that Joe is using the same lab for DNA testing as the Commonwealth used to support their execution of Timothy Spencer. This is important information for the lawyers, and the media. I also decide to send a media package to Joe Jackson of the *Virginian-Pilot*. I was prompted by his many detailed, balanced and well-written articles over the past several months. He appeared fair in his reporting.

The weekend is nearing, it's spring and my daughter is heavily involved in her soccer games. We have a tournament in Delaware, which means a road trip with another soccer mom and her daughter. When I arrive in Delaware I send a second package to Joe Jackson. Joe calls while I'm at the game. I'm screaming, cheering Jen on. He is tickled to hear, if not be included in, a sports game. As a natural result of Joe becoming an almost everyday part of my life, I was happy to share these events with him. I wanted to offer him some momentary distraction from the cement walls that were closing in on him.

In order to ensure Kitty Behan received the materials, I follow up with her, and I tell her of Richard Reyna's letter, outlining the information about the contents of food in the victim's stomach when she died. I hope she will be excited about this compelling new discovery. The New York firm didn't seem to care, nor did they act upon it. Briefly, I speak with Bob Smith and Don Lee about Joe's investigation. I'm concerned about the timing of Richard's investigation and the evidentiary hearing. We need to give Richard time to do his thing. Don agrees again to assist in continuing to fund Richard's investigation beyond what the New York law firm can. At night, I put together a package for Joe Taylor, an investigative reporter for the Associated Press.

Part of my time and attention is taken up with plans for Jen's going away party that I'm giving her at a restaurant and movie theatre, along with the finalizing of my divorce and some nasty accounting bills that have to be challenged.

Another fact requiring my attention is David Pruett's confession to Helen Schartner's murder. I speak to several people at the South Carolina and North Carolina Death Penalty Resource Center to inquire about it. I need to find out what David Pruett said about killing Helen Schartner, and if there is any credibility to it. I talk to Joe Jackson about the issues at hand, now 99 percent certain he will do the story.

I'm now desperately searching for another lawyer, a reputable one that can help us. I remember the name Brian Powers. Surprisingly, he is candid and offers information that most would not. He informs me that he spoke with Assistant Attorney General Robert Condon who had said, "Joe out-litigated the other side and would have won if he didn't take the stand."

In his letters, Joe reiterated that at trial he was outdoing the prosecution. He was making them look bad, while attracting people to the courtroom to watch him in action. I wasn't sure if it was his own imagination or he was just bragging. Brian's statement offered validity to what Joe told me months earlier. I did know that Joe's ability to understand the law and write his own motions in a highly complicated death case was superb. He was amazingly intelligent and strong-willed, yet he was at a distinct disadvantage. I remember now the judge's comment that Joe may well have walked out of the courtroom if he hadn't taken the stand. A *pro se* defendant almost never wins, especially in a murder and rape case. An innocent man believes all he has to do is take the stand and tell the truth. The system will work: I'm innocent! Ask how many exonerated persons in our country felt the same way. You would be surprised.

"I'm sorry," Brian said, "I can't take the case." Brian works in a labor law firm. "Give Joe my best. I think a lot of him. He's a brilliant guy, very articulate." Brian pauses, then he says something very forcefully that shocked me. "He was railroaded!"

Did I just hear those words? I must be dreaming. It's the first time I hear another person who has knowledge of this case come out with a statement that is so powerful. Welcoming the confirmation, I let it sink in with relief. This is promising news in my first investigation into the innocence of a walking dead man.

Feeling exhilarated now I call Don Lee and ask if he will handle the evidentiary hearing. "Sure," he answers. "But, Lori there's a new director and he's one of the best in the country, ask him! Also, please have Richard call me." I agree to do both.

Chapter 8

~Suppressed Evidence at Trial~

In two months, freedom as I know it is about to change. Law school begins in August. A quick trip to Boston lands me a cozy home in Needham, right across from the train station. At $2,100 a month it's more than I care to spend. I choose its ideal location due to its proximity to Jen's new school. Having accomplished this major goal I continue feeding information to the *Virginian-Pilot* and Kitty Behan, while I wait for paperwork on Watson. I find a little time to pamper myself—the hair salon and a massage help to preserve my identity. And serve as a much needed escape from the desperation in someone else's life that I am now caught up in.

Jennifer's music performance is tonight at PDS. I'm joined by Walter, who always finds time to support his daughter's musical endeavors. I wouldn't say "talent" since she hated the violin lessons she once took. Jen's talent wasn't hidden. It was on the soccer fields, or basketball court, or any sport where she shined. She was also a terrific singer, even without a single voice lesson. She even landed a solo in her eighth grade play.

Early the next morning, I call West Virginia and Barbour County courts for more paperwork on Watson.

Before I know it, the weekend arrives. It is usually my only source of relaxation between intense jaunts of work on Joe O'Dell's case. Jennifer and I drive to the zoo and witness the birth of a baby goat. We stop briefly at a carnival and then head home. On Sunday Jen has a soccer game. She scores the only goal, the winning goal, in a final score of 1-0. A parent's dream. Monday I start back on Joe's case. Realizing I need to contact all sources of information, I reach out to Joe's only sibling, Sheila, his younger sister. Until now I had no reason to talk with her. Joe had informed me that she abandoned him long ago and hadn't visited him in years.

Meanwhile, Joe Jackson is hot on prosecutor Alberi's trail. A phone call alerts me that the *Pilot* will soon print another story about a case of suppressed evidence by Alberi. Obviously, the information I am uncovering about the prosecution is not limited to Joe's case. Dangerous games unfold when those with enormous power choose to ignore the foundation of the lawyer's oath to *serve the courts, and the people*. All people.

Richard Reyna phones me to share good news. "Don Lee agrees to pay my expenses." Yes! My persistence is starting to pay off. Knowing Richard has by now received the stack of papers I have inundated him with, I feel comfortable in asking the inevitable question.

"Richard, what do you think about Joe's innocence?"

Richard is blunt in his reply—to him it is rather clear-cut. "Joe should have been out five years ago." (I suspect due to the results of the DNA tests). His words offer another alignment to my growing concerns. They also cushion the isolation I have been feeling for some time now, easing the struggle of fighting alone. I am building my team. Joe's team. My opinion alone won't free Joe O'Dell. I know that. I am fighting against ruthless, powerful figures of authority who are not interested in the truth. And I have only scratched the surface of this grave of deception. Richard asks me to have Sheila call him.

The more I delve into Joe's case, the more I become aware that something is radically wrong. My alarm doesn't fully sink in until I start to acquire information from additional unexpected sources. Joe

Jackson becomes one of them. He is talking to me about Dr. Joseph Guth, the defense team's scientific witness, who had been scheduled to testify in O'Dell's case, but never did. My reading of the record indicated that he started to participate in the trial before something happened to change his mind. I couldn't pinpoint what it was. I did, however, have Dr. Guth's report, which didn't seem to reveal much. Joe Jackson got more. He ventured off to the courthouse to review O'Dell's files, boxed in the back corner of the records room. Numerous boxes piqued Joe's curiosity, but he was selective in his choice. A letter dated May 16, 1986 from Dr. Guth to the trial judge, caught his attention. In this letter, Guth explains how he had been deceived by the Commonwealth about the evidence.

"The Commonwealth had lied to him about having all the evidence to review and had purposely left out exculpatory evidence, evidence suggesting Joe's innocence," says Joe Jackson.

I can hardly believe what I am hearing. Coming from a third source this was powerful new information. Joe continues, "I spoke with Dr. Guth and can sense he is afraid of Alberi." He went on to say that Guth "echoed" all that I had told Joe Jackson (about soil samples, etc). Then came an unexpected compliment. "You added credibility when you sent me material, but now I have even greater respect for you." Joe was beginning to see that I wasn't fabricating my concerns about the evidence, the misrepresentations, the suppressed evidence, witness intimidation. "Joe, I'll send you Guth's testimony. I'll get it from Centurion Ministries. I think you should see it," I offer.

Not long after my conversation with Jackson, I share some of this information with Joe O'Dell. His response was that of disbelief. I sensed he was pleased the reporter was taking his case seriously.

Jen's school is having its annual parade, and I must attend. It's a big event for the kids. Afterwards, I make a quick trip to the mall, leaving Jennifer with some friends at school. As I return through the majestic tree-lined street to the school's entrance, I notice the parking lot is empty. I begin to look for Jennifer. She is nowhere in the immediate area. She is "missing." In a panic I grab several school personnel and we start to search for her. Forty-five minutes later we find her in the woods by the brook, playing with her best friend Kaitlin. It was the longest 45 minutes of my life.

****

It's the weekend and I am swamped with work on Joe's case. I spend many hours copying and reading transcripts for Joe Jackson. It's amazing what I find each time I scour the transcripts. The more I dig, the more I become aware of witness tampering and suppressed evidence.

The drive to continue prodding into the facts to get at the truth is irresistible and consuming. Like a magnet pulling me across the room I am drawn to the other side. I cannot see what I want until I get up close, close enough to have walked across the entire room. I felt I was only halfway there. I am still walking, my pace slow and deliberate. In the scheme of things it's just the beginning. I have no idea where this journey is leading me.

As I am placing the chicken in the oven for dinner, the fax machine rings. Dr. Guth's letter comes through. It's six pages long. As I sit down to read, tears begin to well up in my eyes. I discover, thanks to Joe Jackson, yet another piece of evidence that supports Joe O'Dell's claim. The contents of the letter only deepen my resolve. Dr. Guth again confirms Joe O'Dell's worst suspicions, and then some.

Joe had filed a motion for the preservation of evidence to have his own experts examine the blood evidence. It was denied. He also challenged the scientific reliability of the "expert's" opinion on the blood and semen evidence. It, too, was denied. Furthermore, he asked for everything the prosecution had, and never got it. Dr. Guth made it all jump out, first in his letter to the court in March and then again in

May. The electrophoresis tests were scientifically impossible to reproduce since the blood evidence had not been preserved. At that time, in 1986, the State Crime Laboratory and Police Department maintained a practice to preserve evidence in DUI cases. I suppose a rape and murder case did not rise to the same level of importance for the Commonwealth of Virginia. Bloodstain identification was hampered due to mildew on the evidence, having been left sitting at room temperature in a back room for six to nine months. It was further compromised when the detective put all of Joe's clothes together in the same bag when he picked them up from Connie Craig's house. The evidence shows they never identified or labeled his clothing separately, just "one bag of clothes." It gave rise to further suspicion when they went back to Connie's house a second time to retrieve another jacket. There seemed to be no chain of custody in this case. The judge apparently had another opinion. Apparently, his opinion wasn't compromised by this:

March 27, 1986

Dear Judge Spain:

At your request and that of Mr. O'Dell…I have obtained the physical evidence in this case from the Virginia Beach Department and examined it for the purposes of: 1. Determining whether there is sufficient preservation of the evidence for a thorough forensic laboratory re-examination…Certain requests for scientific documents were made in my letter of January 7, 1986 and have not been allowed. Hair and fiber evidence appears properly preserved for microscopic re-examination…However…Numerous slides were improperly marked with a marking pen on the glass ends and these labels are difficult or impossible to now read. Due to the severely limited ability to re-examine the stain evidence, the previously requested documentation is an absolute must if I would ever be asked to render opinions regarding whether these procedures could have yielded the results as reported by Ms. Emrich. At present, I am unable to say whether any of the

State's test results have any scientific basis and whether proper control samples were utilized. I reiterate my previous request for these documents and information to provide Mr. O'Dell with expert-level information on the meaning of these results.

Interscience Research, Inc.

Joseph Guth
Laboratory Director

And the letter Joe Jackson discovered which took me to my knees:

May 8, 1986

Dear Judge Spain:

...I have run into many new and serious omissions which make the necessary task [*sic*] (of evaluating the evidence) impossible to complete..before [*sic*] the trial date. Furthermore, I have just had a meeting with Mr. Ray and investigator Mr. Tom Collins and discovered that extremely important physical evidence collected by the state was either never evaluated or analyzed or was analyzed and would not be introduced at trial. I was deceived by the Commonwealth as to its existence. At the time I picked up the evidence, I was assured by Sergeant Wray Boswell that what I was in receipt of was all of the physical evidence of the case. If this additional evidence contained facts substantiating Mr. O'Dell's position, it will never be brought to light by the Commonwealth attorney (emphasis added). It must be made available to Mr. O'Dell's forensic science expert to analyze or re-analyze it so that all relevant fact are available to the Court. In this case, I **believe the sin of omission is just as serious as the sin of commission since it can lead to a miscarriage of justice. The Commonwealth has definitely morally and ethically committed the former** (emphasis added).

I will not be able to complete the hair comparison re-evaluations due to the following causes: The individual hairs collected from various locations of different sources have not been labeled or documented properly...Conflicting evidence documentation from the crime lab precludes my understanding the exact sources. For instance, the Report of Autopsy, page 1 reads "No obvious foreign fibers are noted under the fingernails. Several hair and other fiber are picked off from both the body and from hands adherent to the dried blood on the hands." I am provided with a set of 94 microscope slides in which two are labeled Rt. hand nails and L.H. nails. The medical examiner did not see these large hairs but the crime laboratory prepares and analyzes these two hairs! Furthermore, Jacqueline A. Emrich, the examiner of these mysterious hair samples indicated that they were "unsuitable for comparison" while my examination shows they are totally suitable for comparison purposes!...This lack of laboratory performance creates strong doubts in my opinion as to their accuracy, credibility and real scientific capabilities and knowledge...

In my discussion with Mr. Ray and Mr. Collins, **I was informed that soil and plant samples were taken from the crime scene. I was also informed that impression casting of footprints and tire tread tracks, along with exemplars were obtained by investigators. Soil and debris particulate along with these impressions could either put Mr. O'Dell at the scene of the crime or vindicate him! The state crime lab has not mentioned this evidence in any of their reports and did not even acknowledge or proffer its existence! The lack of Mr. Tests's [sic] candor and cooperation in the matter of my physical evidence review is tantamount to the concealment of evidence** (emphasis added) and I am requesting that the court provide the defendant's expert with total access to it so that it can be independently evaluated in an unbiased manner...something which it apparently has not been subject to up to now! All of the physical evidence reported by the state is, at best, circumstantial and "class-type" evidence, in contrast to "individual type evidence" (such as latent-fingerprints)...

Interscience Research, Inc.

Joseph Guth
Laboratory Director

The Commonwealth did not produce the footprints casting impressions because they did not match Joe O'Dell's footprints. It took several months, and only upon questioning did they offer this exculpatory evidence. If they withheld the castings because it exonerated Joe O'Dell, they surely withheld the soil sample testing results for the same reasons. Burnside, the first public defender, Dr. Guth, and now I, want to know what happened to the soil samples. No defense worth their salt would have left that stone unturned. It was a huge hole in the prosecutor's case. But this wasn't just a defense question anymore, this was about suppression of evidence. A *Brady*[72] violation of the worst kind if it's exculpatory. I was sure they did the testing, but just like the shoe print did not match Joe O'Dell's, I felt confident neither did the soil samples taken from the field match the soil on Joe's pants. We would never know the answer. The record revealed they never brought it up at trial, and downplayed or ignored its existence when Joe or Paul Ray attempted to obtain it. The judge didn't seem to care. Alberi and Test were smart. Delay discovery long enough and it won't get into the trial framework. They almost succeeded with the footprint casting and did succeed with the soil samples. What else were they hiding?

I finally hear from Richard Reyna. He has been otherwise engaged in a rather important case. The Alfred P. Murrah Federal Building in Oklahoma was bombed on April 2, 1995. As one of the best in the country, Richard was called upon to investigate the case of Timothy McVeigh. I was not surprised. He was in great demand. I knew I was lucky to have him on my team. We speak briefly and I bring him up to date. At the same time I'm busily preparing for my daughter's extravaganza, her farewell party.

Sixty-seven kids arrive for the smashing celebration. The UA movie theatre is closed to the public, open to Jen and her friends. At the conclusion of the movie we stroll next door for a private party in the back room of TGI Fridays. Her friends had made and signed a poster

---

[72] *Brady v. Maryland* 373 U.S. 83 (1963), was a landmark U.S. Supreme Court case in which the prosecution had withheld exculpatory evidence from a criminal defendant.

board for her that I would save for Jennifer over the years. Walter hosted the party and enjoyed every minute of it. He was going to miss his little girl.

The ping-pong of my life continues as Monday morning rolls around and I am hard at work again. By now it's apparent to Joe that in me he has a partner, someone who believes in him and is ready to fight for him. My feisty nature amuses him. Occasionally, he reveals his amusement with bursts of laughter on the phone.

"I can see you now, little girl, the boxing gloves coming on. I can talk this mess now with you because you are there and I am here, but I know when to keep my mouth shut," Joe laughs.

Joe refers to me as a little girl. I may come across as a large, over-bearing woman when I go after what I want, but I'm not. Like the lawyers who were similarly surprised when they first met me, Joe was shocked at my petite frame. He refers to it in jest from time to time. I find it endearing, enjoying his kindness and protective nature. It was the two of us against the world.

Updating the law firm in New York is always high on my list. I call Jeff to offer him the information that I have discovered recently, both Dr. Guth's letter and the prosecutor statements about having a garage full of Joe's stuff. He appears interested. Bob Smith calls to discuss the same. This new information has incensed me. I inform Bob that we, meaning him, have been conservative for over ten years. No more! I'm asking them to leave their comfort zone. While thinking about new lawyers for Joe I decide Don Lee cannot handle this, so I give all of my information to New York. Jeff calls Joe's sister Sheila to ask her if she will testify at trial if Joe's case is heard on the *Simmons* issue.[73] The *Simmons* issue addresses the fact that the prosecution informed

---

[73] *Simmons v. South Carolina*, 512 U.S. 154 (1994). In *Simmons*, the U.S. Supreme Court recognized that when a prosecutor seeks to establish future dangerousness before a capital sentencing jury, due process entitles the defendant to rebut by presenting information regarding his parole ineligibility.

the jury that Joe may get out of prison if given a life sentence. "No other sentence will stop him except death," they told the jury. This was false and misleading. A life sentence meant just that. Joe would never have gotten out. Of course, Alberi and Test didn't care—they would frame whatever they needed to say to ensure the jury gave them what they wanted—a death sentence. The judge should never have allowed this in the Commonwealth's closing argument, but he did. Jeff wanted Sheila to testify about whether Joe poses a "future danger" to society. During the sentencing phase, to obtain the death penalty, the prosecution instructed the jury that Joe was a danger to society, even with the knowledge that a life sentence meant he was ineligible for parole. Sheila could be helpful to us if Joe was to get a shot at a fair sentencing.

I am trying to flush some information out of Sheila so I spend several hours talking to her on the phone about her conversations with Connie Craig and what she feels is an abuse of the process concerning Joe's case. I am trying to help her to help us. I find my mind wandering to Joe Jackson and the more important issue of the DNA testing and Joe's innocence. After my conversation with Sheila I call Jackson and he informs me there is a big article coming out. He says that he will mention the same lab that was used for DNA testing to execute Timothy Spencer has revealed DNA tests that are favorable to Joseph O'Dell. It is only one of a series of such articles. "Lori, I'll try to cover Joe's Internet page and the information I've uncovered about Stephen Test. But don't hold me to it," he says.

The news of media coverage for Joe offers a glimmer of hope that I'm starting to make a difference. I am working on the third package of material and finalizing my work with the New York firm on the affidavit from Sheila concerning what we feel may be evidence in Joe's case held in Test's personal possession. I also revise the Internet piece to include the Virginia death row article by Joe Jackson and June Arney, revealing the problems depicted in other cases. I am mounting a strong case of opposition to the "mountain of evidence" the Commonwealth of Virginia claims to have on O'Dell. In comparison, the evidence I am finding, which the jury never heard, dwarfs the trial evidence. I am learning the rules of the courtroom, and the importance of presentation. Though I am not a lawyer yet, it's not difficult to see its effect on the outcome.

The next day Joe Jackson phones to confirm he will be covering Joe's Internet plea. It is scheduled to print on Monday, June 12. I expect all hell to break loose when it does. In preparation, I call David Baugh to inform him of the upcoming event. He offers to represent me if I need a lawyer. "Come on now," Baugh says. "Alberi is a public figure." I know the rules regarding public figures and libel and defamation. The standard is much higher for them and requires malice.

Chapter 9

~Internet Splash~

Twice a year, in June and February, the LSAT is administered for all those who seek its punishment. Since I had taken my first exam during a time when I was in extreme pain I decided to give it another whirl. I put some time aside to review for the exam, hoping to improve my score. I take the exam in mid June and pray for improved results, which I received several months later.

After five years of separation Walter and I have an appointment with the judge for our divorce. We arrive with one lawyer, mine. In unison we reach out and hold each other's hand while waiting for the judge. Loving each other, but having let too much "water" under the bridge, we were saddened to have reached this point. The judge inquires if this is what we really want. She must have been thrown off by our demeanor. I gather it's not the norm for two people to be holding hands upon a dissolution of marriage.

Meanwhile, for months Joe and I have been planning the unveiling of his Internet plea for help. The day finally approaches for its launch. To the best of my knowledge, it's the first time a death row inmate has used the Internet to cry out for help. Finally, Joe O'Dell has a voice. I alert Joe Jackson that the piece is up. Success with a new address, www. gbiz.com/odell. Just two weeks earlier, a lawyer in Illinois listed a site for a prisoner who also claimed he was innocent. We pioneered the same idea at the same time. However, his reached the Internet several days earlier than mine, making the inside pages of *People* magazine. No contest, pure coincidence. Surprised by the result, I was slightly disappointed it wasn't Joe's plea—he, too, needed publicity. My purpose was to expose the truth and reveal what was being blocked from the world. I needed to tell everyone about Joseph O'Dell.

Joe Jackson's article is *front page news* in the *Virginian-Pilot*. Channel 13 calls for a TV interview. The Internet story has the media competing for my comments so it almost guarantees the story will hit the papers the next day through the Associated Press. I inform the New York lawyers of this small success and Jeff now wants to get involved. He calls Joe Jackson to explain in greater detail the DNA evidence, the results of Lifecodes' report and Fed Ex's him a package of material. I think he wants his name in the paper. I am so overwhelmed I can hardly contain myself. So is Joe O'Dell. This is the first time someone is listening, actually hearing what he has to say. With the media rolling, I can now take my long-awaited trip with Jen to the beaches of Cape Cod. It's finally summer.

By now Joe Jackson is well aware of the extent of my knowledge and source documentation. I have more material in my possession than one could ever imagine. Joe comes up to the Cape to meet with me. He wants to talk about Test, Alberi and Lifecodes. I indulge him, but remind him that ultimately it doesn't matter what anyone thinks. What matters is what the court thinks. And how politicians can and do influence the court system. I am only now realizing this.

One of the missing pieces of the puzzle is Joe's expert, Diane Lavett. I wanted to talk with her about Alberi's threat, and her opinion that Joe was framed. I add that to my "to do" list. That afternoon I telephone John Reid, the cop who transported Watson from jail. He informs me that he's getting a divorce and leaving his house in just two weeks. Good timing—I may have otherwise lost him as a witness. He agrees to an affidavit.

The following morning arrives more quickly than I would have liked. I am in the middle of packing for law school. I work the case most of the day and prepare an affidavit for John Reid that is three pages long. I am interrupted from my packing by a call from Diane Lavett. I'm quick to ask for her help. She was one of the first witnesses I discovered who had been threatened by Alberi. When she agrees to an affidavit I am more than surprised. She also agrees to speak to Joe Jackson and may give us an "on record" statement.

Believing this case deserves *national* media attention I call *Time* magazine and speak to a woman named Andrea Sachs. I fax her the *Virginian-Pilot* story and the Internet piece, as well as the "Proof of Innocence" editorial written by John Flannery, an attorney who has a heart for the innocent, and who is aware of the systematic problems in such innocence cases. That evening I plan for my trip in the morning to the law office of Paul, Weiss, Rifkind, Wharton & Garrison. I am finally getting access to *all* documents in Joe's case.

~Discovering Hidden Secrets in Boxes~

I love going to New York. It is invigorating to be amongst millions of people, watching them pass by in a variety of dress, style and nationality. I thoroughly enjoy taking in the smell of roasting chestnuts and absorbing the feel of such a powerful city. I arrive at the prestigious law office on Avenue of the Americas. As I enter the reception room Alan Effron greets me and walks me to his office. After two hours of briefing him on the case, he chaperones me to a large conference room where I have the privilege of sorting through all of their files and boxes of materials related to the O'Dell case. The office is majestically decorated with marble floors, cherrywood walls and pictures of esteemed partners draping the hallways leading to corner offices overlooking Manhattan.

Laid on top of the table are several boxes of seemingly organized material. I methodically sort through the files until 7:00 p.m., gathering information. With little time to read it all, the copy machine allows me to take home scores of documents, including all of Paul Ray's notes, investigators' reports, and very privileged, confidential information.

The legal files are packed, along with our suitcases, at the conclusion of soccer season. Leaving behind another school year, Jen and I head to our summer home, as if on autopilot, allowing familiar smells, and the sensation of beach sand under my feet, to permeate my mind.

~Reporter Visits Cape Cod~

Anxious to see what's in the files I don't even allow myself to settle in before I begin to read. The first file contains the lawyer's notes (Joe's co-counsel, Paul Ray). Each page is marked with an identifier. I scour each one, looking for the reason Ray refused to turn them over, and why the prosecution tried so hard to prevent us from getting them. The answer becomes apparent rather quickly. My jaw drops and my eyes stare blankly at the words before me. I have to read it twice just to be sure. Scribbled on the pages is evidence that appears to reveal a cover-up. *Cover-up? That sounds awfully strong*, I question myself. Nevertheless, these words have now entered my mind. I highlight all the important information. Some of it now serves to fill in the gaps. Other words leap out at me as if from a foreign script, as if adding them would change the outcome of the play I'm watching—the characters coming alive with every document, interview or picture that I see. I have to keep working. Joe Jackson is coming to my house and I need to be prepared. He arrives at 8:00 p.m., too late for a meeting tonight, allowing me some relief. The next morning, we meet at 9:00 a.m., for what turns out to be a twelve-hour day. Together, we are going through all of Joe's files and confidential notes of Joe's co-counsel at trial. Joe Jackson's eyes are the first to read some very confidential, yet revealing information about a very complicated, yet really simple murder case. Jackson is amazed at John Reid's affidavit and surprised I have Reyna's report. It's a Tuesday, a work day. Joe's presence is no permission to refrain from my work. He watches me in action, conversing with the attorneys on the phone. He can see I am running the show, at least the investigation. At the end of the day we long for the taste of New England seafood so I take him to a tourist's favorite restaurant in town for lobster at Thompsons. By 10:00 p.m. I am mentally exhausted, having worked hard to provide him with everything he wants—information that has never been seen before. Information that most likely is unknown even to O'Dell's attorneys, having been buried in the voluminous stacks of papers.

I am sifting through the papers and come across the letter that Joe's scientific expert wrote to him while he was in jail awaiting trial in July 1986. He had always told me that she thought he was framed, but I felt that was such a strong word, perhaps it was just Joe's interpretation. I was wrong. The letter is marked as an exhibit, but says "refused" on it.

> Dear Mr. O'Dell:
>
> On Saturday I received from Mr. Ray the lab notes and photos of the electrophoresis results. A draft affidavit is on its way to Clive. Basically, it says that the photos are horrible, *the results taken at face value exclude you from among the group who could have raped the victim and that differences exist between the lab notes and the lab report. Changes in the results in the lab report follow a pattern of **deliberate attempt to frame you*** (emphasis added). I am sincerely worried that the trial will start on the eleventh since I won't have time to prep Mr. Ray and I am moving…If the trial starts on the eleventh, I will get there if it's humanly possible. I feel very strongly about what the record shows for that crime lab, and I intend to protest in court.

Sincerely,

Diane K. Lavett[74]

Alberi's threat to Lavett, as I discovered early on, was just that. A threat, nothing else. I recall his letter to her where he mentioned he was going to interject and suggest Ms. Emrich hire a lawyer and sue her for libel. In private, privileged communications between a lawyer and his client, a lawyer can say whatever they want. This letter, though an intricate part of his defense, was most likely marked "legal mail" and though was not from Joe's lawyer, it was part of his legal defense. The fact that Alberi read it was frightening. It meant they were monitoring his mail, his *legal* mail. The fact that Alberi admitted to having knowledge of this letter seemed to be indicative of the fact that he had no fear of having broken one of the professional rules of conduct. I was getting the feeling that this man felt he was above the law. Was he? Was Joe framed? Diane Lavett thought so. I continue to dissect the files, recovering even more alarming evidence.

While sorting though the mass of papers suddenly I come across some interviews with the jurors, post trial. One of the jurors admits to having a trial party after Joe's conviction, where all the jurors gathered to celebrate and to compare newspaper clippings. *How sinister.* I myself had already been a juror at this point. We just did our job. It never became a "bonding" experience, and we certainly did not feel it either morally or ethically correct to celebrate a conviction. It was our civic duty, not a celebration of any kind. I found this highly disturbing.

I am now feeling overwhelmed by the things I am discovering in Joe's files. I am even more discomforted by the notion that I am the first person to discover them. I imagine it's impossible to read an entire record, and even harder to delve into another attorney's notes on

---

74 Letter from Diane Lavett to Joseph O'Dell, July 29, 1986 (on file with author). See www.loristjohn.com for a copy of the original document.

a case. Perhaps they thought, *It's all in the record.* Or is it? I was finding that the record only holds what gets into the courtroom. What doesn't get in is an entirely different story.

As I scan through the trial attorney's notes and read the pages before me I am blanketed with an ominous sense of violation, like I am discovering someone's dirty secret. And I am. Contained in the notes, individually marked by stamp for identification, is some information that sends chills down my spine. I can't stop reading through the tears that are now building in my eyes. The mixed sense of happiness in discovering helpful information is shadowed by what I am learning. My stomach is turning and it feels as though I am about to be sick.

Albert Alberi and Stephen Test had led the jury and the public to believe that the victim's belongings were never found. When Helen left the bar that evening she was carrying her pocketbook, her keys and an umbrella. The search warrant contained a statement of material facts constituting probable cause for a search of O'Dell's car. It states the "victim's beige purse, car keys with a small light on the chain, and a black umbrella that the victim was last seen with is still missing." In the trial testimony and closing arguments the prosecution made a big deal of the fact that her personal belongings were missing:

> So Helen Scharnter is not found at her car and her personal belongings are not found at her car[75]. The police go to the County Line and find her car there. It's never been moved. Can't find Helen, can't find her personal belongings[76]. They walked around the parameter of the building and walked into the woods. Didn't find her personal property, but, boy, they sure looked hard.[77] Sometimes what you don't find is as telling as what you do. When they searched the defendant's car, they didn't find Helen's purse, Helen's umbrella, Helen's keys[78]. So Helen Scharter is

[75] Trial Transcript, Vol. 24, page 43, lines 8-9. Closing argument by Stephen Test.
[76] Trial Transcript, Vol. 24, page 50, lines 24-25; page 51, line 1.
[77] Trial Transcript, Vol. 24, page 52, lines 2-4.
[78] Trial Transcript, Vol. 24, page 68, lines 7-9.

not found at her car and her personal belongings are not found at her car. I put it to you, ladies and gentleman, that the defendant got her into his car after hitting her over the head, put her in the passenger seat, and drove her across the street to the lot behind the After Midnight Club; took her out of that car after having disassembled her clothes and started the sexual assault in the car, and carried her back to the area in the weeds where her body was found[79]. Why is this rational or reasonable to believe? Because the defendant is a frequenter of the After Midnight Club. It's a place he knows. It's a place, further, he knows that opens later than other places and a place where no one would have been at 11:30 or midnight[80].

I am thinking to myself now *interesting contradiction, it's an after-hours club, meaning after 12 a.m., and Joe thinks no one would be there at 12 a.m.*? In at least five different statements in closing arguments the prosecution makes certain the jury believes all of her belongings were never found. Her pocketbook and keys were never found, but I am in utter amazement by what is presently staring me in my face, a black and white photograph which is marked R20009. I am staring at a photograph of a black umbrella. It appears to have a bent handle. I feverishly scan through the notes and find scribblings by Paul Ray, "umbrella, bent" (R20923) "umbrella, need it" (R10931). The umbrella *was* found. Paul Ray knows it. Why didn't he tell Joe? Why wasn't this brought out at trial? Where was it found? Was it the murder weapon? The biggest question of all, how can a prosecutor state it was never recovered—repeatedly? Did they tell Paul Ray not to share this information with his client? Or was that something he did on his own? Why was it not shared with Dr. Guth? Was it suppressed like the shoe casting and soil? I am fuming now, finding it inconceivable that this court-appointed team, Alberi and Test, could use their power to manipulate the very system they are sworn to fairly represent. In an

---

[79] Trial Transcript, Vol. 24, page 43, lines 17-23.
[80] Trial Transcript, Vol. 24, page 43, lines 17-23.

article by Frank Overton Brown, Jr., 'A Modest Proposal', he quotes
the oath taken by newly sworn in attorneys:

> Raise your right hand, please. Do you solemnly swear or affirm that
> you will support the Constitution of the United States and the Con-
> stitution of the Commonwealth of Virginia, and that you will faith-
> fully, honestly, professionally, and courteously demean yourself in the
> practice of law and execute your office of attorney at law to the best
> of your ability, so help you God?[81]

Brown describes the phrase "courteously demean yourself in the practice of law" to mean that each attorney is "binding himself or herself
to an ethic of reciprocity which is part of the very fabric of our legal
profession. Courtesy and civility are synonymous words. Courtesy is
accepted as behavior characterized by graciousness and consideration
toward others".

I am wondering now who the criminals in this investigation really
are. I'm also starting to understand why Joe never trusted his attorney
at trial, and why he set him up one day. It was a brilliant way to find out
whether his attorney was sharing confidential facts with the adversary.
I remember Joe telling me that the prosecutors claimed he had a gun
and used it to beat the victim. They wanted to know where he bought
his pellet gun. In an effort to find out whether Paul Ray was sharing confidential information with the Commonwealth, Joe told Paul
Ray he purchased a gun at a different store than the one he did. Not
long after, the prosecutors executed a subpoena *duces tecum* (a com-
mand for the production of papers, documents or other tangible items
of evidence) and served that very same store, the wrong store, not the
one where Joe actually purchased the gun. It was a defendant's worst
nightmare. Joe was not only fighting the state. He was also fighting his
own lawyer.

By this time my eyes are glued to the notes and I'm scanning the

---

[81] Senior Lawyers Conference, *Civility and Professionalism*, Virginia Bar.

pages for anything important. I notice something that causes me to stop, to reread the page, once, twice, now four times. I see something that has always preyed on Joe's mind, but until now I could find no evidence to support his suspicions, his futile attempts to get discovery at trial. The prosecution never alluded to the fact that the victim may have had a room at the Executive Inn that evening, sharing it with her boyfriend. Yet there, right in front of my eyes was a full search of the motel in which the bar was located. Joe always told me about this, but I doubted him. The notes cast a shadow on my doubt. The black hole in this death row mystery reveals a different record than the one transcribed in the courtroom. There was nothing in the court record about a room, or even a search of the motel rooms. Ten years later, I am reading an unfamiliar record like it had been saved for my eyes. In Paul Ray's notes I now see a chart of the motel rooms, just six of them. On top of the chart in the right hand corner I see Ike Wright's name. Below his name is the name Helen Schartner and room number "203." My body freezes, unable to fathom the reality of the substance I am taking in through words spilled on a useless piece of paper at the bottom of some box. Does this mean that Helen and Ike had a room that evening? Joe had been telling me all along that he had filed a subpoena, wanting to obtain the invoices from the motel to show who stayed there that night. He was unable to get them all, many were simply not produced, listed as "missing." I wondered why. So did he. Was the motel ever investigated by the police; did they search the rooms?

Joe told me that the Travelers Insurance Company had hired an investigator to defend the Executive Inn against a lawsuit from the murder victim's family. I was not so sure I believed it for I never saw it anywhere in the papers and there was no evidence of this at trial. Yet here, before my very eyes, was an investigation unfolding that never reached the courtroom. Evidence that suggests that Ike and the victim shared a motel room that evening. Room 203. It would haunt me until I could find more information about this room. Hauntings of Helen's ghost are reaching through the page as if to tell me who really killed her. It reads:

> Motel Room- p/o (police officer) went into room. No fingerprints, no keys to car, no pocketbook.
> Dick Harper (employee)- bed remade or made. Killed in room?
> Dick said no blood in room.
> V (victim) planned on staying in motel room.

The next page has original markings on it—a black-penciled drawing of the configuration of six rooms in the motel and the names of Helen and her boyfriend. Room 203. As I move to the next page I find additional references about the room. *County Line* is marked on top of the page and right below it are the names of staff that were employed there. To the right of the name Dick Harper it reads: *according to Bill Moore the victim had a room at the Executive Inn.* And again on another page, on a *To Do* list, Paul Ray writes "Conf. with Collins (conference with Joe's investigator), and under that he scribbles *Dick Harper-Room-Victim.* My own suspicions about Paul Ray were forming. It was beginning to make sense now, why he refused to turn over his notes to Joe's appellate attorneys. Why he wouldn't even talk to them. Why his notes had to be court ordered. He was told by the prosecution not to talk to Joe's attorneys. I recall reading that in the court record. Now I know why. Instead of sharing this information with Joe, it was shared with the prosecution. *They* knew what was contained in Paul Ray's notes. Privileged information belonging to Joe which, instead of burying Joe, could bury the state. The Commonwealth always counted on the laid back attitude of Joe's appellate attorneys. They counted on the fact that no one would actually read the entire record, including Paul Ray's notes. And if they did, they wouldn't even care. They also counted on O'Dell's lawyers never wanting to challenge another attorney. Worse yet, the system. Who were these two prosecutors and why do they seem to invisibly sew shut the mouths of those who could help O'Dell?

I was becoming frightened by the possibilities. Room 203 would ring in my head for days, even months.

So, too, would the photograph of the umbrella. The circular wounds on Helen Schartner's head were reported to have been caused by a blunt object, possibly a gun. But it could have been the circular end of the umbrella handle. Why no mention of the umbrella? Why wasn't this brought to the jury's attention? Why didn't Paul Ray insist on bringing this up upon examination of the police officers? It clearly raises doubt, reasonable doubt. Once more, I feel like I just discovered a dirty secret. Unfortunately, I have.

As I continue to devour the pages before me, I land on one labeled "Joseph Moore." An interview with Moore seems to have brought out the following facts:

> Saw: clothing, tire tracks, footprints, found a belt, observant-drag marks.
> Pictures: body moved by the time pictures taken. Pictures different weren't exactly the way they were.
> Room: Executive Inn.
> Wet and muddy at the body site. Someone walked around it. Couldn't make it out.
> Path: wet and muddy.
> After Midnight Club - parking lot filled up at 2400 (12am)-packed.

On the same page it states:

> 0730 /6 Feb /Wed.
> Controversy- body not there at Wed morning-0730. Body put there during the day.

The above information alone meant nothing, but I recall the letter from Joe's investigator immediately after his review of the police reports and evidence upon Joe's arrest. It revealed that a witness, Jeff Elliott, stated he walked by the area where the victim was found at 7:30

a.m., the morning of February 7, and there was no body there at that time. It meant she had to have been dumped there during the day. The victim's body was noted to have been only damp and not soaked from the rain. This would suggest she was not lying in the drizzling rain all night long, but dumped in the field sometime later. Another witness I now needed to find, to hear what he had to say. Did the police ignore him? Why didn't Paul Ray subpoena Jeff Elliott and question him on the stand, giving rise to further reasonable doubt? If Helen's body was not there at 7:30 the morning after she left the bar, Joe *could not be the murderer.* He was at work that morning, and for the entire day. A solid alibi. Swept right under the carpet to keep the floors clean, it never made the trial record. The jury never heard it.

The notes also seem to confirm my suspicions. The parking lot of the After Midnight Club was packed that evening. It was ladies' night at the Executive Inn across the street. Customers would eventually leave there and walk across the street, or drive, to continue partying. Ladies' night drew a crowd of approximately 350 people. At least that's what the notes say. It would have been impossible to viciously attack someone at 12:00 a.m., rape her in a bucket-seat Camaro and carry her body to the field immediately adjacent to the parking lot, dumping her only a few feet away, in plain sight of patrons coming and going to the club from the parking lot.

Paul Ray's notes were littered with question marks. One of the questions pertained to the cigarette butt found lying near the body. It was introduced at trial as *Joe's* cigarette.

In Ray's notes, were the comments "cigarette butt, saliva testing? Fingerprints?" On another page: "Paper excellent for fingerprints. Paper—does a good job. Carter (expert witness)—never done it—fingerprint."

He was questioning why it was never tested, but I had to wonder, why not test it himself? It never occurred to me before this. The Commonwealth would never miss an opportunity to tie O'Dell to the murder. Why did they ignore this, or did they? As I read further I would discover why. There was an interview with Joseph Moore, the drunk who found Helen's body. The notes reveal that Moore stated he dropped a cigarette butt near the body when he discovered her. It was *his* cigarette.

I felt like a steel ball had just been swung into my stomach. Why on earth then, if the defense knew this, did they not insist on testing the butt? If the interview of Moore revealed this information, why did the prosecution suggest it was O'Dell's cigarette butt? Even though it was a Marlboro and O'Dell smoked Winstons, they still suggested it was his, struggling in every possible way to tie him to the crime scene. Joe O'Dell was masterful at his trial, but he failed to bring this up. Perhaps he didn't know. Is that why Moore never testified at trial? It would have meant they had nothing to tie O'Dell to the crime scene. The footprints didn't match Joe O'Dell's and they had nothing else to tie Joe to the scene of the crime. Maybe *this* would work? It was a pitiful yet successful attempt to make the jury think they had proof of Joe's presence there.

The next morning Joe Jackson and I meet again. The *Pilot* is paying for his limited time. He has only one day to get what he wants. We proceed to go through the files. By now, Joe is mostly copying it all. He wants to bring it back to Virginia. Paul Ray's notes had the phone number and name of the insurance investigator, William Honbarger, for the motel. Joe Jackson listens as I call Honbarger and ask if he would be willing to speak with me. He is not reluctant, just curious. He speaks freely, answering my questions. He acknowledges he was hired by the Executive Inn to investigate Helen's murder. "They were defending a lawsuit filed against them by Helen's family," he says. Honbarger was at Joe's trial and performed his own investigation at the request of The Travelers insurance company. "I recall someone had a room at the Executive Inn that night. I don't remember if it was the victim or someone in her party," Honbarger says. I almost fell to the floor upon hearing these words from a stranger. He actually knows important information and is telling me the truth. I now realize that what is shaping up is a *cover-up*. I recall the testimony of Ike Wright. He drove from Powahatan that evening to see Helen. It would have been impossible to drive back that same night. Powahatan Correctional Center was approximately two and a half hours away. It made sense to get a room. The convenience too tempting. No need to go anywhere after a night of drinking and dancing with your girl. Drunk or not, just walk upstairs for some late night sex. After all, he didn't drive over 140 miles just to dance with her. Wright's testimony was convenient. He used his sister as an alibi. It was never corroborated, nor was his sister asked to testify to support his alibi. Then again, Ike Wright wasn't on trial. He was a cop.

Joe Jackson is watching me from the corner of his eye. He is witnessing my commitment to the case and can see my frustration, can *feel* it now. He calls his editor at the paper and leaves the following message:

"I feel Joe O'Dell is innocent. We need to expand on the DNA. I'm upset it was cut out. It's a stronger case than Stockton's."

I'm sure he said this for my benefit, but I'm also sure that Joe Jackson shares a deeper concern about this case now. Dennis Stockton was a man on death row who claimed innocence as well. He never made it. The truth was executed along with Stockton. Whatever that truth was.

Jackson finishes by 2:00 p.m., in time for a quick lunch. He heads back to Virginia in the late afternoon. I believe he will give an accurate account of what I'm uncovering. Jackson appears to be a man of high integrity. I hope I'm right. Risky moves are often made in pure desperation, especially in sharing very confidential information that has been either ignored or concealed for the past ten years. The sad thing is, evidence like this shouldn't be hidden, nor finally discovered like the very last egg at an Easter egg hunt. During this hunt I'm finding too many eggs that should have been picked up by the defense and presented to the jurors in a basket full of reasonable doubt.

While still at my home, Jackson had suggested I talk again with Honbarger. I call him, hoping for more information. He is getting older and cannot remember specific details, but he is pleasant and wants to talk. Honbarger tells me that he was impressed with Joe O'Dell at trial. He sat through the trial as a result of the lawsuit and looked for evidence to support the Inn against the family's lawsuit. Honbarger says, "I was impressed with Joseph and I don't think he did it. He out litigated Alberi. I think Alberi just wanted a conviction." I catch my breath. Honbarger continues. "Mr. O'Dell was very polite and neat in his appearance. He was sharp as a tack and I was impressed with his questioning of experts. I had serious reservations that he did it. The state did not carry the burden of the proof. I recall Alberi on the blood evidence. I was lost and dozing off, but when Joe spoke about it the jury sat up and took notice. The coroner said there was no struggle, clothing was not torn and the pantyhose not ripped. Joe would make a fabulous attorney. He should go to law school. One other thing, the room was on the south side of the building and that's the same side her car was found. It seemed to be of importance in the investigation. One thing for sure, he's going to be exonerated. While Alberi and the others are six feet under Joe will still be fighting." Honbarger says he saw a record of the hotel check-in but doesn't recall the name or time. He doesn't remember the names of the people with the victim that night, or even that she had a boyfriend. Just that the person who checked in the room was either Helen Schartner, or someone who was in her party that evening, or someone connected with her. He tells me they had reservations. *That's one hell of a statement from a disinterested party*, I am thinking. He says he will call the manager of the Executive Inn to ask who had a room. Without my suggesting any numbers he remembers *room 203*, but can't be sure. "Couldn't be 302" he says, "because there was no third floor." How could this have not been introduced at trial? A possible room for the victim and her boyfriend, or someone in her party, or connected with her? It was all so relevant to Helen's movements that night. Who was she with? What were her plans that evening? Or better yet, the motives of those she surrounded herself with?

If the investigator for the insurance company could uncover such revealing evidence I'm desperate for an answer as to why Joe O'Dell could not. The record is replete with O'Dell's futile attempt to get the invoices of the Inn's reservations that night. In his letters to me, Joe explained how hard he fought to obtain all the reservations of that evening, and how many were missing. He was sure they were hiding something. Joe was not paranoid. I'm finding this more suggestive of something that's just a little suspicious. There *was* a reservation. Honbarger saw it. Joe did not. Paul Ray must have known about it. It's written all over his notes. This reservation could have, and would have, put a completely different spin on the picture painted by the prosecution. It was too dangerous to allow O'Dell to get hold of it. It may have allowed him to win. Sweep it under the carpet where the rest of the dirt goes.

It's no secret that once the police focus on a suspect, they often close the door to other possibilities. Especially when they find a suspect with a criminal record. Makes it even more likely they have their man. Whether it's human nature, laziness or just plain ignorance, it doesn't matter. The fact is, it happens more often than people know. More often than we would like to believe. When it happens to other people it doesn't affect us. "If it doesn't affect me or my family why should I care?" is an all-too-common reaction. Even among my friends. At that moment the stark realization hits—the system does not guarantee the truth. The truth can so easily be buried deep in legal motions, suppressions, courtroom wit, procedures and rules that make no sense to the average person. No sense to me at all.

As I comb through the documents I gaze across the table and notice a page labeled "Joseph Roger O'Dell. Confidential. Criminal Record." In 1958, at the age of 16, Joe was sentenced to three years for stealing a car and joyriding. First conviction, grand larceny-auto. In prison, Joe hooked up with a guy name Bobby. Upon release, the two new friends went on a spree of robbing service stations and supermarkets. They were labeled the "silk stocking bandits." Eventually caught, they were charged with five counts of armed robbery and unauthorized use of a car, accounting for a total of eleven felonies at the age of 19. During his time in prison, and in 1964, a homosexual attacked Joe with a knife. Joe defended himself, but jailhouse snitches got him a 20-year sentence for second degree murder. He was released in 1974. In 1975, Joe was convicted of robbery and kidnapping. He served seven and a half years before being released in August 1982. In total, he earned 14 convictions on his criminal record. Not a record to be proud of.

To the general public a list of 14 felonies leads one to believe Joe committed 14 separate crimes during his lifetime. Eleven were committed by the time O'Dell was 19. Twelve, by age 22. Joe was no model citizen. He came from a tough neighborhood, hung out with the wrong crowd, and later became an alcoholic by his own admission.

Knowing he had a past criminal record impacts the prosecution and the jury. However, in my evaluation I am trying to find out one thing and one thing only: did he do *this* crime? In one of Joe's letters he confides his thoughts when he was arrested for the rape and murder of Helen Schartner. At first he felt God brought him to his knees in an effort to save him. In his mind he justified the wrongful conviction, believing he was lucky to have been brought in, or "I would otherwise be dead now." But after a while it didn't feel like much of a lesson anymore, and it became harder and harder to justify his incarceration for something he did not do.

I call Mr. Honbarger again, but he is ill and asks me to wait a few days. I quickly get off the phone to allow him to rest. Days pass and I muster the nerve to call him again. We review his statements and I ask him if he will sign an affidavit regarding what he has told me in private. He agrees. I am grateful and relieved. In the context of the sworn statement (dated July 25, 1995- See Exhibit IV) he explains:

> I was employed by the Travelers Insurance Company to defend
> the Executive Inn against a lawsuit by the victim's family for neg-
> ligence arising from the establishment. During my investigation I
> interviewed several people who worked at the County Line, and oth-
> ers who would have any knowledge about either the victim (Helen
> Schartner) or Joseph O'Dell, the suspect. After a complete investiga-
> tion I found nothing to link the two persons together. I do recall that
> the investigation revealed that either the victim, someone who was in
> her party that evening, or someone connected with the victim, had a
> room at the Executive Inn the evening she was murdered.
> During my investigation I had occasion to speak with Virginia Bul-
> lard, the manager of the establishment, and I recall that she showed
> me the reservation; although I saw a record of the check-in, I do not
> recall the name or the time involved. I do remember that the room
> was on the southside of the motel and that the victim's car was found
> on the southside of the motel. This seemed to be of importance dur-
> ing the investigation. The room 203 seems to ring a bell, although
> I cannot be sure that was the room. During the investigation the
> police were apparently informed of the room at the motel and they
> concentrated their efforts on that one or two rooms in the motel. I do
> not recall how they knew about the room, just that they did and they
> concentrated on that one or two rooms in the motel.
> I spent several days observing the trial and it was my gut feeling that
> Joseph O'Dell was an innocent man.
>
> William Honbarger

The notes I was now uncovering confirmed what Joe O'Dell has
been telling me all along. The police did not share Honbarger's investigation with the defense, and if they did, Joe O'Dell knew little about
the results. He fought hard for the invoices to show that someone had
a room at the motel. While the Executive Inn was able to produce the
record for the insurance company, they never did produce that same
record for Joe O'Dell, even though they knew his life hung in the balance. I wondered, how on earth could this not have been brought up at

trial? Then I remembered, Joe represented himself.

Chapter 10

~The Threats Begin~

Relishing the idea of a weekend, I am grateful for any relief I can get. After such an intense week I am feeling myself again. Relaxing means paying bills, cleaning house, and the mundane chores that are part of family life. I mail a package to Walter. It's his birthday. I send a photo album of Jen. I am also expecting company. It didn't take long to discover that having a beach house brings out friends like flies. My best friend from high school is visiting for the weekend with her family. It would be nice to have some company, I thought. The fourth of July in Chatham is always a big deal. Main Street is closed down and families line the street with lawn chairs and strollers. Blankets cover the lawn of the Methodist Church, in front of the library and town hall, while hundreds of tourists wait for the festive parade to paint colors in the streets. Balloons fill the air, and cotton candy and popcorn litter the ground. Because I live in the town village, I can stroll down the block early in the morning and set down three chairs, claiming our spot for the parade. My girlfriend brought her three daughters, Janie, Jackie and Jordan. Jennifer was mine. The four J's. At night, a local babysitter watches the kids so Diane, her husband and I, can enjoy a candlelit dinner overlooking the ocean. Afterwards, we enjoy some country dancing in the restaurant bar. All of this a great respite for me—Joe's case consumes so much time and energy—physical and emotional.

The next day proves to be delightful, as if specially ordered for the thousands of tourists that flock to Cape Cod for the 4th of July holiday weekend. Eighty-degree temperature is accompanied by a clear, bright blue sky. We load the trunk with assorted beach chairs, buckets and shovels, and remember the big yellow radio that lays on the beach towel, to drown out the noise of screaming kids nearby. While I love to share my home, I welcomed the sight of their car leaving my driveway. Company can be exhausting, so I pass on the 4th of July fireworks.

Since summer means beach time, I signed Jennifer up for swimming lessons. I recall my mom did the same for me. I took lessons at a chlorinated indoor pool with a YWCA instructor. I was *not* a good swimmer, but I wanted something different for my daughter. I wanted Jen to be great, to be able to hold her own in the water. At least not drown if she were ever in a life or death situation. The town offered lessons at 10:00 a.m. at Oyster Pond. Jennifer hated swimming lessons. The water was murky and sometimes cold. On the other hand, jellyfish loved swimming in Oyster Pond and seemed to ignore the unwelcomed screams of the children who shared their water by the dock. When the water was clear enough to see, Jen would dodge them. Otherwise feel the pain from their inevitable sting. When the water was murky, which it often was, it was the luck of the draw. As a typical parent, I tell her "swimming lessons are important." Jen wasn't convinced. The result was she quit when she was old enough to voice her opinion, and influence mine.

Though it's a sunny and beautiful beach day I work on Joe's case all day. Joe Jackson phones to discuss his pending article on Joe.

"Lori, Alberi is getting nervous," Joe says. "He's threatening to sue the newspaper."

I also learn that Alberi is upset about the Internet piece. He told Joe, "It convicts an innocent man." Funny I'm thinking, that's exactly what I'm trying to convey. Alberi also reminds Joe that the *Virginian-Pilot* is a party to a libel suit because they gave out the address to the

Internet. I know this is absurd. He's a public figure and everything said in the Internet piece is founded on court documents. Alberi is reaching, throwing out whatever will stick. The possibility of being exposed is too frightening for him. It wasn't enough to intimidate witnesses. Now he's threatening the newspapers. It's a sign of desperation. It means I am shaking things up. Until now no one cared. No one even knew. Alberi could add one more conviction notch on his belt without question. He never dreamed a petite blonde from the northeast would get hold of these papers, or have reason to care what they said. He counted on the fact that Joe O'Dell was a convict and no one would listen to him. But here I am. Our voices, Joe's echoing from death row, mine from suburban America, transcended through words from secondary source documents, emulating our claims with a foundation that could not be disputed. I smile to myself. Alberi's threats don't bother me. Instead, I'm amused because I know I am one person he will not stop. He can't touch me. Perhaps he has finally met his match. Someone who dares to stand up to him, someone outside of his influence in Virginia Beach. After Joe Jackson and I end the conversation I enjoy a pleasant evening out with my daughter. Lobster at the local Squire, followed by a baseball game on the town field. Traditional Cape Cod style. I gaze over at her seated beside me on the bench and drink in her excitement as we watch the game. The sounds of laughter we share tonight are powerful doses of medicine for me.

Although Jen, at this point, will only voice disdain for her swimming lessons, she dutifully complies with her mother's wishes, dreading the mornings they arrive. As my daughter is learning the backstroke, I am backpedaling through my paperwork. I'm now working on the lawyers and media together, providing packages to new attorneys to gain their interest, and sending more material to Joe Jackson. That evening Jen and I go to the Harwich Theatre. I think I enjoy the children's plays more than she does. In time she would decide, like swimming lessons, that it was not for her. She would one day mouth those dreaded words to her mother, "Mommy, I am too old for this; it's for kids." That day would come at age twelve. For now, it's a great cultural experience to enjoy together. The Harwich Theatre offers opportunities for the performing arts to children all over Cape Cod. Truly talented kids participate in the summer program, some aspiring to a career of acting, hoping to use this small town playhouse as a platform to display their talents. We watch a fabulous performance of *Rapunzel* that took me back to my own childhood. I grew up wearing ponytails and pigtails. My dirty blonde hair was parted in the middle and fell over my shoulders, draping my entire back, landing at my small waist. They were ready targets for the boys at school, who enjoyed flipping them from behind me either in class, or at recess when it was easy to escape detection by the teachers.

Whenever I leave the Cape during the summer months I know I will slide out of town with ease. It's coming back onto the Cape that the locals dread most, especially on a Friday afternoon. For most of us we would rather jump ship than return in heavy traffic with the maddening weekenders. I am already dreading the ride home. Unfortunately, I have to return to Jersey in order to finalize my move to Boston. Without knowing exactly why, I feel a little uncomfortable as we arrive. The location of my house, about ten minutes away from my ex-husband, and the more than a decade of memories, contributes to my uneasiness. Since the divorce there has been a new strain on my relationship with Walter which escalates my urge to move away. A fresh new start is what I need. Early the next morning I retrieve the dog from the kennel and pack up the leftover dishes in the kitchen. I'm not home long before something strange happens. I have a friendly relationship with those around me, including my mail carrier. She makes a point to stop by the house while I am packing the car. With a questioning tone of voice, she informs me that I am being investigated.

"For what?" I ask.

"My boss wants to know if you get a lot of express mail and well, if you just get a lot of mail. He asked me if I thought anything illegal was going on at your house," she says. With a shrug I tell her, "That's ridiculous. Thanks for the heads-up."

Certainly I have not kept a low profile. No surprise there. I have indeed been sending express mail packages to the lawyers and press, but so what? This must be the work of Alberi. I had learned during the course of my investigation that his brother was a secret service agent. Are they trying to intimidate me? I immediately call Joe Jackson.

"Don't worry," he tells me. "You're protected a bit by the *Virginian-Pilot*."

In other words, they know what's going on! Alberi is now lashing out at me. He knew I was the source of the release of new information, evidence he hoped would remain silent as a corpse. But Joe wasn't dead yet. I wasn't immune to Alberi's tricks, but I am immune to his threats. I've done nothing wrong.

Before I leave town I hop on the commuter train to New York. During my last visit I was unable to search through the remaining three boxes of O'Dell's files. This is now my last chance. When I move, and while in law school, there will be no opportunity to go back. No telling what I will find this time. I spend the entire day combing through the files, copying everything that looks even remotely important. Before I leave I make it a point to meet with the partner in charge, Bob Smith. During the course of our conversation it becomes apparent that this is just a *pro bono* case to him. The urgency or reality of Joe's innocence doesn't seem to phase him in the least, no matter what I share with him. Damn. I'm working harder than ever yet feel I'm up against a brick wall. There is no enthusiasm, not even a little concern. Maybe that's the way an elite firm operates. Maybe the lawyers can't show any emotion. Tinkering with someone's life though has to be different. We are not litigating a property dispute or a wrongful termination action. It's the difference between one's last breath and a lifetime of them. No matter what I find, it won't matter if Joe's representation won't use it. If they don't believe in him. While I scan the papers in the last two boxes I find *two* autopsy reports. Each with different dates, notes, telephone numbers, new clues for my investigation. I stuff them in my briefcase and head out the door to the bustling streets of Manhattan.

****

Moving to a new city is always stressful—moving, period, is always stressful. For our very last night in New Jersey Jen spends it with Walter while I do a myriad of last-minute errands.

The movers arrive early. I plan on moving some things to Cape Cod and the rest to our new home in Boston. While at the Cape awaiting the movers, Joe Jackson calls. He has spoken to Holmes, Joe's investigator at trial, and found out that the bloody clothes from trial were never kept in an evidence locker. They were stuffed in an unlocked storage room in a back office at the police department. Apparently, they were full of mold and bacteria when they were shipped to Lifecodes Laboratory for DNA testing. Jackson is now satisfied as to the condition of the clothing and why it was not tested further. Holmes also stated that he spoke with Tim Bougades, who told him that Joe O'Dell had blood all over his face when he saw him in a fight across town from the murder scene. He had asked Joe if he was alright. Bougades testified at trial that he saw a "dark substance" on Joe's face. I wondered why. Holmes confirms my suspicions. Alberi and Test went to Bougades' garage and intimidated him prior to his testimony. An interview with Tim revealed how angry he was to have been confronted like this. The prosecutors banged on his door and yelled at him, trying to favor his testimony against Joe O'Dell. I wonder what the prosecutors said. Perhaps they threatened to shut down Tim's nightclub business. His father owned the Brass Rail and Tim was the manager of it. It wouldn't take much to shut down a club in Virginia Beach. Especially if one had connections with the cops in town, as any prosecutor would. The investigator's notes support what Jackson is telling me. This was critical corroborating evidence for O'Dell's alibi. It had to be discredited by the prosecution. They couldn't have an eyewitness testify that Joe O'Dell was just in a fight at 1:00 a.m. across town, miles from where the murder victim lay dead. So they intimidated the witness to say it was not blood they saw on O'Dell's face but a "dark substance." Why, if Paul Ray knew this, did he not bring this out on direct examination of their witness? Why did the trial transcript read only a couple of pages when it came to Tim's testimony? I add Timothy Bougades to the list.

The very next day Jen and I move to Boston. We enter our new residence with excitement, me more so than Jen. My enthusiasm is contagious, helping to ease the stress of the move. In the midst of unpacking, Joe O'Dell calls. He is agitated when he hears the news about Bougades. He could never understand why Bougades was not up-front at trial. He believed it was because Bougades had hit Joe's girlfriend with his car and they had exchanged words. This explains Joe's line of direct examination of Bougades at trial. He didn't know Tim was threatened by Alberi. Another piece of vital information never shared with him by his co-counsel, Paul Ray. It would have been crucial, and fodder for direct examination, to have solicited from Bougades that he had been paid a visit at his home, and threatened by the prosecution. I had Paul Ray's notes now and for the first time Joe was hearing things that he should have been told years ago.[82] Why was Ray apparently working with Alberi and not his own client? What was so powerful as to make a defense attorney ignore his ethical obligations?

---

[82] Paul Ray's notes, and a copy of a telephone message from Kathy Dombrowski reveals the reason at least one of Joe O'Dell's witnesses never testified at trial. She had been assaulted by a black man who threatened her with a gun to "drop out of (Joe's) case or (he would) kill her." See Paul Ray's notes (on file with author).

Chapter 11

~Political Posturing~

In preparation for law school Jennifer and I settle in our new house in July. Creating a home with a comfortable atmosphere for Jennifer is important to me. Meanwhile, Jen is outdoors making new friends on our first day here. I have not spent but three hours in total relief from the case when I get a call from Joe Jackson. "The story won't go until August, Lori, I'm sorry. This will give you and Joe an opportunity to say what you want though." I take a deep breath. "Oh, and by the way, can I have a picture of you for the front-page story?" "Sure," I reply.

I pounce on this extra time to strengthen Joe's claim of innocence. First, I draft an affidavit for William Honbarger concerning the room at the Executive Inn. Then I draft a letter to Travelers Insurance company to release their records of notes. What Honbarger doesn't remember, his notes will. Next, I contact the New York firm—Paul, Weiss, Rifkind, Wharton & Garrison—and tell them we must get Collins' reports, the Holmes' report (investigators at trial), and the shore patrol report which substantiates the fight. "I need these reports ASAP, please." Finally, I reach out to Richard Reyna, who is otherwise tied up with the McVeigh case. I am careful to avoid any loss of contact. I cannot afford to lose him.

For ten long years, Joseph O'Dell has been begging for someone to listen to him. Letter after letter, phone call after phone call he has reached out to literally hundreds, maybe thousands of people. And always met with disinterest and/or distrust. After pleading for an ear to listen to what he had to say, saying and doing exotic things just to draw attention to himself, Joe finally gets to speak to the press. It's July 18 and Joe is interviewed by Joe Jackson for the very first time.[83] I can't imagine the flicker of inspiration it must offer him. With that accomplished I take a break. Jen and I have tickets to the magic show at a local theatre in Chatham. Laughter is often the best medicine and this night it fills my heart, helping to relieve the ache I feel inside for Joe.

Richard finally calls back. He is knee-deep with the Timothy McVeigh case and can't get back to Joe's case until August. "Okay," I say. He offers a pal from El Paso, but I decline. I want only him.

Joe calls me and he sounds somewhat uplifted. "Lori, I had an interview with Joe Jackson and I think it went well. He asked a lot of questions about my past and I answered them all. Thanks for pulling this together."

A summer in Cape Cod would not be a summer at all if one didn't take the ten minute flight to Nantucket for the day. It's famous for its beautiful beaches, great restaurants and shopping. Jen and I marvel at the splendid floral arrangements that fill the boat-shaped window boxes along the cobblestoned streets. New England quilts and Nantucket baskets grace the shop windows, luring tourists as they stroll by. Miles out in the ocean Nantucket can be covered with heavy fog at times. It's not unusual for the fog to slow the flights down, or stop them altogether. Heavy fog that day causes us to miss the 6:00 p.m. flight home. Instead, we hop the ferry over the Atlantic and get home in the early evening. As I started to fall asleep I have thoughts of Joe. I

---

[83] My notes reveal that Joe Jackson had interviewed a police officer in Virginia Beach by the name of Linda Zabrecki. Earlier in my investigation I learned that a cop name "Lisa" stated that Joseph Moore (the drunk who found Helen Schartner's body) was protected by the police. The statement was so unbelievable that I had earlier held off on forming an opinion of its veracity until Joe Jackson told me that Zabrecki agreed with Lisa, that Moore is "protected due to O'Dell's trial." This was the rumor around the cops in Virginia Beach.

wished Joseph O'Dell could have strolled around Nantucket this day, a free man. Away from death row, away from the politics of his case and away from the life I knew he once had.

~Media Games~

While time has passed since the Internet article came out, it must be weighing heavy on Alberi's mind. The distribution of the newspaper that morning had long transpired, but the Internet piece wasn't going away. It remained out there for millions to read, gathering supporters from all around the world. I was wondering when Alberi would threaten me, too. I didn't have to wait long. The phone rings at my home in Cape Cod. It's an unfamiliar voice. He must have tracked me down. Alberi identifies himself and asks for my address. I am cool—I offer him a P.O. box number in Kendall Park, NJ. He then asks about the Internet. My answer is curt.

"I am a spokesperson for O'Dell and believe in his cause."

"So, you admit to being the author of the Internet piece?"

"I admit to nothing. If you have any further questions, I suggest you call my lawyer."

We hang up. I suppose that was meant to scare me. Instead, I prepare to secure my assets in case he decides to file what the courts call a "frivolous" lawsuit. While one is ethically obliged not to do so, I knew one thing for sure: Alberi did not play by the rules. I gift my jewelry to my friend and close the bank account which holds my law school tuition money. Meanwhile, my best friend calls a lawyer friend in California. "No reason to be concerned," he says. "He's probably blowing smoke." I agree, but I don't want to take any chances.

Following this subtle threat, I phone David Baugh and share my conversation with Alberi. He's not surprised. He had agreed to represent me if I ever needed it. Secured with counsel I phone Alberi. He doesn't pick up. "Hi Al, this is Lori Urs. I had a conversation with my lawyer, David Baugh, and he advised me to tell you if, in the future, you have any questions, to please call him. Thank you very much. Bye!"

I'm amused at riling him up, especially knowing his rival would be at the other end of a lawsuit, should he dare. I think I am beginning to enjoy this game.

The summer is going by quickly. Somehow I manage to enjoy it while still focusing my time and attention on Joe's case. Little did I know, while I was enjoying my summer, I had started an all-out war with Alberi. He becomes so furious with me for releasing the evidence I uncovered that he begins to use others for his dirty work. I receive a call from Andy Sebok in Virginia Beach.

"Lori, you won't believe this. Humphrey (Commonwealth Attorney and Alberi's friend and boss) has spoken out through the media. You may want to see this." I immediately call the lawyers in New York and have them fax me the article. It's full of lies. Not misrepresentations, full blown lies. *Humphrey has lost it.* He must have some close ties with Alberi to stick his neck out like this.[84] Otherwise he is just plain ignorant to the truth. Either way, I immediately start drafting a letter to him. Knowledge is power. With my knowledge I can pinpoint specific testimony in an instant, and refute lies by directly pointing to where the truth is, through a variety of sources. I was a force to be reckoned with and I wasn't going away.

The letter in the *Virginian-Pilot* by Humphrey is so full of lies that I could not let it go. He openly called Joe's lawyers "liars." How dare he? I was not going to let this happen. I call Alan Effron and urge them to respond. They are hesitant. I can't reach Reyna so I type a Letter to the Editor of the paper as my response to the allegations and false statements made by Humphrey. The next day I speak to the editor of the *Beacon* newspaper and fax her my response. She wants me to call

---

[84]   Alberi was seeking a spot on the bench during this time. So, to avoid any further negative publicity he started to use Commonwealth Attorney Humphrey to fight his battles in the media.

her on Tuesday to check on space for Friday's edition. I find out Bob Smith is writing directly to Humphrey and copying the paper. Finally, I have them fired up. I instruct Effron not only to address the issues attacking the lawyers, but that he must also support his client as well.

The McVeigh team has cut Richard some slack, allowing him to commit to Joe's case for a few days. He asks me to call him in the morning.

On the same day that I send my tuition to law school I receive a certified notice addressed to my P.O. box in New Jersey. It's probably Alberi. Seconds later I'm speaking directly to C.C. Holmes (Joe's investigator). It's clear he harbors no warm feelings for Alberi. I can also sense he is afraid of him. He says there is no justice in Virginia Beach. He willingly offers to Fed Ex the package of his notes of Joe's investigation. I'm aware that he worked with Paul Ray, causing me to question his allegiance. I must be cautious in my dealings with him.

My dining room table is beginning to look like a research area for an elite FBI operation. I make a feeble attempt, for four hours, to clean if off so that it can be a table for meals, if not for our guests. With the case heating up, the stress of this investigation is starting to reveal itself in my aching body. Adding to the stress, Joe O'Dell is now worried about me going to Virginia Beach, he is afraid for me. I'm not entirely sure I believe in his sincerity. I still maintain some doubt in everything he says. I have to. One thing I have learned so far is that he has every reason to be concerned. The prosecution do not play by the rules and it's apparent they will do whatever they must to protect this conviction. Does that include hurting me?

My focus returns to the newspaper article and Humphrey. Knowing the lies need to be refuted I contact the editor of the *Beacon* newspaper. She asks for support on the letter and I refer her to Joe Jackson's files. I establish what I feel is a good rapport.

****

Law school will begin in two weeks. I don't have much time left before I will be consumed with a different type of reading, different from the myriad files I still have in front of me. I am finally getting somewhere with the investigation. I realize this means the Commonwealth is not too happy with me. Richard Reyna calls to tell me he cannot go to Virginia. Damn. I was counting on this before I entered school. I then receive a call from Joe Jackson and listen intently as he describes his interview today with Commonwealth Attorney Humphrey. Joe says Humphrey yielded. He had to. In the next few minutes I learn the humiliating experience Humphrey went through this morning. Jackson entered the Commonwealth Attorney's office with more information than Humphrey was prepared for. Seated across from the attorney, Joe went over the entire article in the *Beacon* newspaper, point by point. It quickly became apparent that Humphrey did not know the record. One of his statements was that O'Dell's lawyers hid the DNA report and would not turn it over. Jackson reached into his file and pulled out one of the many documents I discovered during my search of the record. It's a letter to the Attorney General's office offering to turn over the DNA reports. Humphrey backpedals and proceeds to tell Jackson that he was "speaking by memory." Joe then asks, "Do you want us to come back after you've read the record?" "Yes, that would be great. Thank you." We nail Humphrey, who should be furious with Alberi for making him look like an ass.

Point by point, Joe O'Dell and I refute each and every lie Humphrey stated in his editorial. Point by point, citing the trial court record, affidavits, and source documents we make our case. Finally, after almost ten years, the public is learning the truth about the evidence. The editor faxes me a copy of the article. It's work well done. It's scary how easy it is to fabricate or exaggerate the truth. Most people don't have the source of information to refute such lies. I do. By now I have worked almost one full year on the case—I can pull a document upon request in an instant. That's dangerous for those who wish to distort the truth.

By now, Joe Jackson had a second interview with the prosecutors in Joe's case. He informs me that Stephen Test "does not buy" the DNA, neither does Alberi. How can you not "buy" a result? Especially when it directly challenges the previous serological, antiquated blood evidence from years earlier. The prosecution was able to spout out erroneous information, dodge the bullet so to speak, but I have now provided enough information to those who are looking into this case to prove the prosecution is (and was) not being truthful and they don't like it. Alberi wants a hard copy of the Internet piece, but he won't go to the *Pilot* to get one. He mentions a lawsuit again, saying it's privileged information. "Not so," says Joe Jackson. "It's all in court records." And it is. Joe confirms that Alberi is still nervous. He ought to be, for I am still not going away. I believe I will become his worst nightmare.

For two days I put together a comprehensive investigation report and forward it to the New York law firm, one to Joe and another attorney I'm trying to bring onto the case. Richard Reyna will eventually receive a copy, but at the moment I am teetering on annoyance and frustration. At this stage of the game an enormous amount of money was flowing out of my wallet and I needed my retainer money back. I am not getting paid for my work, nor am I reimbursed for any of the costs I'm covering, seemingly on an endless basis.

Chapter 12

~Law School~

The much anticipated day arrives, welcoming my new experience with a bright and sunny morning on August 24, 1995. It's the first day of orientation. True to what I have been told, I'm not disappointed by the stressful and confusing day, but I must admit my nerves are shot. Exhaustion creeps into my body by day's end. I dutifully sit in front of the camera for what will become my pass through the halls of the school, and then I pay for half of my law school books. The following day, I slide into the bookstore to pick up my photo ID and purchase the second half of my books. As I cart them to the register I am contemplating how I will carry them to class. The books are both numerous and heavy. I glance down at my assigned homework on the paper tacked to the wall and calculate it isn't much. I can keep my plans to return to the Cape. I leave at 7:30 a.m. for our retreat back to the Chatham beach house. I study from 10:00 a.m. until 9:30 p.m. This tedious schedule may appear to be an unwelcome change in my life, yet I find I am settling into this crazy new habit called OneL[85]. Not surprisingly, Jennifer busies herself without complaint. After returning to Boston, I find the next day requires only five hours of reading time.

As forewarned by the lawyers on Joe's team, the real test is about

---

[85]   "OneL" is a reference commonly used by lawyers for the first year in law school.

to begin. It's the official first day of law school. My first class is Civil Procedure with Professor Cox, a tall thin man with wire-rim glasses framing his small head. Having read the book OneL, I was not surprised when, after the professor asked the first question no one raised their hand—except me. Having mustered this courageous act, and having gotten the answer correct, I was now the student both admired and hated. I was not nervous when I raised my hand, surprisingly with an enormous amount of confidence for my first day. My classmates approach me after class, congratulating me. "You didn't even appear scared," they said in bewilderment. Well beyond many of them in age, fear was not in my vocabulary.

That evening, somehow I find time to work on Joe's case. I had to respond to Commonwealth Attorney Humphrey's attempt to discredit our response to his lies in the *Beacon* newspaper. I fax a letter to Joe's lawyers, the editor of the newspaper and Joe Jackson, disputing each and every lie, one by one, citing the trial transcript and court documentation that could not be disputed.

After jumping the train for the second day I arrive early, ready to tackle OneL. Again, I raise my hand in class. Again, I am probably despised by my fellow classmates. But I'm enjoying my thirst for knowledge way too much to care. Incredibly, I find I'm always confident of my answers.

Having made it through my third day of law school, I find I am actually loving this fascinating and wonderful experience. I thoroughly enjoy learning this foreign craft called the law. It all seems so logical. I fit in well with the students and thoroughly enjoy my professors. I feel quite comfortable briefing cases (outlining the issue, rule, analysis and conclusion, or otherwise known as IRAC). And while it's all supposed to be intimidating, somehow it is not.

As the evening approaches, I quickly turn my attention to Joe's case and make a phone call to the editor of the *Beacon* newspaper. "I plan on getting the article in the paper next week," she tells me.

She also says that Humphrey has the final shot at rebuttal. Unaware of editorial protocol I find it interesting the state has the last shot. Though the bantering back and forth is a play on words, it is essential to correct the record in this fact-finding mission I am on for Joseph O'Dell's life.

As the days pass I find myself having less free time than I envisioned. Second thoughts challenged me about my decision to go it alone in tackling my law school schedule and Jennifer's needs. I decide it wise to arrange for a nanny. My search leads me to Joy, a wonderful nanny from England who turns out to be as close to Mary Poppins as I am going to get. The smell of bacon and eggs rise to the top of the stairs as Jen and I giggle over the reality of having a meal other than cereal for breakfast. I am equally delighted to have all of our clothes washed, pressed and folded by the time we return home. Neat, well-organized, and a very responsible girl, I am enjoying Joy immensely. We are so lucky to have her in our home, even though it was only for one year. And the added plus: I have more time to work on Joe's case.

Soon after I'm settled into the new routine, I receive news of an "en banc" hearing regarding Joe's case. On a *sua sponte* motion (which means on its own) the Fourth Circuit Court of Appeals moves to hear Joe's case on December 4, 1995. It's unbelievable relief. It also means we have a lot to prepare for in the next few months. I will need to call all the lawyers to coordinate their efforts. Reflecting on all it took to get to this point, feelings of elation are suddenly combined with nervousness about the unpredictable. Somehow the universe is playing a major role in this. In fact, I can hardly concentrate tonight on my law school studies.

At this point I realize I must take some time off on the weekend to rest. I clearly see the continued need to balance my life, the void of my family becoming greater with each passing day.

The decision is to have Sunday evening to myself. Somehow the movie *Nell* turns out to be the antithesis of what I need. Even though it's one of the most depressing movies I've ever seen, I'm still thrilled just to have the evening off. With a bit of relief, and knowing I have prepared for my first law school exam the next day, I feel ready. Afterwards, my new law school buddy, Joanne, and I, study in the library from 11:30 a.m. to 6:00 p.m. to finalize our statutory memo research. The following day we study again from 9:00 a.m. to 10:00 p.m. If ever one was put to the test of commitment, law school would win my vote.

In the meantime, Alberi is *still* furious with me. In typical fashion he sends me a certified letter, addressed to an old P.O. box in New Jersey. Not wanting to be distracted from what is important at this time I elect to return it unopened. On the same day, I receive a copy of the motion to the Fourth Circuit Court of Appeals to reschedule the oral argument. By this time I have read numerous motions and though I'm not a lawyer I know what reads well. This motion is well-written. After realizing my time was not needed for numerous redrafts, I have second thoughts about the certified letter from Alberi and wish to read its content. When I call to retrieve it, it's too late. The letter is now en route back to Virginia.

Halloween night is finally here. Delightful distractions like this feed my soul for some fun and normalcy. Masks covering our faces while adorned in costume, Jen, Joy and I walk the streets of the neighborhood for some good old-fashioned trick or treating. With camera in hand the continued flashes illuminate the street. I love creating memories from priceless photographs such as these. With my bag half full of candy I slowly disappear, fading back out of sight and into the house to study the rest of the evening.

By this time I was developing a very close relationship with Joe. Through my work and the intensity of my devotion to the case we became inseparable, obviously in mind. Whether I actually am able to help him or not seems secondary to him now. He finally has someone who believes in him, in seeking the truth. I feel his elation and I'm sucked into its power. In the course of this struggle I too developed a strong attachment to this man. I am not simply an advocate. I am his only source of help, or hope, for life. It's a powerful combination that draws at your inner soul and challenges your traditional notions of what is acceptable, the "norm." I have always found myself challenging those things, not liking the inevitable uneasy feeling I get when I am simply following the crowd "just because." So I allow myself to get closer to Joe. It's almost impossible to be a champion for his cause and not develop some feelings for him as a person, as a man whom I now feel is wrongly accused.

I'm seeking another attorney to replace David Baugh, with whom I had some disagreements. My search draws me to a fellow named Moody Stallings. I need to find potential counsel to be ready for a lawsuit in case Alberi sues. Moody takes the case. I sense I can trust him. Feeling blessed to have this new attorney, I smile when he comments on my "relationship" with Joe.

"So tell me, how do you have a relationship with someone on death row?"

The answer, which I don't provide, is simple. It is not a relationship, it's a connection caused by the union of two people in an intense battle over a human life. It's the sharing of private information, it's the challenge to learn the truth, even if it's not what you want, it's working together side by side (or death row to suburban home) to fight for the truth when others are fighting to suppress and/or destroy it.

The more the Commonwealth fought to hide the truth, the stronger my conviction became to protect Joe O'Dell.

****

November in Boston can be downright bone chilling as the cold ocean air rises over the city. I stay warm indoors and study all day again, preparing my outline for Civil Procedure. It has fast become one of my favorite courses. Though I love them all, Civil Procedure outlines all of the procedures one must follow to gain access to the courtroom, something Joe O'Dell cannot get, and may never get.

In keeping with the balance, in the back of my mind, and motivation for follow up, was the claim by the prosecution that O'Dell's lawyers selectively tested the clothing. The prosecution sought to discredit the DNA results. The lawyers are not doing anything about it, so I decide to take this one on as well. It means a phone call to the director of Lifecodes Laboratory, the lab that conducted the DNA testing for Joseph O'Dell. I speak with Michael Baird.

"Michael, there are allegations out there that the clothing was selectively tested in the O'Dell case. I need to find out what happened here".

"Lori, it was not selectively tested. We tested whatever we felt would yield results, with no direction by the lawyers", he replied.

I ask for a letter to confirm this and he agrees to send it tomorrow. As simple as this task was I have to wonder, why wouldn't O'Dell's lawyers do this themselves? If not for Joe, it protects them from the slanderous comments being thrown around by the Commonwealth concerning their integrity. As usual, I'm the only one who is looking after Joe's best interests. With this out of the way I grin when I think to myself, *let's see how the Commonwealth reacts to this one.*

Joe O'Dell would not even have had the money to do DNA testing if it were not for Percy Ross from "Thanks a Million". It's a reason to reach out to him, so I locate him and phone him personally. After thanking him, I talk to Nancy, his editor, to inform them of the DNA results in Joe's case. I don't believe anyone ever bothered to do this. I am sure they must be interested. I make it a point not to ask for anything. Right now I am simply appreciative that someone actually cares.

Knowing the oral argument in the Fourth Circuit Court of Appeals is fast approaching, I decide to book my reservation for Richmond, Virginia for an overnight stay. I want to be present this time.

I try to book as far ahead as possible to keep my expenses down. The amount of money I'm spending is secondary to my mission, yet I'm aware of its ever-increasing cost to me, both monetarily and otherwise.

~On Trial, DNA Testing~

Finally, after several months of working with Joe Jackson at the *Virginian-Pilot* newspaper, I get the call I have been long awaiting. Line by line, Joe reads to me over the phone the article that will appear in the paper. He is breaking it apart from the bigger story he's written on Joe that will cover the front page and two full pages inside.

"Lori", Jackson says, "Joe will be featured in the front-page article "On Trial, DNA Testing". It will be part of the bigger story, but it's a great intro to his story."

"Thanks Joe, I've worked so hard to get the truth out. I appreciate all you're doing to investigate his case."

I am thinking the DNA story will be powerful news to the reader. It will reveal all the lies by the Commonwealth and will now contain Lifecodes' letter, refuting additional allegations of misconduct. I can hardly wait to see it all in print. The public is entitled to the truth. The victim's *family* is entitled to the truth. My goal is to have everyone form their own opinions once they have all the information. *But let then have all the information, not state filtered misinformation.*

I continue preparing for my law school exams by creating the well-known outlines that become my Bible for studying. I am also preparing for a Thanksgiving visit with Joe. The flight from Boston to Virginia gets me there Wednesday night, in time for an early morning prison visit. While we had decided on an early visit, so had every other inmate in the system. After only visiting from 8:30 a.m. to 10:00 a.m. I am bumped (made to leave to accommodate another visitor). It's a busy time for inmates. I can hardly expect more. I feel the strain of the visit being in the midst of convicted murderers and inmate spouses. I am uncomfortable with the environment. There is no getting used to it. Nor do I wish to try.

Upon my return, I contact the media for coverage of Joe's story. I talk to Joe Jackson to confirm the timing of his article. Then I speak with attorney Bob Morin. I need to check his availability in case we are successful in getting an evidentiary hearing for Joe. He agrees to keep the idea open. I like him. He sounds authentic. Morin says he finds it hard to believe that the attorneys in New York refused to ask Michael Baird for a letter to defend their integrity against allegations of misconduct. He likes me too, I think, mentioning something about my "drive".

Because I'm trying to assemble a strong legal team I'm now making some incredible contacts. After reading about Karen Palmer, the publicist in Mumia Abu-Jamal's case, I contact her in an effort to gain national exposure. I also overnight a package to Nina Bernstein at the *New York Times* and fax information to Zachery Brown at the *Boston Globe*. I am hitting the most prominent papers on the east coast. Maybe *someone* will listen.

Next I call Stuart Taylor at *American Legal Magazine* and speak to the publicist again, and then Joe Jackson. Joe says that his story on O'Dell is the longest story he has ever written. It's scheduled to print this weekend.

Alberi must be feeling the heat for I finally get his letter. I'm not surprised by its content. Dated October 19, 1995, he alleges false statements are being made by *Virginian-Pilot* reporters and presumes they are coming from me. He encourages me to put aside my personal commitment to Joseph O'Dell and to give portions of Paul Ray's notes to the reporters to "set the record straight." He threatens to sue me, for the second time. In his first letter to me, three months earlier, he pointed out that "a publication of information which you know is false or have a high degree of awareness is false will require me to deal with that in a professional manner." He denies all allegations stating he can prove they are all false. I am amused now as I know he is not being truthful here. I know the facts and then some. I also know the law regarding public officials concerning libel or defamation. Alberi is scared and needs an outlet. That would be me. I am not afraid. I have done nothing but speak the truth. I fax the letter to Moody Stalling.

If there is anything more important than a woman's hair, I am not sure what that would be. I would drive hours for just the right stylist and in fact that is just what I do. I make the necessary trip to New Jersey for my hair stylist to highlight and cut my hair. Finding it also a break from school for me, I stop in Connecticut for my best friend's birthday party. And then, something big happens. Something I hadn't seen coming. On Saturday, December 2, 1995 Joe's Internet story appears on the front page of the *New York Times*. The headline reads, "As Executions Increase, Appeals go to the Public." Joe's picture, with the caption "Innocent on Death Row: Virginia. DNA Proves Man's Innocent—still awaits execution" instantly generates international Internet support on his website, the source of the article. While I had been feverishly working to expose Joe's case, little did I know his Internet piece was the second one in less than two weeks to hit this new social networking tool—the world wide web. It was hailed as the new social medium for inmates to reach out to the world, to express themselves in a way unlike ever before. For us, it was simply a way to express to anyone who would listen, what they were doing to an otherwise powerless man. The results were indeed powerful. Behind the scenes Alberi was now even more determined to stop me, but I had no way of knowing this. Not yet.

I return to Boston to prepare for my trip to Richmond for the oral argument before the Fourth Circuit Court of Appeals.

~Court Before the Last Resort~

December 5, 1995 is our potentially life-altering court appearance. I watch and learn as the lawyers stand and seemingly speak rehearsed lines, memorized for days, perhaps weeks. It was a battle of skills, a match being played out in open court. It all seemed fair enough until the end, when someone from the Attorney General's office stood up and, for the second time, misrepresented the DNA results before the court. It took all my willpower not to scream. With the lack of authority to correct this I watch in horror as they misrepresent the facts about the blood evidence. O'Dell's lawyers, as conservative as they are, say nothing. This time, a few days later, I call the clerk at the Fourth Circuit to ask what could be done. She tells me to file a motion to supplement the oral argument. "This way, even if they turn it down, they have to read it." *Good move*, I thought. Now I am getting advice from a non-partisan participant. The advice more likely should be coming from our own legal team. *Strategic games* I am thinking, *just like chess.* No wonder my father was such a great lawyer. He was President of the Chess Club.

Meanwhile, I study for my exams, preparing my contracts outline and studying for torts. During a break I call Michelle Brace at the Virginia Capital Representation Resource Center and encourage her to persuade Bob in New York to file the motion necessary to supplement the record. I knew it would be a challenge for him. I fax a media package of 30 pages to Channel 13 in Virginia and speak with Jonas Kant at the Innocence Project in New York. He informs me that Barry Scheck is not ready to come on board. They suggest that I not involve the media and they offer to find someone if, ultimately, they are able to help. It's a little late for that. I am far too deep in at this point. As a novice I feel I cannot retreat. If I could just get the truth out, Joe's life would be saved. I fax Jonas Kant the DNA article anyway. Immersed in my exams I continue to study for midterms, torts and constitutional law.

With midterms over, I am relieved to have a brief break before school starts again. I had studied hard, really trying to grade as high as I could. I would love to be able to join the *New England Journal on Criminal and Civil Confinement* as a law review student. It's a high honor that would offer me the chance to write about O'Dell's case. This stays in the back of my mind as I prepare for another visit with Joe. On my break I do what I always do—visit with Joe from December 29th to January 2nd. This is my New Year's Eve gala celebration. Not like the extravagant events at the Hyatt in Princeton, New Jersey, or the ones in New York at some famous dance club. This gala would be at a high security prison in the sticks of Virginia, amongst murderers, rapists, thieves, and heavy security. The guards would do Joe and I a favor and bump others first, giving us more time together. I had asked for their assistance because I travel so far for these visits. They are crucial in keeping Joe's spirits strong, and equally crucial in keeping the coals hot for the fire of injustice burning inside me.

To supplement our phone conversations and to enjoy something more private, Joseph starts to prepare tapes for me. They are tape recordings which reveal his thoughts, his moods and his everyday living. Joe is starting to feel protective over me. He starts sharing some deep thoughts and conversations in a comfortable way. I welcome it. Before I leave the prison gates I sign for the package of three tapes he has prepared for me. By now, Joe was writing me on a daily basis. The tapes were a welcome change. It was the one time he could express himself without being interrupted or monitored on the prison phone. They were prepared in the confines of his cell, on his own time and when he felt like talking. Not when he was forced to talk by the prison phone scheduling system. I loved getting the tapes. It was a chance to find out more about Joe, and listen to his voice which I enjoyed. It was eloquent, with a touch of that southern accent that I find so appealing. He is gentle, kind, considerate and always patient. I am amazed that my conversations with him are as easy as they are. If I were in his shoes,

I would be yelling at the world. When I return to the hotel I listen to one of the tapes:

> When I get anxious and upset your strength and fortitude inspire me. I never had anyone do that for me. People always said, "you'll never be anything, why can't you be more like your cousin," and so on. I didn't have anyone to teach me. The boys would beat me up at school and chase me home. I was skinny back then. My father saw this and yelled at me and told me to go out there and fight them. I was more scared of my dad than of the boys so I did and I was surprised I kicked their butts. He was always calling me dumb ass or stup ass. I remember one day when I was trying to help him fix his car, I was a small boy and he asked me for a wrench. I didn't know which tool it was so I gave him two or three and he yelled at me and said "no you dumb ass, that's not it." He wouldn't just hit me with the back of his hand, he took his fist to my head and beat me black and blue. I had a crappy childhood. My poor mom, she always told me not to pay attention to him. You are always building me up, always saying you are proud of me. You don't know how much that means to me.
>
> I've had a rotten life. Maybe that's why the prosecution thinks it's okay to kill Joe O'Dell, to get rid of a burden on society. But I have changed since I have been here. I am not the same man as I was years ago.

His voice is soothing, comforting to me.

> Lori, you are so bubbly and so sweet and the world is so grumpy and mean. You're really an angel aren't you? You're keeping that from me, aren't you? I often wonder how you could be the way you are and the rest of the world so different.

It confirms my belief that Joe never knew any better. His environment, both in his family and on the streets was never any good. I sometimes wondered whether it would be easy for me to fall into a bad life if I were the victim of a bad family situation, or a poor economic one. Somehow I could identify with him. I am not sure how. I just knew I could.

> Joe Jackson called and I don't know why he asked but he wanted to
> know if I were to be executed what my thoughts would be. While
> I told him I'd be thinking of Lori, he replied, "I thought so." I will
> share more with you. My every thought would be of you. I'd be lay-
> ing in bed thinking of you. When the clock struck 9 I'd be thinking
> I'll be going to another world. I wonder who will take care of her,
> love her. I would want you to be happy, I'd be crying because of the
> cruelty of it all, how much it would hurt you. I'm innocent of this
> crime but she's hurting too.

It was more than I could bear listening to.

> I love when you share yours days with me (laughing). I have such
> sweet memories remembering you sledding with Jen, it makes me
> smile. You are the all American dream. All you do is innocent and
> sweet. You go to soccer games, to the movies. You are serious about
> everything you do. School, raising Jen…but you take the time to be a
> little girl. You sit at home and watch movies all by yourself when you
> could be going out. And boy, when you get on something you are like
> a bloodhound, you don't stop.

Joe and I are a lot alike. We are thorough in our work and we are
sharp-witted. He has a great sense of humor and always seems to be in
a good mood. I have shared with him that I do not have a life now. All I
do is work on his case. He tells me I have more of a life than I think. He
remembers me saying, "I shouldn't be talking with you." It must have
been out of pure frustration, but it hurt Joe nevertheless. I was feeling
overwhelmed, like my entire life was Joe's case. It was.

> Lori. You are making great contacts now. These contacts will be in-
> valuable one day to you. You have your precious daughter and law
> school too. You may think I don't have a life in here but I do. My
> mind is not incarcerated and my soul is not incarcerated. Only my
> body is.
> I do all I can to keep my sanity in this place. You would not believe

what it's like. One time I put a tape recorder to my door and taped the sounds of death row. Guys are nutty on the row. The death row sounds are crazy. It's scary. It even scares me. Guys meow, not sure what that's all about. The night sounds are the eeriest sounds, the word death row, no one could understand.

I should draw you a picture of my cell, the table and swing out chair. I have to move every 90 days. For security reasons they move all the inmates. I keep my cell spotless and some of them are disgusting. I have been on death row for nine plus years, locked up eleven. I've kept myself clean, no drugs or anything. Homosexuality is filth. I tell the guys not to joke about that stuff. Sometimes I want to file an eighth amendment violation.

I am always pleased to hear his tapes. The laughter in his voice and the amusement I afford him lighten my heart. It makes me feel like I am helping him through this incredibly insane time. He giggles when he recalls my conversations with him. He is amused both at my accent and unusual determination.

~Environmental Effects on Criminal Behavior~

There are varying philosophies concerning the study of criminal behavior in an attempt to study the source of it. I have always thought one was a product of their environment more than anything else. Joe grew up in a very dysfunctional family. His father drank and beat both Joe and his mother. Joe started running away from home at the age of ten. His only form of transportation with no money was hitchhiking. Back then it was much more common, and almost acceptable, for kids to stick out their thumb for a free ride. Unfortunately, he found himself in the company of some fast people. When his father would finally come to pick him up at the police station he acted cordial and concerned in the presence of the police, until he got his son in the car, where he would beat Joe mercilessly. Joe kept running away and eventually picked up a new interest. Cars. He loved cars like most teenage boys do. Fast cars. Mostly he enjoyed racing them and driving all over town. His first real brush with the law was his arrest for stealing and joyriding cars. The judge sent Joe to reform school which was no help to the now wayward boy. At the age of 16, Joe was handed a three-year sentence in the penitentiary. During his prison time he got word that his father was beating his mother, so while on road camp, he attempted to escape and was shot in the back of the head. He returned to prison to complete a four-year sentence—a year having been added for his attempted escape. Joe left prison when he was 20 years old. That year, having met new peers in the prison environment, his crimes escalated when he and Bobby Watts robbed five convenience stores.

It was at The Beaumont School for Boys that Joe's negative behavior was further influenced. The environment was not suitable for nurturing young boys. Instead, he describes a place that seemed to facilitate anger. In the lawyer's files I had found a three-page synopsis of the school. In it he shares his experience.

> Joe: Beaumont School for Boys is just another name for reform school… Juveniles are sent to Beaumont for various reasons by the courts. Some are there for committing murder, rape, stealing cars, breaking and entering. Some for running away from home. The age of the kids sent to Beaumont range from six years to 17 years old. The normal stay is six to eight months.

After describing the facility and its various "cottages" for housing placement he described the guards.

> Joe: B-Cottage was for new arrivals, and the "House Father", which was a guard who lived in the cottage with his family, was "Deadeye Nelson." He was called "Deadeye" because of having a glass eye that stared straight ahead all of the time. He was a cruel person and beat the kids unmercifully at times…There have been boys caught in homosexual acts by Captain White, and by the

Captains and Monitors. Most of the time these kids do it out of fear. There was a lot of bullying and fear amongst the kids there. I was very fortunate that I was a very big boy, and could take care of myself... I never had any problems with any of the boys there. Sometimes the punishment for infractions of the rules was a whipping by what was known as the "Black Beauty". The Black Beauty was a flat board cut out of solid oak. It was shaped like a small boat oar, and had holes drilled all through the flat part that hit the buttocks, and it usually brought blood. I received ten licks from it once for running away...and I NEVER forgot it, and didn't want an encore...There was a sewing shop for the little boys, and it was run by one of the guard's wives, who looked like a witch. One day the woman's husband came back to their apartment in the cottage early, and he caught two of the boys in bed with his wife. He killed one of the boys and beat the other one almost to death. He only got probation, and still kept his job there.

One of the boys who worked in the dairy was caught masturbating into the milk. None of us would drink milk after that... Another boy got caught screwing a female mule, and the Black Beauty wore his ass out. There was no solitary confinement back in those days, but it came later after I left, so the only punishment was beatings and loss of privileges, standing with the nose against the wall during leisure hours. I escaped one time with two other boys, and was caught several hours later. I was made to run around the ball field with no belt and no shoestrings. And every time I would try to pull my pants up, which were slipping down, a guard would slap me across the ass with a belt. The guards had encircled the field. After that they beat me and then shaved my head. Then put me in the FORCE, which was for troublemakers or those being punished.

We were not allowed to talk until the House Father told us we could talk. If we were caught talking, whispering, etc, we would get slapped up beside the head and put on THE LINE with our noses against the wall...this would last for hours, and would go on for days until the House Father thought you had enough. I was always getting slapped by Deadeye Nelson. He hated my guts, and every chance he got he beat me. The beatings continued until I was released. I came out of Beaumont full of hatred and hostility.

This, of course, did nothing to help Joe, or teach him right from wrong. Instead, it taught him just the opposite. Thus, when he left the school Joe continued his joy riding in stolen cars. Finally, the judge sentenced him as an adult, placing him in prison with murderers and rapists at the young age of 16. At that age if you weren't tough, you'd better pretend you were if you planned to survive.

I recall reading in Joe's memoir about his first night in prison. He got word that someone was planning to make him their "boy." Joe defended himself with a zip gun. The other inmate may have gotten hurt, but Joe's integrity and manhood were preserved. Joe wasn't so lucky several years later when a notorious homosexual made advances toward him, threatening him with a knife. On that date, July 12, 1964, Joe was 22 years old. In the account I read, Joe went berserk, stabbing his attacker numerous times defending himself. Almost three weeks later, Lloyd Bess died in the prison hospital, according to an autopsy report I found in Joe's files. Joe's confidential prison psychiatric report mentions his deep fear of being attacked, *before* this occurred.

On March 25, 1964, while in custody at the State Farm Penitentiary, Joe wrote a letter to the Director of the Division of Corrections expressing his concern over losing his good behavior time, acknowledging what he thought was a problem in adjusting to the State Farm. He mentioned he was nervous and flew off the handle, losing his temper for no reason. He thought he needed psychiatric help. Joe expressly requested to be moved from State Farm back to the penitentiary, C-Building (which I believe is segregated from other inmates). He ends the letter. 'Sir, I hope you don't think I'm feeling sorry for myself, *I just want to get along.*"

Two days later the director asked Dr. Harry Brick to see Joe, stating, "The boy in his letter seems to have some realization of his trouble."

Dr. Brick interviewed Joe and wrote to wrote to the director,

"O'Dell appeared alert, dejected, depressed, restless and tense, relating his difficulties as follows: "On December 26th I had trouble with two guys and tried to kill them with a pick. Every time people are talking I think they are talking about me. I lost my good time and everything. I sweat, shake and am nervous. I can't talk—I am afraid I am going to hit someone. It isn't the work but I don't know what happened to me since I have been here." Dr. Brick went on to state his conclusion that "The general impression gained is that O'Dell is mal-assigned and should the Classification Committee see fit to re-assign him to another job in the building or some other place, this would certainly help to release the tension of this young man."

Before trial for the murder of Lloyd Bess, Joe's lawyer had him evaluated. In his evaluation the doctor reports the following.

> This fellow seemed to me to be a little different than so many of these inmates that I have seen in the past. So many are arrogant, defensive and are pictures of complete denial, even denying that they have ever committed a crime, but this fellow talked freely about himself. Some things happened to him in the last couple of years and he has become intensely frightened. Back in December 1963 he had feelings that some man or men were plotting to kill him…I believe he told me that something happened sometime after he had been sent to a road camp. He stated that this particular man had made some homosexual approach to him and he rejected the man and became afraid of him. He spent almost eleven months in solitary confinement. While he was in confinement, his mind was at ease and he did not feel so upset mentally…He told me that all along before this happened (when he stabbed Lloyd Bess) he was afraid somebody was going to kill him, that he would get up in the middle of the night and throw chairs at anybody that would be walking down the aisle in the dormitory. He was doing this for a purpose. He wanted to be put in solitary confinement. He apparently was making some sort of attempt to get himself protected. He told me he told Dr. Harry Brick about this but no one would do anything about it…In the penitentiary, as I have known it in the past, certainly part of it could be real (Joe's fear of being killed) but I do not think that all is. This fellow is literally scared to death.

...He says now that he would jump somebody at the drop of a hat, an inmate, but he does not feel like this toward the guards. I asked about the guard who shot him when he escaped and he told me when he went on back to the same camp after he was caught and taken care of medically he was friendly towards that guard and had no feelings against him.

As I noted in a previous chapter, Joe was charged with second degree murder and was given a 20-year sentence. Another statistic for his growing rap sheet. At the same time I wonder why, when it was clear from the record that Joe recognized his problem and reached out to get help, he was ignored. It was not only Bess, but Joe O'Dell, who suffered the consequences of ignoring his pleas for help. The system failed them both.

When I return home I re-organize. I need to prepare for the hectic pace of law school on Monday. Since I feel I know the law and did well on midterms I'm determined to stay current and organized in the second semester to ensure finals are a breeze. Organization is key if I am to work Joe's case efficiently—there is so much to do in the next two to three months. At times it's easy to become panicked due to the serious nature of Joe's situation. But I will not give up. I will fight to the end. While I am focusing on what I need to do I'm also staying attuned to Joe's emotional needs.

Taking the time to listen to Joe is easy for me. He is going through hell, waiting on everyone to pull together what appears to be an easy task of showing something went really wrong here. But the procedural wheels of the court don't allow that, especially having been barred in his appellate issues due to his lawyer's mistake.

Somewhere, somehow, people outside of us are seeing our struggle from the other side of the mirror that we feel is black.

Chapter 13

~24 Hours in Cyberspace~

The Internet piece about Joe's struggle has come to the attention of the director of a project which has been launched to identify the most compelling Internet sites in the world. And one of them is: *Joseph Roger O'Dell: Innocent on Death Row*. Rick Smolan and Jennifer Erwitt are creating what is termed a masterpiece. It is called *24 Hours in Cyberspace: Painting on the Walls of the Digital Cave Photographed on One Day by 150 of the World's Leading Photojournalists*. The phone rings. It's one of the directors of this project.

"Lori, I am from *24 Hours in Cyberspace*. We saw Joe O'Dell's website and are intrigued with it. We would like to include it in our project."

"Can you tell me about it?" I ask.

"Sure, it's an unprecedented one-day event that will bring together the worlds' top photographers, editors, programmers and interactive designers to create a digital time capsule of online life. It will feature 200 of the most compelling photographs pulled from 200,000 images taken on February 8, 1996. The 150 photographers who participate will focus their lenses on the human face in cyberspace. It will document the new ways we interact, work, learn or conduct business, and how it is changing people's lives. People like Joe O'Dell. The collage will be full of remarkable human-interest stories, complemented by stunning photographs, including exiled Tibetan and Mexican Za-patista guerrillas seeking political support or medical assistance via the internet, an electronic journal of a four-year-old's battle with leukemia and a Virginia man who is on death row for a murder he claims he did not commit, lobbying for a new trial on a webpage. People's lives are being dramatically affected by the online world."

I am ecstatic. I can hardly believe what an opportunity this can be for Joe. It's the attention we have been trying to garnish for his cause. Someone, somewhere out there has heard him. I wonder how many others have heard him as well.

"Joe, I just got a call from these people who want to include you in a cyberspace project." I am not hiding my enthusiasm.

I attempt to explain what they want. He gives me permission to speak to the Department of Corrections for clearance. I put the wheels in motion, devoting my energy into making this happen for him. The Department of Corrections turns down our request. *24 Hours in Cyber-space* calls to ask for their approval. They, too, are turned down. They don't want Joe's case known around the world. This kind of publicity is unheard of for a death row inmate. My mind is in overdrive now.

It is at this time that I call Michael Radelet. He is a well-known author and researcher on cases of innocence. I ask him to review Joe's story. He agrees to make a statement on Joe's innocence if he feels it is compelling. I am working every angle I can, reaching out to anyone who will listen.

Slowly, the media starts to take pick up on Joe's plight. Out of the blue, ABC News calls to talk to me about the DNA evidence. They are not informed about scientific evidence and I'm beginning to become learned on the subject, having the ability to educate others on its pre-cise meaning. This is an interesting development in the reshaping of my life. After my conversation with Radelet, I put together a package for him and then speak to Scott Diehl, a well-known scientific expert, to ask if he will do a statistical analysis on the ten enzymes of the blood that were tested at Joe's trial. The weekend arrives and after spending twelve more hours pulling together packages, I forward them to the Innocence Project in New York, Attorney Bob Morin, and *24 Hours in Cyberspace*.

In keeping on top of the lawyers, I phone Bob Smith and discuss a rebuttal on a motion before the court. I insist the Lifecodes report be included as an addendum to the motion. I am somehow attempting to direct the lawyers to do whatever is necessary to get the truth out. I know I need to keep a watchful eye on them, otherwise they may fail to protect Joe.

By now the media is catching on to the DNA debate. Joe's case is instrumental in this debate. The touch of my remote brings me to CBS News where there is a piece on DNA. They are interviewing a man who was released from prison based on DNA evidence. "If DNA can convict, it should also free the innocent!" They refer to Joe's case. Without missing an opportunity I call the producer of CBS to discuss Joe's case and the issues pertaining to last night's story. I'm trying to find out how one can rely upon serological evidence that is antiquated when new, sophisticated DNA evidence is definitive in nature. I call Frank Chafari, an expert on serological evidence, to get his opinion.

Surely, Joe and I must be doing something right for we seem to be attracting attention. I am definitely getting people to notice the inherent unfairness about refusing a simple DNA test for someone who has professed his innocence from the moment he was arrested, throughout his trial, and for ten years afterwards. The beauty of this argument is that if the prosecution were so certain of the mountain of evidence, so convinced in their sentence of death for Joe O'Dell, they would jump at this opportunity to confirm his guilt. The truth is, the DNA evidence to date suggests the blood they have been saying was the murder victim's blood may not be hers after all. In fact, the only conclusive test confirms it is not. Damming information for the Commonwealth. The media is picking up on this DNA controversy and I am right in the middle of it.

In my life I would never have expected a call from *60 Minutes*. Joe's case has caught their attention as well.

"Lori, this is Jill Landes from *60 Minutes*. I wonder if I can talk with you about the case of Joseph O'Dell. We are looking for information on DNA evidence."

I am more than happy to comply.

Suddenly, I receive a call from David Wydecka, the attorney for Richard Townes, a Virginia death row inmate who is scheduled to die on January 23. He wants information on Alberi. The word must be out on the street that I am the one who has a mountain of my own evidence, damning evidence, on the character of Mr. Alberi, and the way Joe's case has been prosecuted. I engage in a lengthy conversation and tell him all I know.

School is back in session and time is at a premium now. Moot court competition has me all fired up to compete at my best. That challenge is coupled with the challenge of actually getting to school now. There's no denying it's winter in Boston. A northeast blizzard has hit forcing white powdery drifts of snow to rapidly accumulate. Shoveling heavy snow from my driveway and walkway only bring pain, creeping its way into my back once again, reminding me of the drift of snow that challenged me when I hit black ice two years ago. I can't afford this now. I have no time for this.

Protected from the heavy winds and chill outside, I am comfortably reading in the warmth of my Boston home. I *really* love law school. Unlike most law students I find it a wonderful experience. And I read with such enthusiasm. In the midst of the quiet surrounding me suddenly I hear a thump from the room next door. Jennifer just fell out of her bed onto the hardwood floor. I scoop her up and place her into my bed. The two of us are dependent on one another, coupled with a strong mother–daughter bond.

In the meanwhile, Jane Gottsman from *24 Hours in Cyberspace* is mad as hell. She wants the telephone numbers of the law firm and the Governor's office. She wants media access for her project! Time is running out and she wants O'Dell's story to be included in their project. "It's a compelling human interest story," she says. After two weeks of denials they decide to move ahead with the story, using me for the photograph instead. Anything to help Joe. I call my prisoner rights professor and ask for his help in gaining access to the prison nearby for a photo shoot. He puts me in touch with the local sheriff. I am quick to tell him the story. Within 24 hours they clear the way for a photo shoot at an abandoned prison, the commissioner having stamped the affair with his approval. The photographer for the photo shoot, Steve, is stunned. "Even my wife, a photographer for *Newsweek*, couldn't get into the prison!"

How does one dress for a photo shoot in an abandoned prison? Wanting to portray the role of Joe's lead investigator and advocate, I decide a suit will do. I meet Steve and his assistant at the old jail to begin framing an online photograph that will travel the world. For Joe, it was a dream come true. A chance to tell his story.

During our photo shoot something else is happening in Virginia. People are waking to a fresh cup of coffee and page one of the Metro News, *Virginian-Pilot*. The denial of media access to Virginia prisoners is important to Joe Jackson and Laura Lafay, who co-author the story. Timing is everything, especially in the media. It wasn't the insanity of refusing DNA testing to an innocent man on death row that captures their attention, but the fact that now the prisons want to deny inmates access to the outside world. It struck a nerve for reporters. The only way society can monitor what's happening inside the walls of death row is to have access to its inhabitants. "*Internet project is denied access to death row inmate.*" Why is this news? Because "more and more, access to inmates is being restricted." As the photographer was framing shots for the Internet project, the media was taking shots at the Department of Corrections.

The middle of February offers spring break for law students. For me, it offers uninterrupted time on Joe's case. I spend the next two days revising the Internet piece when suddenly I get a call from a supporter, who advises me that the Attorney General's office is telling the press there is a DNA match. I am amazed at their gall. Being in such high-powered positions, one would think they have advisors. For if they are so ignorant to mislead the public, to report on information erroneously, knowing that a court of law has already ruled there is no match and the result of the jacket "inconclusive", what else are they capable of? I strike back. For the next hour I draft a letter to Senior Assistant Attorney General Mark Davis, to educate him on the law and the ethical standards that attorneys must abide by. Here I am, a law student, and I'm writing to the Attorney General threatening his office for misbehavior. However strange this was, I knew I was right. My letter of February 19, 1996 read:

Dear Mr. Davis:

It has come to my attention that you and/or your office have been disseminating misleading information pertaining to the O'Dell case. I assume that you would be current in your knowledge concerning the legal status of the above mentioned case, but in light of the fact that you have allegedly just given outdated information to a public citizen, I write to better inform you of the facts as they exist.

The state appears to maintain a position that the original DNA testing results, as stated in a report, is valid evidence in this case. The state is mistaken. Just as it was highly unethical to misstate the DNA evidence in front of 13 federal judges, and against Rule 46 g(1)c of the Fourth Circuit Court of Appeals, I believe it also unethical to misinform the public as to the current status of the DNA tests in this case (see Rule 46 g(1)(d). *In Re General Motors Corporation, 61 F.3d 256 (4th Cir. 1995)*, Attorney James Butler was sanctioned for continuing to cite an order which was overruled by the court. He was sanctioned for continuing to refer to an order from the court in an erroneous manner. Similar to this would be the continued reference to a DNA test result which is contrary to the findings of U.S. District Court Judge James Spencer. Therefore, it is essential that I write to inform you of the legal status of the DNA test results, so as to avoid any possible future misrepresentation coming from your office.

As I am currently studying the law, it is of utmost importance to me that the facts of this case be clearly and honestly stated before the public and the courts. As evident from the most recent motions before the Fourth Circuit court, that does not appear to be the case here. I implore you and your office to read the full record to be better informed as to the problems evident in this case. The procedural history of the DNA hearings before the courts and the final order from Judge Spencer follows:

1. On October 23, 1990 a DNA hearing was granted before Judge Owen of the Circuit Court of the City of Virginia Beach.

    Expert testimony:
    Defense: Dr. John Edward Spence
    Record locator: JA02601
    As to the shirt "demonstrates an exclusion", as to the jacket (JA02604) "it's inconclusive".

    Defense: Dr. Scott Diehl
    Record locator: JA02632
    "A comparison of the shirt and the victim's blood, I concluded that there was a mismatch-that the band patterns did not match - they did not originate from the same individual."

    State: Richard Guerrieri:
    Record locator: JA02750
    "You do have an exclusion. As for the jacket, I would not say possible match, rather I would say my inter-pretation would be that it is inconclusive in my mind."

    Result: All experts concluded that the blood on the shirt was a DNA EXCLUSION and the blood on the jacket was INCONCLUSIVE and NOT a match. Due to the state's refusal to preserve the blood evidence there was natural degradation of the blood. A DYXS14 probe was utilized in bringing the misaligned bands together to show a flawed 3-probe match. This was proven to be in error, by all expert witnesses and federal Judge James Spencer.

2. August 4, 1994 - DNA hearing before Judge Spencer of
    the U.S. District Court for the Eastern District of Virginia.
    Decision: September 6, 1994.
    Record locator - page(s) 23-32.

    Court Decision – Judge Spencer rules that the DNA evidence proved NOT to be the victim's blood. The shirt was an EXCLUSION and the jacket was INCONCLUSIVE. The originally stated match was an error! This was proven by expert testimony and ordered so by the Federal Judge.

    Pursuant to the above, it would be highly misleading to inform any-one that there is a match between the blood on O'Dell's jacket and the victim's blood. It has been proven in a court of law NOT to be a match. To continue to mislead the public and the press would be highly unethical and prejudicial to the administration of justice. Accordingly, we ask that you and your office refrain from making such erroneous statements to the public.

Thank you for your time and attention to this very important matter.

Very truly yours,

Lori Urs

I copy all the lawyers, Alberi, and the *Virginian-Pilot* newspaper, sending the letter by certified mail to ensure they receive it and take note of its importance.

Sensing the increasing importance of the DNA issue, I revisit the possibility of obtaining Barry Scheck's support. His name alone may bring recognition to the validity of the importance of the DNA exclusion. When I phone the Innocence Project I am able to reach Jonas Kant. He instructs me to get him the autorads and Lifecodes' report—he thinks he can help. I update him about having contacted Michael Baden. Kant says, "That was a good move, Lori. It will help bring Barry on board." I am building a team of the best experts in our country. As a result of Richard Reyna's report, I had called Michael Baden who was well known for his work in the O.J. Simpson trial. I ask if he would review the autopsy report *pro bono*. Many experts are sympathetic to an indigent client. He was gracious enough to agree. Baden confirmed what Richard had said about the contents in the victim's stomach. I knew then that we were building a strong case for Joe's innocence. At the same time, I'm acutely aware that I must continue working the case.

With my moot court brief completed, I hand it to my professor when I return to law school. Having established a good rapport with my constitutional law professor, and most of my professors, I am comfortable in the law school environment. I find their teaching methods superb, thereby continuing to enjoy this law school experience tremendously.

Soon thereafter I receive news that the Seventh Circuit has ruled on the *Simmons* issue. It means Joe may receive a re-sentencing hearing. It's at least a great beginning for us. While Joe and I are not focusing on his sentencing issue, the lawyers are. It represents a reprieve. This new development means the court will likely find that Joe's constitutional rights were violated when Judge Spain allowed the prosecution to argue future dangerousness, without rebuttal from the defense, knowing that a life sentence meant life without parole. Joe and I are focusing on his freedom, not a life behind bars.

Sitting back on the embroidered sofa in my living room I suddenly feel a rush of pride in my work. I am finding that while I work so hard I have a love for it. Working hard is much easier when you are on a mission, when you *believe* in what you are doing. I find something else is occurring as I become the voice of support for a death row inmate. I'm discovering that *I* can learn from *him*. Joe is patient, humble, intelligent, soft-spoken, but convincing. Most of all, he is my new best friend. I can and do share everything about my life with him now. He is a constant source of support in my own life. I'm surprised by this, for it's the most unlikely connection that ever existed. Working together feels like an eternity.

Still strategizing for results, I have not forgotten about obtaining new lawyers for Joe. I still think I can convince Bob Morin to take Joe's case. Bob is up for a judgeship nomination. I persist anyway until he agrees to talk to his partners about taking Joe's case if he's not appointed. The news is uplifting.

Back at school I am readying myself for my first mock oral argument. Law school can prepare you for some things, but not most. I'm excited to argue my case in a real courtroom, except it's at night and no one will be watching except our class. As I move forward toward the podium my knees are shaking. *Oh no, it's my turn.* I'm forced to speak. When I open my mouth and form the words aloud, all the nervous energy seems to literally drain to my feet. Just as quickly as I speak I feel a renewed source of confidence and enthusiasm. I argue well. Not long after this oral argument I will enter the Moot Court Competition. My professor wants me to try out for the National Moot Court Team.

It's now March and snow has begun to blanket the ground—a soft white cover speckled with tiny diamonds, sparkles from the rays of the sun. My attention is on the falling snowflakes, when I am startled by the loud ringing of the phone. Joe Jackson is on the other end. I can hear him breathing. With hesitation in his voice he begins to tell me the article can't run unless an affidavit is filed in court. I am taken aback by this strange news. Within seconds I call the editor of the *Virginian-Pilot*, William Burke, to confirm this new development. He conveys to me that he can't do a thing about it. "May I speak to your boss, publisher Dennis Hartig?" I ask. Dennis is curt—he echoes what I already know. *Won't do it*, is all I hear. I am being stonewalled as to the real reason for this sudden request. Immediately, I telephone Bob Smith.

"What's in it that's so important to everyone?" he asks.

"I'm afraid I don't know Bob," I reply. "As soon as I find out you'll be the first to know."

The answer to this mystery, I later discover, lies in Virginia Beach.

****

During the year 1996, public outcry for the imprisonment of wrongfully convicted individuals became widespread. A growing movement, still prominent today, started focusing on the use of DNA testing to exonerate the innocent. As a result of my work on Joe's case, I have been asked to speak at the Northeast Region, Human Rights Public Hearing sponsored by the National Commission on Capital Punishment. The hearing will be held in Philadelphia on March 25-27. I have been selected to speak with Barry Scheck and Kirk Bloodsworth (one of the first inmates to be released by DNA testing). Scheck was widely known for his part in the "dream team", responsible for freeing O.J. Simpson from his murder charge. Our panel is addressing DNA evidence and innocence. I have a lot to say. The list of speakers includes esteemed members of the scientific and legal communities, and political figures from across the country. I am honored to be asked and quick to say yes.

The death penalty community is a small one. The names of those involved are equally as small. Those who oppose the death penalty are seen as liberals, or radicals. This perception is changing as we attempt to change the landscape of the legal process to allow DNA testing for those who claim innocence, especially those facing a death sentence. The irreversible sentence underscores the necessity of being right.

By now I am well aware that the prosecution has enormous power, and that I am being blocked in presenting Joe's story. I couldn't believe the media would actually crumble in the face of a lawsuit. The requested affidavit was an attempt to cover their asses. It was a precursor to the fact that the newspaper would not print the story at all. After spending an entire year feeding the *Virginian-Pilot* source information, opening my files and risking the investigation by allowing a reporter an inside scoop, they fold. Why? Of course, none other than Albert Alberi. In Alberi style he threatened to sue the newspaper. The editor tells me point blank, "We just can't risk spending a quarter of a million dollars on a lawsuit." Where they got that figure I don't know. I was crushed. This proved to me that people with money, or power, control the world. I was not going to let that happen on my watch. I was more determined than ever to overcome this new stumbling block. One that would kill Joe for sure. Between the lies in the paper, the courtroom, and being blocked from telling our side, I had no choice. I *had* to go national. I need to acquire some power and persuasion of my own. The only way to capture attention was to bring in some credibility outside of myself, a prominent national figure. Who could stand up and represent an innocent person on death row more than the incredibly devoted nun, Sister Helen Prejean? By now I was well aware of her role in the death penalty community. I knew she was the author of *Dead Man Walking*. I had seen the astonishing film as well. I decide to track her down. I get hold of her by telephone while in the lobby at law school. Someone answers on the other end of the receiver.

"Hello, this is Sister Helen Prejean. Can I help you?"

That was all she had to ask, for after that moment I went furiously into a ten-minute dissertation as to why she had to do just that. It may be my only chance to win her support.

"Yes, Sister. This is Lori Urs. I need help badly on a death row case. The man is innocent and can do a DNA test but the state won't allow it and there's a jailhouse snitch who lied about his confession and there's prosecutorial misconduct, intimidation of witnesses, and I can't get anybody to listen. Maybe, just maybe if you were at a press conference with me, they would finally listen. Would you help me, please?!"

She must have sensed the desperation in my voice—the urgency to save a man's life. It's not like going to court and winning a big settlement. Or filing a motion to quiet title on a property. It's a human life—one that will be extinguished for all the wrong reasons, and then *no one* will ever know the truth. It was killing me. She agreed. Sister Helen informs me that she knows Michael Radelet well.

I was not the picture of what a person would consider a lawyer at that very moment. Perhaps a death penalty lawyer, but certainly not a corporate lawyer. I shouted, "Oh my god, I can't believe I just got Sister Helen!" In a fury of phone calls I inform the lawyers and eventually Joe. Joe seems pleased, but was clearly refraining from too much elation. He was measured in his emotions. It's understandable, considering he has been on death row for over nine years now, never thinking it would come to this. Joe tells me that the prison has just taken his blood. We, too, want to secure his blood so I ask the lawyers to get a sample of it for future testing. This would be an insurmountable job, to ensure first that it's done, and then to protect the chain of custody, which is especially vital in this case.

Shortly after talking to Joe, I phone Sister Helen back to obtain her permission to use her name in the media. She graciously agrees.

****

Spring flowers are finally blooming with the increasingly warm air leading to the last day of law school. It's time to finish my class outlines in preparation for the final exam. Most students dread the first year of law school. I loved it. For the next two and a half weeks I study religiously for my final exams. I study hard, enjoying the challenge at the same time.

Jennifer is now finishing the year at an elite private girls school in Newton, Massachusetts. A Catholic school, they employ headmasters,

nuns, and have church services for all the girls. The year ends with a
formal celebration. Now that school is behind us both, I can concentrate full time on Joe's case. This means lining up the next investigation. The legal files gave me access to the names of jurors so I track
them down. I need to talk with them. Did they know about the umbrella? Did they know his alibi was a solid one? Did they know that the
jailhouse snitch lied? Did they know the DNA test reveals the blood is
not the victim's blood? I had to let them know. I called them all, at least
the ones I could locate.

Legal visits have a privilege attached to them that does not attach
to a regular visit from a civilian. I have been visiting Joe O'Dell as a
"friend" on the prison's visitors list, but our visits were much more
than that. I was his investigator, working intimately with, in fact, of-
tentimes directing his law firm on the course of his investigation. It
was at Joe's request that they finally list me as a member of their legal
team, to afford us confidentiality during our discussions at the prison.
The lawyers and Joe concurrently sent letters to the warden, requesting that I be recognized as a member of his legal team. Finally, after
over a year and a half of intense study and investigation, it was Joe who
insisted on this, not his lawyers. Joe and I were directing the course of
his investigation. We were blindly forging ahead.

Chapter 14

~Legal Visit~

Delighted that summer has replaced a damp wet spring my beach house provides a welcome change of pace. As part of my divorce settlement, Walter generously ensured that his daughter and I could summer every year at a home on Cape Cod. In other words, I can hang the shingle in my name.

As usual, Chatham offers a wide array of summer activities for Jennifer, including antique shopping, small playhouses, craft shows and outdoor water activities. This year we decide to buy a boat. An 18-foot Boston Whaler with extra seating and a built-in ice chest. I know nothing about boats other than the fact that it looks like fun. After a two-hour course we are officially boating enthusiasts. The Boston Whaler is a sturdy boat, built not to sink. That's the kind of boat I wanted. Since I knew nothing about boating, I at least wanted to remain afloat. Of course, I expected Jennifer to learn boating with me, and she soon earns the title "boating mate". The currents have a way of messing with your careful plan to anchor the boat near the beach or sandbar, or dock it upon return. I was hard on Jen, always expecting her to be capable at this. We became a team. It was a great opportunity to entertain friends and enjoy a day at the beach without tourists. Somehow we manage to score the first slip at the boat yard. The guys who work there are always wonderful, willing to help us with whatever we need. I was told by them, "If you can boat in Chatham, you are good anywhere." Chatham is known for its sandbars. The tides must be watched carefully—you are easily at the mercy of their patterns, stuck in the middle of the ocean on a sandbar, or deserted on an island if your boat is beached when the tide goes out. Boating in Chatham is the most peaceful thing I have come to learn on the Cape. Jennifer and I can slip right up alongside the hundreds of seals at South Beach, or stop and sunbathe on the incredibly lovely bird sanctuary of Monomoy Island.

No matter that it's summer time I still have work to do. It's June 23, and I am on a plane to Richmond, Virginia to arrive at the prison in Boydton for my first *legal* visit with Joe O'Dell. I'm excited to see him and to share the week's events that will unfold ahead of me.

I arrive at the prison gates at 9:00 a.m. Unaware that I was the cause of an underlying commotion in the prison in anticipation of my arrival, I casually walk through the front doors. The guard at the desk welcomes me. Guards are scurrying about while I stand here unaware that my presence is what's causing this reaction. As I gaze around I notice the warden, the assistant warden, and several guards are frantic. One of the guards leans over to me and whispers, "I haven't seen anything like this in my 17 years here!" Soon I learn that my visit was changed from Building One to the visitors' room. Building One is the room in which attorneys visit with their clients. I am immediately not comfortable with this. Why am I being singled out and handled differently?

I finally get in an hour and a half later. The warden wants me in his office. I obviously comply. I am seated across the desk from a man who appears to be the Wizard of Oz. While he is a man of power, he doesn't aim to grant wishes. His job is to ensure prison security. Somehow I am seen as a compromise to his comfort level. He asks about my relationship with Joe and whether I am his wife. He should know the Department of Corrections turned Joe down when he requested a "contact" visit after submitting a concocted Indian tribal marriage certificate. The document had no legitimacy and the warden knew it. Suddenly he wants to recognize it. I have to wonder what his angle is.

"Do the lawyers know about your relationship with Joe?" the warden asks.

"Of course they do," I reply. "I've been investigating this case for over two years now and I am part of his legal team."

He ponders this and replies, "Well, I will let you in this time."

He then spits out strict instructions that I must follow, such as passing papers. He wants me to hold the paper up first so the guard can see it. Though this is ludicrous and not the protocol any lawyer must follow, I agree. He also informs me that I can take a total of four pictures of Joe. Two standing up and two sitting.

I have my camera with me and a tape recorder. Everything is X-rayed before I can enter the room in which Joe awaits me. He'd been wondering for half an hour what was holding me up. He knew it was prison politics. I am grateful the warden allows me to take pictures of Joe and record our conversation. To my knowledge it's the first time in years, other than prison ID photos, that anyone has taken a picture of Joe.

In the visitors' room a long table stretches across the room. I place my briefcase and investigative notes, along with my camera and tape recorder, on the table. My eyes lock on Joe as they lead him through the stream of doors heading my way. My eyes are drawn to the handcuffs tightly anchored on both wrists. I ask the guard to remove them. That is my first concern, not my first thought, as I lay eyes on him and feel his presence without the existence of a wall or bulletproof glass between us. Immediately, I feel the difference. I can *feel* his presence now. The guard walks Joe to a seat across from me and removes the handcuffs.

I reach out and gently grab hold of Joe's hand. He places the palm of mine in his. His smile mirrors my own, having reached this pinnacle point in our work together, and the naturally forming bond that has developed between us. The guard asks if I want our picture together. I am so concerned with protocol and appearances that while this would be considered perfectly fine between lawyers and their clients, I politely decline. However, I do take one photograph of Joe and tape our entire conversation, unaware at this time that it may be our last visit, or that this photograph will be seen around the world. How could I know this unplanned journey would lead me to places unknown and circumstances so unfamiliar and challenging? Indeed, the photograph I just snapped will become the only picture of Joe O'Dell since his incarceration over ten years ago. I discuss my plans for the upcoming investigation and share with him the details of my comings and goings. My time over the next week will be spent in Virginia Beach. I will return next weekend to share the results of my work. I share the stress of it with Joe, silently on a piece of paper. When he sees the words "I can't stand this anymore, help!" He replies by drawing a picture of a face with tears falling from the eyes. Even now we are prisoners of our environment. In the afternoon I kiss him goodbye and leave him behind. Our touch lingers as I move into the seemingly dangerous world of street investigation.

For the next two days I search for witnesses and find Jeff Elliott, Carmillo (Bud, otherwise known as Timothy Bougades), and Dana Wade. I also meet with Joe Jackson briefly. Stopping at Bay Vending, I hope to find and speak with Joe Moore. The place is closed. A neighbor reluctantly tells me he is living with "Whitey." I had heard that name before and know it's Whitey Cooper.

"Do you mean Joe White?" he replies, "Yes."

"Where is he?" I ask.

They won't offer me an address. Only that it's around here *somewhere close by*. "Moore is banned from the area around Bay Vending because he physically threatened a girl," a neighbor tells me. When I find I'm not getting anywhere, I move on. I need to check out the

Executive Inn and scope out room 203. It's nighttime and I approach with caution. Room 203 is in the back on the far right side, adjacent to room 201, the room on the end. It's a sleazy looking place in the dead of the night. Late night truckers are idling, parked in the back by the trees. With the key to the room in my hand, my feet hit the outdoor stairs leading up to the room, each step bringing me closer to the end of Helen's life. The bargain basement room gives me the creeps when I open the door. My eyes dart about the interior before I quickly retreat. *I need to get out of here.* Within seconds the motor of my car is running as I hightail it out of there and hurry back to the Holiday Inn where I will be staying the night.

I spend most of the next day at the circuit courthouse. A clerk makes the physical evidence of Joe's case available to me. Several minutes pass before I'm allowed to enter the room where, laid out on several tables, are numerous articles of clothing, and the rest of the evidence I have learned about only on paper. Right before my eyes are Joe's clothes. They are stained with blood. I am taken aback by the sight of it all. There it is, his jeans, jacket, Lifecodes' swabs, cassettes. *Everything* is here. Latex gloves protect my hands as I list the articles of clothing.

1. Blue jeans with what appears to be dirt and blood on two main areas of each leg.
2. Checkered shirt with what appears to be blood on the sleeve.
3. Gray quilt type jacket with maybe blood on it too.
4. Reddish buttoned downed shirt.
5. A heavy brown coat with fur on the collar.
6. A lightweight tan men's jacket.
7. The victim's purple skirt with what appears to be dirt on it.
8. The victim's short sleeve blouse with what appears to be blood on it.

I counted three jackets and two shirts. Just how many articles of clothing could Joe have on at one time? After photographing the clothes, and before I leave the courthouse, I stop in courtroom number 9. I hear Alberi is trying a high profile case. I want to see this man in person. Slowly, I open the courtroom door, careful not to disturb the proceedings. Stepping inside for a few seconds I stand by the door. Alberi looks straight back at me. In an inescapable moment our eyes lock the glance I hoped to have of him unnoticed. Unmoved by his gaze, I smile at him, letting him know I am not afraid.

While in town I don't miss the opportunity to call Presswalla. He refuses to give me a copy of the autopsy pictures without a court order. Why of course, he's Alberi's right hand man. Presswalla justifies his actions by informing me that Joe sued him. He is not warm to the idea of helping him now. If I were Joe I would have sued him too. His handling of the case was suspect. The court documents revealed that much to me.

With only a few days in Virginia Beach I reflect upon Paul Ray's pre-trial investigation notes and focus on the man who walked by the victim's body at 7:30 in the morning. Joseph Moore discovered her body at approximately 3:30 in the afternoon. Paul Ray's notes were clear that *Joe Moore saw someone crouching in the bushes near the victim.* He was spooked and took off. This never made it to trial. Now, in my early stages of learning, I knew that a piece of information such as this would cast doubt on Joc O'Dell's involvement. At 7:30 that morning O'Dell was at the front door of his lover's house, Connie Craig. Joe left the fight in the parking lot at around 1:30 a.m., stopping at a 7-Eleven to clean up (because there were no paper towels in the bathroom of the bar he was at) and then stopped at two other after hours clubs at the beach. Why was Moore not questioned more thoroughly? What information could he provide about the person crouched in the field near the victim's body? If she was dumped there, as the police contended, then the murder happened elsewhere. Where on earth did it happen? If it occurred in O'Dell's car, as the prosecution claimed, it would have more than a few drops or smears of blood. The blood would be spattered everywhere. And there would be fingerprints all over the car. Except there were none. Was she murdered in one of the abandoned trailers in the field? It was a well-known fact that after a few drinks at the After Midnight Club bar patrons used the trailers for some hot late night sex. The bloodied mattress discovered in a trailer also never made it to trial. I want to find and speak to the people that could help me, but I don't have time to interview all the witnesses. I have a death penalty coalition meeting in Washington, D.C., where I am asked to speak on Innocence and the Death Penalty. Georgetown University is hosting the event with a panel of recognized experts in the field.

The drive from Virginia Beach to Washington, D.C. seems to fly. I have a lot on my mind. I had heard that the *24 Hours in Cyberspace* project was on display at the Smithsonian Museum in Washington. I wander off to pay a visit to the historical event. Of the approximately 131 photographed human interest stories from around the world few were selected for display. Mine was one of them. As I walk through the museum I begin scanning the walls for the prison photograph I had posed for. I am struck by the variety of photos painting the walls with emotion, capturing human interest stories from around the world. To my right I observe my photograph, hanging adjacent to one from Stellenbosch, South Africa. In that photograph are four women and ten children in a tiny room, one bathing in a tin tub. The Community of Living Water, a development group of an impoverished South African township, had been using the Internet at a nearby training center to gather information on adult-literacy programs and farming skills. I was struck by the significance the Internet played in effecting people's lives around the world.

In the midst of everything I had started arranging for the press conference that Sister Helen agreed to. I had to take advantage of her generous offer to assist us. Because time is precious now while still in Washington, D.C. I arrange to meet with the public relations woman at the Washington Marriott Hotel. We review our plan for the press conference I'm arranging on Joe's claim of innocence. Having been chosen for its location, the hotel sits across from the Capitol. The small room will have theatre style seating, a podium, and microphone for the speakers. I leave Washington and head back down to South Hill in the early evening hours.

The weekend visits with Joe are always up for grabs on timing. This time we are allowed to visit for three hours. Due to the pressure I'm putting on exposing the truth in Joe's case the Commonwealth decides it's time to strike back. I'm now forbidden from seeing Joe as part of his legal team. They will find a reason to justify their decision, but I have work to do so I put aside that issue for the time being. I must take advantage of my limited time with Joe. Arriving at 8:30 a.m., I'm anxious to share the news of my work during the past week. As a result of the prison games I am back to visiting Joe from behind bulletproof glass.

In the evening I work on setting up what will be a powerful press conference for Joseph O'Dell. Strategically I arranged it in Washington, D.C., far from the corruption of Virginia Beach.

On Sunday I usually visit with Joe, but this Sunday I have a meeting with one of the jurors, Carol Kelly. It was an important interview. She agrees to meet me with reserved kindness. It was evident she wanted to know more about what the jury did *not* see. By this time she had read a lot about the DNA evidence in Joe's case and it caused her some concern. Carol's background as a nurse practitioner led her to instruct the rest of the jurors that the serological blood evidence was like a fingerprint. Wasn't there something inherently wrong with that, even against Joe's constitutional rights? She couldn't have been more wrong. It was critical to Joe's case that the jurors know that the blood evidence meant only one thing. That while the victim had Type O and the blood on Joe's clothing was Type O, 40 to 45 percent of the population also had Type O blood. Serology is only capable of *excluding* an individual as a suspect. Scientifically, it *cannot include* a person as the perpetrator. This I had learned from my subsequent research and as was depicted in the judge's ruling on a hearing regarding the new DNA results. In his ruling Judge Owen stated (in reference to the Commonwealth's expert):

> ...the conclusion that she reached as a result of those tests (serology) was not that there was a match between the shirt and between the victim's blood or between the jacket and the victim's blood, but rather that on the basis of her test results, it could not be excluded that there was in fact a match. In other words, there was not a direct opinion that incriminated, but rather a failure to be able to exclude the result that was sought to be offered by the prosecution in that case. The court is of the opinion that the serological evidence produced at trial was not flawed, that it was in accordance with recognized standards in existence at the time; and while it may be that current testing methods would have produced a different result, that that does not justify the issuance of a writ of habeas corpus.[86]

In short, it alone wasn't enough to convict. Unfortunately, the word "match" was let loose like a cannonball. The prosecution elicited testimony from their expert that the blood on Joe's clothes was "consistent" with the victim's but that word would be modified by the prosecution, and the media, according to their needs to convict or sensationalize. The judge never stopped the Commonwealth from inappropriately referring to it as a "match". Paul Ray did nothing to advise Joe to file a *motion in limine* (motion made at the start of a trial requesting the judge rule certain evidence not be admitted at trial) preventing the Commonwealth from using this language. And the jury was uneducated about scientific procedures, as was the majority of the public.

When I left Carol's modest home I felt I had established a good rapport with her. My goal was to offer her the evidence she needed to formulate an opinion, an opinion based on all evidence, not just

---

[86] Stenographic Transcript at 262-263, *O'Dell v. Thompson*, (CL89-1474) (October 23, 1990).

the evidence she heard at trial. We exchanged information freely and she willing described her misunderstanding of the significance of the serology blood testing. She was also concerned about not having been presented with all the facts I was starting to share with her.

After a brief drive back to South Hill to visit with Joe, I return to Carol's home. This time I share my notes with her. I discuss the fight Joe was in the night Helen Schartner was murdered. For three hours, I explain it all. Carol is learning about things that never reached the jury, and becomes more concerned with each court document I show her. This leads me to believe we may just have another ally on our side. By the end of our visit she agrees to give me an affidavit regarding her misunderstanding of the blood evidence, and how she had influenced the jury with her opinion.

The next witness on my list was Dana Wade, one of the girls at the bar with Helen that fateful night. Approaching her house, I pull over to the curb and reach for my cell phone to request an interview. Instinct tells me never to give a witness time to say no. Preferably a knock on the door and face-to-face meeting would have been better. I reluctantly chose to call first. Dana was stern in her refusal to meet with me. I could tell she was hurt. I learned she had many nightmares. Dana wanted Joe dead, she said. I could also tell she was tied with Alberi and Test, like many witnesses were. The prosecution had informed witnesses that they need not talk to the defense. In fact, they *told them* not to talk to the defense. As any defense attorney knows, this is unethical. Joe O'Dell brought this to the attention of the judge, who held a hearing on it and admonished the prosecution. Unfortunately, it did nothing to stop them. I drove away thinking *I'll be back.*

The next morning I return to Carol Kelly's house, and over a cup of tea with her we review her statement. With the affidavit in hand she leads me to two banks before finding a notary. Prior to having it signed, I read it to her, and tape-record it to ensure she does not later claim I threatened her, or that she was under any duress. I don't trust the prosecution. After the affidavit (See Exhibit V) is notarized I thank Carol, give her a hug and leave. I drive to the courthouse to research public information that may lead to more witnesses.

Immediately afterwards, I decide to write my press conference statement for the big day. Although it's nearly three weeks from now I am eager to get started.

That next day at the prison, Joe and I get very lucky—a visit that lasts four hours. It's amazing what I have become grateful for now. Long before today, Joe's watch had stopped ticking. Suddenly, in the middle of our visit it started ticking again without having been touched. Joe and I take it as a sign of renewed energy. A sign of life. However small or farfetched our grasp was for anything positive, we grabbed onto whatever could help carry us through this fight, together.

Chapter 15

~Rising Stakes~

For almost three weeks I take to the beaches of Chatham, West Dennis and my favorite, the National Seashore in Wellfleet. Chatham is the only place I know where you can ride on the sand dunes. Jen's friends pile into my Jeep Cherokee and we venture out for the ride. First, we stop at the air pump station to slowly release the air in our tires. Next, we set out for the path that's far enough down the sand dune trail for privacy, yet not too remote. But I'm not satisfied with a slow drive over the bumps. What's a sand dune ride if you can't have some fun? So I push the pedal to the floor, and like a little girl, I'm giggling with the rest of the kids in the Jeep. Our music is blasting, the sun beating down on us as we drive out to the seaside. It's always been one of my favorite activities on the Cape. I revel in this joyful time, for in just a few days I will be in Washington for a press conference with Sister Helen Prejean, Richard Reyna, Steve Hawkins (President of the National Association against the Death Penalty), Barry Scheck and Kirk Bloodsworth. I have to enjoy life while I can, and balance it for the sake of my daughter, and my own sanity.

On July 22, I board a flight to Richmond to retrieve Richard Reyna. We review the investigation notes and talk our game through during dinner. A press relations woman shows up at 9:00 p.m. and we have a conference in my room for two and a half hours. My adrenaline must have kicked in because after only four hours of restless sleep, I awake feeling well. Today's date, July 23, will have an entirely different meaning for Joseph and I, exactly one year from now.

The press conference is scheduled for 1:00 p.m. In my hotel room, while waiting for time to pass, I hear a knock on my door. I open it to discover the angelic face of the person who was on the other end of the phone three months earlier in the lobby of my law school. Sister Helen and I greet one another with a hug. It's refreshing to be in the company of another advocate.

Richard, Sister Helen and I stand before the press to discuss Joe's innocence. Barry Scheck joins us by teleconference. One by one we lay out the reasons why DNA testing should be allowed. What does the state have to lose? If they are so certain of his guilt, they should seize this opportunity to confirm it. It seemed like a reasonable request to everyone there. Each of us answers questions pertaining to the case and the blood evidence, and all that we had uncovered to date. We are planting the seeds of doubt into anyone who will listen.

That evening in my hotel room I am delighted to receive a phone call from Jennifer.

"Mom, you got a letter from law school."

I ask her to open it. Jennifer reads its contents and as soon as her words come through the phone, I start screaming with joy from my hotel room. I ask her to read it again, just to be sure. Having graded at the top of my class I was invited to join the law review journal, *New England Journal on Criminal and Civil Confinement* at the New England School of Law. I couldn't have been more pleased.

The following morning I leave for Cape Cod. I'm under incredible stress because our investigation is compromised by the Department of Correction's refusal to allow my legal visits. My own research reveals we need to file a civil rights action lawsuit to protect Joe's rights. But no one was doing that. I put that on the back burner, however, I need a break from the mounting pressure. Though I'm pleased about the press conference, I'm also very tired. Every relaxing moment is taken to reenergize myself, as I become painfully aware that this train ride I'm on is not going to stop anytime soon.

Inevitably, no matter how hard you try, the press always seems to get something wrong. It's complicated stuff—DNA molecules, exclusions, inclusions. What does it all mean? I read the story put out by the *Virginian-Pilot*. They got it wrong. I immediately pick up the phone and call one of the many contacts I have at the paper. I need a correction on the DNA evidence. They printed that it "links" Joe to the crime. It did just the opposite. She gladly agrees. That's one less battle I have on my hands. I cannot allow inaccuracies to kill Joe.

A story had recently been printed concerning Dennis Stockton and the United Nations' concern over his execution. This news offers me another avenue to use for Joe. Irene Knoben at the United Nations is receptive to my call, and my offer to share Joe's plight. She agrees to call the U.S. government to express her concern over Joe O'Dell's case, and the human rights issue it presents for the world.

****

August lies just ahead and Jennifer and I soak up the sun and enjoy boat trips to the outermost beaches where nature's beauty is the most pristine. Often we stroll down the street to the candy store, and in Chatham tradition, visit the bandstand for the Friday night bunny hop. With music, popcorn and blanketed family gatherings, it's a preppy establishment's ideal picture. School is only weeks away and my free time will be severely limited again.

The time finally arrives, forcing us to leave leisurely summer days behind and pack for Boston. School begins on Monday. It's Sunday evening when we arrive at our new home in Newton. I had to give up our place in Needham and locate a small rental in Newton. While

Newton is a town for the affluent, I feel anything but that when we walk into our tiny house, not well furnished, for almost $2,500 per month. It would have to do. I look around and smile—this entire house could fit in my husband's living room. I promised Jennifer it would be short-term. She never once complained.

While last year I was thrilled to be in school, I now had so much on my mind with Joe's case I couldn't concentrate. Here I am in the middle of a huge case that I have spent almost three years investigating, and I feel time is running out. In my second year of law school and after only three days, I take advantage of the long Labor Day weekend and fly down to Virginia. I'm still struggling with the Department of Corrections over my legal visitation rights with Joe. Somehow the *Richmond Times Dispatch* got wind of this. They set me up for a front-page article without any warning. Innocently, I believed they truly cared about the violation of Joe's constitutional right of access to legal counsel (myself). All they cared about was a confrontational story. The lawyers inform me that to file a lawsuit, Joe first needs to be denied a legal visit with me. So I set one up. The prison informs me it cannot be done. I advise them that I will be arriving on that pretense. Apparently, Frank Green from the *Richmond Times Dispatch* saw this as a modern day showdown. I saw it as a violation of Joe's rights, and an impediment to our investigation. The *Dispatch* runs an article on this challenge and is now referring to me as "Joe's wife." I am furious at this point.

On my drive to the prison in the early morning hours, I'm preparing for a legal visit. The *Richmond Times Dispatch* has staked out their position, waiting for my arrival. The photographer's camera is in my face when I attempt to enter as a member of O'Dell's legal team. After all, *I am* the chief investigator. The New York law firm instructs me to visit "under protest." I need the visit as a basis for our lawsuit. I enter the prison and inform the guard at the front desk that I am here for a legal visit. Instead, they allow me to visit Joe as a "spouse." This is all too bizarre since they know I am not Joe's wife. So I play the game. I call the lawyers and they instruct me to go in. Again, I am clear in announcing I'm here for a legal visit, "but will accept another form of visit only under protest." Either way it's considered a contact visit, except one is monitored, the other is not. The prison is masterminding a way to get me off O'Dell's team. I am now in the middle of a new chess game. The prison has no basis for the sudden recognition of me as Joe's spouse. This bold move reveals they are determined to win this chess game. They are referring to me as Joe's wife for one reason only. To discredit me.

If someone was to mention the O'Dell case, it would be no surprise that my name would pop up somewhere in the conversation. It was well known that I was behind the enormous fight to get Joe a new trial, or at least a chance to prove his innocence with DNA testing. The Commonwealth knew that I was the force behind the new energy blossoming in O'Dell's attorneys. The one who stirred up a new investigation in Virginia Beach. The one who is now compromising their death sentence by calling attention to its weaknesses. And the one who is so daring as to bring this case to the public's attention through the media outlets, despite their attempts to stop me.

I enter the visiting room as a member of Joe's team, under a "spousal" visit. My intention is to secure and sustain Joseph's legal right to effective assistance to counsel. Tension is written all over my face. Joe notices it. He is more relaxed, feeling we ought to take advantage of whatever opportunity comes our way. I try to appear calm. I can't let them know I am sweating this. Conversation with Joe develops either in code, or in writing, where I can shield my words from the ears and eyes of his captors. I suck it up and simply leave when I am done with business. Relief hits me when I let the door swing behind me on my way out to the car. Several miles from the prison, while still driving, I break down and cry.

Then my mind focuses on the next task on my way back to Virginia Beach. I have an interview with Carolyn Watson, the jailhouse snitch's former wife. I had tracked her down and felt she could offer us some insight into the reason behind Steven Watson's fabrication at trial. I briefly stop at O'Sullivan's Wharf to talk with Tim Carmillo (Bougades). I want some answers about Joe's alibi. I need more specifics. "Tim isn't here," the bartender tells me. I move onto Carolyn. After two and a half hours of talking, she agrees to give me an affidavit. She's sure Steven made up the story about Joe O'Dell's confession. If Joseph O'Dell had confessed, she would have known it. She tells me that Steven is probably afraid to tell the truth now for fear he will get in trouble. She confirms my strong suspicions. But I need more. It's after hours when I handwrite an affidavit, fearing if I leave, I may never get one.

Religiously, I return to the prison. It's a weekend and I never miss a chance to visit with Joe. The next two days are tense, pressure is building. We seem to be able to relax on the third day and have a pleasant visit.

Some of our tension is abated when I get word that the American Civil Liberties Union (ACLU) will seriously consider acting as counsel for our lawsuit against the Department of Corrections. I had contacted them to help me gain access to Joe O'Dell. They were not the only ones. I had contacted several law firms and was desperately reaching out to anyone who would help us. Knowing Joe's lawyers would never have done anything on their own to help, I was beginning to see what Joe was telling me, his attorneys didn't believe in him, they were not fighting for him. He was right.

****

Jen's first day of school arrives and I am back in Boston. I also start my second year in law school. I have already started law review and I engage in my first exercise of "tech checking". Writing a brief and citing cases is complicated stuff. Legal research and methods are foreign to me. Most of us were not on top of our game after the bare-bones course on legal writing. Law review sharpens those skills and forces you to learn the proper way to write and cite cases. It would teach us to hone our writing skills. While I was learning to write, my darling daughter was learning to play football, after having tricked me to join a peewee football team.

The dreaded day came when I watch my beautiful young daughter on the football field. I can hardly believe my eyes. *Is that her?* She has on shoulder pads, knee pads, and a helmet to protect her face. My heart is pounding hard as she takes to the field to practice with the boys. She is the *only* girl on the team. No doubt, especially at the age of twelve, the boys will want to teach her a lesson—girls shouldn't play football. They would teach her in their own way. It wouldn't be pretty. Jen was prepared for this. I was not. To my surprise, she held her own and played like a champ. I was so very proud of her. After a game at school, soccer practice with the traveling team, and then football practice with the peewee football team, Jen climbed into the tub that I had drawn for her at home and sank into the warm sudsy water. Her football uniform was full of mud. Her body was sore. I had never seen her play so hard and for long. It was truly an inspiration to watch her display of determination.

September 10, 1996. In the midst of dead silence while sitting at home with a book in hand, the phone rings. It's Joe's New York lawyers. They don't often call, so when they do I know it's important. Joe's lawyers had filed a brief in the Fourth Circuit Court of Appeals after the district court denied Joe any relief. Having been warned about the Fourth Circuit I was afraid they would not look favorably on Joe's case. I was told by every attorney I had spoken with, and numerous legal experts in the country, that the Fourth Circuit appellate judges rarely grant relief for an inmate. Judge Luttig was a member of the panel of judges. I was worried about him. Word on the street was that he was biased, unfair in his opinions due to a personal matter. I researched the rumors and found there was truth to them. Judge Luttig's father was gunned down, murdered in the driveway of his own home. In a victim's statement given by Luttig at the sentencing hearing he wrote a four-page letter asking for the death penalty. How can this man be unbiased in any death penalty case he is reviewing? We questioned the move to file a motion asking for his recusal. If granted, we'd win. If denied, it would only serve to anger him more. The lawyers decide not to rock the boat and let it be. I'm not so sure I would have done the same.

Here I am standing in the kitchen listening to Alan, the young associate on the case. He is tepid and proceeds slowly with deliberation, somehow afraid to speak. The reasons for his trepidation unfold as he utters his first words. I am trying hard not to break down.

"Joe was turned down by the Fourth Circuit, Lori. We're sorry," said the young associate on the case.

The words "we're sorry" pierce my heart. The Fourth Circuit is the last court of appeals, the court of last resort. It's a well-known fact that it's always a long shot to be heard by the U.S. Supreme Court. Joe's chances were slim to none. When I hang up the phone, my knees buckle. Never in my life has emotional pain so crippled me. I lay on the cold stone kitchen floor and cry in gut wrenching sobs.

There was no question in my mind what I had to do. With deliberate urgency I withdraw from my second year of law school, enroll Jennifer in Princeton Day School back in New Jersey, plan to move her in with her dad and sublet my house in Newton, all in a week. Having just joined the Pop Warner football team I know Jennifer will miss that, but I also know she'll be happy to be home with all of her old friends. At this point, I had worked three long years on Joe's case and had witnessed firsthand the lies and corruption that would keep him on death row. The injustice of it all ate at my soul. I had to free Joe O'Dell—no one else would.

I call Pat Schwarzschild and everyone I can think of to enlist their help for the clemency petition and appeal to the U.S. Supreme Court.

Feeling his own pressure, Bob Smith calls from New York and informs me there will be another $10,000 designated for the investigation. The money will be used for Richard Reyna. I am still *pro bono*. In preparation for the next stage of this battle, I make the drive with Jennifer to New Jersey. I'm torn about leaving my daughter. Walter is there to greet us when we arrive at his home. With a hug and kiss good-bye, I set out to return to Boston where I had packed up my things and was ready to move to my house in Cape Cod. It would become my base for what now appears to be an insurmountable battle against the Commonwealth of Virginia. I had to work harder, become more creative.

Chapter 16

~The Jailhouse Snitch~

My first goal is to wrap up the statement of facts for the lawyers. After reading the opinion from the Fourth Circuit, it is easy to see how the courts fail even the innocent. By the time the facts got that far, especially in a highly publicized case such as O'Dell's, they were twisted, mischaracterized, or just plain misunderstood. I was livid as I read through the summary.

Staying up half the night I prepare an eight-page document outlining the factual errors in the Fourth Circuit Opinion.[87] This same document would later be used as an appendix to the Petition for a Writ of Certiorari, Volume II, *O'Dell v. Netherland*, 117 US 631, 189A. There were citations to the trial transcripts, court opinions and scientific findings, in an effort to help the attorneys help Joe. I was afraid all along if we did not supplement the oral argument, if we did not refute the Commonwealth's lies, they would become cemented in the record in a way that would be irreversible. I laid it all out, point by point, cite by cite. I knew the case cold, dead cold and the lawyers knew it. They welcomed my help.

Joe and I are both scared. His life is literally hanging in the balance. It would only be a matter of time before they set an execution date.

---

[87]   See website, www.loristjohn.com, for a copy of the document.

Back at school, members of the law journal had sent my *status on review* and voted to deny my re-entry in the future. I draft a letter to the *Journal* with a copy to my constitutional law professor and mentor, Elizabeth Spahn, concerning my protest about their decision, and asking to be reinstated when I return from my leave of absence. I get the sense it's a political decision. I am confident Professor Spahn will go to bat for me. She supported my decision to take on this monstrous battle, having forewarned me of the difficulties I was about to face.

Civil rights attorney Steven Rosenfield, from Charlottesville, confirms that the ACLU will act as co-counsel in filing the civil rights action. Finally, we get some minor relief. The complaint against the Department of Corrections will be filed October 1, 1996.

Under guidance, I attempt to bring in other investigators from Norfolk, Virginia. It does not take long before I'm aware that the investigator I'm interviewing has an alliance with Alberi and Humphrey. He says he would stake his life on them. He flat out refuses to believe they would threaten the newspaper. Alberi seems to have everyone in his pocket. Can they not see through the facade? I now believe I cannot trust *anyone* in Virginia. Joe is upset. We both take a deep breath and move forward with our plan.

With time running out in the procedural process of Joe's appeals, I call Richard Reyna to continue our investigation. Two components are crucial. Without the alleged "confession" they had nothing to tie Joe to the crime but the blood evidence that is now challenged by new, more sophisticated DNA tests. We need to prove Watson lied. We also need to prove Joe had an alibi. I have to find the sailors he fought with in front of the Brass Rail the night of February 8. If they provide a statement and blood samples, perhaps we can prove the blood came from them and not the victim. They need to be found.

On my way to Virginia I make a pit stop to see my daughter. Jen is doing fine but, of course, we miss each other. The car seems to drive itself in warp speed when I arrive in Virginia just five hours later. As

I drive I think about the timing of my denial to visit Joe as part of his legal team. It came immediately after the press conference with Sister Helen Prejean. I didn't think it was coincidental. The prison authorities, and mostly the prosecution, were getting scared. I am getting too close. To what I do not know, but I'm about to find out. I remember what Professor Spahn told me before I left school.

"You are fighting the state, Lori, and you will never win. It's a battle, not a war. Remember that," she said.

She told me I was gifted. "It's a gift and a curse," she said, "because it's hard work." I know exactly what she meant. It's the hardest thing I have ever done in my life. As I make my way down Interstate 95, all I can do is pray and believe that God will guide me and give me strength and direction. I am not afraid at the moment, just curious about what I'll find. Joe needs me now and I will not let him down. Emotionally things are not easy, on us both. I miss law school and my daughter, but I know what I have to do. I plan to stay in Virginia for three weeks, perhaps a month, working and rallying support for Joe O'Dell.

I had arranged to pick up Richard at the Richmond airport. It's a long drive to West Virginia, where Richard has located Steven Watson.

By this time I know Watson's history—his criminal record and stacks of legal documents I have gathered from court records reveal a long history of burglaries. It also reveals he was facing some pretty serious time in prison for a breaking and entering charge that he was arrested for while housed in the same cell block as Joe when he was arrested. I had developed a visual of this man. Tall, lanky, greasy dark hair. A slimy low life who would stoop to anything for his own benefit, no matter what the consequence to another man.

Richard and I spend the night in Charlottesville, and the next morning we head to the mountains. While Richard is driving I watch us get deeper and deeper into rural West Virginia. I have never been anywhere like this so I have no idea what to expect. We're climbing the mountain mile by mile, getting further and further from civilization. I jab at Richard, though I admit I am a little nervous.

"Richard, someone can ram us off the side of this mountain and no one would ever know we were there," I say half joking. Except I'm not joking.

As we climb further into the mountain range I notice my cell phone has no reception.

"Great, Richard. Now if they try to kill us, we can't even call any-one." I'm half kidding, half serious.

I know we are not dealing with honest people.

"Do you at least have a gun on you?" I ask in a quest for some comfort.

"No, I don't carry a gun," Richard says.

Under my breath I'm thinking, *What kind of an investigator doesn't carry a gun?* Maybe I even say it, I'm not sure. All I know is that I am uncomfortable being all the way out here in the middle of nowhere.

A small, quaint-looking café sits off the side of the road, beckoning Richard and I in for some lunch. Mind you, Richard and I are trying to make our way into West Virginia unnoticed. We don't want anyone to know we are there or the investigation will be halted before we get to Watson.

We enter the small café with several booths and four square tables with red and white plastic tablecloths on them. The tables are occu-pied by locals. I'm trying to act nonchalant when I suddenly look at Richard and say, "Richard, why are they all staring at us?" It's at this point that I realize I'm wearing beautiful gold rings on my fingers, have fairly expensive clothing on and have not gotten away from those matching shoes. My nails are manicured and my hair recently high-lighted. Richard replies calmly with a slight smile." You may want to take off some of your jewelry." I nod in reply.

After a quick meal we're ready to hit the road again. For the lon-gest time I don't see any houses. I start to panic. I reach for my cell phone to grasp at any connection with civilization. The signal is dead. I look at Richard and he's laughing. Suddenly, I burst into a deep roar and together we laugh until our belllies ache.

We've been driving for miles now and I *still* don't see any houses. *Where on earth are we?* Finally, we come upon what appears to be an arch in the distance up ahead. "Richard, Richard, there's a house over there." Wanting desperately to see life anywhere I am all too excited. By this time Richard, a seasoned investigator must have either been getting really annoyed with me or found me entertaining.

As we approach the structure, down some long dirt road, Richard first notices it's a school for boys, an institution of some sort. *Great, now all the thieves, muggers and incorrigible kids are around us.* We laugh again, but we know our ride is not a joy ride.

Our desire to arrive incognito is foiled. As we approach the center of Elkins, West Virginia, we realize that we almost leave it before we know we got there. If it hadn't been for the big parade we were now driving through, we may have missed it altogether. I'm looking around for a guy with black greasy hair, wondering if he's walking amongst us now. Richard and I get out of the car to check it out. It's the Mountain Forest celebration, whatever that means. It obviously means a lot to the folks in town. There are TV cameras everywhere. Richard and I decide to get out of Dodge. We quickly slip away and back into the quiet streets of Elkins.

Elkins is a small town in West Virginia with homes that are, well, modest. We find the road to Watson's house and pull up to 26 Diamond Street. It's a small once-white house. The porch is rotted out and the place needs painting badly. No one is home. We decide to pay a visit to Watson's attorney of record for the breaking and entering charge he was facing at the time he was in jail with Joe O'Dell. We find the lawyer's office and, without having an appointment we take a chance, apologize for the intrusion, and insist it was unplanned. When we explain what we are doing there, he tells us to return with a letter from Steven Watson. We need his consent to look at privileged information. I am learning legal rules and procedures. Some of them actually make sense. We leave and as we head back to the motel, Richard talks about his experience with other Virginia lawyers on death cases. There is no passion. Paper is pushed, motions are filed, briefs are filed, but few really take it to heart. Richard and I share a similar style, allowing us to bond in our quest for justice.

I know we need to secure several affidavits now. I try to fall asleep, knowing that in the morning I will meet the man responsible for sealing the conviction that sent Joe to death row. I wonder how I will feel when I actually lay eyes on him for the first time.

It's 10:00 a.m. as Richard and I approach the Watson house again. I stand next to Richard as he knocks on the door. A woman answers, I presume it's Watson's wife. She has dark hair, big brown eyes and is about 100 lbs overweight. She greets us with caution, not knowing if we are cops.

"We're looking for Steve Watson," Richard says.

My heart is racing, wondering if he will come to the door. From behind this woman I see a tall, lanky man with greasy black hair—exactly as I had visualized Watson. We're standing outside on the porch as we shake hands. He invites us inside.

I remember reading a statement from one of the prior investigators. He interviewed Watson several years ago and said Watson seemed to suggest that O'Dell may *not* have confessed. The statement would have made me go back to revisit Watson, but apparently no one else could see the doubt in the words he conveyed to the investigator. Watson was still under the thumb of the prosecutor, who he called right after the visit. Strangely, Steve would later make a statement that the investigator offered him weed, anything to discredit him.

Joe O'Dell knew this and was very worried for me. He never pushed me to investigate Watson because he was afraid what Watson might say about me. Maybe that I offered him sex, who knows? Joe knew one thing, and that was Watson had lied and helped put Joe where he is today. I had to get the truth. I knew Watson had lied. It was obvious as daylight.

Charlotte Watson invites us to sit at the breakfast table in the small, slightly dirty house. Suddenly, Richard and I hear the sound of police on a radio dispatch. Watson has a transmitter set up in his kitchen to listen to the cops as they play out their day. I'm not at all surprised by this. If he's a snitch, this would be right up his alley. He explains the technology to us and seems to even be proud of it. We listen. Let him talk. Listen. Let him talk. We are befriending him.

Richard states our business calmly and in a non-confrontational manner. He asks Watson to tell us what happened. He gets him talking. I watch Richard's style, see him engaging Watson in conversation, trying to make him comfortable. Instead of attacking him, he occasionally interjects, "I'm having a little trouble with that, it doesn't seem to make sense." We sit and talk with the Watson's from 10:00 a.m. to 5:00 p.m. sharing lunch in his home. Slowly, I feel Watson coming around.

Strangely, I do not hate him. In an odd kind of way I can relate to him. I'm not sure where this is coming from, but I feel an understanding from him as well. We talk about Joe O'Dell and how he is facing execution for a crime we are certain he did not commit. We talk about Watson's testimony at trial and ask him to remember what he can. We don't accuse him. We simply ask, and listen. At first he says he does not remember much. Then he says he's not sure O'Dell really confessed, he may have been bragging. I could tell Watson needed a way out. He had dug a hole for himself over ten years ago. Dignity has a way of making people do strange things. He can't come right out and say, "I lied." As we gain his trust and build a "friendship" with him and his wife, he begins to open up.

At first we talk about his hearing problem. He said it was the reason he was transferred to the medical block near Joe O'Dell. Charlotte adds that as long as she's known Steven, prior to his arrest and incarceration with O'Dell, he's had hearing problems. This is helpful information. We ask her to give us an affidavit swearing to this. It gives the prosecution a way out, to not look so bad. We are trying everything we can think of to build our case. It also helps pave the way for Watson to allow him to talk more freely, and he does. By the end of the day I could hardly believe it when Watson finally says, "I want to recant. How do I do this? Can we get a lawyer to write a statement?" Those were the words—the truth—I so desperately needed to hear. They are the words I feel certain will help save Joe's life.

Steve has grown to trust us, and we him. He is scared and needs a way out. Deep down I believe everyone has good in them. I pray everything goes smoothly and that we don't lose him any time in the future. *Thank you God*, I say silently. It would be easy to relish our progress, yet I know there's still so much to do.

It's Tuesday morning and we are up and out the door at 8:30 a.m., ready to meet with Steve at 10:00 a.m.. As we near the front stoop, the curtain is drawn back and Steve is watching us approach. I can sense he's anxious to meet with us. In less than 24 hours we have developed a good rapport with him.

We spend most of the day with Steve and Charlotte. At one point Steve exclaims that he needs to clear his conscience. A feeling of relief and satisfaction starts to come over me. Truth is all I have been after in this case and I am uncovering it, one stone at a time. Charlotte also agrees to give us an affidavit, swearing to Steve's hearing problem. She even provides us with documentation to support it. I'm hoping it leads the way to some movement in the case.

We must have made an impression with the Watsons as their daughter Roslyn stayed over last night just to be there when we arrived that morning. Approaching the house, Richard and I notice they had decorated. A Halloween monster is nailed to the front door, awaiting our arrival. Nearing the monster it suddenly makes a ghostly noise.

Startled, I jump back ten feet, causing Charlotte to laugh hysterically. There were no pretenses. There were no boundaries to the truth. Together we enjoy some relief to an otherwise tense situation.

Steve decides to write his thoughts on paper and jots down all he can remember about Joe. At that moment I just wanted to jump up and hug him. But I know the battle is far from over. One had to be mindful that the prosecution would attempt to claim that we intimidated Watson, or whatever they would say to discredit us, or Steve. The pictures we take during the day show an altogether different scenario. We will leave them a set before we depart. Charlotte is making lasagna for dinner and invites us to stay. We politely decline.

That evening, back at our motel, Bob Smith calls to inform me that Joe was granted a stay of execution. We have until November 7, 1996 to file our petition to the U.S. Supreme Court. Between Watson's recantation and this news I'm on cloud nine. I can hardly wait to tell Joe at 8:00 p.m. tonight, when we are scheduled to speak.

Richard believes it would be powerful if Steve went on the air to recant his statement at trial, and plead to the governor for Joe's release. The impact this would have on so many people brings a smile to my face. *Yes, it's show time.* I believe it's the first time in history that an informant pleads to the governor for clemency for the man he helped put on death row. "It's a great plan, Richard," I say. Somehow, when I first met Steve I knew he was going to help us.

My hotel room phone rings at 9:00 p.m. It's Joe. The pressure of what we are up against is getting to both of us. He's worried sick about me. The stay of execution had not given him pause for elation. Instead, he knows what to expect if we don't stop this corrupt machinery of death. This bonds us even stronger. He is concerned for my well being. I, for his. We are in a vicious circle now, trying to protect one another.

Listening to his concerns, Joe tells me that Pat Schwarzschild believes Bob Smith is too laid-back and that Joe needs to take control of his case. How the hell she expects him to do that I don't know. She also reiterated, "Let me make one thing clear, I work for you—Joe O'Dell and Bob Smith only." I suppose she meant "not Lori Urs." *What on earth gave her that idea?* We both manage to laugh. The games the lawyers play are mind-boggling. Richard and I are in amazement that they are, well, not so clever, and at times without courage. We are not as kind in the words we use to express our frustration. No one is working, I mean *really* working, for Joe. Here I am working this investigation, *ten years* after the fact. *What on earth have they been doing all this time?*

It's Wednesday morning. I offer to take Charlotte and the Watsons' daughters to Walmart. Steve and Richard stay in the motel. In an attempt to rationalize his behavior, Steve tells Richard he was angry with O'Dell, *that is why he made those things up.* O'Dell told him he would get life with four breaking and entering charges and arson. Steve got scared. He said he thought about escaping, but figured that wouldn't work. So he lied. It was a good way out for him.

Back at the house, Charlotte and daughter Roslyn gave me some of their jewelry as a gift. I am touched by their generosity. It somehow makes me believe they will not turn on us. We just need to keep in touch to keep them strong. I make myself that promise. Before we leave Steve says that he wants to be there when Joe gets out. He also reiterates he wants to write the lawyers, the governor and whoever else necessary to make it right.

Joe calls that evening, but the person I really need to talk to is Jen. She helps me feel grounded. Having to witness such deceit and treachery, even just uncovering it, makes me feel dirty. It's such a completely different world than the one I know.

Tomorrow is the hearing before Judge Spencer to reinstate my right to visit Joe O'Dell in a legal capacity. It is scheduled for 2:00 p.m. Once again, I'm praying. Exhaustion suddenly makes the uncomfortable motel bed look inviting. Before I hit the sheets I whisper, *Good night Jennifer. I love you.* I close my eyes to drift out of reality.

When I awaken my mind turns immediately to the pending hearing. The issue before the court is important. No doubt about it. But Richard and I are doing something even more pressing. We are putting together the lost pieces to the puzzle that came in boxes over the past three years. We again spend the day with the Watsons'. It's Niki's birthday, one of their kids. Charlotte asks us to stay for dinner. This time we accept.

This all seems very odd, sitting in the kitchen of the jailhouse snitch while his wife is making dinner. We are their guests tonight. If someone had told me this two years ago, or even two months ago, I would have laughed in their face. I watch as Charlotte prepares dinner, trying to assist her as any proper guest would. I am washing the vegetables when I turn around and observe her dipping her hand in the butter tub, scooping out butter with her fingers and placing it on the bread rolls before placing then on the table for dinner. My stomach turns, yet I cannot say a word. I must keep quiet. As we sit down at the table to eat I am seated adjacent to Richard. He reaches for a roll. I am laughing so hard inside I can barely contain myself. The right thing to do would be to warn him, but I am silenced by the awkwardness this creates. So I say nothing and save it for a story later that evening when we return to the motel. Steve shares with me that he feels responsible for what happened to Joe. I should be angry but I am not. I am grateful for the truth.

After dinner the Watsons turn on some music. Roslyn is dirty dancing and I watch wide-eyed, like a child witnessing *Peter Pan* for the first time. The girl is *only* 16 years old. Her 40-year-old boyfriend drops by. He's a bagger at the local supermarket. "He has a good job," Steve says. He appears to be intellectually challenged. As he speaks, his high-pitched voice is unnerving. Richard and I can hardly contain ourselves. Roslyn is proud to have danced in a club, probably a strip club. She tells Richard she wants to show off her moves. As I glance across the room Richard is sitting on a chair against the wall. This young girl is now straddling him, offering him a lap dance. In what appears to be a split second, Richard leaps up off the chair as he politely declines. He is clever, friendly, yet careful. Roslyn now turns her attention to me, who has sat in disbelief as she slowly moves across the floor. Yet instead of dancing *for* me, she decides to dance *with* me, taking me out to the side porch. She then attempts to teach me how to dirty dance. Unlike Richard, I indulge her, praying the neighbors aren't watching. Then again, they probably wouldn't care. If my friends in Princeton could see me now it would be fodder for years. *The things you do for your client,* Richard had said early in the investigation.

As soon as we are back at the motel my cell phone rings. It's Joe. Our need to be and stay connected has grown with the intensity of my investigation. We enjoy a wonderful conversation. I'm careful about what I share on the phone. I know our conversations are monitored by the prison, forcing us to speak in code. This must remain a secret, for the moment the prosecution finds out, we blow our chance to finally expose the truth to the public.

I awaken the next morning to find myself spending a couple of hours with Charlotte and the kids. Charlotte suggests getting a tape recorder, just in case the cops and prosecutors pay Steven a visit. They know the game better than I do. She is trying to shield Steven. I tell her if they do not want to talk to the police or prosecutors, they are not obligated to do so. I sense their fear. I casually inform them of their right to have an attorney present. I suppose a tape recording would prevent Steve from facing them at all. Charlotte wants to tape-record the cops and the prosecutors if they come knocking on their door. "If they intimidate or threaten Steve, it would be on tape," she reasons. I agree it's a good idea, but we never do buy a tape recorder for them. It turns out to be a mistake I would later regret. I drop Charlotte and Roslyn off at their house.

It's Saturday, our last day in West Virginia. Yesterday Steve and Richard notarized Steve's affidavit. Before we leave I draft a letter to

Bob Smith with a copy to every person of interest I can think of, including the governor. Steve cooperates to right his wrong and signs the powerful letter. I call Joe Jackson to offer him an exclusive interview. He, like everyone else, finds it hard to believe that Watson has confessed to lying about Joe O'Dell's confession. Richard tells me to write a letter to Centurion Ministries and attach a copy of the affidavit—not as a brag, just to let them know how credible I am. Reluctantly, I agree. They should know. Richard suggests we accomplished this 50/50, working as a team. The fact that this was not done years ago dampens my pleasure. It may be too late. I realize that this is what was needed *just two months ago* at the evidentiary hearing before Judge Spencer. It may have gotten Joe a new trial. Now, we are forced to file it in the court of last resort, the governor's lap. I feel the need to talk to Alberi, Test, and Humphrey while I am in Virginia Beach—maybe after I see the jurors. This new evidence has forced my determination up a notch.

Richard needs to be at the airport early. During our drive back at 5:00 a.m. through the mountains, I pull out the letter that may have offered Joe his chance for freedom just two months prior. Judge Spencer had cited it as important in linking Joe to the crime, and presumably as part of the reason he did not grant Joe a new trial:

> Despite this testimony (the DNA exclusion), O'Dell has not proven factual innocence. Based on the circumstantial evidence introduced at trial, and on the confession O'Dell made to jailhouse informant Steve Watson, O'Dell has not proved beyond clear and convincing evidence that he is factually innocent of the crime of murdering Helen Schartner[88].

Steve's letter in hand, I read it slowly, taking in every word[89].

Richard and I arrive at the airport at around 9:00 a.m., say our

---

[88] See *O'Dell v. Thompson*, No. 3:92CV480, slip op. at 32. (Sept. 6, 1994).

[89] See Exhibit II, Sworn Affidavit of Steve Watson, dated October 11, 1996.

goodbyes, and I drive down to South Hill. I need to visit with Joe. I find comfort in his presence, hearing his voice and watching his steel blue eyes focus on me as I share with him all the fruits of my labor. He looked wonderful and I could see what I felt was the adoration he had for me. Our emotions mix from the struggle to save his life with the emotional bond that inevitably forms between two people in such dire circumstances.

In the evening I call Steve Watson to wrap up the details. Steve offers me money from a potential $22,000 settlement he is soon to get. He wants me to know he's in for the long haul. Of course, I would never accept any money from him and it never comes up again. I know it's a display of his conviction. We plan to share the news on the air in three weeks when Richard returns. Richard, Steve, myself and, hopefully, Sister Helen will announce to the world that the only link between Joe and the victim was a lie.

Before I know it, Joe Jackson is on the phone with me on a Sunday night. He wants Watson's letter and affidavit. Jackson is not happy with the newspaper's reluctance to do the story of Joe's innocence. He says that he will approach the publisher if Dennis refuses to publish it. He reminds me that he has the exclusive with Watson. Believing that no one else in Virginia is trustworthy of such delicate news, I gladly agree. I'm learning to watch my back.

~Making Headway, But Toward What?~

It's mid-October, three years since I stumbled upon this death row saga. The process has seemed more like struggling to win a war than engaging in a battle. The thought of having to engage in this battle with even the lawyers is draining. Somehow I always envisioned one's attorney to be most avid advocate for one's cause. I find myself terribly troubled by the reality of what *pro bono* means to some blue chip firms.

Having won the legal argument on the civil rights action in the district court, our lawyer Steven Rosenfield informs me that I can now legally visit with Joe. I jump at the opportunity, realizing it may be short-lived. My legal visit with Joe is scheduled at 9:30 a.m. After an extensive search by security guards I am deemed to be clean. I wonder if they do this to all attorneys. I am placed in a different room than most attorneys, with a guard standing nearby. I refuse to speak, and instead, I call Steven Rosenfield. I then ask to speak to the warden. Dutifully, they escort me to his office. As I enter his office I notice Joanne Royster, a familiar prison staff member, has accompanied us. I suppose they need a witness. I inform the warden that I have a problem with the guard in the room.

"What is the problem?" Warden J.D. Netherland wants to know. "It's not unusual to have a guard in the room."

"As far as I know, Warden, it is not the norm," I reply.

"Isn't it, Joanne?" The warden beckons her to acquiesce. Joanne remains silent. The warden asks what I want.

"I want the guard in the box," I tell him.

The "box" is a small enclosed room adjacent to the visiting room they had offered us for this "legal" visit. I knew little as to whether we could be monitored there as well, but it was one step removed from us. He agrees. Then I bring up the camera in the room and ask if it is audio. The warden says nothing, but Royster jumps in and affirms that it is not hooked up.

"See, I didn't even have to answer," the warden chimes in.

As if I believed anyone at this point.

"Do you want an electrician to show you the cut wires?" he asks.

I inform him that his word is good enough. It should have been, but in all honesty it was not. He calls for an electrician ASAP. A short walk down the hall takes us to the room we are supposed to have for our legal visit, which is actually the visiting room for inmates who are afforded contact visits. We walk directly toward Joe. The warden engages in pleasantries with him. Then he pulls a chair to the area where a camera hangs from the ceiling and draws a wire out of the wall to prove it is not hooked up. The guards, Cruthfield and Royster, Joe and I, all laugh. The warden then asks if Joe wants the other camera wires pulled. Simultaneously, we reply, "No, that's fine."

Joe and I proceed to engage in a clandestine meeting until 3:00 p.m. I can't wait to share our latest victory. I watch his face as I slide the affidavit across the table, along with the letter Steve Watson wrote to Bob Smith and the governor. A slight look of satisfaction comes across Joe's face. I know his emotions are measured as a result of the roller-coaster ride he has been on since 1985. I can sense that the guards like Joe, they allow him to enjoy a cigarette in the bathroom, twice, against regulation, but with the blessings of the powers watching over him.

Later that day, Steve Rosenfield calls to inform me that the Commonwealth has asked the Fourth Circuit for a stay of the injunction which has allowed me legal access to Joe. Steve spends the entire day preparing his brief.[90] They have asked for Judge Luttig. Can they do that, I ask? Hand pick your judge? No question why they want him. He has a bone to pick with murderers, any way he can. At 6:30 p.m. the clerk of the court informs Steve that they are deciding whether a panel of judges will hear the request, or whether Luttig himself will have that honor. I see immediately the distinct difference between Steve and Joe's lawyer Bob Smith, who refused to call the clerk on a life or death matter. Zealously advocate for your client…those words are jumping off the page now. I am seeing for the first time a lawyer who is doing

---

[90] The author learned this was so unusual that to this day Attorney Steve Rosenfield talks about the expeditious manner in which the court handled this matter. Specifically, Judge Spencer granted relief on Monday. The Fourth Circuit, through Judge Luttig, granted a stay of the district court decision on Tuesday. On Wednesday the state filed its brief with the court and my civil rights lawyers filed their brief on Thursday. Friday, a panel of the Fourth Circuit Court of Appeals heard oral argument and rendered an opinion the same day reversing Judge Spencer. Rosenfield quipped that the court system can run like a smooth running machine when they want to reverse a judgment in favor of a condemned man.

just that. The *Mecklenburg Sun* picks up the story for its front page. The AP wire follows to make it national news. The positive, energetic display by Rosenfield, and his belief that Joe's lawyers did not act as though they cared, helps me feel I am not alone in this game. Shortly thereafter, I listen to Bob Smith as he tells me, "It's all up to the media – a successor (petition) is unlikely." I disagree. I will have to tell him tomorrow if he cannot do the successor petition the right way, he has to let me know. He is dead quiet when I mention witness intimidation, prosecutorial misconduct, suborned perjury. Words too strong for a corporate attorney sitting in an ivory tower. They argue with me in recognizing the reality of what those words mean. They do not want to help Joe.

I take the opportunity for another legal visit before leaving South Hill. The court had not yet rendered an opinion, so I'm free to engage in privileged communication with Joe. In the "box" is Motley, a small, thin guard who appears not to have the physical strength to defend himself in a prison situation. With him is another guard who is one of Joe's favorites. He teases Joe about being his "look-alike." Theirs is not the kind of relationship one would expect from a captive and his guards.

Meanwhile, I wait to hear back from the media. I must get them out to Elkins, West Virginia before Watson changes his mind. One never knows when a witness will lose faith and fortitude. Or worse yet, be threatened by the "other side". Tomorrow I will retrieve Richard from the Richmond airport.

Channel 7 can't do the story until Monday so I offer it to Channel 13 in Norfolk. They confirm they will be in Elkins on Friday. With Joe Jackson scheduled to arrive on Saturday, our plan is set in motion. Channel 13 promises to air the piece on Monday and Jackson will print it on Tuesday. I pick up the phone to call Watson. "It's so good to hear your voice," Steve says. Excited about the interview on Friday, he tells me Charlotte will have to clean the house. He also tells me that he misses me. "Joe O'Dell is lucky to have you in his corner, Lori." Roslyn screams hello from the background. "We'll see you at 6 p.m. tomorrow night," I excitedly tell Steve. Before I end the call he asks about the statute of limitation for perjury. He is afraid the prosecutors will go after him. I dance around the issue to buy some time. I need him to do this interview first, *then* I will engage in legal discussions with him.

Prior to leaving for Richmond I swing by the prison to pick up a tape from Joe. Soon afterwards, Richard is in my car and we're on our way to Elkins. I am running on fumes at this point.

In a highly unusual move, a jailhouse snitch is now publicly admitting he lied at trial. Steve Watson is on the air with Channel 13, discussing how he fabricated Joe's confession. I sit in awe at the remarkable event unfolding before me. Emotion tears at me while I fight any form of outward expression of our triumph. I appear calm. Richard and I had prepared Steve for the interview. We didn't want the reporters to throw him off guard, as they are known to do. In half an hour Watson tears the Commonwealth's case apart.

"I took innocent statements that Joe said and changed it to help myself. I have lied and I feel responsible for Joe being where he is today. I want to publicly apologize to Joseph O'Dell. I am sorry for what I did. If I could take it all back, go back ten years, I would."

Watson pleads to the governor to stop the execution and investigate the case. He is sincere in his apology through the camera. For the first time in what may have been years, if not a lifetime, Watson is dressed in a pair of dark blue slacks, dress shoes, a blue shirt and a tie. He appears credible, but they *had* to ask,

"Why should anyone believe you now?" questions a reporter.

"I had charges on me back then and I was afraid. I have changed. A great burden has been lifted off my shoulders. It has taken me ten years to get up the courage to tell the truth," said Steve.

A female reporter then turns to me. She ambushes me about rumors the prison is spreading about my being married to Joe O'Dell.

"No, Joseph and I are not married according to Virginia law, according to *any* law," I respond. "The Department of Corrections is simply trying to defocus the public about the facts of the case and move away from the issue of innocence."

She asks me where it will go from here, now that we have this recantation.

"We hope and expect that the court, when they hear the recantation and all the other exculpatory evidence that has come to light, will conclude that Joseph O'Dell's original conviction cannot stand."

I am beginning to sound like a lawyer.

Next, they interview Richard. He states that the prosecution must have known Watson was lying. He mentions the soil, the fact that they needed a link between Joe and the victim and the fact that the prosecutor had nothing. They needed Watson. As most reporters often do, she threw in her own bias.

"You don't have any relationship with Joe, do you? Sounds like your beef was that he didn't get a fair trial."

She didn't get it. Could she not see that we had more than an innocent man who never received a fair trial? I started to distrust the media more than ever.

Today we made history in the Commonwealth of Virginia. I am sure that no jailhouse snitch has ever publicly confessed to having lied at trial, apologized to the condemned, and at the same time, solicited the governor's help to overturn a conviction.

That evening, Joe and I finally get to talk on the phone. As I discuss the day's events, Joe takes it all in with amazement. "Joe, Watson asked me to give you his P.O. box number." The man who has helped put Joe on death row, now wants Joe to write him. I am not surprised when Joe agrees. "Sure, I'll write him." Joe is not the monster the prosecution wants everyone to believe he is. In over ten years in prison, and on death row, he received only one infraction—it was the day the prison opened personal mail between Joe and I. He was standing up for me. Because he yelled at them, they wrote him up. It was the first and last report on file.

Joe Jackson arrives Saturday morning. Just prior to that I receive a devastating call. Joe doesn't have much time left. The motel clerk hands me a message that Joe is trying to reach me. I quickly phone the prison and instruct them to have him call me. This is when I hear that the Fourth Circuit has turned us down, meaning I cannot have legal visitation with Joe. Worse, Joe now has a date with his executioner on December 18, 1996. For the first time in a long time tears glide off my cheeks. Joe and I try our best to reassure one another. In need of some comfort I approach Richard. His seasoned approach to these cases doesn't allow for sympathy. When I drop him at Watson's house the next morning, I return to the motel to call Sister Helen. She would tell me what to do. As if knowing that I need a miracle, she answers the phone.

"You need national attention, Lori. Try *60 Minutes*," Helen tells me. She agrees to help. Inexplicably, I sense I am being guided throughout this entire journey.

As promised, Joe Jackson arrives to interview Watson. I tape it for evidence, sitting on pins and needles until he utters his last words, "I'm sorry." Afterwards, Richard and I visit with the Watsons before leaving town. All I want now is to see Joe. The mind-boggling news of his pending execution is drawing us closer to the end of the nightmare we are desperately trying to avert. It's not long before I arrive in South Hill. I do my best to calm him.

In the evening, I return to my motel room and fax a letter to *60 Minutes*, sharing Watson's affidavit, the ink still wet with his signature. Steady in my goal to see justice unveil, the trip back to Chatham draws me closer to it. I know Watson will be on Channel 13 in Virginia by the time I arrive home.

There is comfort in knowing Joe Jackson's article will tell it like it is. On the front page of the morning paper is Watson's recantation. The courtroom lie is now completely exposed. Perhaps *60 Minutes* will find it newsworthy. Helen has contacted Josh Howard, the senior producer, and a friend of hers. The memory of my fax machine is documenting the spread of Jackson's article across state lines.

Meanwhile, from his desk at the law school, Professor Nyquist reaches out to me.

"I miss you, we all miss you. When are you coming back?" he asks.

He wants to know if Sister Helen will speak at the school. I assure him she will. "The church I belong to Lori has a declaration of life—victim's families who don't want their murderers put to death. I'll present Joe's case to them. I expect around 50 people will write to the governor," he assures me. That's 50 more people who will support Joe O'Dell. A click interrupts our call. The voice of Steve Watson quivers in fear. He is seeking reassurance and support from me.

"Steve, has anyone come to see you yet?"

"Not yet," he sighs, understandably relieved. "Don't worry, I'll stick by you."

"Stay strong, Steve. Please call back in two days."

To protect myself, I tape him when he acknowledges, "No, you didn't harass me." I have seen Watson turn on a previous investigator. The last thing I need are false claims surfacing if he receives a visit from the government. The fact that he likes me is helpful in keeping him in our corner.

The next morning I awake and head to the kitchen for my morning cup of tea. The red light on the message machine is blinking—it's Bob Smith in New York. I hit the message button and suddenly Bob's sullen voice is saying, "Joe's date was officially set at 2:30 p.m. by the Circuit Court of Virginia Beach." This is not the way one would like to learn of a date with the grim reaper. The news reminds me of the fact that Joe's life, so much now, depends on what I can do for him. *People have to care*, I think. *They simply must.*

We have two options to file a petition for certiorari with the U.S. Supreme Court, November 7 or December 9, 1996. Joe insists on November 7. I agree. We don't want room for mistakes. The Commonwealth has proven less than forthright, and downright unethical, when it comes to fairness. They would insist we are procedurally barred if we file after November 7. I call Bob to confirm his understanding of Joe's wishes.

I phone Kris Sperry and Dr. Silverstein, both forensic specialists. Upon my request for assistance I'm met with the puzzling question, "Why wasn't this done before?" I have no answers for Sperry. I was tired of defending the law firm. "Lori, the lack of evidence doesn't mean much, but the lack of soil samples on Joe's shoes is important." I make note of this when he refers me to a pathologist in New York. I share my progress, in code, with Joe.

Joe is all too aware of his pending walk to the death chamber when we argue over Watson. He is fearful of Watson's capabilities. "Lori, I worry about what Watson may say about you," Joe says. He wants to protect me from false allegations, or anything leading to an attack on my credibility. I assure him everything is alright. But honestly, how can I? This man had no trouble lying to a judge and jury after he swore on the Bible to tell the truth. "This is dangerous territory," Joe reminds me. I try to comfort his fears while smoldering my own.

That same evening Walter calls to inform me that his best friend is leaving his wife. It's strange how close we still are. I miss that about us. It's ironic how polar opposite he is from Joe O'Dell. Though ours is a marriage that failed, it was not from the lack of love, but from circumstances. I didn't know it at the time, but as my time became totally consumed with Joseph O'Dell he began to take on many roles in my life. It was natural as I had no one else to fill them. Although it was bound to happen, I was still focusing on one thing and one thing only—the truth.

****

October is such a beautiful month in New England. Still warm enough to enjoy the remaining days of "Indian summer". I awaken early that morning to singing birds and the sound of bells chiming from the village church. I gaze at the clock on my nightstand. It's exactly the same time Joe told me he loved me, two years ago. "No, I had said to him, you just think you do because I'm helping you." No matter he has a fiancée named Cheryl Murden. They met during his trial when she befriended him and fell in love while he was fighting for his life. She stood by his side ever since, silently. Shame, or fear of being shunned, kept her relationship with Joseph largely a secret. I was fearless, unafraid to stand up for him. I had no personal attachment to him, unaware I was developing one as I tenaciously fought for his freedom. Joseph confided in me that he never had anyone who believed in him. His parents, especially his dad, were abusive and would always make fun of him. His mother was overindulgent and without strength to protect her children from their father's wrath and beatings. Joe was unused to loyalty and such fierce commitment. Ours was becoming a highly unusual relationship—full of love, fear, hope, laughs, heartbreak, honesty, sadness, joy and dedication. It was a most unusual situation, and one that would never have developed had it not been for our predestined paths. It was certainly outside of my wildest imagination.

Early Friday morning I fumble through my black book for Dr. Michael Baden's number. After the third ring he answers in his jovial tone of voice. He asks me to fax him the information I want him to review. I am quick to convey the urgency of the situation, explaining that Joe has a December 18 execution date. I forward to him six letters and documents, as well as the PGM blood results, performed by Virginia's amateur scientist prior to Joe's trial.

I am now determined to find John Nutter, and to learn what his blood type is. I need to confirm that the blood on Joe's clothes could have come from one of the sailors he purported to fight with that evening. I telephone his mother in Upton, New York. I am friendly. She responds the same.

"It's funny, just the other day I pulled the records of my children's blood type, but John's wasn't there. I think he's O negative."

After hearing those words, I refrain from screaming out, "Oh my God!" She offers to confirm John's blood type by calling the pediatrician. Before we hang up I ask if she will provide me documentation as proof. Our conversation leaves me with the strange sense that I am being *guided* in this journey. I often wonder where my energy or direction comes from.

It's now imperative that I find the man Joseph fought with that dreadful night. I need to verify Joe's alibi, and the source of blood on his clothing and in his car.

Chapter 17

~Joe's Hospital Visit~

Early Saturday morning I receive an unfamiliar phone call from one of Joe's friend's on death row.

"Lori, this is Roy Smith. Joe is badly sick, you need to do something. The nurse just took his blood pressure and told him there was nothing wrong. But Joe's in bad pain and he just threw up."

After thanking Roy for the alert I immediately call the prison. The guard in charge is indifferent to my inquiry. He informs me that Joe has already been seen. "That's all they intend to do," he mumbles. "If you want to call back, speak to the assistant warden in a couple of hours."

I hang up and call Joe's lawyers. I explain the urgency of the matter before they offer me Bob Smith's home phone number.

"Bob, I'm sorry to bother you. We have an urgent situation. Joe has been sick for over a week now. Days after he had complained of stomach pain, he saw a doctor. The stomach pains started on Tuesday and Joe said it felt like a knife in his belly. A few days before that he was taken to the prison doctor who gave him a flu shot. She informed Joe it was being administered to all asthmatics, but Joe said none of the other inmates seem to have gotten the shot. The doctor put something in his mouth and it turned a color. He immediately left the room and came back to repeat whatever test he was doing."

Bob promises to call the prison. I then call Joe's sister Sheila and tell her to call the prison. She phones a family friend and the two of them call the warden to inquire about Joe's condition. The more calls I can get to the prison, the more they know people are watching. They cannot ignore the situation.

While gone from the house for a morning cup of coffee I miss Joe's call, twice. He had been taken to the prison medical center. I receive an update from Roy Smith who says that two guards came to escort Joe out of his cell. Having heard nothing from Bob I call the assistant warden and talk to him for ten minutes. He's curious about how I have learned that Joe was sick. "I received a call from someone," I tell him. "So, you talk to Joe every day?" the warden asks. "Yes, I do. And I've also spoken to a doctor who says that an inflamed pancreas is serious and Joe's condition cannot not be ignored." They are responsible for his care. Bob calls me five minutes later. The assistant warden told him everything was okay. "Of course they will say that, Lori." Bob acknowledges that persistent calls will let the prison know of everyone's concern. I agree.

In an attempt to escape this insanity, I take a drive with a law school friend and return home a bit less frantic. Around six I call the prison and a pleasant guard informs me that Joe just got back from the hospital. "They took him to the emergency room." For a death row inmate to be removed from the prison facility it requires an act of Congress. I knew our phone calls had encouraged them to take action. It's not long before the phone rings. It's Joe. His voice sounds tired and strained.

"Five cop cars, two civilian cars, the van I rode in and a backup car escorted me to the hospital," he says. "They took me to South Hill Medical Center with a helicopter following us the entire way. When I arrived, there was a SWAT team outside the hospital. They had SWAT hats on and machine guns. All this for me! The state trooper asked me about the jailhouse snitch article and the nurse asked if I was the one with the wife in the newspaper.

Meanwhile, the cops who had surrounded Joe in the emergency room kept careful watch as they waited for the doctor to take Joe in. The hospital had no idea how to handle a death row inmate who had to be taken to X-ray. They phoned Mecklenburg. The warden instructed them, "Keep him handcuffed at all times." They think he has a bleeding ulcer. His pancreas is fine. He will have to return on Monday or Tuesday. Thankfully, they gave Joe medication for his spasms. Joe tells me that one of the state troopers ran to get a doctor when he was having a spasm in the emergency room. It was a display of empathy that apparently surprised Joe. What we all take for granted as a simple doctor's visit, is a very different thing for those incarcerated.

After a quick break to the grocery store I return home to a missed call from Steve Watson and a call from Mike George's mother, Dorothy. Mike is another death row inmate, awaiting his turn. Her message was urgent, directing me to phone her at any hour. I phone her right back and she tells me that Joe says he's dying. "He needs to talk to you." I tell Dorothy it was all taken care of and not to worry. It's amazing how resourceful Joe can be when he needs to reach out to the world for help inside. He had acquired quite a team of people who connected him to a world that could place controls and demands on those who controlled him. The alternative was to be at left to the mercy of a high security prison whose only goal was to keep you alive until they killed you.

~Forensics, Corruption and the Media~

It's always rejuvenating to my soul when I return from a morning church service. When I feel alone, or when the ethical challenges I am seeing start to eat at me, I need spiritual intervention. The sermons my minister so eloquently preaches to us on Sunday seem to be tailored just for me, yet I know there are others who can and do resonate with his words. They serve to lift my spirits and allow me the peace I need to escape from a world I have entered that wreaks of havoc.

While I engage in a mindless afternoon I find myself in front of the TV watching a show on forensics. I am learning about bugs and botanical debris. Perched on the edge of my chair with my eyes wide open, my ears are attuned to every word the scientist speaks. Of course it's useful information that I can apply to Joe's case. I now have another goal—I need to contact the experts. Steve Watson calls and tells me no one has come to see him yet. He adds that his brother stopped by and told him he was crazy to admit he had lied. Steve seems to be strong, standing by his conviction to tell the truth. I am encouraged.

I am equally as encouraged the next morning by a call from Joe Hamlin from *60 Minutes*. He is reviewing Joe's case and will get back to me later in the week.

Next, I reach out to three forensic specialists in Florida. One of them, Carlisle, agrees to perform soil comparison testing. To acquire his approval I alert Bob Smith who updates me on DNA testing. "Barry Scheck called and has offered his help." They intend to call the prosecutor regarding DNA tests with a statement such as, "You think he's guilty, we think he's innocent. Let's settle this once and for all." I wonder what changed Scheck's mind. Perhaps he's spoken to Michael Baden. The step to facilitate DNA testing offers me a glimmer of hope. Adding to this, the law firm announces that the petition for certiorari is completed. They are sending me, Joe and Clive Stafford Smith a copy for review. Bob Smith sounds upbeat. I thank him for his efforts.

Briefly I speak to Jen, whom I miss terribly, and then to Joe, four separate times during the day. He says he needs me near him. However, I am focused on Nutter. I need to find something to get someone's attention. The execution date is 60 days away.

The fax machine is spitting out Dr. Carlisle's credentials as I'm conversing with Peter Finn from the *Washington Post*. Trying to get all our ducks in a row, the phone calls move from Bob, to Barry Scheck and then to Michael Baird from Lifecodes Laboratory.

Meanwhile, I am fielding phone calls from NBC's *Dateline* and *60 Minutes*. Not sensing that I have anyone's complete cooperation, I wonder how much false information the prosecutor is feeding them. The frightening truth is that the prosecution, and the Commonwealth in general, have tremendous power in the dissemination of information. The media has no reason to suspect they are not being honest or forthright. I know differently, and it's an awful position to be in. A sense of pure helplessness runs through my body as I listen to the distorted facts Alberi has been giving to the press. They are quickly losing interest, and because I'm an unknown source, the media is steering away from the story. Then, the bomb I have been waiting for hits and I do all I can to hold on.

~Threats from the Attorney General's Office~

"Lori, I need to talk to you. A special agent came to our house this morning to see Steve. I told them he wasn't here, even though he was." Charlotte's voice is quivering.

"Tell Steve it's okay to talk to them. You have nothing to hide, just tell the truth," I say. Immediately, I call one of Joe's attorneys in Virginia and am quickly reminded that my naiveté will kill Joe. As anyone who watches TV crime dramas knows…never talk to the cops! Steve Rosenfield assures me they won't arrest Watson. It would mean they were admitting that he lied. It would also mean extradition, and with a Democratic governor it probably won't happen. Charlotte is anxiously rambling while I'm realizing Joe's worst nightmare concerning the Commonwealth attorneys and their tactics is coming true. Charlotte says the agent asked if Richard or I threatened Steve. She told him, "I didn't see anything like that, they didn't talk around me. You'll have to talk with Steve." The agent warns Charlotte that Joe could get a new trial with the recantation. Worry consumes Charlotte while Steve is bordering on a breakdown. "Have Steve call me between 7 and 8:00 p.m.," I tell Charlotte. "Okay Lori, but he won't go out in the light. He's afraid the agent is watching." Steve's lawyer wants money to help and the defense team cannot pay the bond if Steve's arrested. And Charlotte certainly doesn't have bond money. This concerns me.

Richard warns me that the cops will use whatever Watson says against him. So when I get Steve on the phone I suggest that he not speak to the agent. "The lawyers all say it's the worst possible thing to do," I advise him. Knowing the prison is listening in, I attempt to share this new development, in code, with Joe. Soon we are arguing. The tension is high, my phone bill even higher, with my unreimbursed monthly bills averaging $1,000. The costs of this investigation are becoming more than I can handle. I find some relief and passage into normalcy when I speak to Jennifer before she drifts off to sleep. "Everything is going to be alright," I whisper to her. Before I go to sleep I pen this message in my journal.

> Tonight I feel the awesome weight on my shoulders of Joe's execution. I realize how much I have made a difference in this case, yet I need to do more. I have so many emotions yet I know the tender and delicate ones lie far beneath the others, for protection. I'm scared, yet I fight with all I've got. *60 Minutes* or *Dateline* will be a breakthrough for Joe. I pray whoever does it will do it right and look after Joe's interest and not just their own. Such heavy decisions, who to trust. It's all I can do to stay calm and rational. I miss Jennifer - more than I'll admit to myself and therefore to others. I feel so out of touch with her. I pray she's still the same little girl and that her strength in school and sweet love at home remains the same. I know she misses me and it's hard on her too. God, help me through this. My strength is only your hand and guidance. I'm running on pure love for fear has crept into my heart. My work for Joseph could never be compared to another's, I have completely devoted my life to him and his freedom - Lord save us. I love you Jennifer.

Early the next morning I'm on the phone with a newscaster from

60 Minutes, who informs me the prosecutors told her of Joe's extensive criminal past, blood in his car and the "match" from Lifecodes. My work has doubled, for now I have to combat this in sharing the truth about the evidence. I am furious that the prosecutor has willfully ignored *their own expert's opinion*, and continues to refer to the DNA test as a match, as opposed to the only viable result, which is an exclusion. With the pressure mounting everywhere, Joe calls to inform me that a guard named Kevin Lutz at Mecklenburg has agreed to offer an affidavit stating that former death row inmate David Pruett had confessed to the Helen Schartner murder. Joe wants the *lawyers* to call him at prison, not me. Lutz told Joe that Pruett had told other guards as well. "Why aren't your lawyers following through with the Pruett confession?" Now the guards are helping Joe.

Since *60 Minutes* is now slanted toward the prosecution, I decide to give the story to John Block at NBC *Dateline*. Bob Smith was unavailable to correct the *60 Minutes* view of the Fourth Circuit Opinion and Alan Effron never bothered to follow through, even though I had asked him. As if knowing I need help, Michael Radelet calls this morning and cheerfully exclaims the affidavit concerning the snitch is strong. He agrees to give *60 Minutes* a call. His assistance will help corroborate evidence of Joe's innocence. If the lawyers won't help me I'll get help wherever I can!

Finally, when Alan calls the guard at Mecklenburg, he tells me that something is fishy. He was transferred to personnel, who wouldn't give him any information. They said he was not there today and would not comment on yesterday. It's obvious the prison knows something is up with Lutz. They *must* be listening to our calls. Damn Alan for saying his name on the phone last night with Joe. My mind is in turmoil. Never have I been so involved with such deceit, lies and the strong urgency to execute an innocent person. They are pushing hard. God, please help me regain control.

~International Plea~

Meanwhile, on the row, they are walking Joe Payne to the death house. The mentally torturous ordeal has a heightened effect on Joe. He can't escape the fact that he's next. Somehow I force myself not to care, realizing I must conserve my energy to save Joe. Truthfully, I need to think, or rest, but I can't. The clock is ticking too fast. Forty-six days left until Joe's execution. I need a miracle.

By this time I had figured out that Joe was not going to receive any media exposure in the United States. The prosecution has interfered with each and every attempt I made, by either threatening to sue the media outlet or skewing the facts to convince them of Joe's undeniable guilt. Joe's lawyers were doing nothing to help. I knew I had to reach foreign sources if I was to get Joe any justice. I decide to reach out internationally and get the names of people in the French and Italian media. One particular journalist takes an interest in Joe's case, displaying frustration that Virginia's 21-day rule would not allow new evidence after 21 days of conviction. DNA evidence of innocence was not enough. This inflamed the journalist's sense of justice. She wrote about Joe's case in a front-page article in the well known Italian newspaper, *Corriere Della Sera*. The newspaper reached over 4 million readers. Immediately, I saw a huge influx of emails on Joe's website.

In what would normally have been good news for Joe, he was focused on activities at home. Having seen an entire front page and inside newspaper article on Joe Payne's claim of innocence, Joe was, of course, greatly disappointed. He knows he has a case stronger than Joe Payne, but no one will listen. The reality of the situation has made Joe deeply depressed. Joe needs nothing less than a miracle. We need a break. *Anything* will do.

The kind of break I wanted was a positive one so when I receive news that Watson recanted his recantation I am horrified. On November 5, 1996 the cops pay a visit to Steve. Agent Williams informs Steve he had better call Robert Harris and "straighten this mess out or you will be charged with perjury in the morning." Steve's fear took control, overriding his conscience—he gave in and called Harris. Instead of asking Steve what happened, in a desire to hear the truth, he put more fear into Steve's heart. "Did she offer you sexual favors or did they offer you weed?" Even for Harris this must have been an all-time low, but not outside his reality. Harris wanted to know how long we were there. He told Steve he would be sending a cop back to his house tonight for a recantation of the recantation. Steve, in a panicked state, and afraid of going to jail, commits his hand to paper and that night, writes a three sentence recantation stating he was coerced. Joe O'Dell was right. He knows the game. He's played it with them before.

Steve is now sadly expressing to me what he has done, looking for a way to make it right. He draws strength from my resolve to keep on fighting. I am thinking fast as I pick up the receiver to call Mike Gooding (a newscaster) to tell him of the Attorney General's intimidation. With Steve still on the phone, we reach the *Virginian-Pilot*. Steve agrees to hold to the recantation he swore out for the governor and the people, and for Joe O'Dell. He wants to fix what he has now done. David Baugh agrees to represent Steve in Virginia if he is charged with perjury. Next, Watson pays a visit to his lawyer, "who is not very helpful," says Watson. Too dirty, I presume. Easier to leave this one alone.

Soon thereafter, I speak briefly with *Dateline* and am informed they have spoken at length with Richard Reyna, but were rushed when they spoke to Bob Smith. Why am I not surprised? An inmate's attorney is crucial when it comes to innocence cases. Joe never had this. In my eyes, and his, it was and is killing him—both literally and figuratively.

I am preparing the affidavit for Steve to sign concerning the Attorney General's intimidation. I conference him in on a three-way call to NBC *Dateline*. He bravely agrees to talk to them. Steve Chang questions Watson and I can feel his uncertainty until the very end when he tells Watson that he admired him for what he was doing. Chang wants

Lifecodes' full report. It's obvious he's been talking with the Commonwealth. I must counter this with subsequent courtroom expert testimony from the federal hearing on this very issue, and the judge's conclusion that the scientifically conclusive result deems the blood is *not* the victim's.

I realize that both Joe and I are at our wits' end.

"Steve Rosenfield please," I ask his secretary to put us through.

When he answers I confide in him how I am feeling. "I can't take it anymore, Steve." He patiently tries to calm me down. "I'll call Chip in the morning." Chip is one of Joe's lawyers. Before he hangs up, Steve tells me, "Someone needs to take control of the case and get affidavits from experts." I am not hearing anything I don't already know. We've been told this before.

The Attorney General's office ups the ante. They returned to visit Steve, Charlotte tells me. As a result, Steve admitted himself into a psychiatric clinic. He is now going to give an affidavit to the Attorney General's office *against* Joe. I have Charlotte read his letter to me and I am sickened. It speaks of how he cares, but "Joe confessed." My highs are at their lowest and my lows can't get much lower. I am grasping now for the truth to be heard by anyone who will listen. I feel like David up against Goliath.

In need of a social event in my life that has nothing to do with prisons, death row, or the scum that serve in political offices, I get into my car and drive to New Jersey to see my daughter. Her friend's bar mitzvah will serve as an excuse for me to have some fun. My life has become so introverted with Joe and this case that I forget what it's like to socialize. It doesn't take long before I am laughing, disguising the pain I feel for Joe deep inside my tired body. The next day Jennifer and I enjoy the Jets and Patriots game. It's the best day I have had in over a year. It's *so* much fun to spend time with Jen, just the two of us.

NBC *Dateline* is getting cold feet. They still want to do the story, but need to convince the executive producer. I ask Barry Scheck to help influence the result. For half an hour he speaks to them about the blood exclusion and inconclusive results. "What Lori Urs says is right about the DNA." Barry says PCR testing is more definitive than when Roger Coleman performed DNA testing. Roger was a Virginia death row inmate who professed his innocence for years. His DNA results, posthumously, confirmed his guilt. Barry emphatically states, "Only sperm testing will be conclusive for the state." We strategically talk, outside of NBC, about how to approach DNA testing given the petition for certiorari.

The next day I reach out to Kitty Behan from Arnold and Porter. Kitty casually advises me that they will execute Joe if we don't do new DNA testing. They will rely upon the Fourth Circuit opinion. *Dateline* is *still* not sure they want to do the story. The producer believes it's too "iffy." *Have they not read all I have sent to them? Can they not see the fabrication of facts the prosecutors keep regurgitating?* If one is not committed to reviewing all the evidence, studying the court opinions and following it closely, they can easily be swayed by the prosecution. It's becoming clear that in this game one needs to be open minded, or the game is over. Unfortunately, most people are not.

"I'm going to die, Lori." Joe say the words that stab me in the heart. I refuse to listen. I can't talk about it. I know I'm supposed to be supportive yet I cannot think of his death.

To understand the expert testimony I contact Dr. Spence and Dr. Diel. Bob says we don't need an affidavit, just their testimony. I disagree. One never knows when a tragic accident can prevent testimony from reaching its destination. An affidavit tells a statement, whether the affiant is dead or alive. I decide instead to move on to something else. I use my time to update the Internet petition. Several weeks earlier I started a petition to capture all the responses to Joe's case from Italy and around the world.

In the morning I receive a phone call from Kris Sperry's secretary. "He is absolutely not interested in helping with this case. He's busy," she mutters on the phone. Unconvinced of this sudden change of heart, I press her for more information. My sense is he's been tainted by Dr. Presswalla, the Commonwealth's medical examiner. I tell her this is leaving me in a bind, this last minute pull-out. She then mentions a fee. "For what, he hasn't done anything yet?" I still have not learned the game. Perhaps money would have changed his mind. *Of course Lori*, I am self-muttering now. She tells me she is sending all the information back. "He knows who you are." *Exactly what is that supposed to mean?* The prosecution will stop at nothing to discredit me. But, why not perform additional DNA testing? It would confirm their conviction and prove Joe's guilt. The answer is clear to me and to those who know the case. The evidence is circumstantial at best and does not directly link Joe to the crime. They cannot take a chance. It would make them look bad. Alberi has not given up his quest for a judgeship nomination and Governor Allen seeks a seat in the Senate. Big aspirations can only get stifled by a wrongful conviction.

~Legal Strategy~

In the back of my mind I am still pondering how to approach the misleading facts laid out in the Fourth Circuit court opinion. In the death penalty world, the number of lawyers who are more dedicated to their clients than their careers is small. I had come to learn the names of those who were either brilliant and or devoted to excellence. George Kendall's name was one of those on the list. I call his office to discuss strategy on how to best correct the factual record in the Fourth Circuit, the court of long known ill-repute to death row inmates. As I reflect upon the enormous task of how to correct the record without making the court look bad, I start gathering all the relevant court documents to compile my support for this endeavor. Before I start working, I reach out to Steve Watson's family to see how he's doing. Rose, his sister, has become the designated family contact.

"Rose, this is Lori. How is Steve? Please tell him I'm thinking about him and wish him well. Stay strong."

Rose explains to me how scared Steve is of perjury charges.

"Steve says he's having nightmares of cops at his front door," Rose tells me.

She tries to convey to me that Steve felt much better when he told the truth, but they don't want to hear the truth. He hasn't called the Attorney General's office yet. I suggest to her that Steve do nothing until he is well. I let her know that the letter he sent to me about his recantation being wrong is nonsense. I know better. They are clearly words spoken from the Attorney General's office and put on paper for effect.

Just before I start to put pen to paper I decide to put a package together for a German news reporter. It can't hurt. No one seems to care in the U.S. Perhaps an international source cannot be reached by the prosecution, or have the same effect as it does in this country.

For the next three days I work on pulling together all the corrections to the numerous factual errors that just came from the highest court hearing Joe's case. During this time I'm also recruiting the Roman Catholic Diocese. Bishop Sullivan's office agrees to write a letter for Joe and will get others to do the same. Desperation knows no religious boundaries so I also reach out to the Episcopal Bishop who agrees to do the same.

Charlotte telephones to say that Steve wants to talk to me. He's home from the hospital.

"I thought you'd be angry with me, Lori," he says in a pitiful tone.

"No, Steve," I assure him. "I understand you are scared, but it's wrong what the A.G.'s office is doing."

"Lori, they didn't care about the truth. Never once asked me about it. Sure, I'll sign another affidavit to what happened and how I felt threatened by them. Charlotte agrees to sign one, too."

I can tell Steven is not strong and I am not confident he will stand by the truth. I decide to wait on the second affidavit until last minute.

On November 16, 1996 I receive the certiorari petition in the mail. As this is our last shot at hope, my eyes are peeled to the pages as I start to read its content. It does not take long before I'm feeling betrayed. There is nothing in it about innocence. They don't plan on addressing the actual innocence claim. I leave a message for Bob and Alan to return my call. The morning doesn't pass before I receive a call from Bob. He agrees to look at the factual section and directs Alan to discuss it with me. After its revision, the petition is clear and persuasive, focusing on the *Simmons* issue.

I suppose when you are recruited from a blue chip law firm you can expect to be pulled in on a Sunday if your client is about to die. After church service I return home to a day of phone calls. Debo (one of the attorneys at Paul Weiss) and I are furiously working on the factual errors for half the day, pulling together all the citations. We are assembling it as an appendix to the petition for certiorari. The lawyers are working hard now.

After finalizing the factual errors, and strategy for the clemency petition, I fax it off to Paul, Weiss, Rifkind, Wharton & Garrison. Peter Finn from the *Washington Post* and Frank Green from the *Richmond Times Dispatch* are both interested and are now looking at the material. The top-notch lawyers' meeting is tomorrow and I have brought them all up to speed. Joe O'Dell's fate is in their hands. I wish I could be there. Just as I am finishing up with them, I hear the phone clicking. I know it's a call from Joe. In all of our wildest dreams I would never have imagined hearing such extraordinary news from Joe.

~Italian Intervention~

"Lori, you will never believe this. I just received a letter of support from Italy. It's someone really important."

Joe reads to me a letter he received from the son of a powerful woman in the Italian Parliament. They have written to the Italian ambassador and other influential and powerful people here in America and have told Governor Allen they can get the whole Parliament involved if need be. But she hoped the governor would do the right thing. I'm thrilled to hear this news. Maybe it will be the thing that works. Still, I keep praying for Joe.

With every inch forward I still feel that Alberi is trying to push me two feet back. Joe has expressed reservations about the *Washington Post*. He has more reason not to believe in the media, but I'm trying to still have hope. I have to. Peter Finn tells me he spoke with Alberi, who is pushing Joe's criminal past as a reason to execute him. He says the blood doesn't matter and the blood in his car was substantial. What?! I am incredulous. The blood was the only thing they had at trial and now it doesn't matter? I am perplexed at the power Alberi has over the media and confused that while the record is clear on the facts, the evidence is so easily distorted because most reporters will not read enough to learn the truth. Joe Jackson was the exception. However, I didn't know that, yet.

I feel Joe's tension as we argue about the *Post* interview. I am trying to protect him and it's coming across all wrong. I feel he's falling apart—he hasn't been himself for days. I reflect upon what I just thought and realize how absurd it is. This man is about to be killed and *I feel he's falling apart?* When I hang up the phone, my tears flow freely. All my energy has been zapped, my faith stomped on by the reality of possible defeat. Somehow, an hour later, I feel something odd calm my mind and body. It is telling me not to let this interfere with my faith. Joe needs me now. It is my spiritual leader.

Finn and Kilpatrick are looking for materials, so I send them a copy of the crime scene photograph of the victim's bent black umbrella and all the information about Watson, along with the facts as outlined for the Fourth Circuit. Joe's voice on the phone today sounds uplifted, and I smile when I think he has rejoined the living. I read him a letter that I wrote to him and he cries. It's amazing how much we are in need of each other's support. Essentially, that's all we have.

Meanwhile, I check out Joe's criminal record in Florida. I contact his trial attorney, Moses Meide. Moses confides in me his feelings of Joe's guilt in the kidnapping of a convenience store clerk. Joe's story is, of course, different. I decide to read the trial transcript for myself and assess the veracity of the victim's testimony.

Peter Finn calls and interrogates me about the "Indian" marriage with Joe. I should have known this was coming. I explain to him the nonsense of it all and that it was something Joe unilaterally did, explaining it was not authentic. I suggest he call Steven Rosenfield for a further explanation.

"Peter, I don't want to be in the papers. This story is about Joe's innocence; let's try to keep our mind on the ball."

I fax him the same request to ensure there is no misunderstanding of my intent to simply get the facts of Joe's case right. Finn, however, senses a sensational story. "This is too good, Lori," Finn mutters over the phone with almost a chuckle. Still, I'm praying someone will focus on Joe's innocence.

That evening the lawyers call and for an hour we go over the certiorari petition. I fax them all of my citations and finally after midnight, I collapse in bed. I will finish my work for the lawyers in the morning, followed by some chores around the house that have escaped my attention. That next day I have dinner with a friend at the Impotent Oyster in Chatham and relax with a glass of wine and a fine clambake dinner.

Chapter 18

~The Alibi Witness~

As I step inside the front door I hear the phone ringing in the kitchen and make a mad dash for it. I grab the phone and hear Richard Reyna's excited voice on the other end.

"Lori, John Nutter's mom says John said yes, he was in a fight with Joe. He told her the prosecution flew him in (200 miles) and paid for his food, motel, and then when the trial was reset, they never called him back. He said they didn't call cause he would hurt their case. He said Joe was obnoxious and that the fight didn't happen exactly as Joe said it did, but *it did happen.* John's type O, Lori. We got our man!"

This was great news and I hung onto Richard's every word. He said he would interview Nutter in person. It would mean a trip to Florida.

Prior to visiting the sunshine state I have other things on my agenda. Next week is Thanksgiving and I plan to spend it visiting a man condemned to die. I am now suddenly recognized, again, as Joe's "spouse." It's the prison's continued way to discredit me and to cast doubt on my work. I change focus and concentrate on the next few days, remembering the advice of one of the lawyers, "Pick your battles, Lori," I was told about this issue.

On my way to death row for the holiday I plan to visit with Jennifer in New Jersey. Frantically working, I set the pace to finish before leaving Cape Cod. Peter Finn is falling for the prosecutor's Lifecodes' claim. He doesn't understand the factual errors of the Fourth Circuit, nor does he understand that a factual finding in a district court cannot be changed. Although I am laying it out for him and offering him all the solid court records and expert testimony he needs, he is simply not getting it. He may be a loose canon, or our best ally. I can't tell which. One thing I do know is that he is digging hard. More important things are happening now.

~Breakfast Before Death?~

Michael Baden's pleasant voice urges me to the fax machine for his report on the victim's stomach contents and head wounds. He also faxes it to the attorneys. Michael confirms Richard's thoughts in his letter dated November 25, 1996. My jubilation exudes with a loud "yes" to no one but myself.

> Dear Ms. Urs:
>
> I have reviewed the autopsy report, scene and autopsy photographs and investigative reports that you forwarded to me relative to the death of Helen C. Schartner.
>
> Ms. Schartner was 44 years old when she was found dead of manual strangulation on 2/7/85. In addition to the evidence of strangulation, semen was found in the vagina and multiple lacerations were present on the scalp. These lacerations are consistent with having been inflicted by many different types of blunt heavy objects including tire irons, hammers, metal pipes, the handle of a heavy knife or a handgun, etc, depending on the configuration of that object.
>
> The autopsy report does describe about 100 grams of "a residual meal: containing identifiable fragments of "potato, tomato, and some greens ..." **In my opinion, assuming Ms. Schartner had not eaten any such food from 8:30 p.m. to 11:30 p.m. while at the County**

Line Lounge, she would have had to have eaten this food after she left the nightclub and about 2 hours before she was murdered. (emphasis added)

I would be pleased to discuss this matter with you further should you wish to do so.

Very truly yours,
Michael M. Baden, M.D.

There is no evidence, nor any testimony, that Helen ate at the County Line Lounge. This means that she left the County Line bar and went out to eat with someone before she was murdered. It also suggests that the wounds on her head could have been from any circular object, not necessarily a gun as was testified to at trial and argued by the prosecution. This was big news. It directly challenged the prosecution's theory that she was killed immediately after she left the bar. It also cast doubt on their "theory" that Joe had somehow raped and killed her before driving several miles down the street to a fight at the Brass Rail, which was reported and confirmed by police reports at approximately 1:15 a.m.

When I hang up with Michael I call Larry Mueller in California. He is a population geneticist who has agreed to help. As an expert in serology testing, he informs me that you can have the same ten enzymes as another person and still have an exclusion. The prosecution in Joe's case had serology-tested ten of the 15 enzymes to claim the blood of Helen Schartner was "consistent" with the blood on Joe's clothing. Larry went on to say that Lifecodes' band shifting theory is bullshit. "It's the worst lab. You *can* share similar DNA patterns," he says.

Mueller's opinion is mirrored by a Louisiana case, *State of Louisiana v. Quatrevingt*, 670 So.2d 197, 206, *reh'g denied*, (Mar.29, 1996); *cert. denied*, 117 S.Ct. 294 (1996), two other court cases, and by all experts before the District Court, including the Commonwealth's expert in Joe's case. In *Quatrevingt* the defendant asserted that the trial court erred in allowing evidence of DNA testing to be introduced at trial. Specifically, he claimed that under the well known standard of admissibility for determining reliability of novel scientific evidence set forth in *Daubert v. Merrell Dow Pharmaceuticals, Inc.*, 509 U.S. 579, 113 S.CT. 2786 (1993), the procedure used by Lifecodes to correct for band shifting is not a reliable methodology and should have been *inadmissible*. In that case, and after a review of the scientific background of DNA profiling and the Standard for Admitting Scientific Evidence, the court addressed the specific method of correcting for band shifting. Dr. McElfresh testified that "Lifecodes is the only laboratory which attempts to correct for band shifting and still declare a match." The defendant's experts, Drs. Cohen and Jazwinski, disputed Lifecodes' claims and testified there was no way to correct for band shifting and that generally scientists disregarded such results. He remarked that he was extremely disturbed that Lifecodes independently created a correction factor—"their own personal fudge factor that no one else accepts"—noting it had not even been documented. Dr. Cohen observed that without the correction some of the bands in the case would be outside of Lifecodes' own "match" criterion of 2 percent deviation.

Dr. Jazwinski further informed the jury that no valid methods existed to correct for the bands and that Dr. McElfresh's claim that Lifecodes' method has been peer reviewed was unfounded. In the court's opinion it refers to the fact that the jury was well aware that a serious dispute existed over the DNA testing by Lifecodes, and that other labs, including the FBI, would not have attempted to correct the bandshift, but would have declared the results *inconclusive*. The court refers to the findings in *DNA Technology in Forensic Science*, National Research Council (NRC), National Academy Press (1992). The report specifically states, "For the present, several laboratories have decided against quantitative corrections; samples that lie outside the match criterion because of apparent band shifting are declared to be "inconclusive". The committee urges further study of the problems associated with band shifting. "Until testing laboratories have published adequate studies on the accuracy and reliability of such corrections, we recommend that they adopt the policy of declaring samples that show apparent band shifting to be 'inconclusive'." The court opinion cites jurisprudence from other jurisdictions which had deemed inadmissible DNA results which have employed correction for band shifting. In two other cases, *People v. Keene*, 165 Misc. 2d. 108, 591 N.Y.S.2d 733 (N.Y Sup. Ct. 1992) and *Hayes v. State*, 660 So.2d 257, 1995 WL 368405 (Fla. 6/22/95), the courts rejected Lifecodes' correction method for band shifting under the *Frye* test, relying in part on the NRC report. The *Frye* standard is the "general acceptance standard in the scientific community" used by courts.

Simply stated, you cannot use a "DXYS14 probe" to bring together bands that have shifted and then call it a match! This is what Lifecodes did in Joe's case and what the Commonwealth continues to refer to when claiming there is a "match," although they are aware of the above referenced cases, as well as the testimony directly from their own experts. They were also painfully aware that Judge Spencer found, after hearing testimony from both sides, that the "match" referred to in Lifecodes' report of the O'Dell case was scientifically not acceptable and, therefore, accepted the correct conclusion that it was "inconclusive." The only other DNA test performed by Lifecodes resulted in an *exclusion*, as also concluded by Judge Spencer in his September 6, 1994 opinion.

It always bothered me that novice serology expert, Jacqueline Emrich, had been allowed to testify. Worse yet, Joe O'Dell was not given the opportunity to challenge her testimony with his own expert. The expert he did have, Dr. Guth, was intimidated by Alberi and Test when they wrote to him and requested, by way of a subpoena *duces tecum*, a listing of all his property and equipment. They wanted to see if he paid taxes on all his assets. They filed this request with the IRS. This would intimidate Guth they thought, and it did. They would stoop as low as it took to get rid of any witnesses that could help Joe. In the mountain of files I had read there was a certificate of analysis by Dr. Guth, issued after Alberi's tactics. His analysis of the footprint casting confirmed results that the footprint found at the scene was not Joe O'Dell's, nor did it belong to the witness who found the body. His analysis stated the tire evidence "does not allow a particular vehicle to be associated with the crime scene". Regarding blood and seminal stains he reported, "From an early point in this re-evaluation, it was plagued with the problem that preservable evidence was not only mis-packaged by police evidence technicians in the field (such as multiple, stained garments being placed within the same paper bag wherein cross-contamination might have occurred) but the preservation methods in the evidence storage room were inadequate to protect the labile biochemical and serological characteristics of the stains for future testing." Finally, regarding hair comparisons, though the medical examiner's autopsy report states, *"no obvious foreign fibers are noted under the fingernails,"* Dr. Guth's report indicates that two hairs sent to him for re-examination were identified by the state lab as having come from the victim's fingernails. Guth's examination of those hairs revealed they were consistent with the head hair of Joe O'Dell. Understandably concerned, Guth criticizes the Tidewater Laboratory, stating the "origins of these two significant hairs is unknown since no adequate chain of custody voucher has been found (or turned over by the Commonwealth Attorney) between the Medical Examiner's collection of evidence and its receipt by the Tidewater Laboratory. He then lists the following questions raised by his finding(s):

1. Were these samples mistakenly labeled from sources other than their true ones?
2. Were there in fact no hairs found under the victim's fingernails? If not, where did these originate? Why did this evidence get misidenti-

fied or mislabeled?

3. Could "cross-contamination" of one source of hair with another have occurred to account for these findings?
4. Were these occurrences "accidental," a result of poor procedures, human error or intentional?
5. Why is there no chain of custody in receipts between the Medical Examiner and the Crime Laboratory?
6. Could other hair evidence in this case have suffered the same lack of integrity due to similar causes?

Joe O'Dell and Paul Ray decided not to use the report because it identified Joe's hair was "consistent" with the surprise two hairs suddenly showing up as having come from under her fingernails. Guth's report, however, lists so many problems with the result that I would have used it regardless, pointing to the fact that there is incontrovertible evidence that the medical examiner did NOT find any hairs under her fingernails. This raised further doubt, and support, as to the unreliability of the testing performed by Emrich.

It's pouring as I make the six-hour drive to Princeton to visit with Jennifer. It's the only bit of reality I have centered in my world. My heart melts when I see her after having been away for so long. Jennifer runs to my car and hops into the front seat. I lean over to kiss her and hug her tightly. We both look forward to spending the night before I must drop her off at her father's house. My next drive will be the eight hours it takes me to reach South Hill, Virginia, the night before Thanksgiving.

On the Tuesday before Thanksgiving two guards stop in front of Joe and Ronnie Hokes' prison cell and ask how they want to die. Ronnie doesn't answer. Joe told them electrocution. The neighboring inmates gasped when they heard this. What Joe really wanted to say was the meanest thing he could think of because he was so hurt. But he didn't.

I arrive at the only motel in South Hill and get ready to spend an hour, or four, depending on the holiday visiting crowd, with Joseph

O'Dell. We calculate that 11:00 a.m. will give us a good shot at spending more time together. On Thanksgiving Day I am thankful to visit with Joe for 4½ hours. The time passes quickly as we enjoy a casual visit, meant to unite our souls to strengthen us in the coming days.

The next day, just before leaving the motel room, my cell phone rings. Richard is ecstatic about John Nutter.

"Lori, Nutter has agreed to meet with me. He also still admits to being in a fight with Joe."

This news is almost too good to be true. Richard will be meeting with John at 6:00 p.m. tomorrow night. Nutter promises to help in any way he can, within reason.

I'm at the prison to visit with Joe at 11:15 a.m. We are bumped shortly afterwards at 12:30 p.m. Having read the morning paper, we were both aware that Governor Allen was front-page news with three executions scheduled for December. It's all we can do to keep the faith so we agree not to discuss the news. Feeling tense, I try to shake off my headache. And I'm instinctively aware that I am distancing myself from Joe. The thought of helping him after he is released and spending time with him is difficult to imagine. He has been so tortured, I feel it would haunt me. The reality of this all is so overwhelming. But it would be foolish to allow emotion to cloud my mission. I try to ignore the feelings.

Right about now Joe and I agree not to talk to the reporters. He wants it quiet for the governor. His scheduled death is only weeks away. I have never felt so at odds in my life.

During our visit on Sunday Joe tells me he is preparing for the reality of being strapped to the electric chair. His statement paralyzes me. He is nervous, even with the news about Nutter. "Lori, I am at the end of my rope. I cannot believe my lawyers are asking for clemency instead of a pardon. I am innocent!" I had discussed the legal standard with the attorney and he said it was "clear and convincing evidence" of innocence. What more do we need? The lawyers are still not fighting.

Only Richard and I are. I silently ask for God's help.

Today is the scheduled "spousal" visit with Joseph. It's such a strange concept, but the lawyers suggest I go along with it. We have one hour. For the first time in over three years, Joseph and I can embrace, touch hands, even run our fingers across one another's face to see if we are real. Is this a dream, or a nightmare for us both? As Joe walks toward me, I can see he has no handcuffs on. I later find out that he had requested that—he knows how I hate to see him restrained. Our hands are joined the entire hour—his so warm, strong yet gentle. Our conversation centers around the case and, of course, each other. At one point the clock indicates it's 10:40 a.m. and in what appears to be five to ten minutes later, it is 11:10 a.m. We are relishing every second of this hour together. Joe takes his hand and touches my cheek. His fingers move to my chin. He brushes his hand across my face, savoring every touch, every moment, memorizing it until again. I wipe his eye and softly brush a speck of tissue off his other eye. I, too, savor the human touch, the intimacy of being next to one another while looking directly into each other's eyes, absent bulletproof glass to distort them. I am reassured. Our dedication and resolve is at its strongest. When it is time to leave I lean over the table separating us, reach my arms past his shoulders and around his neck, and kiss him goodbye. He slides his hand down my back and rests it beneath my waist.

All my life I had wanted a man to love and adore me with all his heart. And to show me in ways so tender. Blinded by confusion in my marriage, I couldn't see that I had it right in front of me, reality testing its existence. How strange it was to have this man, a man so outside of my world, one I would abhor had it not been for destiny, to be the man who would wish to fulfill those dreams. The way he touched my face, my chin, was the first time a man had done so. So lovingly, and with such adoration. It was a woman's dream. But not this way. I was tortured by its reality.

Ready to leave South Hill and the barbed wired prison behind me,

I'm back on the road home. On the drive I phone Cellmark Diagnostics to set up a blood draw for John Nutter. I phone Richard the next morning to hook him up with the lab and lawyers. Nutter's blood has been drawn with a strong affidavit supporting his position. The affidavit eliminated the need for the 1988 "telecon" between the lawyers and Nutter. They had spoken to him eight years earlier and never did a damn thing about it.

The car quietly approaches the pristine neighborhood in Princeton where Jen's friend lives. A brief cordial visit allows me to depart quickly for the Hyatt Hotel, where Jennifer and I relish each other's company before I must return her to school the next morning.

~International Help~

I am always surprised at how desolate Chatham is in off-season. It's incredibly eerie at times—this quaint fishing town that's covered with fog so often the locals laugh when they say, "Just wait a minute and the weather will change." The sound of crushed seashells welcome me home as the tires of my car roll across the driveway well past sunset. I am missing Jennifer terribly, having witnessed her growth spurt this year in just a 24-hour window.

Morning frost covers the manicured glades of the grass in my backyard as I watch the glistening of the sun's rays trying to peek out from the morning fog. Standing at my kitchen window with a cup of tea in my hand, in the quiet of the hour, the ringing phone interrupts my thoughts. I hear an undeniable German accent on the other end. It's Andrea from the German newspaper I had contacted. The story on Joe will run next week. A quick "thank you" is followed by a smile as my mind takes me back to yesterday.

The long drive to Cape Cod encourages musical company with tunes from a CD I had mixed some time ago. George Strait muffles a call on my cell phone from an unknown number. Six rings later the caller identifies the number as a national broadcast radio station in Rome, Italy. The man on the other end is expressing his excitement that the Parliament has collected 150 signatures for Joe's cause! In a strong Italian accent he requests an interview, live at 10:30 a.m. I have just 15 minutes to prepare. In anticipation of the call, I pull off the busy highway to quiet the noise and concentrate on what is happening. Did he just refer to me as Joe's wife? I don't correct him—it's not an important matter. What matters is that someone cares. When he calls back I answer on the first ring and for five to eight minutes I dutifully answer questions and speak about Joe's plight. As I speak, this reporter interprets my words to all the Italian listeners. They seemed enthused when they learn I, too, am of Italian decent. I am not shy in discussing American apathy. By comparison I note how the warmth and compassion of the Italians make me proud to be one. "Henry Kissinger pardoned a dog in the states. If that can be done, we should ask for the pardon of a human being," I begin to rile them up. The interviewer asks, "What do you want to tell the world?" I speak clearly and without reservation, "People should call or write the president of our country and the Governor of Virginia and *please, fight for what is right*." My voice is strong with conviction as I utter the words, "We must all unite for justice." It was a great interview. As I veer off from the shoulder of the road I'm somewhat in disbelief. At the time, I am unaware of the power of this phone call, and the chain of international events that will follow. For the moment, I am simply grateful to be heard.

Joe's sister draws me back to death when she calls to tell me she wants to see her brother prior to his execution. I am stunned by her sudden desire to visit Joe after never having stepped foot on death row in the ten long years of his existence there. Far from complaining about it, Joe always told me of his disappointment in her. The thought of death changes people. But I am not ready to think about death. I am still fighting for life.

Frustrated with the disruption of my own life, I decide to bring normalcy back. Maybe if I have my hair trimmed this morning and visit with the girls at the salon, it will lift my spirits. It doesn't work. No matter where I go or what I do I still feel so incredibly alone. With Joe's execution set for less than two weeks away the tension is unbearable. We get into our worst fight ever with our final words in high pitch before he hangs up on me. In over three years he has *never* hung up on me. I hate it when people hang up on one another. It's a sign of such disrespect. I am hurt, but I also know I'm trying to control these last days because everything else is so out of control. Joe is doing the same and resents me for this. I couldn't possibly blame him. Just before he hangs up I find out why he is freaking out. Beaver, his friend, was killed tonight. Murdered by the Commonwealth of Virginia in a judicial execution. I have learned through the years that most of the inmates don't show any emotion when a fellow prisoner is put to death. It stuns Joe every time.

Chapter 19

~Deathwatch~

Joe O'Dell is now on "deathwatch". This means the guards watch him every hour on the hour. Having heard from other inmates who have temporarily escaped death, he knows the hell of Greensville, the place of no return. Many of his friends have walked the dead man's path. It is beyond my imagination how he manages to survive each day with the knowledge of the date, exact time and manner of his own death. He is so close to death now that he tells me he would kill himself if it weren't for me. At this point I believe him. With thoughts of gas chambers, lethal needles and electric chairs running through my mind, I am numb. I cannot write anymore nor can I talk to anyone. His words echo in my ears, once again, "Lori, I'm going to die." My heart sinks and I do all I can just to hold on. Psychologically they are trying to destroy him, torturing him all the way until they kill him. I will him to hold on. I haven't given up. There's so much more to do.

~Italy~

Little do I know on the other side of the world a government with strong convictions against the death penalty is rallying to Joe's aid. I'm standing in the kitchen of my Cape Cod home when a call from Italy

284 LORI ST JOHN

comes through.

"Are you Lori Urs?" the Italian man asks.

"Yes, this is she," I reply. Who is this man?

"Hello." He speaks with a wonderful Italian accent. "My name is Luciano Neri and I am from the Italian Parliament. I wanted to speak to you about the Joseph O'Dell case."

I can hardly believe what I'm hearing. Italian Parliament? Why are they calling me? I listen intently as Mr. Neri describes his interest in the case and offers his help. He explains that ever since the story hit the front page of the newspapers in Italy, it has been talked about all over the country. He feels he can get the backing of the entire Italian Parliament. We agree to talk soon again.

Feelings of desperation give way to the notion of optimism and hope when I receive another call. Someone from the Italian Parliament is asking if Joe O'Dell can be interviewed in front of the American Embassy on Tuesday morning. Apparently, all members of the Parliament are working on an official declaration on Joe's behalf. I'm not sure how I intend to pull this off, but I quickly respond, "Yes!" What currently is stirring on the other side of the world is something I couldn't possibly know.

Just two days earlier, two prison guards had approached Joe's cell. They had snapped his picture for an update and asked again how he wished to die. I suppose the picture is meant to memorialize what he looks like just days before they kill him. Sort of like the first picture they took of him when he was arrested. The difference of eleven years was startling. The man with a full head of dark brown wavy hair with a bright white smile and piercing blue eyes, a toned body and bounce in his step, was now almost bald, his bounce long gone. His eyes had lost any life to them, his skin was now pasty white. "I'm not going to die," Joe replied to the request to choose the manner of his death. "I hope not," replied the guard. Still, they were going to place four guards outside of his door from 11:40 p.m. to 12:00 a.m. just in case he changed his mind. Two showed up. They never asked him again, but camped out as promised. While seated outside Joe's cell, Joe asks if they would like a cup of coffee. "Yes," one guard replies. "How do you want it, cream and sugar?" Joe's character was revealing itself in what I always said spoke volumes about oneself. In times of adversity you can tell a lot about the character of a person. I was not surprised by how Joe could seemingly distance himself from the reality of the role of his keepers. They were there to be sure he did not commit suicide before they killed him. There to guide him to his death, literally, over the next few days. I cried when Joe told me this.

Meanwhile, Larry Mueller, the population geneticist, calls from California to offer a statement about the ten enzymes and how it is possible to have ten enzymes consistent with another person and still have a DNA exclusion with the same blood. In short, the fact that ten enzymes of the blood on Joe's clothes were the same as the victim's meant nothing. Nothing at all. It seemed silly that one would need such a statement in light of the powerful testimony of the DNA exclusion. But the prosecution would argue that the blood tests at trial showed a match and no one would know this was untrue. At trial the experts could only opine it was "consistent." Alberi and Test preferred the word "match."

With only a few days left to live, Joe insists on seeing a copy of the certiorari petition. He wants to see a paralegal or lawyer in the morning for fear the lawyers will screw it up. It's strange because without having the knowledge I now possess, I would have thought he was paranoid, or just overly excited. He was neither. They had an uncanny way of screwing things up and easing the path to execution. Nothing is easy on the row, or from the legal ivory tower in New York City.

There is now only time for last minute details and the press. By now I am well aware the Italians are strongly protesting Joe's fate. Amnesty International in Italy interviewed Joe. I received their nine questions ahead of time and prepped him to ensure he was prepared. The interviewer called me back to say how moved she was. Joe also spoke with Georgio Morelli, a newspaper reporter from New York who had called Alberi, who, in his usual style portrayed Joe as a dangerous man. The reporter acknowledges Joe's past crimes were 30 years ago and agrees the prosecution is using this to kill Joe, instead of focusing on the evidence. The reporter blurts out, "I hope the prosecutor doesn't prosecute me now!" Joe and I laugh. We relish the opportunity to speak to an intelligent man who can see through this game.

Frank Green of the *Richmond Times Dispatch* is after a sensational story about Joe's execution. I can feel the bloodthirsty excitement as he asks me about Joe's choice for the electric chair. I clear my throat and offer a comment. "Joe was forced into a decision. It was a personal and private choice which he did not know was to be released to the public. He is not seeking media attention. The only thing he ever wanted from the media was for them to state the facts of his case of innocence, accurately and properly."

I can hear Frank typing away in the background. I have no confidence the quote will be correctly stated. But I did learn that the Italians were putting pressure on him to print Joe's story.

The Italian Parliament members' support has reached 80 percent. The official declaration to stop the execution and allow DNA testing for Joe was signed this week. It will be presented to Governor Allen next week. To the best of my knowledge, this is the first time in history that the Italian Parliament has officially supported an American inmate in this way (See Exhibit I).

Time has a way of coasting when every minute counts. Staying focused on remaining strong I fight the fear of next week and the conflicting emotions it brings. While I care about this innocent man, I care *more* about the lies that are being used to justify the state action, and even more about the manner in which the prosecution is able to suppress or lie about the evidence of innocence that has surfaced. I believe if Helens Schartner's boyfriend, Ike Wright, were to stand up and confess to her brutal murder, they would ignore him, just as they have Steve Watson. It's a sickening thought, and leads me to fears about my own safety.

The quiet from the lawyers stirs me. I desperately need to know what is transpiring with the experts I have summoned to help us— Michael Radelet, Michael Baden, Barry Scheck and Governor Allen's personal pilot, John Rocovich. I decide to give the lawyers until Monday before I contact them myself.

Emotionally distraught, I remind myself that my suffering pales in comparison to what Joe is going through. Gently, Joe says to me, "Don't be scared." He warns me that he'll be in an orange jumpsuit, his head and leg completely shaven. He is not allowed to brush his teeth without first asking the guard, and must look at a large clock hanging directly on the wall in front of him, reminding him what time he will draw his last breath on earth. There is nothing to do. Nothing but wait to die. Every move he makes will be recorded, like a caged animal in an experiment. It sounds more like an archaic and barbaric ritual. Inwardly, I promise to protest this the rest of my life.

Normalcy to my world returns just briefly when Professor Nyquist calls and informs me that he's glad I'm coming back to law school. The law journal has agreed to defer my membership for one year. He'll fax me a copy of the letter. His kindness doesn't go unnoticed, nor my appreciation for having someone who likes and takes a personal interest in me.

****

Support from the Italians is strengthening and they all want to hear what Joe has to say. He is only days before execution and his story is powerful. I'm awakened at 7:00 a.m. by a phone call from Italy. Joe joins me on a three-way conference call. It's a radio interview and the show is scheduled for a full hour. I am impressed by Joe's demeanor.

His voice lacks anger. One can hear his sincere desire to be heard, to have the truth told about the evidence. He asks for no sympathy. His voice, soft yet strong, engages the audience in his fight for life. When the interview is over, Joe and I spend another hour on the phone, just the two of us. We are closer than ever in this seemingly impossible battle.

In the meantime I collect Watson's videotape for Governor Allen's private viewing. I want him to see it for himself. My patience is gone; I'm now angry with Steve Watson for lying, once again sacrificing Joe for his own well-being. These last minute details are all I have time for. In just a few days I leave for the death house in Greensville, Virginia. I whisper to myself, "Everything will be fine," in an attempt to assure myself, and against impossible odds.

I spend the entire next day on the phone. Sister Helen calls three times. She is trying to involve *Prime Time Live* to put pressure on the governor's office. For the first time in a long time I allow myself to feel emotions hidden deep inside, my words silenced by the sound of sobs. At first Helen is quiet. She hesitates before telling me not to worry because she knows full well if there was ever a time to worry, it was now. Immediately after we speak, I regain my resolve and phone Bob to remind him *he* must contact John Rocovich and John Dowd. One of the lawyers calls to ease my mind about the clemency petition and tells me what I already know: there is no evidence of guilt. "Don't worry, Lori, Bob should do the rest." When the lawyers suggest we send the clemency petition to the general assembly members, I agree.

The Italian press manages to cajole me to give them one last interview before I depart for Virginia. Joe calls and describes what he expects for the day of processing at Greensville. Apparently, there are no secrets on death row. Those that receive stays are only too shocked and brutally honest in sharing the horror that occurs only hours before their scheduled death. Joe tells me he will be X-rayed to make sure there is nothing inside him. They don't want him to kill himself before they get to him. Joe says to me, "Be strong." When we hang up I call Chaplain Bob West to gather strength.

Charlotte Watson's guilt is mounting when she calls me at this awkward time to read a letter Steve wrote to the Attorney General.

"Charlotte, I know he's lying. You both have to live with this lie. What goes around comes around. God will sit in judgment, not me."

On my way down to Virginia, I attempt to put on the face of a normal mom as I briefly visit with Jennifer. Who am I kidding? Such a casual visit would be impossible, the tension and stress too powerful to ignore. I chose instead to shield her from my emotions, leaving with a forced smile, hiding my own fear.

December 12, 1996. Thirteen days until Christmas. The holiday is nonexistent for Joe and I. When I arrive in Emporia I stop at the Greensville Correctional Center to prepare myself for tomorrow's visit with Joe. Entering the town of Jarret is akin to driving down the path to hell. My emotions have been bottled up, ready to explode, threatening to blow off the tight lid I have kept on them. I fail to maintain composure as tears stream down my cheeks, dripping to the car seat. Immediately, my thoughts turn from myself to Joe. I pray for him more than for myself.

After checking into my motel room, I jump in my car to find a liquor store. I know now I am under tremendous stress because I don't even drink. I think *just in case. I might need it.*

While at the motel I call the analytical testing center to make arrangements for them to ship Joe's blood to Cellmark for possible PCR testing. I also need to call Michael Baird at Lifecodes tomorrow to arrange the shipment of everything to Cellmark and inquire about XY chromosomal testing. The New York law firm says it will take 13 days to do the testing. I'm exploring all options and believe if I can prove the blood was from a man and not a woman, this would free Joe. But it has to be done more quickly. We don't have 13 days.

The clemency hearing is today at 2:30 p.m. All day I reflect on a conversation with the lawyers about Joe's alibi witness, wishing they'd call. They had informed me that John Nutter's blood contained four of the same enzymes as the victim's blood, but he was a PGM 1, not PGM 2-1. Since the prosecutor's expert suggested a mixture of PGM markings, I had to review the significance of this. Previously, I had called Richard to inquire about Joe's alibi fight at the Brass Rail. We reconciled Nutter's recollection with Joe's statement. The time and location frame fit. Nutter should be brought forward to substantiate Joe's alibi and to release his statement that there was no blood on Joe at 1:15 a.m. when Nutter first saw him. I'll plan to fly him in with Richard on Monday. Tuesday we'll do a press conference, whether the lawyers like it or not. If cert. (short for certiorari) isn't granted by Tuesday at 5:00 p.m., we'll do a live press conference for the six o'clock broadcast. This is essential if and only if certiorari isn't granted, which I now believe it will be. The lawyers think the *Simmons* issue is ripe to be heard. It's an issue that can save Joe's life.

Feeling sleepy I contemplate calling it a night when my thoughts are interrupted by a call from Debo at 12:45 a.m. For half an hour we speak about the possibility of a reprieve for Joe. It is almost impossible to close my eyes after we hang up.

Back home on Channel 3 my friend tells me Joe's case is on the news. They are still referring to me as his wife. It's amazing what will stick in the media. I don't have time to correct all the errors. It's easier to ignore the annoying news.

~The Death House~

I schedule my arrival in Greensville one day prior to Joe's arrival to be sure I'm here for him just in case he needs me for anything. The day passes and I finally receive his call at 7:30 p.m. Joe speaks softly and explains the nightmare of his day. "We drove right by the Inn and I saw where you're staying." The transport van took Joe from Mecklenburg to Greensville, arriving at 11:00 a.m. As expected, they X-rayed his entire body. Then they submitted him to a familiar, yet humiliating exercise, in which he had to show his cheeks and private parts. He is whispering to me now, "I never knew it was so evil, Lori."

Joe's cell is situated right in front of the "death shower". Strategically placed there, it means Joe is forced to watch Lem Tuggle, another man from death row, prepare to be killed. Joe's eyes are glazed with horror as he witnesses Tuggle taking a shower. Stunned, he watches as the guards hand him his burial clothes, after drying his naked body in preparation for his death. Tuggle's cell is adjacent to Joe. Right before his execution, Tuggle hands Joe his cards. His last words to Joe are "Hang in there, man, it's not going to happen to you." Joe says that all the guards tell him they can't believe he's there. He whispers how they are all nice to him, *even on the way over*, Joe says. It's 9:02 p.m. Tuggle was just killed by the Commonwealth. I know Joe is praying. He is witnessing it all firsthand, evil permeating the walls and air around him.

Outside of his large bare cell on a cement wall is a phone for his use. I suppose it's for those last minute clemency deals, or a stay, when one's pending death is hanging on a single individual's decision. As expected, he's in an orange jumpsuit. He has a metal bed. Cigarettes help calm his nerves. He tells me prior to visiting him, "Forgive my looks, Lori, I don't have a comb for my hair."

I dread my visit there tomorrow, but at the same time, I'm anxious to see him. We need each other now in a way no one could ever understand. We are each other's strength. On that same day I pen this letter to Joe:

Joseph,

If you are going through exactly what I am, I know it's hell, and worse. I have just arrived here and what god-awful evil place. It's as if I'm condoning it by being here but no, instead I'm here for you - to stay with you until the U.S. Supreme Court sends you back or the Governor commutes your sentence. I drove to the prison hellhole and I got the creeps. I turned back when I got there. The immediate surroundings are disgusting. It's good Bob and Sarah will be here because its weird being in a new place - strange and uncomfortable. God only knows the hell you are forced to endure and face the next few days. As I have always said, keep your head up and keep your dignity. Your little one is right by your side. I'm still fighting and will until justice is met. Your innocence will be known to the world. For whatever reason God has wanted us to walk this path, it must be so very important. He must have his reasons, maybe those not for us to understand quite yet. I have truly learned that our life is in his hands. I miss you, cannot wait to see you. I somewhat dread the process, as I know without a doubt you do, too. I am sorry for all those that know no better, they are ignorant and they are blind. In the face of all this we still must stand strong. I am anxiously waiting to hear from you - its already 5:30 p.m. I left the room only to eat. Waiting to hear from your lawyers. Tomorrow I'll be there by your side, to see you. I just called the prison and I guess I may not talk to you tonight because of Tuggle. They said at 4 p.m. the list was approved and you "chose" not to call me. I can hardly believe that. They already know who I am - they must have been given the heads up. They told me that "spiritual advisors" were there to see you. Shit...they better leave us alone! I find this sick, that citizens are involved in the murder of a fellow human being.

It's Saturday night now and I am empty inside. I cannot describe my feelings. I Imagine they are the same or similar to yours. Lord, I cannot believe that we are in such an evil situation. I promise, Joseph, I will prove your innocence. You are my inner drive. I thank God I have you and that I am strong. You have been and always will be my hero. A true hero in the eyes of the world. I am hurting that you have been subjected to such a gross miscarriage of justice. I am sorry, but I will vindicate those rights. Please know that. You have taught me so much Joseph. I thank God for you, each and every day with every breath that I take. Just as you sit numb to this mess, so, too, do I. I feel like I'm in a vacuum, such a strange, unnatural feeling.

Friday, December 13, 1996. Today I find myself driving to the death house. I know I arrive because I see the prison in front of me but I don't remember the sights along the way. I enter the building at 8:30 a.m. to be processed, searched and taken back to the L building. I'm amazed at the size of the prison and the coldness creeping from it into my bones. It wasn't the temperature that was cold, but the atmosphere in which I entered that sent chills up my spine. I finally get back to where they are holding Joe. Nerves shatter any calmness left inside me. I am scared not for me, but for what Joe must be going through. First the guard places me in a locked room with two-way mirrors. I protest, saying I was here first and want to visit Joe where his holding cell is. I know the rules. I smile at the guard and utter "please." Only then am I escorted back to Joe's cell. It's protocol that when there is more than one prisoner in the death house, only one visitor can go into the holding cell area. There was no one there when I arrived. I take a seat in the chair placed in front of Joe and gaze at him, sitting in a small cell. A cot is on the left wall with a single blue blanket and plastic pillow. Against the back wall is a metal shelf where he keeps his legal papers. In the front corner is a steel toilet and sink combination. A grungy white washcloth lays neatly on the side of the sink. My heart sinks and the reality of where I am hits me. I feel slightly faint. Instantly Joe notices. Summoning the guard, Joe asks him to get me a cup of water. After a few minutes, I recover my senses. Every move that Joe makes is recorded. He must ask for a cigarette, and the light to smoke it. I glance around me at three guards talking and watching TV. The reality of a job like this stuns me. Preparing a man to die seems so utterly gruesome. I watch as Joe slowly puts his head to the cold steel bars, looking at me with such love and helplessness, yet he is strong and calm *for me*. A plexiglass partition with about ten little holes in it separates us. It's hard to hear Joe talk over the guards, forcing me to lean in as we whisper back and forth to one another, trying to avert unwelcome voyeurs to our conversation. I stay the full two hours, taking in every word and offering whatever strength I can muster. When

I'm escorted out, I walk past inmates in cages who are hooting and hollering at me, mimicking their behavior on my way in. Before I leave, Joe asks me if I want to become a Catholic. We both would, he says. I agree, though my father is full-blooded Italian from a strong Catholic family who raised me as such. Right now, at this moment, that doesn't matter. If I can ease his pain, offer him comfort, it matters not what religion I am. My father's memory appears momentarily. The sudden vision of my hand in his, walking down the church aisle to our seats, my sisters following, brings an unexpected smile to my face. All three girls are adorned in paisley-colored lace Easter Sunday dresses. In the blink of an eye, the rawness of my surroundings fade the paisley colors.

Not long after I return to my motel room I receive a call from Sister Helen. She is extremely excited. "Lori, Lori, the POPE has intervened! Pope John Paul is requesting the execution be stopped. He even faxed the governor."

Shortly afterwards, my phone is ringing off the hook. I have an interview with the Associated Press and another with BBC Radio in London. Frank Green confirms the story is powerful enough, he doesn't need more material about Joe's innocence. Frank's not exactly interested in the innocence aspect of Joe's story, only the state sponsored execution. Peter Finn had called yesterday; the *Washington Post* story is ready for print. Little did I know the newspapers were not rallying for justice for Joe. They were looking for sales.

Death house rules allow a visitor to return after lunch so I follow the rules and visit with Joe again, for two hours. This time he is behind glass in a small room with two-way mirrors. I'm sitting on a metal chair in a stark room, directly in front of him. It was a more comfortable feeling, sort of like Mecklenburg, and easy to hear him on the phone. I take a deep breath and smile as we both reach for the phone at the same time. I immediately start talking. "Joe, Sister Helen called last night and told me the Pope intervened! Can you believe it?" He was thrilled, yet all along I could see that all he really cares about at this very moment is me. I hadn't eaten lunch and now feel lightheaded. Joe asks the guard to bring me water, tootsie rolls and two oatmeal cookies. The guard retrieves *Joe's* food from his cell and dutifully hands it to me. I sip on the cold water and eat three tootsie rolls. Before I leave I am mindful to hand what I don't eat back to the guard. Joe will need all the strength he can get.

"I can't believe I'm here, Lori." His face puzzled with disbelief.

We talk about Nutter in cryptic language. Before I realize it, it's 3:00 p.m. I know I must leave so I comply, but only because I am forced to.

Back at the motel room I field press calls and then until 5:10 p.m. when suddenly I feel I simply *have* to eat or I will pass out. Trying to shove food down your throat in the midst of such torture is not easy. I can't seem to force the food down. The reality of this entire process is mind blowing, this frenzy to kill a man. Maybe if I bring a burger back to my room it will help. Still, I can't eat. Joe and I manage to talk on the phone from 6:30 to 8:55 p.m. and again from 9:50 to 11:00 p.m. It's love that is allowing us to walk through this. Love between two human beings brought together to fight for justice. That, and God.

When I arise the next morning I find that the Pope's intervention is front-page news in Italy—it has, in fact, only occurred three times. The last being ten years ago. Luciano Neri tells me he will contact the Pope's representatives in America to make sure The Commonwealth of Virginia knows about it. Countering the Pope is Alberi, who, once again, is lying about the blood evidence. This time he's threatening Lifecodes, stating they can be sued for releasing information. Joe is the one who asked and paid for the testing, how could the prosecution sue? First, the Attorney General claims the defense team hid the DNA results, and now the Commonwealth wants to sue because the results are now publicly out there. I find Alberi's claims ludicrous, yet mindful that his threats have worked in the past. It's Alberi's MO.

The next morning I arrive at the prison and Joe and I visit for two hours, the maximum time allowed. Except this time I'm permitted to visit with him inside the "holding area", adjacent to his cell. Joe had seen the article about the Pope and is pleased, but still his eyes hold a look of doom. Joe is now just hours away from his scheduled lethal injection of drugs that will ensure he is no trouble to the Commonwealth anymore. Again, he leans against the bars, as close to me as he can get. This visit is different, softer than the others. We reach through the bars, touch hands and talk to keep our minds occupied. The hours move quickly, and again I must leave. I promise to return at 1:00 p.m. and when I do, this time I'm visiting from behind a four-way mirrored room. I tell Joe that the Italian journalist Georgio Morelli, reports that the governor's office has received over 200 to 300 calls or faxes a day for the past three days. He reports approximately a thousand faxes are coming in from all over the world, but mostly from Italy. Later, I learn the governor's office would finally turn the fax machine off. Governor George Allen wasn't interested in what anyone has to say.

While Joe and I are struggling to make sense of this, Sister Helen is working on getting him some relief. The Associated Press prints her plea for help. The article mentions this is the very first time Sister Helen Prejean is standing behind a prisoner. Never has she intervened to help any one particular person. Joe is the very first. I am comforted by everyone's support, yet I sit here strangely frightened. The only thing that can stop the clock from ticking is the U.S. Supreme Court. The Justices *need* to grant certiorari. I tilt my head back and softly speak out loud, "God, please help us. Joseph doesn't deserve to die."

Yesterday, Joe informed me that when Building L was built ten years ago a skull was accidentally formed in the first cell on the cement floor. Tuggle mentioned it right before he died. "What the hell is this?" he gasped when he first laid eyes on it. Joe is in the second cell. For the first time I am privy to the fact that Tuggle raped and murdered a 20-year-old Vietnamese boy in Mecklenburg back in 1988. Joe says the prison covered it up, creating a story instead that it was a suicide—the boy having hung himself in the shower. The truth was he was anally raped, sperm running down his leg and then choked to death. A state cop interviewed Joe and he told them the truth, but it mattered not. They denied the presence of sperm. The boy had begged not to be moved to the location where Tuggle was. Ignoring his pleas, they moved him anyway. Three days later he was dead.

Finding it unusual, the deathwatch guard tells Joe the Attorney General wants to know everything about him. They are not interested in Ronnie Hoke, only Joe. Joe says it's a profile. They record what he eats, when he defecates and when he sleeps. The guard comments to Joe on how slick he is—seven women a day try to interview Joe, including a psychologist. Today, Joe misleads whoever is listening by talking about a former wife—a psychologist who committed suicide. I believe he could expose some very important people in Florida regarding a prison drug scheme, but he won't tell me the details, believing it will endanger me. I have never quite fully understood what or who he means by this, but I don't ask. Later, I would learn there was truth to this when I discover several letters from a correctional facility in Joe's legal file. Indeed, Joe *worked undercover* with federal and state authorities to bust a drug trafficking trade in the Florida prison system. In an autobiography, Joe laid it out in great detail, later denying its truth due to the likely ramifications on death row. A snitch was a dead man.

As I sit with Joe I hear him claim, over and over again, that he cannot believe he's facing death for something he did not do. He won't say goodbye to me, he says. If Wednesday, December 18 at 3:00 p.m. rolls around, he will call me, but he refuses to talk about the worst. I understand. I have to.

The lawyers have not called me all day. The need to talk to Chip about Nutter and the DNA is interrupted by a phone call from Georgio. When I return to the motel, Georgio tells me of a conversation he had with Alberi. Alberi emphatically told him the governor won't intervene, as if he already knows. Perhaps he does. Perhaps they already spoke. Georgio asks if I'm alone.

"Yes," I reply.

"I don't think that's a good idea, Lori."

"Do you mean for my safety?"

"I don't mean to suggest you would hurt yourself, but maybe you could be in danger. Be careful," he warns me.

Bob and Sarah West are visiting with Joe. "He'll have to call you back," the guard tells me. Instead, I call Professor Nyquist who informs me the *Boston Globe* has printed an article about the Pope.

Anxious to see what the *Richmond Times Dispatch* feels is newsworthy, I rise before dawn on Sunday morning and go to the front desk and grab the paper. Minutes later, after carefully scanning the paper, twice, I find that Frank Green has, once again, lied. There is no story. Later, I find out the *Washington Post* had not printed theirs either. The *Post* and *New York Times* each ran a small piece on the Pope's intervention and was sure to mention the governor's dismissal of it. I can see the indifference of the media and, once again, it ignites my fury.

Being true to prison schedule, Joe and I visit from 9:00 to 11:00 in the morning. Today, he's in his holding cell, me now pressed against the bars that entrap him. He sweetly places his face to the steel and lovingly looks into my eyes with a pitiful expression of helplessness. It tears at me not to have the power to do anything. I wish I could literally free him. Walk over, grab the key and just walk out of here.

Earlier, a female guard had shared a newspaper article with Joe, depicting the torture of making inmates in the death house watch one another prepare for their death. The Commonwealth now has three prisoners in the death house, including Joe, all lined up to be killed just in time to celebrate Christmas. I also learn about a small piece by the Associated Press mentioning the Pope is seeking clemency for Joe O'Dell. The Pope did not just appeal to Governor Allen, he went straight to President Bill Clinton.

Two guards had accompanied Ronnie Hoke's girlfriend, Dawn,

and I to the death house in a stark white van, and two escort us on the way back. This special treatment is reserved only for those whose kin or friends are soon to die. Back in my motel room I am alone with my thoughts. Only Georgio calls to see how Joe is holding up.

The following day I promptly return to the prison for my 1:00 p.m. visit. I am painfully aware these could be the very last moments I see or talk with Joe. During this visit we speak by two-way mirror. Dawn, Ronnie's girlfriend, is in the room with me. Usually I am a very observant person, but in this scenario I find I am almost afraid to look around me. I feel danger, evil surrounding me. Dawn grabs my attention before the guys are brought in. "Lori, look over there at the blinds on the other side of the room," Dawn whispers. The back wall is dark behind the blinds. In horror, I gasp when I suddenly realize it is the execution chamber. We sit frozen by the eerie sounds of the guards behind the wall, preparing for Ronnie's death. They must be able to detach, for they're laughing, kidding around and clapping hands. For almost the entire visit I am horrified by this process. Joe ignores it. Or seems to. However, this morning he speaks more of "if I don't make it," than ever before. He has lost weight, still numb with the reality of his fate. In the afternoon, as if tape-recorded, Joe repeats over and over again, "Where's the evidence?" He cannot, should not, accept this. He is as sad as I have ever seen him. Death can greet someone even before you close your eyes and take your last breath. Joe looked like he was almost there. Without my acquiescence, the term "dead man walking" has attached personal meaning to the debate over the death penalty. Thankfully, during the course of our conversation I am able to see a spark of life. Maybe just a little.

Today only one guard took us back and forth in the death van. Inside the death house I notice many more guards are present. They are getting ready to kill Ronnie—all members of the death squad.

The calendar on my watch says it's Monday, December 16, 1996. I don't need a watch to tell me how many days are left. I see Joe again at the usual hours. He now has two days to live if they plan on carrying out the death sentence as planned. Back at the motel the phone rings at 7:00 a.m. It's Joe.

"Lori, Ronnie will switch up and visit inside with Dawn first so we can watch the CNN interview with Bob Smith."

CNN is doing a story on Joe's pending execution. As usual, the prison doesn't cooperate. Although we are there right on time, Dawn and I are made to wait until 9:20 a.m. to get in. When we finally make it back to the death house, they prepare Ronnie and Dawn for a visit in the booth. Joe and I visit inside, right next to his death cell. The atmosphere is hectic. They are readying themselves for Ronnie's execution. Four guards sit at the table in the corner, two behind me. Joe and I feel each other's tension, but we are both thinking about Ronnie. The incredible pressure is obvious in his drawn face. During the course of our conversation the mounting pressure overpowers Joe. Tears are rolling from the corners of his tired eyes. With all the power in me I remain strong for him and hold back my own tears. I cannot cry. I somehow comfort him and in no time we are back engaging in conversation, trying to savor every moment we have left. Having witnessed my faintness over the ceremonial preparations for death, Joe wants to ensure I'll be okay, so in front of me are three tootsie rolls and a root beer soda. Joe's food.

My return visit in the afternoon does nothing to ease the eerie atmosphere I feel around me. CNN is airing Joe's case at 1:00 p.m., but we can't get reception in the death house. Bob Smith is talking about Joe's case and the Pope's intervention. I wonder what he's saying. It's only a four to five minute segment, but enough to let the nation know Joe is fighting for his life. At 3:00 p.m. the guards come to escort me out. I want to fight to stay, to be there for Joe. I know the next few hours will be hell for him. Resisting the temptation to shout out to his captors, I quietly leave, yet somehow with determination to continue my battle. On my way back to the motel I set up an interview with the governor's office for tomorrow morning. Bob Smith will be conferencing in.

Joe then calls. He is quiet, real quiet as he watches, as if with someone else's eyes, the preparation for Ronnie's death. He is forced to watch Ronnie shower. The shower is directly in front of Joe's cell. Joe is witnessing death number two this week, front row seats. They exchange few words. Joe is visibly upset at what he is literally forced to view. The silence is deafening. He watches people walk in and starts to whisper to me, "I think it's Angelone, and the guys with suits are attorney generals." They walk into the two-way mirror room. Joe watches as they place chairs, one by one, into the room. I am now figuring out that the room I have been visiting Joe in is the witness room. The room where people watch, as in theatre style, but minus the popcorn, a live drama right before their eyes.

At just after 9:00 p.m. they inject fluids into the veins of Ronnie Hoke until he takes his last breath. Joe is only feet away. Caged like an animal, unable to escape his pain. The article that was written in the papers, just days before, concerning the torture inflicted by the Commonwealth by having set three executions, one right after the other, is only an article. The reality is that indeed it is psychological torture. Yet I can't possibly know the enormity of its effect on Joseph.

A half hour after Ronnie's execution Joe summons the strength to call. Joseph whispers, "Ronnie's father and mother cried hard." Joe, too, is now quietly crying on the phone.

With death behind us, the morning arrives like any other. I have a 10:00 a.m. meeting with Mark Christie at the governor's office, as a "family member". As I enter the office I immediately learn from Bob Smith that Joe has been granted a stay.[91] I wonder when Joe will learn

---

[91] The U.S. Supreme Court granted a stay of execution on December 17, 1996. The issue before the court would not be actual innocence, but rather whether O'Dell's constitutional rights were violated under the issue presented in the *Simmons* case. In a shocking attempt to further persuade the court to deny certiorari to O'Dell, the Attorney General, in the

that his life has been spared, for now. Will he live in pure torture for the next few hours, knowing tomorrow is his turn? Or will he be told now? I remain cool. I want to scream, jump and yell, but I don't. The atmosphere is stoic. Christie asks me to step out and he calls the Attorney General's office and then informs the governor. The news had just come in. I meet with Christie, and with Bob by conference call. I speak for 15 minutes to plead on behalf of Joe. Mixing facts of innocence with Joe's central role in my life, I speak. I inform them I plan on proving his innocence, no matter what. Christie is unmoved. As I leave, I notice a press conference on the second floor. Governor Allen walks right by me. I wait for him to come out and when he does I shake his hand and introduce myself. To my disgust I find myself in the role of the lawyerly game. Instinctively, I want to yell at him, tell him how wrong he is to have handled the case with such disregard. Instead I ask him to give the case *careful consideration*. Lawyer's words, not the ones I wanted to blurt out. He smiles for the camera and asks me if I know

respondents' brief in opposition to the Petition For A Writ of Certiorari, misled the court with the following opening sentence:

"In this petition for a writ of certiorari, filed after his state of habeas corpus review, O'Dell deliberately withheld crucial evidence demonstrating his guilt of capital murder: his own experts had matched DNA found on his jacket to DNA from his murder victim. O'Dell grossly misrepresented the facts of his case in that petition and three members of this Court expressed their opinion that there were serious questions about O'Dell's guilt."

In footnote 14, on page 16 of the respondents' petition, the Commonwealth continues to mislead the court (they had already litigated this issue in an evidentiary hearing that revealed there was no match and that the only conclusive DNA evidence revealed the blood did NOT match Helen Schartner, by all experts, *including* the Commonwealth's experts):

"No amount of reconfiguring of the facts by O'Dell can hide the fact that his own DNA experts matched the blood on his jacket to the blood of Helen Schartner."

In footnote 15, page 17, signed by Assistant Attorney General Katherine Baldwin, the Commonwealth misleads the court again regarding Steve Watson, by distorting the facts and failing to include the fact that the Attorney General's Office intimidated the witness and threatened him with perjury charges if he did not recant his recantation.

Joe was granted a stay.

In front of his audience the governor is now discussing how badly he feels for the victim's family—Helen Schartner's family—having to go through Christmas and all with their daughter's killer still alive. I can hardly believe his words and it finally hits me. He would have killed Joe! At least now I know and I must stay on top of this case. This is not a battle anymore, it has become war. Vaguely, I recall the wisdom my professor offered me. A war is almost impossible to win, but we just won this battle. Thank you Lord.

As I leave the Capitol, I see Joe's sister, Sheila. She thought the clemency hearing was today. I didn't have time for her. I have work to do, so I visit with her briefly and rush back to my motel. I am immediately surrounded by the media. I accept their invitation to interview. Two reporters from Rai in Italy—Rai 2 and 1—and Channel One all want my reaction. I also give an interview with the Swiss on a foreign channel. Because I am functioning in a cloud, I am mostly unaware of what is happening outside of our personal death row watch, but I am more determined than ever to fight this fight. I'm on the phone all night until exhaustion finally kicks in as I spend my last night in this dreaded place.

Joe receives the news on a conference call with Chip at the Virginia Resource Center and a reporter in Italy. Just as he finishes hearing about the stay a guard approaches his cell, "What size clothes are you, you're outta here." Joe and I speak only 15 minutes. He is happy, but like me, overwhelmed. Joe came within *24 hours* of death. Right now, I'm feeling only one person could possibly understand, Sister Helen. To be so near death and walk away is mind-boggling. The press is quoting Alberi as saying, "It's just a delay of the execution."

Chapter 20

~Cause Célèbre~

I am confident now that the Commonwealth has no intention at looking at the facts. They are determined to kill Joe. I'm quickly learning who our allies are and who our enemies are, including the press. I phone Chip to let him know who we cannot trust. While the Commonwealth is keen on executing Joe, an entire country is just as keen on saving him. The Associated Press and other media outlets throughout the world are printing the astonishing news. The headline of one article relays it best: "O'Dell Is A Cause Célèbre For Italians."

Never could I have predicted the powerful force of support that is now ensuing from an entire country. Not only did both houses of the Italian Parliament rise to cheer the announcement of the stay, the President of the Senate wrote a personal letter of protest to Vice President Gore. The Mayor of Palermo went so far as to make Joe an honorary citizen. "I really can't remember another story like this," said Vittorio Zucconi, who is writing about Joe for *la Repubblica*, Italy's largest newspaper. "I mean Joe O'Dell got a standing ovation in the Italian Parliament…The last time that happened was when we won the World Cup in 1980…Italian citizens bombarded the governor's office with pleas for clemency and cluttered the Internet with expressions of outrage." It was also reported that an Italian ambassador to the United States went to see the governor's lawyer. Allen, not knowing what to make of this, simply acknowledged it had "turned into somewhat of an international situation."

On November 11, 1996 Rosa Jervolino Russo, from the office of the President of the Commission of Constitutional Affairs in the Camera dei Deputati, sent a letter to the governor urging him to take action to save Joseph O'Dell. It read:

> Dear Governor:
>
> On behalf of the members of the Italian Parliament we are writing to you to express our concern about the case of Joseph Roger O'Dell III. As you know, he is sitting on death row in one of your State's prisons, waiting for execution although a DNA blood test shows that he is innocent.
>
> Mr. Governor, you have the power to suspend the execution and revisit the case of Mr. O'Dell. Please do it. We acknowledge that in your country such a decision may be unpopular, but, please, take into consideration the fact that the State of Virginia is killing an innocent man. This will be your personal contribution to the people of the State of Virginia, whom you represent.
>
> Looking forward to hearing from you the wonderful news of the revision of Mr. O'Dell's case.
>
> We are sincerely and respectfully yours,

The letter was signed by numerous members of the Parliament, and Russo was sure to let the governor know this is just the beginning. They can get the entire Parliament behind them if they must, she says.

On December 13, 1996, the Director of the Vatican press office, Joaquin Navaro-Valls, announced that the Pope had asked his Washington representative to intercede and ask for clemency. The next day it was announced the message had been passed to President Clinton and Governor Allen. Allen knew that millions of people were concerned, and that Joe's support ran high and deep. Would he give credence to any of their concerns?

I set my alarm for 4:15 a.m. I have a 4:30 a.m. interview with an Italian radio station. The president of the Senate in the Italian Parliament will accompany me on this interview. Before I attempt to drift off to sleep I receive a phone call from Alessandra from Hands Off Cain. She wants me to go to Italy. "Sure, I can go for a few days after Christmas."

At 4:30 a.m. I am ready to speak to the radio host in Italy who has much to ask about Joseph O'Dell and my work. I thank everyone for their support. The interview is both emotional and compassionate. The president of the senate announces his support for Joseph and speaks eloquently. I end the interview with, "We love you, and are deeply grateful." "We love you too," the broadcaster replies. The sound of those words fill my heart and echo in my ears for days. The warmth and compassion felt from strangers across the globe gives me comfort. I am not alone anymore.

The next day Georgio Morelli asks if Joe needs money. "Yes," I answer. After struggling with the lawyers to pay for his investigation, we are desperate for any financial assistance we can get. "I will start to raise money in ten days for Joe's defense." He also tells me that Mayor Giuliani's attorney wants to help Joe for free.

Today is the day Joe was supposed to die. Instead I am taking a phone call about Joe's life at 8:00 a.m. to interview with an unknown woman by the name of Augusta from some radio station. I make it a point afterwards to find out which station it is. There are so many calls coming in I can hardly keep track. After showering I'm ready to finally leave this horrible motel. I see the Italian Rai crew has come back for more footage of me packing my car and talking with their reporter. This group, I sense, is not supportive of Joe. I refuse a second interview. I am told they need it for editing, but I wonder. I am now asked about the location of the crime scene and I watch as they scribble notes about the "County Line" on a piece of paper.

"Lori, what is your next move, tell us about your investigation, your strategy. Where you are going?" Not feeling comfortable releasing information, I go back inside and wait for them to leave. I am cautiously skeptical, maybe even a little paranoid.

****

Today is Joe's first day back on death row. I receive his first phone call at 11:00 a.m. After speaking for a few minutes he calls Sister Helen to thank her. We need to stay connected, especially after the trauma of yesterday. He calls again at 11:40 a.m., 12:15 and 12:40 p.m. Expecting his date with death he gave away his money. He asks me if I can drop some off for commissary. After first stopping at a restaurant to eat I then make the miserable drive to Mecklenburg to drop off $140. Our brush with death has changed my demeanor at the prison. I do not smile at anyone, nor do they smile at me. The game has changed. I return back to the Best Western to take some phone calls. First, I have a long and thorough interview with National News Service of Italy. ANSA calls and asks a couple of questions. They, too, want to know what my investigation plans are. I feel like Alberi is lurking in the background. I trust no one now. While my caution may be misplaced, I act out of survival for Joe. I cautiously inform them that there is nothing more to do. Hands Off Cain calls to initiate plans for my trip to Italy. Each day now Georgio Morelli calls me, leading me to believe he is a strong ally for Joe.

The interviews continue in full force while Joe grants a request to Laura Lafay from the *Virginian-Pilot*. She has not been kind to Joe in the past so I am angry with him. I recall feeling upset about a similar situation not long ago. I was trying so hard to protect him, not realizing the enormity of the task. I was also upset about the crazy stories now spreading from one newspaper to the other, like uncontrollable wildfire.

"Joseph, I'm really upset about the news all over the Internet that I'm your wife and that you want your sperm frozen for me. This is crazy, it's getting out of hand!" The frozen sperm story was not Joe's doing but the media going hog wild over sensationalism. The media had taken an old request of Joe's and simply adapted it to me, however unsavory that was.

I phone the news service Reuters, demanding a retraction. With Joe's execution not staring me in the face I have a renewed interest, and finally time, to stand up for *myself*. Joe is upset when I tell him about our "marriage". "Fine, I'll call an old girlfriend. Someone will marry me and that will displace the word that you are my wife." He is crying now, emotionally exhausted from the past few days. The press has added stress to an already stressful situation. The inevitable spin on their stories and the thirst for sensationalism is becoming rampant.

There is a fever in Italy concerning Joseph and his plight. The Italians are incensed over the 21-day rule in Virginia and more so that the United States could possibly consider executing someone with evidence of innocence, however strong or weak it was. Hands Off Cain is feverishly planning my trip to Italy to encourage further support. However, things begin to change when I become annoyed with Alessandra. Not being used to this attention, or how the media works, I'm told that after an all night trip and arrival in Italy at 8:30 a.m., they want to whisk me off to the studio for a live TV interview at 10:30 a.m. I tell her that I cannot take any other interviews that day and need to sleep. Maybe I am just short on patience and need time to recover. She insists I stay at her house. "No, thank you, I insist on a hotel, where Jennifer and I can rest in privacy." I had decided I would bring Jen with me, if she wanted to go. It would be a universal education.

Feeling we need a media blitz about the true facts of the case, I am developing a new plan. I now think about gathering a team of people to get the real facts out in order to blast Justice Scalia's dissent on the blood. Certiorari was granted and the U.S. Supreme Court will hear Joe's case. This was the basis for the stay of execution. Justice Scalia, in an unusual statement, dissented, not joining the other Justices' vote to hear the case. After having read his dissent I had to wonder, how on earth can a Justice of the Supreme Court get it so wrong? I knew that if the factual errors of the Fourth Circuit were not corrected, they would reach the top. But any good lawyer would have learned what the facts were, based on the record. Scalia's dissent was factually incorrect regarding the blood evidence. It was clear upon reading it that it was designed as a press statement. All the lawyers agreed. I need to reach out to Joe—we have to decide who is going to argue his case. Marshall Diane, a death penalty litigator, suggests George Kendall. "Don't use Bob," he says. I must tell Joe to put George Kendall on his attorney list for advice. I need to pull together a new team. It ought to be easier now.

It's finally Saturday when Joe and I can visit together. I'm anxious to see him outside of the living nightmare we just experienced. With a whole new attitude I step through the front gates. After going through the security area, and a pat down from the female guard, I wait for Joe by the electronic door, caged between entryways.

As Joe walks in, I draw a sigh. We catch each other's first glimpse, my face bright with a beaming smile. I had waited days for this. So had he. Our visit lasts four and a half hours, but it seems like minutes. I keep from caring for him too transparently. I am still protecting my feelings, afraid of the future and what it might bring. We speak briefly of the case and a little of us, never too deeply, the fear of breaking down and crying too near the experience. I have a desire to hold and protect him. Will I ever, I wonder? I am already looking forward to to-morrow morning, knowing this is when our eyes will meet once again. Looking into his eyes means he is still alive.

Knowing I must leave to return home by 11:00 a.m. I am one of the first visitors. The smile I usually bring to the prison gates has disappeared. The reality of this fierce battle has permanently wiped the smile from my face. The remaining tension reveals its ugly face when Joe and I argue a bit, over what I don't remember. We put it behind us before I leave. I drive back to New Jersey to pick up Jennifer.

We have little time to rest and enjoy one another's company. My tickets to Rome are at the Newark airport waiting for me. We continue our drive to Stanford, Connecticut where I need to go to obtain a passport. Tomorrow we should be in Cape Cod, just in time to celebrate the holidays.

~Christmas~

At home, Jennifer and I engage in normal family affairs during Christmas. It serves as a temporary distraction from the hell I am living with Joe. Tomorrow is Christmas Day and we need a tree. I make a mad dash to find one. As we decorate the tree and set up the lights, Christmas is brought to our living room, if not in our hearts. I'm pleased to be able to make this happen for Jennifer. She needs some normalcy in her life while her mother is out waging a war. Just in time, and before we are done decorating, Joe calls. From 5:00 to 6:00 p.m. he decorates the tree with us as Christmas music plays in the background.

This Christmas is naturally quiet. While few gifts are exchanged, the real joy of Christmas is knowing that Joe is alive. It is a Christmas miracle. As the day progresses, I finally get the chance to check the Internet site. One view of Joe's page leads to over five hours of retrieving emails from the Italians. 99 percent of the emails were from December 11, the day before I had arrived at Greensville Correctional Center to meet Joe for his pending death. During my review of the emails, I start to prepare Christmas dinner for Jen. After a long several days apart we finally sit down to a wonderful candied ham, sweet potatoes and steamed vegetables. I wonder what Joe is having tonight.

~Taking It Up A Notch~

In my desperate search for help I had discovered John Rocovich was a religious and decent man. He was also the governor's personal pilot. I had sent the clemency petition, and important documents, to John in the hope that he would whisper in the governor's ear to pay particular attention to this case. I am in utter amazement when I receive John's phone call the morning after Christmas. He tells me that only twelve hours after he had received the documents he had dinner with "George," meaning Governor George Allen. I found John to be open, cordial, and above all compassionate. His opinion was that it was a very good petition—it raised doubt. He said if Joe had a decent lawyer at trial, he would be a free man, and if he had a new trial, he would walk. This is not the first time I heard such comments from other attorneys, or those who knew Joe's case. What he had was a lousy, incompetent, court-appointed lawyer and Virginia was doing all they could to prevent Joe from getting a new trial.

John and I engage in intelligent conversation—it's a relief to hear he can see the truth about the evidence. He asks me why Joe defended himself. I tell him about Paul Ray and that I would have done the same thing. John remarks that Joe had "done everything from murder to...," his words drifting off, I couldn't understand. It sounded as if he were spoon-fed the words from Alberi and Test. I tell him Joe has changed and that I studied him and the record cold. He responded, "People are good in prison but when they start drinking they're sometimes a different person." John is a Baptist and tells me in his own church they have prostitutes, murderers and ex-cons who have indeed changed. I, once again, remind him that Joe, too, has changed. He said he thought Joe should not get out but spend the rest of his life in prison, even suggesting he should be in a geriatric prison. He informs me that George was relieved that the U.S. Supreme Court stayed the case and would hear it. I will need to send him a packet of information to ask his help on the 21-day rule!

When I hang up I feel comforted, strangely comforted, knowing that *someone* understands the facts. I also know that Joe's past is taken out of context, twisted by the prosecution. The murder they keep referring to is a case of homosexual aggression toward Joe when he was a young man in prison, after having been sentenced for robbing a convenience store. Lloyd Bess attacked Joe and Joe defended himself— though that's not how the courts saw it with the testimony of a jailhouse snitch. And while an independent death penalty lawyer reviewed this case and determined it would be thrown out and seen as self-defense, that never happened. I had to find out for myself so I got hold of the court transcript and autopsy report, revealing Bess died almost three weeks after the fight. I reviewed numerous documentation, including psychiatric reports, about Joe's fear and concern, months prior to the incident. But this made a perfect sound bite for the prosecution. Joe was always referred to as a murderer, even before Helen Schartner was found dead in a field in Virginia Beach, her clothes stained in red.

"I don't know what George will do, Lori, but I will tell him my opinion. I do think he will be fair with the clemency, but he was irritated by the Pope's intervention (the governor is Presbyterian)". He also said the prosecution went to the governor and said, "This is what didn't get into the trial, it proves his guilt." I was wondering, why haven't we had that same opportunity? It would change anyone's mind. Speaking to John was the closest I would get to Governor Allen. If he couldn't influence George, no one could.

That same day, the day after Christmas, Georgio Morelli visits me in Chatham to talk about Joe's case. The Italian media is pulling me in different directions. Luciano Neri phones to suggest I have my first press conference in the pressroom of the Italian Parliament, and *then* do individual interviews. Luciano is a member of the Parliament and has been instrumental in the publicity around Joe's case. Maria, Alessandra's friend, is angry. She wants a press conference with Hands Off

Cain first. Intuition tells me otherwise. I reach out to Sister Helen for her advice. After discussing it with her, I decide the Parliament serves our best interest. Helen reminds me that Hands Off Cain is a great organization and suggests I work with them, too. The Parliament is interested in Joe's innocence. To Hands Off Cain, Joe fuels the death penalty debate. But this is an innocence case and I don't want Joe used as a tool for the death penalty issue, not now. Helen and I laugh about my victory. It's cause for celebration. We giggle as I remind her I had told Joe Jackson, "If Alberi thinks he is going to stop me, watch. I promise to take this to the world!" I was responding to news that Alberi threatened the newspaper with a lawsuit right before they were to expose the truth in Joe's case. I had delivered on my promise.

"Lori, I'm going to write a letter to the Pope," Sister Helen says. "Can you hand deliver it for me?"

"I would be delighted to, Helen," I reply.

I decide to fly to Italy on January 5th, rest the 6th and interview from the 7th to the 13th. Jen will miss a few days of school, but it'll be worth it.

In preparation for my arrival in Italy, Georgio wants to visit with me. I agree to allow him a couple of days in Chatham. We dine at one of my favorite restaurants, the Impotent Oyster, and say goodnight after a lovely evening. He has brought me all the newspapers clippings from Italy. I am struck by the sheer volume of the coverage Joseph's case has been given. It also reveals a small amount of bad press. To no surprise there will always be bad to balance the good. But Georgio has great connections and I gain comfort knowing he is on our side.

The next day I invite him to dine with me and over dinner he gently offers me advice on how I should dress while in Italy, when I'm at the Vatican, on talk shows, and at the Parliament. He tells me to wear no jewelry. "You are too elegant," he says. By that I think he means I appear too wealthy. I suppose I should look more "humble". I understand he is trying to help but I have never put up pretenses for anyone or anything. I am not about to take such advice.

Jennifer is trying to hang in there while I spend time with Georgio, but she is sick and needs some TLC. She is also finally sick of the case.

During the day Alessandra phones and informs me that the TV show does not wish to pay for my plane ticket if I don't interview with them first. I didn't realize it, but they were all fighting for the first exclusive on Joe's story. I am glad my instincts were correct and that I had decided to work with the Italian Parliament.

The next morning I rise early to do more work on the Internet. After having breakfast with Jennifer I meet Georgio for lunch. We finalize our discussion about Italy and he informs me that he will pay for my tickets. His editor "just wants to prep you," he says. "Many journalists want to see you make your first mistake." The Associated Press, CNN, the *Washington Post*, and *New York Times* will all be there. They are expecting around 30 journalists.

That evening when Joe calls I bring up the rumors about being his "wife." I remind him that the Commonwealth is using this in an attempt to discredit me. I fax Paul Bernstein at the *Washington Post* and request a retraction. He needs to talk to Peter Finn first, he says, and asks if I can wait until Monday. "Yes, that will be fine," I respond. But I'm ready to threaten a lawsuit just to get the truth printed. I don't like this game.

With a moment to spare I phone Bob West and tell him about my conversation with John Rocovich, thanking him for the connection. Bob is Joe's prison minister and the person who told me about John, who he was, and how he might help Joe. He tells me to ask him about the 21-day rule. I still need to work on John.

Now all I have to do is wait for Luciano to call to arrange my trip to Italy.

~Trip to Italy~

New Year's Eve in Chatham is called First Night, a New England village tradition to commemorate the new year with a local celebration. It's something we look forward to every year. This year brings a different kind of celebration. Grateful for the support of the Italian Parliament, I make arrangements with Luciano for my trip to Italy. By day's end, I'm anxious to join in the town celebration. Rounding the Main Street corner, we pass several houses before pulling into our driveway, pausing for the crowd of people strolling to town. After grabbing our scarves and mittens, Jen and I venture out to join the other villagers for the festivities, including the annual horse carriage ride through town. Littered with bales of hay for comfortable seating we all crowd onto the wagon. Jingle bells hang from the horse's neck, ready to ring in the New Year for all the parents and their children. The rhythmic sound of bells is music to my soul. Visitors fill the churches on Main Street, their open doors making way for Christmas songs to flood the streets. Huddled on nearly every street corner parents and their children are braving the cold for a taste of the best hot cider in Chatham. At midnight, and from the rooftop of our home, Jennifer and I stare in delight at the spectacular fireworks over Oyster Pond.

Awakening to a new year, I sleepily rise on this bitter cold morning, wondering what this year will bring for me, Jennifer, and for Joe. My thoughts are interrupted when Kitty Behan calls and asks for the appendix to the cert. and clemency petition. She wants to address the innocence aspect of the case in state court. I am overjoyed. Kitty is a fine attorney and we need all the help we can get. Now that she is a partner, she calls the shots. She wants me to propose to the Italians they pay her expenses. I agree to try to raise some money.

My day is lifted by a phone call from Joe.

"I have a kitten in my cell, Lori. His name is Oreo."

"What does he look like?" I ask.

"He's a black and white kitty, just as cute as can be."

I am touched by this, for Jen wanted to adopt a stray black and white cat in Chatham and name it Oreo. Joe paid the guard $20.00 to bring it in. I can hear it softly meowing in the quiet of his cell. Joe is clearly tickled to have her in his abode. It gives me joy to hear the delight in his voice.

~A New Year, 1997~

The new year promises to test my resolution to be strong. I know the only relief for Joe rests with the Italians, and any pressure they can mount on American politicians. So when Rai TV wishes to interview me, I am waiting with open arms. They arrive at my home in Chatham, Cape Cod with cameras in hand. The hours pass quickly from 11:30 a.m. until 2:30 p.m. when we finally break for lunch at the Squire, a popular touristy restaurant.

In what appeared to be an appropriate setting, I am filmed in front of a mountain of courtroom transcripts and massive paperwork accumulated over the past three years, all of which I took to task to read and memorize with a tenacity that made Alberi want me dead. For what seems like the millionth time, I talk about the evidence. The words roll off my tongue as I describe one by one the lies that have been portrayed about the case, the DNA results, the tire track, Watson, the cigarette and Joe's past criminal history. The prosecution and Attorney General's office have been stating that Joe was charged with rape prior to this case. His criminal record reveals no evidence of being charged with a sexual assault crime. I inform them that it is the Commonwealth's desire to paint Joe as a dangerous man so they can quietly kill him. Finally, they come to the question that bothers me the most. Was I his wife? "No," I softly reply, "I am not."

"There have been a lot of false statements, I see," states the Rai reporter.

"Yes, more than you can imagine," I reply.

I am told they will air this piece when I'm in Italy. Scores of documents fill their arms as they head for the front door.

"I will have Bob Smith get you the cert. petition, and maybe the clemency petition," I blurt out to ensure they have all they need before they leave.

Toward the end of our meeting, I decide to share with the Italian press some photos of Joseph when he was a little boy. Handing the pictures over, I recall what Joe once told me, "The Lord will take me to the very end, but he won't let me die. I have to have faith." I know he lives by those words. I am trying with all my might to do the same.

That next morning Sister Helen calls in a panic to tell me that she is not quite done with her letter to the Pope. I calm her. "Helen, I would never miss the opportunity to pass along your letter. I'm not leaving until next week." We chat briefly until Joe calls, at which point I politely say goodbye. Time with Joe is limited to prison dictated schedules.

"I invented a diaper for Oreo," Joe tells me. "I'm going to patent it."

When I ask what it's made of, he says it's a tissue that he cut a hole in for the tail. Desperate measures for a desperate situation. Oreo was peeing all over the place and he needed to do something. Our chat is brief in this early morning hour.

As I am sipping a cup of tea, a forkful of eggs ready to energize my day, Steve Rosenfield telephones. He knows how upset I am about the Department of Correction's alignment with the prosecution and Attorney General's office, and the continued reference to me as his wife. "Pick your battles, Lori," he advises me now. I take a deep breath and agree that the truth concerning the evidence in Joe's case is far more important than spousal visits every three months. After placing a call to the *Washington Post* to accept their retraction as currently worded, I write a letter to the editor noting my position. Perhaps they will print it. Reuters had called Steve and said they have a copy of the fabricated Indian marriage document. This is their basis for not issuing a retraction. But they do agree not to refer to me as his wife in the future. How easy it is to become married in the press!

As I ponder over what other connections I can make, I call David Bruck to thank him for his support. I inform him about the Italian support and my upcoming trip and rattle off about the cert. petition and the work I put into its appendix. "David, we need you for the briefing, you are the best!" He remarks about the unfairness of the DOC and the marriage thing. Kitty is relieved when she calls to hear I have not become Mrs. O'Dell. She tells me there is nothing wrong with an American Indian ceremony, but I know she, too, does not want distraction from the real issues. It's no secret that I care about Joe, but the reality of our friendship cannot change the facts in the courtroom, the ten-year-old transcripts, the recantation of jailhouse snitches, the contents of Paul Ray's notes, nor the blatant lies the Commonwealth continues to espouse. No amount of personal involvement can change raw fact.

The news of the Pope's support and my upcoming trip to Italy has put a tiny spark into the lawyers. Bob Smith just called to tell me he will go ahead and do DNA testing for Joe. I share the details about my upcoming trip to Italy and news that the National Law Society is now backing Joe. He is still amazed about the Pope's intervention and all the support Joe is receiving from Italy.

"Bob, Luciano tells me that I will be meeting the President of Italy in Milan."

I myself am amazed. I let him know I have recruited Kitty and that I'm trying to convince the firm to go back to the state on the innocence claim for a new trial. Although he appeared pleased to hear this I thought to myself, "*Why am I doing what they should have been doing all along?*"

During the past few weeks I have come to realize that Jennifer needs a strong family unit to support her during my absence. Her father works long hours and the unfairness of leaving her alone is more than I can bear. I make arrangements with one of her good friends to stay with the family while I am away. Tomorrow my daughter will be flying to New Jersey to stay with her friend Kaitlin.

Trying to get off Cape Cod can be challenging at times. Fog decides to cancel our plans when we arrive at the Hyannis airport. Ignoring the Cape Cod weather, I opt to make the drive to Boston where the planes have not been delayed. Our ride to the airport is pleasant, offering us uninterrupted time together before we must say goodbye. My strength, always on the surface in all I do, is about to be tested when I find myself alone in the car on the way back to Chatham. My tears can't hide the realization of how much I will miss her. Regrouping, I ponder all that lies ahead of me. Back in the house, I sit for 45 minutes answering Internet mail from Joe's fans around the world. I await his call at ten that night. Sensing the tension in Joe's voice I know something is wrong. He voices frustration about being imprisoned, something he rarely does. I have little to offer in the way of comfort. Oreo keeps his company for almost a full week.

"Lori, I'm dreading the fact that we won't be able to communicate when you're in Italy. It's going to be pure hell," he says.

I acknowledge his feelings, but I have bigger plans that trump our discomfort.

Knowing that my daughter is now settled with friends I sit here, alone in my home and occupy my time writing thank-you letters to all the religious organizations that have offered their support for Joe. Flames from the fireplace are warming the room as I sit in my favorite chair, reflecting. I recall my old life, missing it and the new journey of my law school education. Sister Helen saves me from further despair when she calls to ask for my help. She is discussing a documentary with some German television producer. He wants information about

Joe's case. For the first time, and only because I am bone tired, I refer this possibility to the lawyers at Paul, Weiss, Rifkind, Wharton & Garrison.

I remember in the morning to call the head of Jennifer's middle school in Princeton to inform them that she will be staying with friends until I return from Italy. They need to be aware of family dynamics in case there is an emergency at school.

Chapter 21

~Corruption of Innocence~

Joe's case has opened my eyes to the reality of political corruption in our country, resting in the hands of those in power whose political careers are at stake. I am firmly convinced this would not be the case if politicians heeded the integrity and moral standards initially demanded of them when they vowed to administer justice honestly, fairly and evenly. The lack of ethical conduct, combined with a display of apathy, has led to the continued incarceration of Joseph O'Dell. But he is not alone. He is among so many others imprisoned in our country whose fate lies in the integrity of those given power by the people. The system has failed. Not only has it failed Joseph O'Dell but it has failed us, you and me—the people. Responsible journalists will see through the mischaracterization of evidence, the distortions and, sometimes, outright lies concerning the factual matters of this death penalty case, including O'Dell's background. But the tendency to believe state officials because we are taught to do so sometimes clouds the minds of those who must be objective. Threats of lawsuits by those afraid of exposure kept Joe's story of innocence from the American media, and ultimately, the public.

Because propaganda exists, shadowing the ability to print the truth, I realize that politics takes precedence over justice. This saddens me as I study the law to become a member of the *justice* system. I expect more from my future colleagues. I shall not accept what others seem to acknowledge with dismay but take no action to correct, and still others who are so unfortunate as to not even know truth from fiction. For Joseph O'Dell the fight has lasted twelve years this February. For me, the battle has just begun.

The U.S. Supreme Court has agreed only to hear a technicality in Joe's case. At best, Joe will get a new sentencing hearing, at worst, another death sentence. Even if successful in the U.S. Supreme Court he still faces death, again, at the trial court.

~Italian Support~

As the brilliant sun replaces the last shadows of the moon, a phone call from Georgio awakens me. His voice is full with anger. "Lori, Bob Smith just gave an interview with Italian Swiss TV and said DNA is ambiguous and he never once mentioned his client is innocent. He was very neutral. Even now, after I have struggled to gain support for Joe's cause I have an editor who is thinking, what gives?" This law firm has hurt Joe all along, I cannot allow them to speak on behalf of his case. I leave a message for Bob that I am completely disappointed by this news.

With a few moments to spare I decide to fax the information needed by the German press for the documentary on Joe. It won't get done otherwise. I phone Luciano to talk about my upcoming trip. Alessandra's group calls soon after, afraid of being shut out. I am stuck in the middle of this struggle, but my concern at the moment is the case, not media politics.

Taking a break to open mail I notice one seems to stand out. It's from Sister Helen. Inside the envelope is her letter to the Pope. A half hour later she telephones me. We speak briefly and I acknowledge the strength of her letter to the Pope. Helen acknowledges the strength of my determination.

Georgio calls again. His prosecutor friend in New York has reviewed the materials. He feels it's the worst miscarriage of justice he has ever seen. These are not words spoken by a prosecutor, causing me to be leery of him, but I heed Georgio's advice to utilize his support. Michael Mozzarella will join us for two weeks while I tour the country. Joe could use a former prosecutor's support.

Before I leave for Italy I tackle my "to do" list. A phone call to a CPA colleague of mine in Princeton will ensure the formation of a not-for-profit fund to handle the money Georgio hopes to raise for Joe. I update Joe's website, outlining a page labeled "lies/truth", detailing every lie and outlining the truth with supporting court documentation, affidavits, legal paperwork and other irrefutable evidence. A letter to the editor of the *Virginian-Pilot* updates him concerning the data in Joe's current website. I manage to remove the tinsel and bulbs off the Christmas tree and pack the decorations for next year. After grabbing some clothes from the cleaners I return home just in time to field two overseas calls. The first is from *Corriere de Serra*. The second is the Vatican Radio. "Lori, do you have a comment about the three executions in Arkansas?" I offer a comment only to the Vatican and direct the newspaper to attend the press conference on Tuesday at 11:30 a.m. I know they'd prefer my statements prior to the press conference, but I politely decline. The Vatican correspondent asks if I would like to meet the Pope. "It would be an incredible honor," I respond. I refer to the three upcoming executions in Arkansas as barbaric and agree to comment further when I arrive in Italy.

Bob Smith assures me he voiced Joe's innocence. I warn him that they hang on his every word and that he must be careful what he says. After all, he does represent Joe's interests. When we end our phone call I fax a well-known attorney named Gerry Spence in Wyoming to ask for his help. I inform him Kitty Behan wishes to handle the innocence aspect of the case and anticipates filing a motion to request a new trial. If I must, and if necessary, I will hire Spence myself.

The Joseph O'Dell Defense Fund is set up in Princeton with a P.O. box number. Kitty Behan confirms receipt of the material I sent her and asks again to have her costs covered, no need for an hourly rate. I agree. I discuss with her the Italian lawyer in New York that Georgio is pushing so hard on me and let her know I am not impressed. She agrees. We need a trial attorney. In my newness to this legal arena I ask her if Gerry Spence is okay and she chuckles. "Yes, he's great!" Gerry happens to be a strong, dedicated attorney who is well known for his tenacity.

With time fast approaching for my trip to Italy, Rai radio wants to interview Joe. I get their list of questions and go over them with Joe ahead of time so he is not ambushed. I want him to be successful in his message and to come across well to the listeners. He doesn't need my help. He is charismatic and steadfast in his approach.

~Rome, Italy~

I have never flown overseas. Though it's a new experience for me, strangely it seems to fit in the picture of this journey to save Joe. I'm also excited to finally meet Luciano Neri, my main contact with the Italian Parliament, and all the other Italians he has arranged for me to visit with. With bags packed, I arrive at Boston's Logan Airport without the slightest idea of what lies ahead of me.

An overnight flight drops me in Rome the next morning. Luciano's friend Giavan from La Rete (the government party that Luciano belongs to and who is sponsoring Joe), Georgio and Michael Mozzarella (the NY prosecutor) all meet me at the airport. They arrive in a blue Mercedes Benz limo. After a couple of hours' rest they call me at 4:00 p.m. to arrange my pick-up. "Lori, do you have a scarf, glasses and a hat? Put them on. The media is all over looking for you. They are even at the airport waiting for you." I do as I am told as we scurry into the car heading straight to the Italian Parliament. I enter the building and am escorted to a small room that is filled with binders with the inscription "Joseph O'Dell." It is obvious this is an important issue to them. Currently, we are preparing for the press conference and there, in this parliamentary room, for the first time I meet Senator Mario Occhipinti and Franco Danieli. They are part of an intimate team of members of the Italian Parliament who have started a campaign to free Joseph O'Dell. After we discuss what is in store for me over the next few days, we go out for an Italian dinner at around 9:00 p.m. We are joined by a reporter from Rai newspaper, who has first shot at me. As we enter the small but elegant restaurant that is frequented by members of the Parliament, I'm immediately noticed by the girls who witness our presence. They are whispering and pointing at me. As always, I just want the reporter to get the facts right and print the truth about Joe's case. When I am peppered with questions I regurgitate the facts all the way up to the U.S. Supreme Court. I also dispel the rumor of any marriage.

One of the main reasons for my trip to Italy is to drum up support and meet the people who wish to help Joe and his cause. They all want to know, "*Who is this person rallying for Joseph? Who is behind this cause?*" My first scheduled event is an international press conference. Little do I know what's in store for me.

Today, January 12, 1997, is any girl's worst nightmare. I had just gotten a beautiful body wave back home. I was in the middle of blow-drying my hair when I suddenly look over at the flat iron and notice the light on the contraption is not green. "*It must be a mistake,*" I speak silently to myself, frantic the mistake was not mine. After removing the plug three or four times to prove it must be the outlet I'm horrified to learn that I'm left with a very uncoiffed look for my first appearance in Italy. I am dreadfully mortified. First impressions are everything, and this is not how I wanted to start off. At first I think about asking someone to retrieve this vital tool for me. Not wanting to appear like a princess, I refrain from such desperation. Instead I do what I can and leave for the *Dinatello Raffi* show that morning, a *national* television show. As we enter, and are formally greeted, I notice Georgio and Michael are each handed $2,000 for "expenses". I am given nothing. I, of course, did not expect anything, yet it rubs me the wrong way to see them capitalizing on my appearance. Georgio had given us great press so I'm mostly offended by Michael's acceptance of any money. It seemed, well, not right.

I was interviewed until 11:20 a.m. The press conference at the Italian Parliament is scheduled for 11:30 a.m. I *hate* being rushed, and on such an important day. I was beginning to regret this first interview. I arrive at the Parliament five minutes late. Photographers swarm from all directions. Flashbulbs illuminate the room as I make my way through the maze of media. I was not at all prepared for this. It looked like it could have been a red carpet event, except not in Hollywood and minus a movie star. NBC, the Associated Press, Rai, and several media outlets are here to memorialize the event. The pressroom is very elegant and I can't help noticing its beauty. I stop in my tracks to admire the elegant and gorgeous decor of the room. We make our way to a long beautifully carved table. In the frenzy of it all I forget about my hair.

There are eight seats at the table and I'm seated in the middle. To my right is Georgio Morelli, Michael, Giuseppe Scozzari and then Franco Danieli. To my left is Luciano Neri, Senator Mario Occhipinti and an interpreter from Amnesty International.

There is an easel upon which I have placed a copy of the Internet piece. And another where I have placed a chart labeled "Proof of Innocence". I field all sorts of questions and notice I am warmly welcomed, the minor exception being the Associated Press, who makes it clear they are not O'Dell supporters. "Is the Parliament going to continue to speak out for one person, or in general?" the AP reporter asks. Luciano is angry and immediately responds, "Joe represents all people and we will fight until we free Joseph." It was the strongest statement made on behalf of Joseph O'Dell since I entered the picture over three years ago.

My speech was prepared, having written it on the plane ride over. First, I thank the Pope for his intervention, the parliamentary members of the national campaign to free Joseph O'Dell, and next all the people of Italy. Then I move onto the documentation. I want to dispel lies and insert truth into the media mainstream.

Afterwards, I interview with *la Repubblica*, Rai, Swiss TV and numerous other media outlets. Immediately following the press conference, we leave for the office at the Parliament and print the AP wires. There we receive a preview of the reporter's interview with me last night while at the restaurant. I review it with Luciano and make only minor corrections.

Finally, Luciano, Giovanni, and his fiancée, and I, go to dinner. They select a wonderful quiet place with superb food and wine. Sitting in a quaint Italian cafe off the cobblestoned streets of Rome is a dream come true for me. I'm immediately comfortable—it reminds me of the holiday feasts I always enjoyed back home with my Italian relatives.

On the way home, Luciano asks the taxi driver to pass the Vatican. He wants to show me the magnificent City and its breathtaking architecture. We also drove by Castel Sant'Angelo, where Pope Clement VII hid from the siege of Charles V's Landsknechte during the Sack of Rome (1527). The Castel was the Pope's fortress, residence and ultimately a prison.

Back in my hotel by 11:30 p.m. I miss Joe's call by ten minutes. My home phone is forwarded to my cell. After I phone the prison to leave him a message he calls me right back. He senses the excitement in my voice as I rapidly explain the past two days' events. "Joe, in the middle of the press conference, the Ambassador of the Italian Republic, His Excellency Signor Luigi Amaduzzi agrees to receive me. Luciano was sure to share this with the press for adequate coverage."

The next day I have a 5:30 p.m. meeting with the Ambassador. Senator Occhipinti and Giovanni (a member of the group, La Rete) escort me to his office in the Parliament. I offer my passport to the guards at the door. In front of the doors leading into the Parliament are five uniformed guardsmen adorned in greenish khaki colored pants with matching jackets decorated with brass buttons. Draped over their shoulders, their capes have red fabric forming a V-shape down their backs. Black berets and boots complete their outfits. Their white-gloved hands each hold a rifle, which is held at attention. They move aside to let us pass by.

Inside the building, in the middle of an arched doorway, stands a single, rather large, guard dressed in a black suit, bow tie and white shirt. He reaches to shake my hand and stops momentarily for a picture before I'm escorted down a hallway to be received by the ambassador. The room is massively elegant. Magnificent artwork tastefully decorates the walls. As I step toward the ambassador he welcomes me with a warm handshake. He wears a double-breasted suit with a red tie.

"Please, take a seat," he directs me.

He first asks me if I believe the intervention has made a difference. I assure him it has, but add that most won't admit it. He is not as sure. A skeptical tone in his voice, doubt lingers in his words. He tells me that the federal government does not control the state criminal court system, so they can do very little. I inform him about the three Supreme Court Justices and their comments in 1991 about Joe's case. He believes that's why they stopped the execution. Now it is I who is not so sure. I urge his continued support and reiterate the importance of using one innocence case in the United States to reveal the flaws of the system to the people. He openly states, "The President of Italy cannot intervene formally a second time. But quietly and diplomatically, he can. Unless there is new evidence." We have a full 20–30 minute meeting prior to my departure. I listen with intent curiosity when he converses in Italian to a member of the La Rete group. I wish I knew the language. We reach to shake hands and he pulls my hand up as if to kiss it. In the awe of the moment it escapes me whether he actually does.

Immediately back at the Press Club we issue a press release about my visit with the ambassador. The ambassador is the right hand advisor to the President of Italy. Luciano jokes with me and says even he has never met him. "It is a high honor, Lori," he tells me.

The very next day I am scheduled to appear on the *Maurizio Costanzo* talk show. I'm told it is ranked the number one talk show in Italy. As I enter the studio I'm greeted by numerous celebrities, none of whom I'm familiar with. I've been told that I will be among a panel that includes the Foreign Affairs Prime Minister Prodi. Staff members check my makeup and hair. I take the little fuss they make over me as a good sign. We are then escorted to our seats on stage. Seated to my immediate left is my interpreter. To my right is sociologist Franco Ferratti, a celebrity singer, comedian Peppe Lanzetta, a woman working at home (which was a novel idea at the time), a doctor, and a man from a boat with lost members. Surprisingly, I'm not nervous. I feel confident and find myself conversing intelligently with all of them. The show is a success and I understand it helps to nationalize the O'Dell cause. For me, I am simply on a mission which is far greater than myself. To others I'm becoming an Italian *cause célèbre*.

To greet the morning listeners on their way to work I am scheduled for a 7:30 a.m. interview on Rai Radio. The program's host is curious why the Italians are supporting this one single case. The broadcast includes various personalities, and many callers. A well-known philosopher shares the line with me. We are informed it was a powerful show, and another success. Before I end my interview I make a statement regarding capital punishment, suggesting those in favor of it might possibly have a change of heart if they witnessed firsthand what I saw with Joe. I don't spare the details of the horror in preparing for one's own death, or how evil the environment is.

I've been scheduled for another Rai talk show at 10:30 a.m. This one is on TV. And this time they make me up and fix my hair. It's a game show and the talk host is reported to be the second largest to the *Costanzo* show. Again, I speak about Joe after a question and answer session earlier rehearsed. I find myself having fun and leave with a photo and autograph from the host.

As I leave the studio and step to the streets, Rai TV interviews me before I continue my scheduled tour of this warm and welcoming country.

Our time is tight and we are now literally running to meet, Luciano Violante, the President of Camera dei Deputati at the Italian Parliament. It is a more casual and laid-back meeting than would be with the President of the Senate, whom I will meet later. He asks me what he can do for me. Before I can respond he suggests a debate in the United States. It's a brilliant idea. We engage in conversation for about 20 minutes and take advantage of a photo op by his desk. I leave with another friend by my side.

We break for lunch in mid-afternoon and during lunch I'm interviewed by a reporter from *il manifesto*. I inform her about the fundraising campaign. She offers me a gift to give to Joe.

When I return to the hotel I'm told to pack for a trip to Umbria. I will be staying at Luciano's house as my stay in Italy continues. We hop the train and arrive in the evening. Joe calls at 11:00 that night. He tells me that earlier in the day he had passed out as a result of low blood pressure.

Lucian's blue French car takes us up a dirt road to his stone house. It sits on top of a mountain in the Umbrian countryside. Quietly secluded, the old, but beautifully renovated, stone home is exactly what I need to escape my frantic pace ever since I got to Italy. Luciano promises a ride on his horse as I walk past their stall, chickens running everywhere.

By mid-morning the next day, after a restful night in the guest bedroom, we are on our way to Perugia to meet with the president (the president of a region is like a governor in the U.S.). I am warmly received and find myself in a stately office even nicer than that of the President of Camera dei Deputati. Our interview is taped by Rai TV, Channel 3. I relay the posture of the case and statistics of the death penalty and give thanks for their support, while reiterating that the battle is far from over. We pose for photographs, after which I proceed to a conference room where I meet with the vice president of the city of Province. We, too, memorialize our visit with photo ops. Before I leave he offers me a book of Umbria and a pin of his city for my lapel.

On our way next to see the Mayor of Perugia, Gianfranco Maddoli, we walk down the gorgeous center of town enjoying the brilliantly sunny day. I find myself feeling so comfortable in this foreign, yet familiar country. I'm not among strangers. They have become my friends. The expressions of love and compassion offered to me are unparalleled back home. The mayor embraces me, we engage pleasantries and there are more photo ops. He, too, offers me gifts, a book of Perugia and a pin of the symbol of his town. He also gives me a copy of the letter he wrote to the American ambassador to request Governor Allen's halt of the execution. Accompanying us is a woman who is a secretary to the bishop, who is now head of all the bishops in Italy, and is in the Vatican. She will call him in the morning to see if she can set a meeting with Pope John Paul II.

Basilica Papale di San Francesco (St. Francis of Italy) was built in 1230 as a world center of peace. It was built in three stages through the 1500s. It is the mother church of the Roman Catholic Order of Friars Minor, commonly known as the Franciscan Order. The basilica is one of the most important places of Christian pilgrimage in Italy. It is next on my tour. I am learning about St. Francis for the first time. Father Nicola gives me a complete tour and shows me the three levels of tiers of this beautiful church—the Upper Basilica, the Lower Basilica and the crypt. I learn about the five clusters, which represent different religions, all to unite as one. Next to the basilica stands the friary Sacro Covento. Its imposing walls are cascaded with Romanesque arches. As I stand in the midst of them I am overwhelmed by the history surrounding me.

As I pass through the church library, my eyes focus on manuscripts from the 12th century, the tombstone of Francisco, and the place below, the bottom tier, where his bones are laid. This is where I pray. The paintings all over the ceilings and walls were created by only three artists, I am told.

During the tour I am introduced to Father Julius, head of the Franciscans in Assisi. It is a recognized honor of which I am humbled to receive. After the tour, and in response to my question regarding what message he would like to give me to aid in my work in the United States, he hands me a letter he had just drafted. Rai TV photographs this unique tour of the grounds. And they don't miss the photo op in the exchange between Father Julius and I. The formal greeting extended to me indicates how much support Joe O'Dell is getting in a country that has no reason to care whether he lives or dies. At the conclusion of my tour, and as I speak about the death penalty case, including Joe's pending execution, tears start to fill my eyes. Just as quickly, and upon saying goodbye to Father Julius, I am now crying tears of joy. The sanctity of the moment and the knowledge that people had gone so far out of their way for me, for Joseph, is overwhelming.

Next we leave for Todi, a place the *New York Times* once wrote was the most desirable place to live in the world. A huge crowd of people is waiting outside the building I'm about to enter. Walking past them I notice a sign announcing my presence. This is a formal meeting, to discuss my involvement with the case and the death penalty in general. The session runs smoothly. Included with me is an organization of politicians who wish to start an international campaign to abolish the death penalty. They want me to head it. The Mayor of Todi, Ottavio Nulli Pero, walks in to greet me with kisses on both cheeks. He presents me with a picturesque book of Todi and a letter from the bishop, who has apologized for not being able to be here. We all, around a dozen of us at this point, depart for dinner. That evening, the television station broadcasts my meeting with the governor (president) and Father Julius. I am back at in Luciano's house by 1:30 a.m., after one of the most memorable days of my life.

I slip my jeans on and prepare to stroll around the grounds and view the beauty of the Umbrian forest around me. Luciano has agreed to let me ride his horse. As I mount her, he is holding the reins. He jumps on his favorite and slowly we head toward the hills and through the mountain forest. From the top of this mountain it looks like you can see forever. My eyes search for the horizon but never quite catch a glimpse of it. After a peaceful morning ride we dismount and tie the horses to the rail. Later that morning, Luciano takes what he refers to as his "mountain car" and we use it to climb the mountains to a breathtaking spot where we are literally above the clouds. Marina, his lovely wife, and friend Ann, come along. We stop to see his friend's magnificent wild horses on the way down the mountain. I am surprised to see them approach the car as he calls them one by one. Three black and one caramel color with white markings. They are quite tame for wild horses, allowing me to stroke their mane.

At 5:30 p.m. we conduct two television interviews with the mayor of Castello. The photographers are snapping photos continuously. The mayor mentions that he hopes for a positive outcome and that the next time he sees me it is with Joseph. He even says that Joe's battle is his battle, too. I am deeply touched. As we walk through the local square, everyone seems to recognize me from the Costanzo talk show which had aired on TV a few nights earlier. Some of the townspeople comment and greet me with warm smiles. Later that night Luciano helps me go through the photographs that had been taken over the last few days.

"Let me write down who the dignitaries are on the back of the pictures so you'll remember their names," Luciano offers.

This will help me prepare proper thank-you cards. I'm thinking about Jennifer and Joe now, wishing they could join in the splendid day I just had in this country I now love.

Today I leave for Rome. Annibale, Luciano's friend, is driving me to her house there. Before I depart, I kiss Luciano and his wife good-bye and thank them for all their wonderful hospitality. Giovanni greets us when we arrive and takes me to the Parliament where I drop off my belongings. I call Mecklenburg prison to leave a message for Joe to call the lawyers on Monday at 5:00 p.m. for a conference call. I learn here that the Parliament has arranged for a one-hour evening flight to Palermo.

The next morning Giovanni comes for me and prepares me for the "ceremony". The mayor is about to officially make Joseph Roger O'Dell an honorary citizen of Palermo. As we approach, there are cameras and photographers everywhere. Mayor Leoluca Orlando speaks first.

"Palermo has a history of death and this honorary citizenship for Joseph O'Dell means we are saying no to death and yes to life! This is a small gesture but an important one."

He speaks of Joe as one who is probably innocent. I reach for the microphone and thank everyone for being here.

"Mayor Orlando, please know that while this may be a small gesture in your eyes, to Joseph it means the world. I am grateful for your generosity. Joe wishes to share a message with you as well. With his deepest gratitude he is honored to receive the citizenship and for your support in his case and against the death penalty. Joseph looks forward to the day he can place his feet on the soil of your country."

Because this quote was a great "sound bite" (as I would later learn) it was splashed all over the newspapers. As the mayor hands me the citizenship papers, one woman in the audience cries out, "Why Joe?" to which the mayor responds, "Because he can and did thank me for my commitment to save his life."

Then we are escorted into the mayor's grand office, which is more suitable for the vice president of a country. I inform him about the details of the case and the need for the support of the European Parliament of which he is a member and has some influence. I am seeking support from countries such as Germany, France, Spain and others, to join in our fight. I then recite the procedural posture of the case and the need to overturn the 21-day rule.

The mayor says, "Lori, I am leaving for Brussels in the morning and then to the European Parliament. I will give you my number in Brussels. Please fax me a brief summary of the 21-day rule and what needs to be done." The next day, while in Rome, I do just that.

Before I leave Palermo, and while still in his office, the mayor mentions that at this very moment there is a press conference in the next room and the subject is genocide. He then suggests a photo op with the square behind us. He opens the huge windows and we step onto the balcony overlooking the picturesque square. Once again, we pose with the citizenship papers. Mayor Orlando is courageous, a good person and I like him immensely. In a display of solidarity he exclaims, "Next time you come, Joseph will be walking the square with us."

I'm now scheduled for a tour of the Sicilian Parliament. I am being escorted to the "red room", where important meetings take place. On one of the balconies there are two dates inscribed for their significance. One is 1130, which was the beginning of Sicily, the first government. The other is inscribed 1947, which is the date Sicily won its independence.

I walk through the elegant Sicilian Parliament building toward the president's office. We stop in the dining room where our lunch is served at a long, elaborately carved wooden table. Afterwards, I'm presented with a "medal" of the 50th anniversary of Sicily, a Sicilian emblem and a book, all gifts from the president. I am deeply moved.

Palermo is famous for their puppets, so the Parliamentarians indulge me in a little shopping. During my stroll through town I notice my name on several large posters, announcing my appearance at 6:00 p.m. at the Palace, a public meeting house.

Prior to lunch I had spoken at the law school in Palermo. Arriving to an audience of around 400. On stage, I sat among a professor, Alfredo Galasso (a very famous lawyer), a judge from Rome, Michaela DelGaudio (an old Parliament member from the Camera dei Deputati) and two students. I spoke about Joe's case and the procedural vs. substance problem in our American court system. Sensing they were not convinced of his innocence, I quickly went over the evidence. At the end of my presentation I took questions and met with students on stage.

The town meeting was well attended. I was seated in the center and to my left was Professor Galasso, then Judge DelGaudio and next a philosopher (who was very good!). I spoke against the death penalty mostly, at times interjecting Joe's case and his innocence. When approached by an intern for Amnesty, and without much thought, I truthfully inform him that Amnesty had not been particularly helpful to Joe or his cause. The intern tells me that Amnesty is bureaucratic and afraid to challenge the government.

It is Martin Luther King Day in the U.S., so while I wanted to have a conference call with Joe and his attorneys, that wasn't going to happen.

The next morning I depart for Rome. I had wanted to do some sightseeing while there, so Giovanni arranges for one of the girls in his office to take me around. The tour took me to the Coliseum and the Roman ruins. Four thousand years of history laid out before us. Afterwards, we tour the Roman Catacombs, where I see the Catacomb of San Callisto. Here I witness the ancient underground tunnels of tombs and learn this is where, in the third century, nine Popes were buried. I relish in the ability to be a simple tourist and learn the history of a country that is taking on my battle. The day ends with an interview back at the office with Rai International. Though a difficult reporter, the woman I talk with is important. Her organization will reach the United States, around the world, and publish in their international magazine.

After my interview, in the early evening, I meet briefly with Rosa Jervolino Russo. She is the President of Constitutional Affairs and has been instrumental in getting the Parliament's help for Joe. She's a very busy woman, but graciously takes the time to greet me. She is not pleased that Luciano's group, La Rete, has not included her. She and Luciano share a few words and she departs. I thank her immensely for her help and support. We kiss goodbye.

I am now ready for dinner with the "team" with Calogero (Rino) Piscitello, Giovanni, Luciano Neri and Senator Mario Occhipinti. Franco Danieli and Giuseppe Scozzari cannot make it. They choose a spot where the elite members of Parliament dine and there I enjoy a relaxing evening free from the press.

On the way back to my hotel, the cab gets lost causing me to miss Joe's call. Immediately, I call the lawyers and Debo informs me he is on the line with Joe. Joe is upset. We have not spoken in five days and our lifeline has become disconnected. Our conversation is measured due to Debo's presence. Joe had called Richard Reyna, who wants me to call him when I return to the U.S. I could tell Joe is relieved to hear my voice after he states, "No more trips to Italy!" He wants me home where I'm not so far removed from his lawyers and continued investigation. The lawyers inform me they are waiting on Barry Scheck to give directions for the DNA tests.

Back at the hotel, Luciano calls with delight in his voice. "Lori, they will receive you at the Vatican tomorrow!" I hadn't thought about the reality of it all, not yet. After a good night's sleep, I anxiously awaken early for Luciano, who collects me for a visit to the Parliament office. It is there we prepare for a 5:15 p.m. meeting at the Vatican. I phone Kitty Behan and inform her of the details of my tour in Italy.

She's amused and tells me the *pro bono* committee is looking at Joe's case, and that the papers are looking good. Kitty reminds me that she is waiting to hear from me about the costs of the firm being reimbursed. I assure her that it is not a problem, that the Italian Parliament is raising money, and artists were donating money through their paintings. She requests at least two hours of my time upon my return to go over the details. Before we hang up, Kitty promises to reach out to Bob Smith to see if they can work together.

It's now time to be escorted to the Vatican. I am anxious and nervous about being received by the third highest official at the Vatican. Monsignor Gabriele Caccia is the assistant to the Secretary of State, who is directly below the Pope in authority.

As we near Vatican City I look up in awe at its magnificence. In my hands are three things, Sister Helen Prejean's letter, court papers about Joe's case, and a cassette tape directly from death row to the Pope. I am struck by the thought of the meeting that lies ahead of me. Approaching the Vatican it is quickly apparent by the amount of security that this is not a casual visit. I obtain a pass to enter the building and proceed in. They are expecting me. Inside, the Vatican is breathtaking.

Dressed in a long black robe, Monsignor Caccia is a mild-mannered, warm and kind-hearted man. Instantly, I feel a kinship with him. We arrive at his office where we sit to visit with one another.

"Monsignor, Sister Helen Prejean asked me to deliver this letter to the Pope. I also have some documents on Joseph's case and a tape from him addressing the Pope. Will you be sure that he receives it?" I gently ask.

"Yes, Lori. I will personally deliver them myself."

I thank him for the Pope's intervention, assuring him of our gratitude. Nearing the end of our meeting he leaves briefly, returning with a small box in his hand.

"This is a gift from the Pope."

I open the white satin box with a symbol of the Vatican on top etched in gold. Inside is the most beautiful rosary I have ever seen.

"I will pray for you and Joseph," he says.

I thank him for his kindness and support. We embrace before I leave.

Prior to my visit with Monsignor Caccia I had a meeting with Father Gino, a short man with glasses that fit proportionately with his face and expressions. A jubilant fellow, Father Gino is the main writer for the Vatican newspaper. The Vatican newspaper, *L'Osservatore Romano*, is printed in nine different languages, including English, Italian, French, German and Spanish—its voice is far reaching. Father Gino tells me he's been fighting the death penalty for 25 years and that he was one of the first Catholics to speak out against it. He was admonished and prevented from writing about it further. He has since written and published a book in Italy on the death penalty and asks me if I would like to see it. "Of course, Father," I reply.

"Would you like to see if you can get it published in America? You would have to get it translated into English first," he says.

"Yes, I will try, Father. Where would you want the money to go?" I ask.

"To groups against the death penalty," he responds.

I think to myself that I should start my own as I haven't found one that would fit the bill. I'm honored Father Gino trusts me and has asked me to perform this task. He then tells me that he has connections with the BBC and wants to do a TV program with me. Father Gino won't interview with any other TV stations as he believes they are not serious. Unfortunately, I'm scheduled to leave Italy in another day so there wouldn't be enough time for this. I promise to do the interview when I next return to Italy. Before I leave I tell him it was important that he knew Joe was innocent and he said, "Yes, I know." I then reiterate a few facts concerning the state's fabrications. It's hard *not* to talk about it.

When I return to the Italian Parliament, excited to share my visit at the Vatican, my new friends ask to see the rosary. As I open the box they appear surprised. I offer it to their outreached hands. "Lori, that is not the rosary that's given to everyone. I think it may be the Pope's personal rosary." I was awed by this statement and would not know its truth until months later.

****

After ten days in Italy, meeting, dining and staying with a variety of new friends, it is time to return home. Yet, as I board the plane and head back to my country a tinge of sadness falls over me. Here in Italy, we are supported. We are loved. Back home we are alone, hated by the Commonwealth of Virginia. The long plane ride home offers me time to readjust.

I slide back easily into the routine when I arrive home, alone, in Chatham. Today, my first day back in the United States, I pray. My small hands clutch the rosary given to me by Pope John Paul II. I raise it to my heart, gently kissing it as I lay it against my chest. I vow to cherish it for the rest of my life.

January 25, 1997. My schedule has etched itself into my sleeping habits so I awaken early and talk to Joe several times throughout the day. I forget that he has just missed death by less than 24 hours and is still on edge. The experience has actually left me wanting to distance myself from him personally, too scared to face the ugly truth. My threats to leave him, or the case, don't help. I have such mixed emotions about my involvement that, at times, I just want to run away—find my way back to normalcy. There is nothing normal about my life now. Knowing Joe is in a fragile state, I remind myself to think more of him and less of my own needs, especially when I hear him break down. A crying death row inmate can crack any tough facade one carries. Listening to him sob now as he speaks of Ronnie Hoke's death weakens me. "God has prepared me for everything but that," Joe says. The look on Ronnie's face haunts Joe everyday.

"God did not want you to see such evil ahead of time," I offer in consolation. *Oh my gosh. Did it slip? What does that mean? That he may experience it again? Not if I can help it*, I convince myself. The experience has traumatized Joe, and without knowing it, me too.

Chapter 22

~Dangerous Alibi~

The need to be near my daughter overshadows all else, driving me to pack for a trip to Princeton. I need to see her beautiful face and feel her presence in my life. In preparation of my return to New Jersey I locate a one-bedroom condo in Lawrenceville. Although a tiny apartment, *it's only for four months,* I tell myself. More than most road trips, I'm looking forward to this one because at the end of it is my shining star.

It doesn't take long before Luciano calls from Rome. He and several members of the Italian Parliament had expressed their desire to be present at the U.S. Supreme Court for oral argument in Joe's case. I am extremely impressed with their resolve. During our conversation, I encourage Luciano to ask for tickets in advance. "There is limited seating," I advise him. I offer to assist in making this happen. I also request the addresses of the Parliament members who wish to visit with Joe. Before leaving Italy they had advised me of their interest in seeing the man they are rallying for. I would need their complete information to arrange such a highly unusual visit.

To the best of my knowledge this is the very first time dignitaries from a foreign country will be walking the same path of the condemned when they arrive at Mecklenburg Correctional Center to see Joe O'Dell, the man whose cause they now call their own. To keep the momentum going I call George Kendall. He expresses excitement about my Italian trip, eagerly sharing his amazement at the unfolding of events. George suggests the Georgetown Law campus as a location for the debate and refers me to Stephen Bright. Taking the advice from a dignitary to conduct an international debate requires I invite the prosecution and Attorney General's office. For now, I mentally create a list of panelists; Stephen Bright, a strong advocate against the death penalty, is teaching at Georgetown Law; Bob Morin is now a judge in Washington; and Father Darian, who also teaches at the law school. This will draw national attention for Joe in the legal community. It also affords us the chance the get the truth out about the evidence, which means now I also need a DNA expert. Wanting the most notable expert in the field means a call to Barry Scheck. My mission now is to organize a press conference, and forum, in Washington for an international presentation of Joe O'Dell's case.

Despite the fact that Frank Green is still focused on sensationalism, I remain focused on educating him about the case. I agree to send him photos of my time in Italy. Not long after, he books a trip to Italy for February 17, 1997, to spend an *entire week*. This must be one of the perks he can squeeze out of the newspaper. I agree to hook him up with Luciano. Luciano can prepare Frank's interviewees, to ensure nothing backfires.

Meanwhile, my move to New Jersey has made for a hectic few days. Jen and I arrive at the Lawrenceville apartment and we both realize it's much too small and not at all well-appointed. We decide to move back to the townhouse in Somerset. I have decided to stay there for my last two years of law school. Or at least a year, to make this place a home for Jennifer. I spend a great deal of money furnishing and fixing up the townhouse for our comfort. Jennifer had wanted to return to her friends at the Princeton Day School, which meant a transfer to the Rutgers School of Law for me to finish my law school education. It was easy to do after grading at the top of my class, and onto the law review journal *New England Journal on Criminal and Civil Confinement.*

The phone rings and instantly Luciano's voice is hurried with excitement. "Lori, Ratzinger, a Vatican representative and the second highest official and speaker for the Pope, announced that the Vatican's position will be against the death penalty in *all* cases."

Three days later, I would find out from a Vatican representative in Washington that the Pope will soon announce this. If true, Sister Helen tells me this is the first time in two thousand years that this has occurred. I am elated. Helen is ecstatic. The news serves to bond us together even further. It's an amazing accomplishment. This shift in the Catholic religion is a direct result of our battle, and Joe's case. And Sister Helen's letter, hand delivered to the Pope.

The next morning I am on the phone with Channel 8 in Richmond. Richard Real is interested in my trip to Italy and wants to discuss it, or so I think. After a brief interruption, Richard calls me back and urgently wants an interview. He states his producer wants to schedule it for Monday. They don't want to wait until next week when I will be in Virginia to see Joe. I wonder what's up. I tell him that I'm only interested in discussing the evidence and ask for a half-hour to do so. At the same time, I'm thinking I want to meet with Detective Dunn from the murder investigation to face off with him.

The following day, when Helen and I speak again, I ask if she'll participate in the forum in Washington on March 18. We end the conversation with her referring me to Ron Tayback of the American Bar Association. She wants to stay with her friend Kris, who is dying of cancer. For the first time, and as we say goodbye, I tell her I love her. She replies, "I love you, too."

Shortly thereafter, the Arnold and Porter law firm reaches me. "Please hold for Kitty Behan," says a voice trained for setting up conference calls. "Let's meet next week to discuss Joe's case," Kitty suggests. She also wants to set up a death penalty organization. Through my conversation with Father Gino and others, I realize this is exactly what I should do now, but I gently respond "no." I need to keep her focused on Joe and his new trial. Kitty promises to set up a meeting with Father Darian and myself.

I waste no time in reaching Ron Tayback at the American Bar Association to request that he speak at the International Forum. He is kind and engaging, willing to come. "I can't make the 18th. I can be available on the 19th," he explains. "Lori, I heard about your trip to Italy. I have some ideas on how Italy can fight the death penalty here in the U.S.," Ron says. He is a great contact. Before we hang up he tells me he doesn't understand why Paul, Weiss, Rifkind, Wharton & Garrison have not asked for an amicus curie brief on the O'Dell case. I am not surprised.

On Monday, Richard Real, from Channel 8 in Richmond, Virginia, is at my front door with camera in hand. I diligently speak about Joe's case for nearly three hours. It's easy to share details about my recent trip to Italy, and the overwhelming support we have from the Italians. I have a good feeling that perhaps, maybe, this will be the first time a story is told without changing the facts. I want so much for the facts to come out regarding Joe's innocence. Catching me off guard, and at the very every end of the interview, Richard asks me what I thought was a rather odd question. "Do you love Joe O'Dell?" I am taken aback by his question, sensing there is more to it than he reveals. "Certainly I care for him and love him as a person, I am fighting for his life," I reply.

Only twelve days later, after receiving the tape of the aired show, having run to the mailbox thinking, finally, the truth will come out, I find out *they had tricked me.* They fooled me into believing they were running a story about my trip to Italy and Joe's innocence. Instead, they did a show on "lovers behind bars." I was livid! I contact the American Writers Association—surely there is something unethical about tricking someone as they did me. I wanted an apology, and admission of a mistake. As I would later discover, this organization protects its own, just as the officials in Virginia were protecting their verdict.

Since Sister Helen probably won't be able to attend the press conference, I reach out to Clive Stafford Smith, who readily agrees to assist. Clive mentions that he would really like to help Joe, adding he will be there if Joe is freed. I need a lawyer who is not afraid to speak out on behalf of Joe. In preparation for the press conference I work on hiring a good PR firm in Washington. To be ready, I reserve a room at the Press Club in Washington for March 17.

Meanwhile, I continue nesting to make an attractive and comfortable home for Jennifer. The comfort of this house is beginning to make it feel like home. But soon I would take Jennifer from this home to the home of Joseph Roger O'Dell, bridging the stark difference between the two.

It's mid-February and I'm driving to Virginia to see Joe. Not wanting to leave Jennifer home, I reluctantly decide to take her with me. It will be the first time she meets him, the man who has consumed my life for over three and a half years. I think it's time. Jen had just returned from a three-day trip to Cooperstown, NY to visit the baseball hall of fame. It was mini-week at school. I missed her so much when she was gone that I scooped her up after school and together we are taking this unique road trip. Dinner is our only pit stop, as we make our way through Virginia in the pouring rain, finally arriving at 10:45 p.m. I hate driving in the rain.

Tired of leaving everyone at home, I had even decided to bring along the family dog, Taffy, our yellow lab. Having claimed shotgun, Jen leaves Taffy riding in the back seat of my Mercedes. Cautiously aware of the strangeness in this arrangement my mind is eased when the weekend turns out better than I could have imagined. I worried: will this scar her? Is she strong enough for this? Then I relax as Jen and Joe's eyes light up when they see each other. Like it or not, Joe is a part of her life, too. They had exchanged a few cards and spoken on the phone from time to time. Joe is delighted to be involved in family normalcy, and I'm happy to share this with him. For three days I watch as they smile and laugh together from behind plexiglass in a maximum security prison. Having prepared Jen as best I could for this visit I was relieved that she displayed no signs of fear or discomfort during our visits. "Mommy, Joe doesn't *look* mean," Jen says after one of our visits. On our last day we decide to leave in mid-afternoon to enable our return back to New Jersey at a reasonable hour. I found it easy to have Taffy with us. She added to our family fun on this unconventional road trip.

As the days pass, I continue to work on the press conference. I draft a letter to the ethics committee for *Journalist* concerning the Channel 8 interview, alerting them to the deceit by Richard Real. I'm also updating the Internet piece to include the support of a politician who has joined our team, Senator Patrick Leahy. Conscious of the fact that I need to raise money for the campaign I begin to call religious organizations.

"Meow, meow," I hear on the other end of the phone. Joe now has two kittens in his cell. Oreo is about six weeks old. Feeling depressed this morning, Joe had given them up. The lift of his mood called for drastic measures, and sophisticated bartering. In exchange for Oreo and his brother, Joe gave the guard his Walkman. His pain, replaced with lightness, offers me equal pleasure. Peace returns to his voice. With enough time having passed from our experience at the death house, we are reconnecting. I feel his spirit returning, and the much needed desire to keep fighting.

The date for the press conference is fast approaching. Frank Green calls for an interview. He's still focused on sensationalism as he asks about my relationship with Joe. Kate at Centurion Ministries had informed him that Joe manipulated me into the position I am currently in. I assure Frank that is not so. In usual team fashion, Joe and I have a conference with Kate, who confirms that Green was not interested in Joe's innocence. Instead, he wanted to know about the nature of my relationship with Joe. Kate assures us that she expressed Centurion's belief in Joe's innocence.

Early the next morning Joe informs me that through a reliable source (I am wondering now, a guard?) the FBI is tapping my phone and everyone on Joe's list. Things are heating up and I believe he may be right. I have heard inexplicable clicking on my phone but had dismissed it as just some sort of interference. I recall reading that Alberi's brother is a secret service agent. This would be right up his alley.

Following up on our discussion, Kitty Behan informs me the firm is still evaluating Joe's case and wants to speak to the Italian Parliament. The new partner has expressed some interest. This is a good sign for Joe. But the hotter this topic gets, the more vulnerable I become for criticism and attack. I'm working closely with the Italian Parliament to fight for truth and justice. I realize I'm a target now, subjected to harassment, humiliation and yes, even danger—danger to my life perhaps. I'm becoming more aware of this on my own, and through the concern of others.

The very next day strange events start to occur. Joe alerts me to the prison's search of his cell. It's not unusual for the prison to search an inmate's cell but there was something very different, very odd about this search. For 40 minutes, Joe stood outside of his cell as the guards turned it inside out. Lockdown was just one week ago. Lockdown means the prisoners are confined to their cells as the guards conduct a thorough search for contraband. Now, they are focusing only on Joe. They are looking for legal documents, obviously becoming nervous because, for the first time in history, the Italian Parliament is coming to Mecklenburg. They are looking for *anything* and *everything* now. At 6:00 p.m. Joe calls. When he tries back after the standard 15-minute interval (where MCI gets an additional $3.50 for the reconnect), my phone is blocked. Debo calls to tell me Joe will try later on my fax line. After taking a break and having a quick dinner with my good friend Marie, Joe calls back on the fax line and gets through. Telecom, the phone company, says there is no block; it must have been placed through the prison, they tell me. The games begin.

Birthdays are usually spent around a family cake with candles, presents, flowers and a wonderful dinner at an exclusive restaurant in town. At least they once were. Today's birthday is not like any other. Having passed 40 I am now one year over the "over the hill" mark, creeping slowly, and I do mean slowly, toward 50, the dreaded half-century mark that women usually loathe. The lack of time calls for improvisation. It's no secret that I am fighting the government so my gift is appropriate. Always teasing me about putting up my dukes, laughing at the idea of a petite girl, all of 5'3", firing things up, Joe had an idea of what to buy me. I'm not surprised to learn he encouraged Jen to find some red boxing gloves. Jennifer tells me "I know how much you hate Virginia so when you get angry mom, just use these!" In usual family style, Jen orders me a cake. That evening we all sing the traditional birthday song, Joe included. There is nothing traditional about this scene. Vastly at odds is the difference between this celebration and my past birthdays, where I was gifted with diamond jewelry and limousine trips to New York for a baseball game. The reality of this strange new world has crept into my life ever so slowly. I accept it without question, knowing the bigger picture is so much greater than me.

~Alibi Witness~

For the next few days I prepare for the press conference in Washington, D.C. It is set to include a small demonstration that will be held on the front steps of the U.S. Supreme Court, on the day of oral arguments on behalf of Joe's petition before the court. During these days Richard Reyna tells me I must meet him in Jacksonville, Florida. He's interviewing John Nutter, Joe's alibi witness. I dutifully arrive in

Jacksonville and check into the La Quinta Inn where Richard is also
staying. Locating Nutter wasn't easy, Richard says, but he has a knack
for this kind of work. We are about to meet the man who could have
prevented Joe from greeting death row. In 1986 Joe was sentenced to
death. It is now 1997, eleven years later, and no one has ever met with
John Nutter for a formal interview. *No one.* Not having a clue what to
expect, I take a backseat and watch Richard.

We are in a lower-middle-class neighborhood, in the middle of
a trailer park. This is where Nutter lives. A red Volkswagen beetle
with an open back, engine showing, sits alongside the house. As we
walk toward the trailer, a small black and white dog scurries past us.
A tall, lanky man with reddish hair steps outside to greet us. He looks
surprised, never looking directly at me, speaking only to Richard. We
chat briefly and decide to return after he has showered and is ready for
dinner. One hour later we are at Long Johns steak house.

John Nutter is sure of himself. Cool and laid-back, it's apparent
he resents authority. Still he doesn't look at me, trying to focus on
Richard as we begin our conversation. We laugh a lot, trying to engage
him. When we start discussing the fight with Joe O'Dell, Nutter is
immediately open about it, though remembering it a little differently
than what I had learned from Joe. Nutter is discussing the fight the
prosecution said never existed. He admits to having gotten into a fight
with Joe O'Dell on the evening of the murder, or closer to around 1:15
a.m. when Helen Schartner was no doubt in a struggle for her life. I
can hardly believe what he is saying, and though the version of how the
fight occurred is slightly different from Joe's, he is sure it was Joe. We
ask him if he would submit to a blood test. "Sure, no problem," Nutter replies. I'm thrilled. The day's events lead to a night of tossing and
turning, depriving me of much needed sleep. When I awaken I fear
problems. I can feel the strong attraction Nutter has toward me. I must
be careful in how I handle myself. Richard and I discuss the previous
night's events over breakfast and then rush off to Kinkos. We need to

secure an affidavit from Nutter while we have him in our sight. He appears to be a drifter, unsteady in his address. We waste no time in setting up the blood tests. Nutter is ready when we arrive to pick him up at 4:00 p.m. to escort him to the Southern Reference Lab. At the lab I learn we need to have the attorneys arrange for the blood draw. Clive Stafford Smith had referred me to his friend, Dwight Wells. I call him and ask him to fax a request to the lab. Making plans to arrange for this, and as I am walking away from Richard and Nutter, my back toward them, I sense John is watching me.

For the testing, we are instructed to use a number, not a name. This will assist in privacy issues. John Nutter is amused. Because of this Nutter tells me the nurse wants to know if he's famous. *Infamous* is more like it. Richard and I return to the motel in time for a radio interview that my girlfriend Marie arranged for me back in Princeton, New Jersey. In five minutes I agree to discuss the wrongful conviction of Joseph O'Dell.

For a second evening we all dine again at the steak house. Richard sits across from me and Nutter against the wall of the booth, next to me. It's relaxing and comfortable. Before we head back to the motel I find myself engaging in a game of pool with Nutter. He thought it would be a good place to continue to talk. I agree. As we play, he wages a bet. If I win I get to pick what I want, but if he wins, I must attend his sister's wedding with him. Up until then he was not playing so well and I was doing great, so I agreed. Little did I know he was setting me up. I lost miserably. I now owe him a date at his sister's wedding.

The next day I'm back home preparing for the press conference. In an unprecedented move, four members of the Italian Parliament arrive in New York on March 14 to show their support for Joe. During lunch on Saturday I am interviewed by the *Village Voice*. Sunday afternoon the Italians are escorted by a limo from New York to New Jersey, just a few minutes away from my home. Not knowing where I lived they asked to be dropped off close by. They are at the Middlesex Diner right off a busy highway. After receiving a phone call that they have arrived I grab my keys and hurry to the car. I don't want to keep them waiting. I could never have imagined that I would soon be picking up dignitaries from Italy in the middle of a parking lot, ready to head to a press conference to save a man from being executed for a crime he didn't commit. As I jump out of my car I look around, trying to find them. Luciano is walking toward me waving his arms. My Italian friends are all standing there in the cold with suitcases by their side. We hug and kiss and quickly leave for my home. At the house I fax some material to Clive and share some of the crime scene photos with my new friends and supporters. Then we head out for our road trip to Washington for what will be the biggest press conference in America for Joe O'Dell. On our way down we stop at the Golden Corral in Maryland for a bite to eat. I hated to have to bring them there after dining in the finest restaurants in Italy as their guest, but there was little time for us. I laugh with them at their first time experience in one of America's finest fast-food, buffet-styled restaurants.

"What do we do, Lori?" one of the men asks. I instruct them what to do with the trays as the waitress approaches for our drink order.

"I'll have a glass of wine," Mario replies with a straight face. Instantly I am in stitches. This is not Italy.

"I'm sorry, sir, but we don't have any wine," the waitress replies.

"Okay," Mario says, "I'll take some beer."

Since Italians always drink with their meals, they are shocked, but very amused that the restaurant serves no liquor. Immediately, they notice a rather large woman seated not too far from us and comment that if Italy had restaurants that served food for $8.00 a plate, all you can eat, it would be out of business in two years. "People would bring in the whole family and relatives." We're all laughing at this point. After all this fine dining, I get them to the Sofitel hotel by 11:00 p.m. A tight schedule of interviews fills tomorrow's calendar.

Luciano's first interview is live with MSNBC. Next he moves to

Democracy Now for a taped radio show. Here, we are both interviewed concerning their presence in the United States on Joe's behalf.

Finding time before the press conference, we meet with Clive at the London *Times* to discuss the issues. After a brief visit at the Italian Embassy, where flashbulbs challenge our visibility, we arrive at the Press Club for the 1:30 p.m. media event. I immediately notice the entire room is filled with reporters. My eyes glance to the back wall, noticeably peppered with cameras. At the front table sit four members of the Italian Parliament, Clive Stafford Smith and Dick Dieter, along with a translator that was not very good. Clive led the narration. It was appropriate, as he has stood by Joseph since day one. He emphatically stated that Joseph O'Dell is innocent, and asked, "How much doubt do we need?" Luciano and Franco spoke about Joe and their support for him, also reiterating their belief in Joe's innocence. Next at the podium was Dick Dieter, who spoke just a few minutes on innocence and the courts. Finally, I am grateful to have credible, high-powered attorneys, and dignitaries, speaking out for Joe in his own country.

While in Washington I had received a request to meet with Paul Kourey, another attorney for a death row inmate housed in the same prison as Joe. He informs me he wants to give us the names of those to contact for assistance with witnesses, as well as an FBI agent to conduct a lie detector test for any new witnesses. I am thinking about Nutter now, and wished we had done this with Steve Watson. Paul expressed his amazement at what I had been doing for Joe and mentioned the firm had the *Richmond Times Dispatch* in their hands. We, on the other hand, were being stomped on all over by that paper. Kourey was a good contact, and a face I would see the next day while at the U.S. Supreme Court for oral arguments on behalf of Joseph O'Dell.

My next stop was the American Bar Association where I meet with Ginny Sloan and Kevin Driscoll. Ginny mentions she has a high regard for me. She is now recruiting me for one of their committees. I explain that I would love to help the ABA when I'm finished with law school. I learn that the ABA recently issued a moratorium on the death penalty. Our timing couldn't have been better. Is the timing a coincidence? The news suggests we were making progress!

From there I leave for the U.S. Bishop Conference and meet with Dan Misleh. "Lori, we never did hear from Sister Helen. We will need a Bishop to ask for their help in this case." Bishop Sullivan is now on my list to send materials to in order to garner his support. I tell Dan I will contact Sister Helen and facilitate the necessary communications.

Finally, that evening all the Italian Parliament members and I have dinner at Georgia's, a southern-style cooking restaurant. Alessandra Farkas join us. I am not quite so comfortable with her and, as it turns out, we will be at odds. Luciano is unaware of my discomfort, and her ability for being, well, somewhat too forthright.

March 18, 1997. I look forward to the unfolding of the day's events. The steps of the "Equal Justice for All" building are littered with demonstrators on behalf of Joe, their signs flailing in the air. My gray suit, with a white silk handkerchief in the left pocket, serves to camouflage me in a rather long line of lawyers trying to get in. We arrived late at 10:15 a.m. Authoritatively, we walk in front of everyone; it's *our* case. I am about to sign in when Alessandra pushes me aside and says, "No, not now, I have to go the bathroom."

"I'm sorry, but I'm late and I'm checking in," I reply.

Meanwhile, she had already checked in and had told them she would be translating so they were going to put us in the back. After four years of battling, struggling for the courts to hear Joseph O'Dell's case, this woman was messing with the wrong person. I immediately inform them, "I don't know who told you that but it's not so." *How dare she?* Somehow we manage to sit apart from her. Prior to the oral arguments we are all interviewed by Rai television.

Front row. Bob Smith. Not the one I would have selected for this argument, but most lawyers were afraid to step on colleagues' toes. It's the highest honor for a lawyer to argue before the U.S. Supreme Court.

An honor few lawyers obtain. Bob has been preparing for weeks, practicing with colleagues, undoubtedly for hours. Bob is ready. He's up.
It starts quickly. Bob is sure of himself, strong on his feet. I am taken
aback. He is quick, not stuttering, as he is known to do. I'm incredibly
pleased that he seemingly outperforms Kathryn Baldwin, the representative from the Attorney General's office. Bob is not arguing the innocence aspect of Joe's case. The issue before the court deals with the
sentencing aspect of Joe's trial, based upon the precedent setting case,
Schlup v. Delo[92]. The *Schlup* case stands for the proposition that it is
unconstitutional to argue for the death penalty based upon erroneous
(and misleading) instructions to the jury that a defendant is a danger
to society, when the alternative, a life sentence, means a life sentence
without the possibility of parole.

I listen carefully to the justices and to Justice Souter who expresses
his opinion that it is an "issue of fundamental fairness." One down.
Justice Ginsburg seems to want to find relief under the second exception in *Teague v. Lane*, 489 U.S. 288, 311 (1989). Breyer seems to
lean in our favor. And then we have a favorable appearing Justice Stevens. Justice Scalia is unapologetically obnoxious, but Bob holds his
own. Justice Souter embarrasses Baldwin, almost forcing her to admit
the case (*Schlup v. Delo*) does not present a "new rule." The issue is
whether *Schlup* can be applied to Joe's case. If it is considered a new
rule, they will not apply it to Joe. If the Justices find the issue at hand
is unconstitutional, they would have to decide whether to apply the
law retroactively to Joe. This would require that Joe receive a new
sentencing hearing. More than likely, he would not be sentenced to
death this time around.

Afterwards, Bob conducts an interview with CNN. He doesn't utter a word about Joe's innocence. I am not surprised. Though I understand him not wishing to annoy the Justices, if he does not show that
he believes in his client's innocence, it will be hard to get relief for him.

[92] *Schlup v. Delo*, 115 S. Ct. 851 (1995).

As the oral argument ends, we move toward the exit with the crowd. Most of them are casual observers. For me, it's literally life or death for someone I am fiercely fighting for.

There is a full array of cameras and reporters outside waiting for us. Bob speaks first and then they move on to me. They know who I am, addressing me as Ms. Urs. I respond, stating I felt we had four justices, a mistake I knew right off the bat. A lawyer should *never* speculate about such things, but I was not yet legally trained, so I spoke my mind. I went on to say that the innocence aspect of Joe's case should have been an issue before the court, and then I quickly turned it over to the Italians. I linger to watch Bob in other interviews to ensure he is supportive of his client. Finally, I turn to thank the demonstrators and speak briefly to them. "Lori," one shouts out, "will you come speak at Georgetown?" I say that I will. Another supporter yells out, "I bet you rile things up wherever you go!" As this person didn't know me at all I was surprised by her statement. I was unaware of any reputation or influence that I had on others. In my mind all I was doing was fighting for Joe. When I think back to my childhood years my mother always ribbed me about being a fighter. But I was fighting in my own household for equal treatment, my mom having favored my brother who took care of my invalid father. And I remember that I stuck up for my younger sister quite often. Now, that household fight takes on a whole new meaning as I fight for a man I would never have become involved with but for a twist of fate.

Luciano speaks to the reporters and confirms the Italian Parliament's support for Joe and the belief in his innocence. At the end of his speech we pose for historic photographs on the steps of the courthouse.

During my campaign it was not unusual to speak with so many people over the phone, but never to have the privilege of meeting them in person. Andy Sebok and Sandy Hausler introduce themselves to me on the courthouse steps. They were both Joe's lawyers a long time ago.

I had contacted them in the ordinary course of my work. Andy wanted information on Steven Watson. "Joe needs help with a new trial," I replied. "I can't help there," Andy says. "Andy, you know Watson is attorney client privilege. I cannot discuss this with you." He mentions he called the firm looking for me. I wasn't told. "Please be sure to let Joe know I was here," Sandy adds. "I will. Joe will be pleased."

Michelle Brace from the Virginia Capital Representation Resource Center approaches and offers praise for a job well done. Bob's wife joins her. "Yeah, Lori, how did you get a senator here?" Eyeing the Attorney General and friends huddled by the steps I notice them watching me. I was proud. Proud to stand up to them and finally get some support for Joe.

After a brief stop at the hotel, my Italian contingent and I go off to a wonderful restaurant. Luciano, Franco, Mario and Rino are all pleased to be greeted by an Italian maitre d' and a waitress. Perhaps, finally, they get to feel a touch of their country here in the U.S.

It's now early morning and we are readying to leave for death row. To arrive on time for the limousine I had arranged for the dignitaries in South Hill, we had to leave by 7:00 a.m. Luciano is late and we don't leave until 7:40 a.m. This allows us just enough time to stop briefly for coffee at McDonalds, something I'm sure they are not used to. The notion of driving while drinking coffee would bring a traffic ticket in Italy. The thought has us laughing so hard we decide to pull over so they can mix the sugar in their cup. When we arrive at the Best Western, they immediately start to work their magic to obtain a Cadillac from a local car dealer. Their maintenance man would drive us. We arrive at the prison a half hour later. Numerous media are scattered in the parking lot, including News G (Italian press), *Richmond Times Dispatch*, *Virginian-Pilot*, Associated Press and many others. It's raining, yet like hunters waiting for their prey, they have waited for us. The dignitaries take questions while the rain falls. The guard meets up with us at the front gate to dutifully ask us to identify ourselves. He jots all their names down on a pad. He passes on me, he already knows who I am. When the members of the Italian Parliament are ready to enter the prison a guard comes out to greet them and walk them through the main door. They enter. I leave.

I return to the motel and start making calls, but before I know it the Italians are ready to be picked up. The officials granted them a very brief visit. They asked to see the warden before they left so arrangements were quickly made for their request to be honored. I can only assume they were sure to let the warden know their concerns, and of their support for Joseph. The Italians walk out of the prison at 3:30 p.m. My new friends are now being interviewed by Channel 6, the AP and ANSA from Italy.

David Botkins, a tall thin man in a tan trench coat, stood outside the entire time with a uniformed guard. A spokesperson for the Department of Corrections, he has been a strong advocate against me, and of course Joe. He is trying to intimidate the reception of the dignitaries. It's not working. As I get out of the car, Rino eyes me to get back in. At the time, I am unaware of who Botkins is, only to find out later it was he who had blocked media communication for Joe on more than one occasion.

Back at the motel we grab a snack before the Italian Parliament members have to leave for the airport and their Alitalia flight back to Italy. I reach for the phone to call Richard. "Lori, I'm sorry but I cannot make it to Virginia. We will have to reschedule." Our investigation is postponed. I find relief in his words. Frankly, I don't have the funds for his investigation right now. The press conference and the trip down here has wiped out my bank account. And with the days' hectic events, I am desperately in need of a break.

The next morning I drop some coins in the metal box outside the motel and grab the *Richmond Times Dispatch*. To my surprise, I discover a fairly decent and accurate article about Joe. They are not referring to me as Joe's spouse, but more accurately as a close friend. The message is positive. The paper cites the Italians as saying, "We believe more now in Joe's innocence." It's a small victory, marking a step in the right direction.

It's time for me to venture back north to return home, stopping briefly in Washington D.C. I have recently been told that my picture is one of 50 chosen from around the world to be displayed in the Smithsonian Institute for the *24 Hours in Cyberspace* project. Inside the Smithsonian, in a far corner, I notice my photograph framed on the wall depicting Joe's Internet plight. It's one of many selected for inclusion in their book and now displayed here in the Institute for a couple of months. Later, I learn it will be stored in the Smithsonian's archives—memorialized forever. Not wanting to linger, I make it to New Jersey in time to pick Jennifer up from school, arriving home just in time for Joe's call. I am intensely interested in what he has to say.

"Lori, after the Italians' visit and before they even left, the deputy and other guards at Mecklenburg converged on me, trying to get me to fight back in front of the Italians. They didn't even wait for them to leave. I kept my cool. They asked me about TV. Botkins is really mad about the tape I made for them and confiscated it and the letter I left at the gate—they never received it." It has been okay, and still is, for inmates to leave things at the gate for their visitors. This time was different. The prison did not like being in the public eye, and facing international scrutiny. The guards gave Joe a disciplinary charge for contraband (his TV?) and rummaged through his cell removing his only TV. Joe is now quite upset, and rightfully so. The prison is retaliating because we had the audacity to bring public attention to his case. They couldn't very well have turned down a meeting with foreign dignitaries, but they would make Joe pay for this, teach him who's boss. They would make Joe's life miserable from now on. The very next day they take Joe to the infirmary to draw his blood, without reason. The nurse hesitates and tells Joe the doctor ordered it. I am sure this is no coincidence. Maybe they want to do their own DNA testing. As

Joe walks back from the infirmary, approximately 75 prisoners yell out to him, "Viva Italy, long live the Italians!" This invigorates Joe. I'm glad he now has so many positive influences from Italy in his life. I later learn that prior to taking Joe to the nurse, Joe warned the guards, "Don't come in my cell." The guard later asked Joe, "Would you have jumped me?" "No, of course not," Joe replied. "Keep your cool, you have too much to lose," the guard tells Joe.

For the next few days Joe's nerves are at wits' end. He is pushing me to do more work. "Joe, I have no more money. I need a break." He responds by settling down. It's been a tough push for me the past several weeks and while I know it's even harder on Joe, I need some space.

That same evening I receive a phone call from John Nutter. He says he misses me and "won't give up on me." I tell him it's all wrong and try to discourage him. This is a dance I must be careful to perform well. I cannot lose him as a witness.

Meanwhile, a call from Georgio Morelli lets me know he is upset. He is apparently jealous and quite arrogant at the moment. He wants to know why Alessandra Farkas went to the Supreme Court and not him. The Parliament won't do anymore, he suggests. I make a note to follow up with Luciano. Suddenly a different side of Georgio is emerging. Why is he suddenly so angry with me? I wasn't the one who invited Farkas to the U.S. Supreme Court. While the Parliament has been so incredibly gracious with its efforts to save Joe, I think we need more. But at this point I'm not sure what that is. All I know is Joe will soon die if we don't continue to fight.

Nutter is still calling and I am careful with him. Richard and I plan on visiting with him again on April 18.

By now, Bob Smith is alerted to the prison taking Joe's blood. There have been no complaints of pain and Joe was not scheduled to see the doctor. Bob assures me he will call the Attorney General's office to find out why. As Joe's lawyer, he is privileged to make such calls. I am not. I'm still limited in my capacity to help Joe.

****

Crucial to a prisoner are attorney–client contact visits. Running parallel to that, for an innocent person, is that your attorney believes in you. Bob Smith, after almost three and a half years into the case, visits Joe for the *first time*. He arrives in Mecklenburg at 1:40 p.m. and departs by 3:00 p.m. Though it's a relatively brief visit, Joe feels good about it. During the visit, he shows Bob how he could not have committed the crime, drawing a diagram that maps it out. "Bob is not abandoning me, Lori. I think he is grateful for having done the oral argument." Joe is surprised, as I am, that Bob will stick by him. It has been a contentious relationship and now it was more important than ever for these two to be on the same page. The purpose of the visit was to strategize. We needed a plan.

While Nutter is still a key issue, being protective of one another Joe doesn't want me near him. I tell him I must continue my work in this life and death struggle to fit all pieces together. The Southern Reference Lab sends Nutter's blood to the attorneys by accident, instead of Lifecodes lab. I am horrified by this error. It has destroyed the chain of custody. We don't want to lose Nutter so I agree to destroy it in front of Nutter after Dwight Mills' son Matthew agrees to mail the blood directly to me. Nutter is now suspicious that he has to do a third draw and wants a letter saying he gave blood. I can hardly blame him for being nervous.

At this point Joe and I are not getting along well. We have grown distant and we are now arguing. Up until now we have had a relatively smooth relationship. It would be foolish to underestimate how extremely scared he is these days. Rightfully so, he is afraid of dying. I, too, am scared, but I cannot allow fear to dictate my path. I realize I must get moving and put together some packages for senators or congressmen—we need a couple of politicians in our corner.

I wait patiently for Nutter to call. I need to ask him to *please* do another blood draw.

On April 7 Nutter calls to tell me he has three hours. "Can I do the blood draw now?" I instantly call the lab to arrange it. When it's completed the lab calls to confirm they are all set. Instead of listing the case as a number, with an unknown name, they photograph Nutter and fingerprint him. This was against our instructions. The blood is sent to Lifecodes and I am fuming. I don't learn of this until that evening when Nutter calls. The next morning I phone the lab. "This was not the arrangement," I tell them. This must remain a secret or the prosecution will intimidate Nutter. "You must call Lifecodes and tell them it was sent there by accident and to send it back," I instruct them. This is now becoming a nightmare. "Dwight, this is Lori. I need your help in calling Lifecodes. The lab sent all of John Nutter's identification along with the blood. This is not protocol and must be diverted. Can you help?" It is not uncommon for a lab to issue a number, and not use a name or other identification, for a case in which privacy is a concern. I wanted privacy.

Another unwanted occurrence: Nutter thinks he is in love with me. I keep assuring him he is not. I gingerly tell him I don't want this and he replies, "Lori, I never believed in love at first sight until I met you." *Lord*, I am saying to myself, how on earth am I going to handle this?"

With little time to spare I am still reaching out for help. I place a call to Doug Curtis at the law firm of Miller, Cassidy, Larroca & Lewin in Washington, D.C. I want them to take over Joe's case. Doug expresses interest, but refrains from an affirmative response until he can check it out further. They place a call to Kitty Behan to get additional information. I need an aggressive and brilliant team. At the same time, I am also trying to reach Sir Alec Jeffreys in London, the founder of DNA technology. I need to see if he can offer an irrefutable expert opinion on the PGM theory, as well as the DNA results in Joe's case, which contradict the antiquated serology method of testing over a decade ago.

Luciano is not returning my calls. Our distance is a disadvantage. Frustration snakes its way into my mind. He is my lifeline to the Parliament and we still need their support. Right about now I'm also waiting for the photos from the Washington press conference. They have not arrived. The dignitaries had asked to process them in Italy. I reluctantly agreed. An uneasy feeling comes across me. I wonder whether politics are again emerging into this picture. I take another avenue and prepare a package for Rosa Jervolino Russo. She is a strong ally for Joe. I feel confident she will distribute it for me.

The next phone call nearly sends me over the edge. "Is this Lori Urs, are you the contact person here? This is Lifecodes and we just received a package." Though she had no authorization to do so, Diane from Southern Reference Lab had told them to call me. I quickly deny that I'm the contact person. This is a small community and if my name gets out, the prosecution will find out and interfere with any progress I am making.

"I am only the one who facilitated drawing the blood," I assure her. I direct them to Dwight Wells. The woman at Lifecodes informs me that David (also from Lifecodes) told her this is out of the ordinary. I reply, "No, Holly tells me this is done all the time; the photo and fingerprint is the only thing out of the ordinary". She agrees. At this point we are desperate to do testing, to hell with the chain of custody. We cannot get any more blood from Nutter. I ask Dwight to be sure to get this done. By now I am exhausted. The stress is beginning to take its toll on me.

Throughout this ordeal, I have found that this work can be and often is very lonely. I was warned about this by Sister Helen Prejean. I had no idea what was in store for me when I was assigned this case over three years ago. I naturally reach out to Joe, but he, too, is on edge. He thinks I should be doing things more quickly perhaps. Is he blaming me for things that are out of our control? This is one of those times when I cannot deal with his fears and frustrations, as well as my own.

The sun had not lost its rich orange color that following morning before I reach for the phone to call the man Joe wanted to perform DNA testing years ago. I am now talking with Sir Alec Jeffreys, the inventor of DNA technology. When I have his attention I begin to ask scientific questions about PGM and DNA testing. He explains that the PGM of the victim could mask O'Dell's PGM 1 and that PCR DNA testing is very reliable if we get a traceable sample. It is not so reliable if there is a poor sample to test. "We should condition testing on this premise," he says. What he is telling me is no different than what was said at trial. What infuriated me was that the prosecution would alter the fact that the tests performed on the sperm could not *identify* O'Dell as the perpetrator. It simply could not *exclude* him. Big difference. No testing on the sperm connected O'Dell to Helen Schartner, yet the prosecutor would repeat at trial, and to the courts and the media, time and time again, that the sperm matched Joe O'Dell's. This kind of junk science, and unfortunately in this case, intentional deceit, is capable of sending an innocent man to his death.

Jeffreys tells me I should use David Bonwedle, an FBI guy. I know this man from a DNA article I recently read. I also learn for the first time that Lifecodes bought out Cellmark Diagnostics. This is bad news. "Stay away from them, they are no good. You need independent testing," says Jeffreys. I must relay this information to Joe.

Six years has passed since I separated from my husband. Confused by the presence of men in my life, or lack thereof, I am understandably feeling vulnerable and lonely. I feel that I have disappointed Joe. I don't have the answer. I want someone to love, to hold me. I'm missing the presence of a male companion in my life. But I want the right one, not just anyone.

Yesterday, Bob Smith called Alberi and asked for DNA testing. Alberi called Humphrey and they both defer to the Attorney General's office. As directed, Bob then calls Katherine Baldwin who adamantly responds with a firm, "No. The case is over!" Bob is astonished and on April 23, 1997 he writes an awesome letter to "confirm" their conversation, and his shock over her response.[93] If she does not change her mind, all media will be notified and the Commonwealth will look bad. They will be forced to yield to testing. Or so I think.

Jen and I are needing some normalcy and joy in our life so we bring in a new member to the family. He is a gorgeous black cocker spaniel puppy just six weeks old. We name him Pepper and begin the fun of housebreaking. Perhaps our yellow lab, Taffy will give her some pointers.

Two days later I fly to Jacksonville to meet with the alibi witness, John Nutter. He is a key component to the case, or was until we were slammed with a strong "no" by the Commonwealth to our request to perform DNA testing on the sperm. As I exit the plane and make my way to the gate, John Nutter is waiting for me. I cringe inwardly when he smiles—his stained and crooked teeth reveal a lack of care over the years. He quickly embraces me, leaving me with a rush of embarrassment. He leads me to his pickup truck and as we drive off, the truck is emanating odd and alarming noises the entire, seemingly very long, ride to his house.

In some ways John reminds me of Joe in his younger years. John pulls to a stop at his friend's trailer home. At the kitchen table are two guys and a skanky-looking girl drinking whiskey. All three are drinking whiskey. Two unkempt kids are watching TV. The television set is the most expensive thing in the trailer. *Is this how Joe used to live?* If so, it saddens me. We don't linger long before we head over to John's favorite bar for a drink. I ease into conversation about the case and ensure that we have his continued support. Sensing his strong feelings toward me I realize I risk losing him as a witness. I remind him that I have a commitment to help Joe and I'm not interested in anything personal,

---

[93] See website, www.loristjohn.com, for a copy of the original letter.

but that doesn't stop him from asking me to marry him several times over the next few days. He assures me he won't change his mind.

Completing my work in Florida, John offers me a ride to the airport. He is still persistent in asking me to marry him as soon as I graduate from law school. He later tells me that he cried on the way to work, forcing him to pull over because he couldn't see. I am concerned about this instant "obsession" he has with me. Convinced I can handle it, I throw caution to the wind.

Leaving Florida I'm confident that John is on board, paving the way to contact Lifecodes to confirm the procedures necessary for comparable testing. It is important to use the same exact methodology of testing to avoid the challenge that the methodology is different, hence the results are different. I can hear Alberi raising that issue now.

Over the two weeks I complete the packages I have prepared for politicians and the Vatican. They are a concise, purely factual packet of information. I bind it for the Vatican, including the new motion for DNA testing, along with Bob's letter to the AG's office. Afterwards, I steal some time to drop off the note I received from the Vatican at a local frame shop to memorialize the acknowledgment of our meeting while I was in Italy. I am honored by this, a sure sign of friendship in a united cause.

****

At a middle school dance night there has to be a parent chaperone. As I stand in the corner to avoid the inevitable, "Mom you're embarrassing me," statement, I try to swallow my own discomfort as I watch my daughter slow dancing, in the arms of a boy. They are not holding each other tightly or hugging, yet somehow it still shocks me. At that moment, I decide I must have the long-awaited mother–daughter talk. The appropriateness of the moment reflects upon the day—it's

Mother's Day.

The continuing situation with Nutter is clearly not going away; in fact it's a deepening problem. I must somehow gently let John down. I'm not sure what he will think or do, nor whether I risk losing him for the case.

It's Memorial Day weekend, and I'm visiting with Joe. For the first time I find myself resisting the long drive down to the prison. It would have been an easier way to deal with my emotions had I just stayed home. Mixing my visit with media opportunities for Joe, I have an interview with Channel 6. The interviewer is easy and pleasant to deal with and the ten-minute interview is a welcome one.

The past few weeks have tested Joe's and my resolve to work together. It is during this time that I learn he has maintained romantic relations with his "fiancée", Sheryl Murden, the girl who sat by him during his trial. During the past ten years she had chosen to hide their personal relationship to save her reputation. While he claims to have terminated this relationship, it comes as no surprise. Somehow though I feel betrayed. *He should have told me. Why did he lie? Did he think it would have made a difference in my fight for him? Did he worry I would back off?* If so, he was dead wrong. I was fighting for the truth, to fix a broken system. I realize that I have been drifting away from Joe lately because it's all too painful. I can't face the possibility of his execution. With mixed emotions I look forward to seeing him tomorrow. The situation is far more intense and frightening than one can ever imagine. How did I get here, living on the edge like this?

We were all hoping to file an unopposed petition for DNA testing but, of course, the Commonwealth would never agree to that. So we filed a motion with the circuit judge. Having read it prior to submittal, Joe and I give it our seal of approval. We can only pray for a positive result. It's the only thing that makes any sense. Of course the governor does not wish to "interfere" with the Attorney General's decision to oppose it. *Such a cowardly way out.* How people can play Russian rou-

368 LORI ST JOHN

lette with someone's life is beyond me.

The final investigation with Richard is scheduled from June 6th to June 11th. I don't want to go. John's sister's wedding is that weekend as well. Instead I want to speak at the Rotary Club on Friday about "Law and the Abuse of Power". I call Mrs. Nutter and tell her to have John call me. John has already told her he would be bringing a guest. "Promise me, no talking about the case this weekend," she says. I promise except I know I won't be there. Neither will John.

Obtaining admission into law school is difficult enough, as is a request to transfer. When I receive a recommendation from the Italian Parliament for my application to transfer to Rutgers School of Law I am overjoyed. Quite possibly it will let my application stand out amongst hundreds of others. In the midst of all this I feel like I am in a state of confusion. My isolation from normal social activities, and the comfort of a loving, caring partner, is taking its toll on me. To ease my mind from the distraction I playfully engage with the dogs, eyeing them as they are wrestling together. Pepper is the playmate that Taffy needed during my absence.

Suddenly, I receive a call from Nutter. He's in a panic and needs to get out of Florida. "I'm on my way up to my parents' house," he says anxiously. My bet with him some time ago is now coming back to haunt me. Against my better judgment, I agree to accompany him to New York as promised. I am keenly aware this is not good for me now. I need him out of my life. But what about his testimony, his alibi? This web has just spun another layer of confusion and worry around my already delicate mind.

In the past I would have accompanied Bob Smith to oral arguments for DNA testing in Virginia Beach. This time I await his call. Helen Schartner's family apparently sat with Alberi, wearing yellow ribbons pinned to their lapels. I know whose doing that was. Alberi always orchestrates everything. He is far too personal with his victim's friends and witnesses than a prosecutor ought to be. It's his way of ensuring his position is not compromised. Bob phones to say, "Lori, we just left the hearing. It was hard to read the judge. There is no telling what he will do." In 48 hours we will know. My participation has declined now, in part due to my state of mind, and in part due to finances. My financial situation allows me to do little more. Joe and I have emotionally separated. As a result I am distant. I admit I am afraid. The U.S. Supreme Court will rule in just one to two weeks. We need that ruling to be in our favor. The thought of that, too, failing raises doubt about my ability to handle all of this.

Tomorrow, Jen and I leave for the Cape. I cannot wait for normalcy to return to my life, even if ever so briefly. John begs me to let him come to Cape Cod. He sells me on the idea that he doesn't want to live in New York. He is now following me in his pickup truck, all the way to the Cape. "Mom, just leave him here," Jen rationally tells me on the ride up. Mixed feelings give way to John. It is a mistake that will result in tragedy over a year later. But how could I know? I agree to help him get on his feet.

On June 17, after the usual six-hour ride, I round the bend near Oyster Pond and turn left onto Cross Street. The glorious smell of the ocean touches my senses as I breathe deeply to inhale the fresh air. I visually inspect the outside of the house when we pull into the driveway. I can see I must get busy on the flower boxes and the lawn needs watering. Martha, the housekeeper, had been here to prepare the house for our arrival, making it easy for us to drop our bags and simply relax. At least momentarily.

The very next morning Joe surprises me with a call in the early hours. He unexpectedly stirs emotions in me that I thought were long gone. Almost three years ago Joe called here for the first time. There was a freeness about things back then that surfaces this morning. Joe seems emotionally light-hearted, lifting my spirits. The sound of life in his voice draws me back into the fight, countering the worry, fear and voice of confusion. He is speaking cryptically now, telling me I will receive a phone call. "You'll know who it is, an Italian," he tells me in code. "Don't be scared or flip out." I can only guess at the implication. Fear doesn't creep into my heart. I feel reasonably sure I won't ever get that call. Although we have reconnected, still, I remain guarded.

John Nutter is staying here for a few days until I can find him a place to rent. I offer him the downstairs guest bedroom and make him pay rent. Fortunately, he gets a job right away and begins work on Friday. I am thankful that soon he will be on his own. I have no way of knowing how wrong I am.

Lori Urs with His Excellency SIgnor Luigi Amaduzzi- Ambassador and first advisor to the President of Italy.

Lori Urs with the President of the Senate in Italy, Nicola Mancino.

Lori Urs with Foreign Affairs Prime Minister Prodi at the Maurizio Costanzo Show- the largest talk show in Italy.

Lori Urs at the Vatican, preparing to meet Monsignor Caccia, assistant to the Secretary of State.

Lori Urs being received at the Vatican by Monsignor Caccia Binder.

Lori Urs with Gino Concetti, the main writer for the Vatican newspaper.

Rino Piscitello, Lori Urs, Luciano Neri, Franco Danieli and Senator Mario Occhipiniti at a press conference for Joe O'Dell in Washington, D.C.

Rino Piscitello, Senator Mario Occhipinti, Franco Danieli and Luciano Neri, members of the Italian Parliament who initiated the National Campaign to Free Joe O'Dell.

Italian Parliament members visit Joe O'Dell on death row, Boydton, Va.

Joseph O'Dell- Death Row- 1996.

Bob Smith- Joe O'Dell's
post-conviction lawyer.

Albert Alberi- the trial
prosecutor.

Helen Schartner-The Victim.

Lori Urs, Steve Watson, Roslyn Watson and investigator Richard Reyna at the Watson home after he recanted his trial testimony, admitting that Joe never confessed to the murder.

Press Conference With Sister Helen Prejean, Richard Reyna and Lori Urs.

Chapter 23

~Decision of the Court~

It's June 19th and I know the phone will ring anytime soon with news from the court. I pick up the phone after the second ring. Debo and Paul are on the phone with Joseph. This can't be a good sign. My usual cheerful disposition dissipates quickly when all I hear is silence, each not wanting to be the first to speak. Who will dare share the bad news? "Lori, Joe lost in the Supreme Court." The words reach through the phone like a dagger stabbing me in the heart. Without much hesitation I begin to cry. I should be strong for Joe, but I am not. I just want to get off the phone. As I set the receiver down I burst into tears. Joseph is quiet, more concerned about my feelings than his own. I don't think I have ever cried so hard in my entire life. I scream for my mother as tears are dropping to the kitchen floor. Now, hours later, I am sitting here alone. I believe I am in a state of denial.

Immediately after the decision came down, the Attorney General's office wrote a letter to Judge Lowe in the Virginia Beach Circuit Court asking him to deny the DNA motion. Bob Smith, although on vacation, is so angry we lost he dictates a letter to the judge asking that the motion be granted. Shockingly, the Attorney General's office also calls the governor and the Department of Corrections to set an execution date, July 23. They ask Judge Lowe to sign the order to expedite the process. The lawyers inform me this is highly unusual. Steps like this to fast-track the execution date are not the norm. I already know there is nothing normal about how they are handling Joe's case. All along I knew he was special. Special because he can and is challenging them—speaking truth to power. Authoritative figures don't like that. Especially the ones we are dealing with.

Their overzealous attitude and filing for an execution date to the very same judge who can offer a man the opportunity to prove his innocence seems ironic. I think this judge must feel morally obligated to grant the DNA motion if he himself would be signing the death warrant. I send my own letter by fax and will Fed Ex it tomorrow. This time I don't restrain myself. I must, simply must, have something to say about this.

Reporters are now phoning off the hook. Joe and I take a couple of calls today. We are both numb, speaking in code. "Lori, I'm on security watch now." Of course. The prison officials, including the warden, came to see him to tell him the bad news. A guard named Tony alerts Joe about a security issue. The prison is concerned about the international attention Joe is receiving. He is on heightened security, as are the prison walls.

As I sit here all alone, I cannot imagine how Joe is feeling now with no one to hold or comfort him. He, too, is crying, I'm sure. It's ironic how just yesterday we re-bonded. God's way of reuniting two human beings struggling for justice. He has become the main focus of my life. I had always said, *I don't know why you picked me or why this is happening, and I don't have to know, I'm here for the journey.* I know that people all over the world are sharing in my disbelief and shock. I must have faith that the DNA motion will be granted. It has to be.

My darling daughter has been so incredibly supportive and loving to me today. I couldn't make it without her. Now I have to call Luciano before he finds out some other way. "It's not good news," I say in a shaky voice. "Joe was turned down and we are both afraid." Luciano shares my sorrow and hangs up to phone the Parliamentarians to issue a press release. Georgio calls and he, too, sounds as if he was, or is, crying. I am sure he can feel my pain. During the day, I am still numb with so much pain that I truly understand the meaning of the word "brokenhearted".

Today is Sunday, June 22. and I have just learned that last Friday while in Denver, Colorado for the Summit meeting, Prime Minister Prodi asked President Bill Clinton to pardon Joseph. In the midst of the gathering of world leaders this was appropriate—the case has become an international concern. Italy is now even more behind Joseph than ever before. Georgio says the politicians, the highest ones, are fighting for Joe. Luciano still seems to be less available. Perhaps he's tired, perhaps he is taking flak from someone. I don't have time to guess.

In the midst of all this John Nutter finally left our house. I am incredibly relieved. I need time to focus on Joseph, me and Jen. I need peace more than ever, and to be alone. Nutter is not well. His behavior is frightening. I wish I'd known this before I agreed to help him. Last night he slit his wrist in the guest bathroom downstairs and said he did it because he loved me. He frightens me more than ever now. He knows how dedicated I am to Joe and it kills him, but Joe comes first, before anyone, including myself.

Before I go to sleep I speak briefly to Joe. "Dream of me tonight, peanut," he tells me. "I will." I softly say.

"Hi, Lori, it's Bob," says the voice on the other end. I sense disappointment in his tone. "I have Joe on the line with us. I have bad news." I instantly take a deep breath, bracing myself for almost anything now. "The judge turned down the DNA motion." By this time the call was near ending the 15-minute interval allowed to death row inmates. I ask Joe to call me back and we phone Bob to get the details. Joe and I are hearing the news at the same time, holding onto thin air.

Joe appears to be okay, yet I know he is dying inside, trying to be strong for me. I tried to work today, but I feel lost. I have energy but then none—a strange feeling, one I never had before. I am numb, in shock, and partly in denial. Jesus, how could this be happening? Sister Helen leaves me a message and I return her phone call to give her the bad news. She is quiet. I can tell she doesn't know what to say. She says that she's trying to get prominent TV shows for national coverage. As with Bob, Joe is on the phone with me as we speak with Helen. I sense she feels uncomfortable, not knowing the words to choose. Joe expresses his gratitude.

I then telephone Luciano and Rosa Russo about the DNA denial. Rosa faxes me a letter of encouragement.

Her son, Michelle, translates and faxes me a letter from him to Joseph, and another from Rosa's secretaries (four of them) to Joe. I read them to Joe over the phone, taking in each and every word of love. He is touched. We both are.

Meanwhile, Bob has a conference call with the judge at 4:30 p.m. concerning the execution date. Just prior to this, I receive a call from Chip Woodrum (a delegate) who told me his "source" was down the line with the decision. The judge didn't like getting a letter from a delegate, Mitch Van Yahres. That was my idea, but hell, who wouldn't get all the help they could? The prosecution had the entire victim's family in the courtroom. Chip suggests we request a rehearing and offer proof that the DNA testing would meet judicial standards. I relay this to Bob and he supposedly alerts the judge to his desire to do so. I am told the judge basically responded with, "Don't waste your time." I would not have asked. I would have filed the motion, period. Bob asks for an execution date in August to give him time to litigate the DNA motion. As the judge suggests one, the Commonwealth quickly steps in. "The governor does not have a date in August; he's busy." *Lies to the very end.* I pray inside they all go to hell for this. Bob agrees to the date. Even the judge is suspect about it when he says to Bob, "I hope you do the responsible thing." In other words, try for August. "It's 50:50, Lori, that July 23, 1997 will be Joe's date," Bob tells me.

Dear God:

Please help me. Even more please help Joseph. I have been strong and will follow your lead as your servant. I know that this is all much bigger than me and that you chose me to be involved for a reason. Whatever that reason is I do not complain. Please, spare Joseph. Let a miracle happen to save his life. I am crying out loudly to you, although I appear soft-spoken now. It's because of the very deep wounds to my spirit. Allow me to be unselfish—to only think of him and of myself and those I love second, as they will be there for me, I hope and pray. I have always been unselfish, at least most of the time, so please do not be angry with me if I am selfish right now—I almost need to be to simply survive. I have tried to be a warrior, a woman with passion and with high morals. I have stood up against the system in the face of all that was terrible and wrong. I am not sure of what to expect the next several days of my life but I will trust in you and try to understand. I pray you will give the miracle for which I ask.

I want to sleep, maybe sleep forever, but I know I can't. Can you give me a sign? Tell me what to do please? I am lost now. My spirit, my soul is searching the skies trying to find which way to go. I have no direction, no seemingly known purpose but pure existence right now. Lord, have mercy on us all. Give Joseph the strength he needs to face whatever he will - let him be strong and fierce and hold his head up high in the face of all these evil monsters. Let him retain his dignity.
I must fight until the end. Yes, God, help me do this, I humbly ask you.

Amen.

This morning Joe calls me with the words we thought he would never hear. The guards casually walk to his cell and stand in front of him. Line by line they read the death warrant to him, as if reading a letter from a long lost cousin. I could hear in his voice how it has affected him. He is bewildered, as am I. Last night I received a call from Larry O'Dell, a reporter from AP. It was he who confirmed the execution date of July 23, 1997. I call Bob to ask what he knows. He says there is an order out there but he hasn't seen it yet. Why is it that the AG's office is privy to this news and we are not? If I were Bob, I would call the judge and ask for a copy of the order and why reporters got word of this prior to counsel? I sometimes forget, this game is played much differently. Lawyers will be lawyers and few challenge the system, at least the ones from blue-chip firms, the ones I know. I make it a point to speak to Bob after the weekend and find out more about his conversation with Mark Christie from the AG's office. I know it must have been about the clemency petition. I inform Larry that no matter what, I will prove Joe's innocence.

It's easy to conduct a conference call with a death row inmate if they call you first and you patch in the rest of the team. So when I have Joseph on the line I call Miller, Cassidy, Larroca & Lewin and get Doug, Kate and Paul on the phone. We are strategizing and discussing a successor petition and the clemency petition. A successor petition is authorized by 28 U.S.C. Section 2244(b), which basically governs successor habeas petitions by state prisoners—another shot at justice. While Bob's firm is handling the clemency petition, Miller, Cassidy, Larroca & Lewin is now on board to help in that and all other matters.

"Doug, what do you think about a press conference with Sister Helen? I think we need one to let everyone know what's happening here," I say.

"Sure, that's a great idea, Lori."

Knowing sensationalism runs the media I wonder whether having the jailhouse snitch and Joe's alibi together in one press conference would make a difference. Nutter's affidavit is strong: there's no doubt he was in a fight with Joe O'Dell. There are minor inconsistencies that may be torn apart by the prosecution but the outcome is the same—he was in a fight with Joe. More importantly, he is adamant that Joe had *no blood* on him when he saw him at 1:15 a.m. that morning. This would have been impossible had he murdered Helen less than an hour before that. So, whether the fight was at the Brass Rail (where witnesses testified it may have started), or down the block, really doesn't matter at all.

Finally, I know this new firm is not shy to discuss the truth and will speak out about Joe's innocence. I need an attorney to fight for Joe. I immediately pick up the phone and ring Bob to ask for an extra $1,000, "Because now we have a press conference and instead of $1,250 I need $2,250." Without a fight he calls me back with a "yes". I am in utter amazement that this request has come so much easier than those in the past. Perhaps Bob realizes this is our last hope. I have engaged Riptide Communications to assist us. I phone David Lerner and Sister Helen to coordinate the effort. Sister Margaret calls me back to let me know Helen is with friends in Boston. "You'll hear from her on Monday, okay?"

A renewed burst of energy has surfaced, giving me the drive to read through the clemency petition and make a list of necessary changes and additions. I focus on what's *not* in the petition, and which Joe and I feel is necessary for an accurate portrayal of his plight. When I complete the changes, I update the website to include the fact that the Commonwealth is denying DNA testing and expediting Joe's execution. When Joe and I get a chance to talk it's a bittersweet conversation, with a silent understanding of my fear. Joe tells me a story about a young boy who was in isolation for 90 days for cutting a guard with a razor blade. He just got out and wanted his mom to send him $30. Joe tried to call a friend, Ruth, to see if she could put the call through for him. "I told him, look son, I'll try to call your mom." Joe was showing me that he was a human being. That he cared for others. I do know he has always tried to help others on the row and that his demeanor while imprisoned at Mecklenburg has been nothing less than stellar for almost a decade now. I am thinking of today and what I can do for him. I am not thinking about three weeks down the road. I let my mind escape, wishing he were free as a bird.

Joe and I are start talking day and night trying to stay on top of things. When I get him on the phone I call Luciano and patch him on the line. The air is heavy with sadness. For the very first time, Joe tells me that after we meet this weekend, we need to discuss some things. We had carefully avoided any talk about death. Joe is referring to funeral arrangements. I block it out. Instead, I think about buying some flowers to plant around the light post and in my flower boxes on the windowsills.

Then, suddenly Joe is quiet. He whispers to me, "Lori, before I die I want to know if you will marry me. You have been my hero, the only one who has fought so very hard for me. You believe in me and I love you. Just think about it, okay?"

I promise to think about it, not really understanding what's in store for me.

Being on death row and so close to your own death brings out all sorts of vultures in prison. Joe's fellow inmates are already asking for his meager possessions. One has already claimed his sneakers. I can sense the hurt in Joe's voice. These are guys he has shared things with, been unselfish with when they needed something. They are callous and uncaring and the reality of the row hits hard. To the contrary, and for me, it's a big day. I am on the phone half the day with the lawyers and the PR firm.

Suddenly I receive a call from Walter. He almost never calls me now. It's just after midnight. "Lori, it's not a good idea to marry Joe. I am very concerned about you and for your reputation." I tell him I just want to make Joe happy. I also tell him of my plans to do posthumous DNA testing, and that to do that I need legal status. Being a "family" member offers me that much. Walter says he understands. I am surprised at that and it offers me great comfort. But I agree with him, and worry that people will think I fought for love, not justice. I know that is not true, but will they? I believe in Joe. I don't expect others to understand. All I know is that I must think outside of myself. I want to help another human being. Now I hesitate, not sure of what to do.

Turning over to silence the alarm I notice a message on the answering machine. Sister Helen has agreed to the press conference. In a three-way call we discuss the details. She gingerly offers to be by Joe's side if they kill him. Joe and I simply listen, hoping this is not our reality. She hasn't given up the fight she says. "I'm still trying to get Lisa Cohen at *PrimeTime* to get a story out." We thank her and I turn my attention back to the details before me, strategizing with the lawyers and focusing on the press conference. And I am still hesitant on the marriage idea.

Joe's problems at the prison intensify. One evening an inmate had smashed the phone. As a result, a guard and captain announced, "There will be no phone for 30 days!" Joseph obviously needs the phone badly. We hook up at 8:00 p.m. for ten minutes and when we hang up, I make a note to call the warden to ensure there are no problems with the phone. I must continue to get ready for my trip to Virginia.

Last night I dreamt Joe was in the death house and they wouldn't let us get married. I am not sure which is the nightmare here, the death house or the marriage, but I wake up numb. I'm still not letting my feelings out, guarding them to stay strong. While I'm frightened, I won't stop fighting or having faith. It's a strange combination. And though I am not a particularly religious person, I know God is walking with us. With little time left I schedule a trip to see Joseph. It could quite possibly be our last visit together.

~Last Visit to Mecklenburg~

The irony of my drive down to see Joe is too much. It's Thursday, Walter's birthday, and the day before this country celebrates its independence. America is free, but Joe and I are caged. The stress seeps into every bone in my body. The thought of seeing him for the last time in South Hill is unbearable. Joe calls me on my car phone. I don't know why but I am screaming at him. I am actually screaming *for* him, for his attention and affection. I felt I had shared him way too long with the press, with the world. We shared everything about the case with the lawyers and now he is sharing his wish to marry me with them as well. I am feeling lost, as if I am part of a circus here with no privacy whatsoever. It's becoming too overwhelming for me. For the first time in over four years Joe is screaming back at me. And for the first time ever he threatens to end his life. I assure him I will run my car into another and kill myself first. At that very moment we both break down, crying tears that cannot be seen, only heard, by one another. We listen to each other's sobs in an attempt to gain consolation. Crying together is the only way to release our pain. He doesn't want to die, nor do I want him to. Although I told him I feel all alone, and I do, I needed him now. When I arrive in South Hill I grab a beer and a half, which for me is a lot. I also smoke one half of a cigarette. I felt better, just enough to doze off to sleep in the motel. And sleep is what I need.

Morning comes undisturbed and quickly. The front office was instructed to hold my calls. I plan a 10:30 a.m. visit, trying to beat the odds for an all-day visit. After the normal screening and search of my body for contraband, Joe walks in at 11:00 a.m. We are placed at our favorite end booth. Four death row inmates are here, one gets bumped. Somehow I knew we would have all day. We were now two human beings caring, loving and clinging to one solidarity in the face of death. Joe initiates the forgiveness we both need. I can feel his sincerity through the hard glass wall between us. Spiritually, we connect again.

Before I leave Joe makes sure the head guard, Robinson, carries out two heavy, large boxes he had packed for me. My heart is heavy after hearing Joe whisper to me, "It's so hard to get ready to die, as I did once before." He is thinking about his death, his own autopsy, and then seeing me and Jennifer—the sunlight of his life. He talks of his need for peace of mind. Sensing my reluctance to marry him, he gives me permission to be free of the stigma and entanglement by suggesting I arrange for an annulment when he is gone. He knows my purpose and he also knows it's not for the reasons one typically marries. As I said before, desperate measures call for desperate actions.

Back at the motel Joe calls in the early evening through Ruth. The prison prevents a call to a motel room so he asks a friend to help connect us. We speak twice, revisiting our wonderful day. He is anxious. A reporter has called to talk to him. I know he wanted to speak, but I'm becoming so forceful in controlling his time, the events, whatever I could. It is the only control I have left. I reassure him it's okay not to speak now, telling him it's our weekend. "They will have to wait until Thursday," I say. I had given Georgio and Angela specific instructions. No interviews. We need our privacy. They want exclusives. Joe and I need to bond if we are to get through the next few days. No one could possibly understand this except us.

Replaying Sunday's visit in my head brings feelings of conflict. As Joe spoke of marriage I was dying inside. My heart doesn't want this - how do I get out of this? I don't want to hurt him, yet I have a life, too. I hope there is a development in the case that helps me here. I know I can be unselfish to a fault. But I have to start thinking of me. I know that if Joe were actually released I would have a tremendous amount of stress helping him adapt and adjust to a new life. I desperately want to get on with my life. I miss my life so very much.

On Sunday he had asked me if I would stand by him if he got a life sentence. I lied; I couldn't hurt him now. Not now. I do tell him I can't do anymore on the case. Financially, I can do no more. I was honest and told him I would go back to law school and get on with my life.

Truth is I am feeling that Joe is very selfish. This man is fighting for his life, however the natural inclination is for me to resent him. I have no other escape for the pain. I'm not entirely sure Joe appreciates all I have done, sacrificed so much of my family life. I question his own commitment. During this last visit that question was challenged. I felt I had caught him in a lie and I want to walk out, but I know it may be the last time I see him. He, too, is challenging me, accusing me of breaking promises or lying to him. I hate when he seems to be unfair to me. Hate him for being selfish. But who am I to judge? I couldn't possibly understand how he is feeling now. The circumstances are nothing less than tumultuous, forcing our emotions to surface in all kinds of ways.

With a few days between scheduled events in Virginia I contemplate remaining here to avoid driving back and forth to New Jersey. *It's almost over*, I remind myself. My emotions and stability seem to ride like a current, with me unable to control the flow. This doesn't stop the momentum. I take a call at 10:00 a.m. to conference in with the lawyers in Washington, David Lerner and Sister Helen. It's essential to discuss strategy for the press conference, documentation release and Sister Helen's role. I cannot give up now.

I'm scheduled to pick up Sister Helen at the airport on Thursday morning. The lawyers feel that since David asked about my relationship with Joe I should release information on his proposal. Should it come up at the press conference I will answer, "No comment." I reluctantly agree. Immediately after the conference call, I phone Helen and for almost one hour we speak candidly. I am in turmoil over this decision. "Helen, what should I do? Joe proposed to me and I don't know how to handle this delicate situation. He wants to marry me on July 15th or 16th but I should change the date to July 22nd, this way I have a sense of what happens. Maybe he'll get a stay."

"Lori honey, you and Joe have built an unconditional love, a loyal friendship, based not on sex but open communications. Most people don't have that even in marriage. In the end it's your choice, but follow your heart."

I must consider everything here, including the press—sometimes they are our worst enemy.

"I'm still working on Larry King but he says he won't do the show unless we get the Pope," Helen says. *I suppose an innocent person facing execution isn't worthy enough on its own.*

Chapter 24

~Last Call~

The sun feels heavenly. My body and mind both soaking it up for a brief 60 minutes to help ease the tension. I have not found the time to enjoy the Cape Cod summer days this year. They are fast slipping away from me. I am confident we will be able to do the DNA test and we will prevail—that's the fair outcome.

I pick up the ringing phone. I know it's Joe. He listens while I explain the update, interjecting his agreement about press strategy. He can be so hardheaded and wrong at times (pot calling the kettle black?), but we agree to connect again when we speak to Kate Pringle at 2:30 p.m. Acquiescing that I fall into the same category in character traits as Joe does, I'm not so sure what makes me think I'm right about the press. Nevertheless, I forge ahead with our plan. What I do know is that I have made a wonderful friend in Sister Helen. I am grateful to have her in my life.

July 7, 1997. Joe's words are scattered. His voice uneven.

"What's wrong Joe?" I ask through a three-way call with his "mom" Ruth.

"At 7:30 p.m. the guards walked up to my cell and asked me to step outside. 'How do you want to die, Joseph?' I refused to answer, Lori. I refuse to be led out in chains and a dog leash. The captain then came to my cell and said 'Joe, we are only doing our job'".

I know Joe. He has a good relationship with the guards. He wouldn't want to put them in an uncomfortable position. He signs on the dotted line under "lethal injection", yet he tells me it's really *fuel injection.*

Numbness floods my body and I am fighting back tears regarding the cruelty of it all. I cannot even begin to understand what it's like to be in Joe's shoes. For the first time tonight Joe said he was sure they were going to carry him down to the death house. I sank. I figured we'd get a stay, but he may be right. I told him of my conversation with the lawyers, and the press, and with Sister Helen about the marriage. He smiled. I can't see the smile, but I know it's there. Maybe that will help get him through this. Joe tells me a guard came around and told him Warden Pruett said to put the date of his original request on the form letter, as the Department of Corrections needs a 30-day request period for such things. I had called the warden to ask if it could be retroactive and at first he was hard, but then he seemed to give in. For Joseph's sake I pray it all goes well and he gets the stay and we get our time. There *is* a possibility he will be given a life sentence if he drops the innocence aspect, at least that's what the lawyers say.

The stress in Joe's voice is at first very noticeable, fluttering to and from escape in the form of words that are hollow of emotion. The pages of my notebook are wet from the tears steadily dropping from my tired eyes. The thought of ever returning to the death house torments me. Time has now become our worst enemy. Even if granted DNA testing, I dread the torturous wait. I hurt for Joseph, feel his pain. Just as easily as he must feel mine.

The following day I find myself packing my files and getting everything ready to be put away. It's my way of saying enough is enough. My actions usually precede the cognizant reality of what I want or am doing. I am angry with Joe for having not listened to staying away from journalists. *I am done*, I am speaking to myself now. No one is listening. No one cares. *I certainly won't marry him now*, I am swearing inside my head and sorry for the language, but *what a fool I have been to have given my life to him. I cannot wait for this to be over so I can walk away. Strategy Joe says, he doesn't know what he is doing,* I utter my last silent words. Thursday cannot come soon enough so I can finish my work and go home to my family. I vow to take my life back.

"Lori, today they took my picture. When I walked, the ankle chains cut into my ankles they were so tight." He is not complaining, just sharing his life. I listen quietly.

Feeling I have done all I can I talk myself into thinking I can rest, it's out of my hands now. I just need to follow though with the clemency petition and, most importantly, the DNA issue and successor petition. I feel as though whatever happens I have fought with all I have and have not been afraid of those who have tried to intimidate me.

It's 7:00 p.m. the evening before the press conference, and I have a terrible headache. There is not much left in me anymore. I perform the last minute coordination between all the lawyers and the press and arrange for the receipt of an affidavit from Attorney Steve Rosenfield about the intimidation of Watson by the Attorney General's office. In the late afternoon I speak with Andy Sebok. He agrees to give me an affidavit about the DNA evidence and the Attorney General's lies.[94] Suddenly, I receive an unexpected phone call and additional bad news. The Virginia Supreme Court has turned down Joe's request for DNA tests. Debo was chosen to be the bearer of this bad news. I'm guessing Bob didn't have the heart. Helen lifts my mood with an update that Barry Scheck will be available by phone at the press conference. I know it's because Helen has spoken to him. I sense he enjoys fame and recognition. Whatever it takes. I know he has what it takes to challenge the system.

I will myself to sleep, knowing I cannot appear nervous or frayed tomorrow. I grab hold of the Pope's rosary and pray for Joe's release,

---

[94]   See website, www.loristjohn.com for a copy of the affidavit.

his freedom.

The alarm clock rings at 5:30 a.m. After I dress I leave in time to arrive at the hotel in Richmond by 8:30 a.m. First I meet with the lawyers for a cup of tea and to discuss strategy. Then we move up to room 505 to meet with the PR guy, David, and with Debo. I look down at the 8 x 10 photograph of Joe that Doug has framed for me. It isn't the photo that touched my heart as much as the idea that it is a gift offered by Doug in acknowledgment of my hard work and deep concern for Joe. I hurry off to pick up Sister Helen at the airport. When we embrace I see a beautiful face, so calm and serene. So full of love, peace and goodness. By the time we arrive in the lobby of the hotel the Italian reporters are waiting for us. They want an interview with Sister Helen who promptly responds, "In a few minutes". She knows how to take control. A short while later, we head down to the "Madison Room". It's starting to fill up. I put in a call to Barry Scheck to make sure he's on schedule for a call-in at 11:30 a.m. "Barry, are you going to make a statement"? I ask. "I wasn't planning to, but maybe a short one", he replies. He was planning on a question and answer session. "Okay, then, please be sure to call back at 11:30 a.m.".

The room is full. Joe's family is seated on the far right and lawyers from Miller, Cassidy, Larroca & Lewin are idly talking among the crowd of journalists. We take our places at the table. Doug stands to speak first. I had arranged for Joe to call in and read a statement directly to the press. Doug holds the phone to the microphone as Joe reiterates the facts of his case and speaks about his innocence. "First, I'd like to thank Lori, Sister Helen and my family". His voice is strong, he's articulate, his statement is moving. Sister Helen approaches the microphone. Everyone is quiet. Her southern accent is genuine and effective, having a way of reaching right down into your heart. She pauses briefly when the phone rings. Barry Scheck is on hold. When she finishes her statement, Paul Enzina speaks about the evidence— the *truth* about the evidence with factual support. When the panel completes their speeches, scattered hands are raised across the room. Barry ends up speaking far more than he had planned. He reminds the press, and indirectly Joe's foe, **"The only reason the Commonwealth would not do this DNA test is if they are hiding something."** He is adamant in his opinion. The conference ends and Joe phones back twice to speak to me, and then to Sister Helen and his sister. His first phone call to me is not about the conference. He is concerned about John Nutter. He had just called the Chatham police and told them I was an investigator, that he was concerned for my safety because Nutter may be in my house. The cops actually checked it out. I was embarrassed, yet I understood why Joe was so concerned about me. Nutter is just another witness who indirectly helped put him on death row. He was afraid for me, and protective in his actions.

After the reporters pepper us with questions, we gather in an adjacent room to discuss the results of the press conference and then head downstairs to the restaurant for lunch. We are seated at a large round table. Helen walks in front of me and whispers, "Sit next to me, okay?" I'm happy she wants me near her as I watch her engaging the others at the table. Her ease in conversation has everyone laughing. After dropping Helen at the airport I take the exit to 95 North. I'm thrilled to be going home. For the first time in a very long time I'm actually smiling. I had pulled off a great press conference. And it felt good to have a team of supporters speak eloquently and truthfully about the real facts of the case. I was sure Governor Allen will have to listen to this.

"Lori, it's all over the news, channel 35, 13, 3 and 8," Joe says enthusiastically. I'm happy, though the picture of Richard Real hiding in the back of the room pops into my mind. He knew he did me dirty with his interview, but I have no time for him now.

I finally get to Walter's house at 10:00 p.m. and scoop up Jennifer to take her home with me.

Jen and I set out for Cape Cod the next morning. While we are driving, Governor Allen is pushing to drive another message through the media. Shortly after I arrive in Chatham the phone rings. It's Debo. When I hear his voice I instantly know it's bad news. However, I'm unprepared for this one.

"Lori, the governor denied Joe a DNA test. I'm so sorry," he says. Joe is also on this phone call.

"Joe, I told her the news," said Debo.

Joe wanted to be sure he was there when Debo spoke to me. He wanted, in whatever way possible, to comfort me. To comfort *me*.

I'm in shock, not believing the governor would issue a statement so quickly and without careful consideration. Joe and I speak briefly about what legal strategies we have left and I stay as strong as I can until I get off the phone. Seated on the kitchen floor I weep hard before I finally pick myself up. Joe calls again later—we try to make sense of it all—we can't face what this latest news potentially means.

Though I am up early the next morning it promises to be an easy day. I don't have much to do. Luciano phones me and lets me know he has heard the news. He is devastated.

Later that evening when Joe and I speak I find an awkwardness has arisen. Do I act as if he's dying, or as if there is hope left? There is no script to the scene after the curtain closed, when the judge read Joe his death sentence.

The lawyers finally send me a copy of the governor's statement. I rise early to spend some time correcting the many factual errors written throughout it. The corrections are four pages long. I am going to have to fax this to the press so they know the *truth*, not what Allen wishes to spin to the public.

Helen's call is a sudden surprise. "Lori, listen to me, this is great news. The Pope has just intervened in Joe's case! I sent you a fax, go check your machine. He says he is praying for Joseph," says Helen. I was thrilled—this is totally unexpected.

The phone is once again ringing off the hook as I work with the lawyers. The governor's denial of Joe's request is so full of "mischaracterizations" or lies that even the lawyers are agreeing we need to respond. Paul Enzina drafts the reply. Bob reviews and modifies it and sends it over to me for my approval.

"Lori, is it alright?" Bob asks.

Bob knows no one knows the facts, and the support for them in the transcript or elsewhere, better than I do. Upon its completion I fax a copy of our response to Frank Green at the *Dispatch* and two Italian newspapers, *la Repubblica* and ANSA. The letter reiterates Joe's innocence and is essentially a press release. The lawyers then forward me the press release regarding the federal hearing on the DNA evidence. I couldn't say it was as well-written as the statement regarding the governor's "mischaracterizations". I need to stay on top of the lawyers to make sure they get my approval first.

The papers are relentless now in their requests to speak to Joe so I conduct two interviews for him. I know what he would say at this point and type out his response for a Catholic newspaper and another for ANSA. Tomorrow I will respond to *Corriere*'s request for the same. Kate, from Centurion Ministries calls. "I have an affidavit from Steve Watson, a four-page statement to the cops and Attorney General dated November 6, 1996." Watson is suggesting Richard Reyna and I intimidated him. I need to guide her on how to combat this so I refer her to attorney Steven Rosenfield, Andy Sebok, and the transcripts from all the tapes and videos of our interviews with Watson. Then I phone Bob Smith.

"Bob, what's going on with the clemency petition?" I ask.

"We're focusing on the truth and sentencing aspect of it," Bob replies.

"No, that's not a good idea. We need to follow though with Joe's innocence claim."

"That's a better idea. Whatever you and Joe want." Bob knows we are on our last leg. I must now follow though with Paul and Debo to ensure they update the petition to include Joe's innocence.

Meanwhile, I phone Helen about news from Italy.

"Helen, the European Parliament is going to help Joe. Orlando is a member and he's been talking to them about the case."

"That's great. And I'm going to call Larry King tomorrow to follow up on getting his help." Suddenly we are interrupted. It's Andrea, Mayor Orlando's aide.

"I have wonderful news, Lori. The European Parliament is going to pass a resolution on Thursday and they will be available for a press conference call at 10:00 a.m.," says Andrea.

We are now orchestrating an international resolution to save Joe, and announce it to the world. The magnitude of this success is beyond what Virginia could have ever imagined. To the best of my knowledge this has never happened before. We need to share this significant event.

"Mayor Orlando has plans to come to the United States Sunday night. He's flying to Washington and then to Richmond. He will do whatever Joe wants on Monday."

"Great, Andrea. Be sure to follow through with the request to meet with Governor Allen and to visit with Joseph."

Immediately after we hang up I call the lawyers to set up a visit from Italian dignitaries to the death row house of Joe O'Dell. I also take care of other pressing business.

"Warden Pruett, this is Lori Urs. I need to confirm the details about my marriage to Joe O'Dell."

"Yes, July 23, 1997 is fine."

I know that this verbal confirmation means nothing so I make a note to get it in writing.

As the day nears an end, Jennifer and I stroll down our village street to the town square. She needs some clothes and stuff for camp. I can see the sadness in her face. She needs my attention. I have little to offer now.

Mid-week leaves just one more day before I journey to Virginia to be by Joe's side. With so little time left I ponder the thought of writing the governor. The thought is ever so fleeting before it's pushed off to the side like everything else right now. *Soon, I'll write*, I promise myself.

"Jen, let's go for dinner in town with Alicia."

Alicia is her best friend from school. Our destination: a New England seafood dinner. Carefully tying bibs around our necks we eagerly crack open the lobster claws. Empty steamed clamshells and cups of clam chowder sit carefully near the edge of the table. The brief escape of dining out allows me to talk more easily with Joe that evening.

Joe believes he is going to die. I know this. If I should be thinking the same, I simply cannot. I'm thinking about my stay in Virginia. Knowing what lies ahead, I contemplate having someone with me during my stay at the motel. It is not wise to be alone. Not at this time. The last few years have not been conducive to engaging friends so I wonder, who could that possibly be? At the moment, I can think of no one. A welcoming phone call interrupts my thoughts.

Orlando's aide, Andrea, is trying to send me some information.

"I am sending you a fax of the letter the mayor wrote to the governor and to Angelone for a visit with Joseph when he visits the United States. He has confirmed his plans and is definitely coming. Tomorrow he will call from the European Parliament to announce the Resolution immediately after it happens," Andrea explains.

I can hardly believe what I'm hearing. We were ecstatic to have the support of the Italian Parliament, but now the European Parliament? This is an unprecedented international situation which needs to be broadcast. Perhaps I will conference in a reporter for an exclusive. Even in the midst of this confusion, I recognize how fortunate we are to be up front and close to this miracle. A direct line into a Parliament which represents countries from across Europe is a powerful international statement.

In the meantime, Bill Baskerville of the Associated Press has called to ask me what my role is in Joe's case. When he asked me what my relationship is with him I reply, "I am his best friend, his confidante, his paralegal, advisor and his investigator."

"One has to admire you for your dedication and drive for Joe, and for justice," he says.

Soon afterward I receive a fax from our PR guy. Scanning through it I see a couple of articles about Joe. As I read them I can hardly control myself from calling the lawyers before I am done. The articles mention a "letter" Joe wrote to *la Repubblica*. The letter was morbid. Unfortunately, I can see people are starting to use him. Laura Lafay took advantage of it and headlined an article "Italian Newspaper Farewell to Joe". I immediately call Chip, one of Joe's lawyers down south, to scold him.

"Why are you not protecting your client; how can you let this happen? You can sit there with your humble attitude, but if you were me, Chip, you would be upset as well. No more interviews!" I then call all of Joe's lawyers and tell them, "No more interviews for Joe." If the press has him dead already, the governor has no reason to spare his life. I insist on a positive outlook, even now.

Luciano calls to check in. When we hang up, I rush to the computer to type a three-page summary of my dealings with Watson. This needs to be included in the federal court hearing in the morning, and also the successor petition. I am the only one who can refute the four-page affidavit Watson gave to the cops.

Thursday, July 17, 1997. Joe wakes me in the early morning with a phone call. We are preparing for the RTI Worldwide interview at 10:30 a.m. Right after talking to Joe, I'm welcomed with a call directly from the European Parliament. It's Mayor Orlando. "The members of the European Parliament have just finished meeting and in one hour the resolution will be signed on Joe's behalf," Orlando tells me. I initiate a three-way call and hook the RTI reporter up with Orlando. One minute later Joe calls and I patch him in with Orlando. "Thank you, Mayor Orlando, I so appreciate all you have done for me." Joe is now talking to members of the European Parliament directly from his death row cell right in the middle of the sticks of Virginia. I count this as a victory and thank the mayor for his solidarity.

"Have courage and take care; we are doing everything we can," Orlando exclaims. They speak for five to eight minutes before we hang up. A half-hour later, straight from the pens of dignitaries from around the world, including Sweden, Germany, Belgium, France and Denmark, the resolution arrives by fax. In turn, I forward it to the reporter, hot off the press. Immediately thereafter, I hook Joe up on a three-way call for a TV interview. He is articulate, strong and convincing. The female interviewer loves him. Soon she begins to veer off from questions on her list. I finally interrupt, "That's enough, we must go now." She is surprised at his eloquence and his strength. I respond, "Joseph is an extraordinary man; he is who he is, not who *they* say he is." When asked where he gets all his strength from, he answers, "Lori Urs, for three and a half years she has given me my strength; she doesn't buy it, but it's true." Upon reflection I can hardly believe that modern day technology has made this all possible. I wander how many death row inmates get to speak to the European Parliament right after a resolution is signed in an attempt to save their life. I am beaming now.

The federal hearing in front of Judge Spencer was today at 9:00 a.m. We lost. Kate called and was surprised that I didn't care. I told her about the European Parliament instead. "Spencer said he would like to do the test but it was the governor's job," Kate said. Another way out, I thought to myself. It was his job too, but it's too political to touch. I heard he backed away from his own decision in 1994 and said there was a three probe match. This is unheard of. There is no basis for such a misstatement. Though I am not surprised anymore, the PR guy says, "I hate to be cynical, but maybe the prosecutor got to him." "It's much deeper than you think," I reply.

For whatever reason, Joe and I are arguing for almost an hour now. I am grateful that the last ten minutes of our call is spent making up. I am suddenly aware that we are arguing over crazy stuff. To escape this, Jennifer and I do some shopping in town and then go out to dinner.

In the meanwhile, John Nutter is threatening suicide again. In all honesty, I don't care. I only have so much emotion left and it is reserved for Joe now. After only five hours' sleep I awake to another call.

"I just called to say goodbye," Nutter says. I am furious. I try to calm him down but cannot really offer him any assurances as I have nothing to offer him. I have too much to do in preparation for my trip to New Jersey, and then down to Virginia.

Andrea calls me three or four times to finalize plans with the governor. He called Mark Christie to set a meeting with Governor Allen at 1:00 p.m. on Monday. He then faxed a letter to Botkins for a meeting with Joseph. Though he has not heard back yet from the Department of Corrections it would not strengthen international relations by denying a group of Parliamentarians a visit. As I start packing, a faint smile threatens to brighten my face. Then, Joe's call at 9:00 a.m. reminds me of why I am going down south. I apologize for raising my voice yesterday. Our time is too precious for this. After an hour on the phone in the morning we catch a quick afternoon chat.

"Don't worry about Shadow (my cat), she isn't lost, just look under the bed," Joe says. I had told him earlier she must have run away. Three hours later she crawled out from under the bed. I smiled as I thought of Joe.

"Today they weighed me like a piece of meat and took my blood pressure. It was 110 over 80. I was amazed." Joe is surprised his blood pressure hasn't skyrocketed and quite frankly, so am I.

"Joe, don't worry, the plans are all set for the marriage. I called the court and the Fed Ex package is expected to be here in the morning with the papers I will need."

Orlando faxes me his flight itinerary. He will arrive in Richmond on Sunday. I will meet him at the hotel at 6:30 in the evening to discuss his meeting with Governor Allen on Monday.

Joe and I have so little time now. I miss our easy time, when I could hear his laughter about the kittens in his cell or find him chuckling as I describe one of Jennifer's soccer moves. It's all too crazy now.

In keeping with good strategy, I feel that, as with Joe Payne, it would be helpful to have a juror who is asking for Joe's life to be spared. Joe Payne is a Virginia death row inmate who received a reprieve from the governor in December. His claims of innocence earned him a spot in prison as a lifer. Would Allen do the same for Joe O'Dell? I call Carol Kelly and ask for her support. She says, "I don't feel comfortable about giving a statement for the truth in sentencing issue but I will stand by my first letter to the governor." I recall that she informed him that her opinion would be different had she known the truth about the blood evidence. There would be reasonable doubt about Joe's guilt, she had said. "Carol, I want you to know that I did not mislead you in any way. I *am* the paralegal and wanted you to make your mind up on facts, not emotions". I had heard she felt I had deceived her somehow. She was kind, yet guarded in our conversation. I sensed she would stand firm. I also sensed she felt badly about having shared with the other jury members erroneous information that helped nail Joe's coffin.

If a law firm ever got fired up over injustice it is Miller, Cassidy, Larroca & Lewin. They are furious about Judge Spencer's opinion yesterday. They could not believe he changed his factual finding to say there was a match in the blood evidence. "Lori, I know it won't do any good, but we are going to file a "kiss-my-ass" motion. I have to get this off my chest," Doug tells me. For the first time in this case I witness firsthand some of the same emotions I have been feeling for years now.

Julie Carey from NBC calls and wants to interview Joe. My first reaction is, *screw you, you put us off seven months ago. Now that Joe is about to die you want his last words?* I stick with my gut and tell her, "I'm sorry, no more interviews."

It's Saturday now, July 19th. John Nutter interrupts me at 8:00 a.m. with another upsetting phone call—further proof of his instability. I put my house phone on call forwarding and stop at the post office to drop Joseph a letter. Just before I'm ready to leave, Fed Ex arrives with my divorce decree. I can't help thinking this is God helping us out when we need it most.

I stop at Walter's house. He looks good but I sense he is not happy. A warm feeling runs through me while in his presence. He is, or was, my one and only husband. He insists on making me breakfast. He's an awesome cook. He whips up some eggs, bacon and toast, topping it off with a cup of coffee. He then does the same for Jennifer, minus the coffee. He walks me upstairs and shows me pictures of Jennifer. In his library he shows off his new surround-sound system for his favorite movie, *Top Gun*. The stark difference between a kind sweet wonderful caring man who saves lives, the mansion I'm sitting in protected from the world, and my trip to Virginia to see Joe at the death house, is more than I can bear. It brings home the reality of what my life has become during the fierce struggle to save Joseph. I was sad, somewhat quiet, but I smiled at Walter's willingness to make me happy. When I said I was afraid, he answered, "How do you think he feels?"

~*The Death House*~

Driving to Virginia is like being a blindfolded rat in a maze. I have the music up at times, trying to drown out my anger and forget the world. With my mind unclear I caught myself, twice, swerving into another lane, thankful another car was not in my way. The CD player sang to me the words of the song that has come to represent us. *I'll Stand By You*, by the Pretenders, playing over and over again. It's a song that brings me close to Joe. As I approach the sign "Jarret", a heavy, dark pit drops into my stomach. After another 10 miles to Emporia, I veer off the exit and stop at the light where I suddenly seem to huddle to myself. In this place the outside world seems filled with evil people. I check into the motel where the desk clerk informs me I have a lot of calls. He told them I wasn't there. I offer him a list of people I will speak with and retreat to my room. Joe and I are able to speak for two hours between seven and nine, and then again from 9:30 to 11:00 p.m. Prior to leaving for the execution house Joe sent me his last few articles of clothing. I slip into his blue shorts and tee shirt before bed, somehow thinking this will unite us in strength. Joe and I, our spirits still high, are surviving on blind faith, and love—the oneness we share as human beings.

July 20, 1997. The phone rings at 7:00 a.m. It's Joe. "You always call when I am naked!" I shout as I step out of the shower to dry off. We speak briefly as I prepare to leave the motel in another hour. When I arrive at the death house I notice numerous guards sitting at the main desk. They all know who I am and who I am visiting. I see one guard lean over and whisper to another guard. Canines are in the hallway. After I'm searched by two guards, the visitors (me) are told to stand up against the wall. Two dogs sniff me to make sure I have no bombs or deadly cocktails. One dog, a black and white fluffy mutt, the other, a black lab. I wait patiently until 9:00 a.m. Finally, they allow me to walk over to the waiting van. I feel sick to my stomach. Still, I'm walking with my head held high. Two guards are by my side. One guard will drive and one will sit in back with me. *I must be extremely dangerous.*

I am taken to *the* building, the death house. Immediately, two female guards approach me. One of them says, "You know you only have one hour, don't you?" Joe is right there.

"No," I reply. "No one told me that." I turn to Givens, a mean-looking, burly guard wearing sunglasses and a visor. "You got one hour," he yells out. I look puzzled.

"Why? It's supposed to be a two-hour visit in the morning and two in the afternoon? Why is there a different set of rules for me and Joe; who said so?"

"Department of Corrections, Angelone's office," the guard blurts out.

Of course. I know that. I turn to ask the female guard why and she whispers, "Shhh, they're a bunch of motherfuckers!" I can sense that both female guards know this is wrong and cruel, and that Joe is being treated unfairly. Even in death. There is no humanity in this process. None.

At one point Joe stands up and says to Givens, "This is bullshit. You know people are going to pay for this. I've got nothing to lose, I am not alone. There are people behind me." To that the mean guard responds, "I know, whatever."

Needless to say, Joe is upset the entire visit. I try to calm him by talking about Jen but he stays focused on the evil. His eyes are watery; I've never seen him so angry. As I'm watching him I cannot help but notice the orange jumpsuit he's wearing. He had asked for a shower and canteen but they refused him, even though he has $551 in his account.

"Peanut, they gave me a toothbrush with three bristles on it. When I'm in my cell I'm freezing. They make me wear just my underwear so I wrap a blanket around me." Yet he has maintained his kindness to the guards, he is *still* nice to them. *These fucking guards*, they don't deserve niceness.

"I'm on a hunger strike; I refuse to eat." Joe says. I can hardly blame him. "They medicated, drugged my food. I was fine when I spoke to you and then passed out after eating breakfast." His tongue and his mouth are dry. "It's valium. I woke up just before you got here."

For the entire one-hour visit two guards sit in with me, not like last time, six months ago. When Givens leaves the room, I speak more freely to Joe. "Don't let them get to you, it's not worth it."

"Lori, they will beat me when you leave. Don't come back if I don't call you. And if they do, don't be sad, it's okay. I'd rather go out like a tiger."

At this point I agree with him.

We have no afternoon visit. The one-hour visit was one hour for the entire day! I hate these people more than ever now.

When I return to the motel I force myself to eat. I need my energy to fight now. Joe will call me at 1:00 p.m. We can visit on the phone.

The afternoon is creeping by when suddenly there is a knock on my door. I open the door to Bob and Sarah West from Joe's prison ministry. I was speaking with Joe and had to hang up. I need to call the lawyers to tell them about Joe's physical condition and our visit limitation. Bob and Sarah listen patiently, all the while amused by my efforts on behalf of Joe. They can see I'm still fighting for him. We are about to end our visit when they offer to be with me, to discuss briefly the "what if" phase and any arrangements that need to be made. "Lori, you have to think about that. The body is always ready between 6:00–8:00 a.m. the next morning." I thank them for their concern but decline the offer. The term "always ready" is chilling to me, said with such casualness. I cannot think of this now—I need faith.

I now have just enough time to freshen up and leave to meet Mayor Orlando at 6:30 p.m. He is staying at the Commonwealth Park Suites. When I arrive we embrace and get to work right away. We review the evidence and what to say to Mark Christie. They were reading the Fourth Circuit Opinion errors and had obviously read all the material. I was impressed.

By 9:00 p.m. we're ready for dinner. I feel like I'm back in Italy now. The Consul of Italy for the Commonwealth of Virginia accompanies us, as does Andreas. Somehow they locate the finest Italian restaurant in Richmond which prepares for us a special order. The service is superb and the food extraordinary. We are treated like royalty. They must have known who they were. After we take the last sip of our wine, we head back to their hotel.

As we hug and kiss goodbye, I let them know that Joe asked me to marry him and that I said yes. They know it paves the way for his arrival in Rome should the worst happen. When I departed I felt confident the message to the governor would be clear. Joe O'Dell is innocent. They will present the European Parliament resolution and speak of his burial in Palermo, if need be. Orlando said he has never done this in his entire life, spending three days fighting for a man, when there are thousands of men all over the world in Joe's situation. But Joe is different. I advise them not to speak much about Joe's burial. "Focus on life," I tell them.

Mayor Orlando would later tell me that the Commonwealth refused to allow him to visit with Joe, citing "security concerns". Though Orlando's request for a meeting was with the governor, George Allen sent Mark Christie to meet with the dignitary. "I hope the governor will understand that the European Parliament has voted unanimously to confer the sentence of death to not death, and to make available for testing all the DNA evidence," Orlando said upon his arrival at the governor's office. The Commonwealth's denial of his request to meet with Joe, which infuriated Orlando, fueled a comment by one of the Italian reporters, "So what's (Orlando) going to do? Come to America and help a convicted felon break out of prison?"

~Power Play~

It is now two days before the Commonwealth plans to kill Joe. He calls in the early morning. We speak about last night. When I leave my room I stop to get Joe a money order for $40. I arrive at the prison at 9:00 a.m. and ask to speak directly to the warden. I want to ask him why I am limited to a one-hour visit.

At the moment, I am waiting to see Joe. A female guard named Chapman comes to retrieve me. I know I cannot give anything directly to Joe so I offer the money order to Tammy Brown, the girl at the desk. She refuses to accept it. "No, you cannot leave that for Joe," she spits out. In a fury, I tear it up in Tammy's face and follow Chapman for my visit with Joe. "She would have held the money for you, Lori. Don't let them mess with you," Chapman tells me.

On my way to see Joe we pass by the cages enclosing the inmates out for rec time. I notice a disgusting prisoner open his pants and swing his penis around. I ignore it. Chapman shouts out, "Put that thing back in your pants." I was afraid of encountering just what happened and pretend it doesn't phase me. Inside I'm cringing. The inmates are wearing white shirts and blue pants. As we continue to drive down the road to the execution house where Joe is being held all eyes are focused on the "death van".

I glance at the clock on the wall behind Joe. I can see he's more relaxed than yesterday. He looks at me with love in his eyes and says, "You are so beautiful, you're eyes are sparkling. God, you are so beautiful."

Chapman leans over and whispers, "I don't care what you do. Joe needs some female attention." With that she goes to the phone and turns her back. It was her cue to allow me to show Joe some flesh, if I wanted. I ignore her permission. Joe smiles and starts to tell me that he had left some legal papers for me, but the prison wouldn't take them. We spend half the time talking about the one-hour visit and the legal papers and the messages now going back and forth to the warden's office. Joe looks worn, but his eyes are filled with love and adoration. The grayness in his skin masks any color left in his life.

When our visit is over I'm informed Warden Garrity will see me. Garrity is a man with a rough face, grey hair on the sides of his head and bald on top. He looks like a cowboy without his hat. He is cocky in an administrative way.

As we begin our conversation, it quickly became apparent what was going on—an awesome mind game.

"The DOC has concerns about you," Garrity says in a gruff voice, "but the decision to limit the visit to one hour is mine. It's either that or nothing. The one-hour visit takes a lot of guard time and it's sufficient enough."

"Warden, with all due respect, nothing has changed since December. Why would you change the rules?" I ask.

"It's a matter of credibility. At first, you're married, then you tell the press you will sue if they repeat that."

Oh, I see. They are angry that I made them look bad. I recall when Joe tried to get conjugal visits, he prepared the Indian ceremony paper and the DOC denied it because it was not authentic, or legal. Now, when they want to discredit me, they start referring to me as his wife, recognizing an illegal document.[95]

"My reputation is better than yours, Lori," the warden states.

"No, I doubt that. I am very professional and a highly ethical person who is well respected by the lawyers and my professors at law school. It is only the DOC that doesn't respect me and I don't care about them," I reply.

I smile and offer a chuckle. "What are you afraid of, me?" I am amused now as the warden at Mecklenburg and the guards all admit there is no reason for security concerns.

"No, we're not afraid of you. That would mean you have power and you have no power," Garrity responds.

"What are you afraid of then?" I ask.

"We're afraid of what you might do," he replies.

I laugh. "What on earth could I possibly do? There are guards everywhere. I'm strip-searched. Are you kidding?"

"You might bring in contraband," the warden replies.

I laugh again. "I'm the most conservative, law-abiding person you know."

He is clearly amused, seeing firsthand the feisty woman behind this unique situation.

I finally suggest, "Let's not bicker about this. I want to know about

---

[95] See Appendix, Exhibit III, for a copy of the original letter from the DOC denying such a marriage.

the marriage thing. I don't want to waste my time."

"It's being processed."

He proceeds to talk about who would marry us and asks, "Don't you want Father Jim?"

"Yes, but I cannot reach him," I reply.

The warden is pleasant about the marriage, even accommodating, yet he knows no kindness. "You know you'll only have one hour tomorrow, including the ceremony. There will be no conjugal visit."

I thank him and leave for the courthouse. I request a marriage license application and after filling it out, drop it back at the prison for Tammy to give to Joe. He has to sign and notarize it. It doesn't dawn on me that people must be wondering why on earth I am marrying a man who is to die within hours of our vows. It doesn't dawn on me because I don't care. I'm focused on one thing and one thing only—Joseph.

By this time I need to leave for Christie's office. I call Debo. The secretary answers and I tell her, "I'm getting married." I don't think I realized how crazy that sounded. She was genuinely happy and shouted back, "Congratulations!" I'm now thinking about the reality of this. I call Sister Helen to tell her of my decision. At first, she's quiet, then excited. I sense she's surprised they would allow it. She knows I won't stop, even at death, to prove Joe's innocence. We speak for 15 minutes.

"I'm coming in tomorrow morning," Sister Helen says. "Bishop Sullivan's office will pick me up and bring me to you."

She asks about staying at the parish, then said, "Should I stay near you?"

"Sister Helen, stay *with* me," I respond. "I have two double beds in my room!"

She was happy with that. *This is all so surreal.*

Then, in only the way Helen can do, she starts to make me laugh. No one in the world could have done that at this point but her.

"Lori, when I'm at the wedding maybe I can be a bridesmaid or maid of honor. Oh, no, I have to be a matron of honor."

"You bet, whatever you want!" I reply.

We both start laughing.

Before I leave for the governor's office I call Tammy Brown. I need to pick up the papers to ensure this will happen now.

"We're not sure, the DOC is not sure," Tammy says. "We need to wait to hear from them. Call back in ten minutes." They are stalling and I don't know why.

Ten minutes later I call her back. Still no answer. She will leave the paper for me at the "control box". At 4:00 p.m. they had given Joe the papers to sign and notarize. I'm hoping it goes through.

When I arrive at the prison at 5:30 p.m. the papers are waiting for me. I first have to show my ID. When I do, I grab the papers and return to my motel.

As I drive to the governor's office I accidentally pass the exit. I arrive a half-hour late. As I enter the building I immediately notice a lot of press in the hallway. *How do they know about this meeting?* I am still functioning in my own world of trying to save Joe. A media van notices me and does a quick turnaround. A man shouts out the window, "Are you Lori Urs?"

"Yes I am, but I need to go inside," I call back.

As I sit in the waiting room of the governor's office, the journalists and cameras swarm around me. One reporter yells out, "Can we have a minute?"

"No," I reply. "Not now, I'd rather after my meeting". They quickly move away.

Two hours later I finally get in to see Christie. I look up and suddenly see Bob Smith standing before me. Paul is behind him. I ask, 'How'd it go?" "Good", he says, without offering any other information. I wonder what "good" means. The press are waiting for him. I look directly at him, reminding him we're here on business. "Bob, we should go in, are you coming with me"? He nods and we enter the room. Christie takes a seat across the table from me, Bob Smith, Paul and Debo. This meeting was for Joe's family and I guess that was me, though officially I'm not. All eyes were focused on me and I was ready. I had three messages to get across. I take a deep breath and clear my throat. I could see both Bob Smith and Christie's mouths hone open as I spoke.

> On behalf of Joe's family and friends we are disappointed about the governor's decision to deny DNA testing for Joseph. Although you consider the guilt and innocence aspect of this case closed, it will always be open in your hearts and your mind. We are tortured and are suffering just as the victim's family is. Putting that aside, we hope that governor Allen will be true to his word, what he based his campaign on, and apply it across the board, especially in a death penalty case. Allen's campaign was based on truth in sentencing. I find it difficult for him to ignore his own campaign platform.
> Now, this message comes from me and me alone...

I proceed to tell them why I fought so hard for Joe and the extent of my research of the record. I tried to convey to them the reason for my tenacity and mission for the truth. The second part of the message was aimed at the part that Joseph played in my life as a human being, not a number on death row.

> Joe is an integral part of my life. If you take him away, I will have all the time in the world to fight. This is not a threat, it's just me and who I am. I will prove that Virginia killed an innocent man and it will follow the governor's career path forever. If you commute his sentence, I can go on with my life. I can continue with law school. If not, I will take a leave of absence to vindicate Joe's name. They say he's manipulative but if you were in prison and innocent, wouldn't you do all you could to bring attention to your case, even if it was stupid? All Joe ever wanted was a chance for the truth to be told about the evidence and although I am not happy about the possibility of no freedom, I ask you not to take Joe's life.
> Joe is an extraordinary person. His record in prison is exemplary. He has changed. People are capable of that. Isn't that what we hope for

through incarceration? I believe in his innocence. Please do not take his life.

My speech was not fluid, nor eloquent or articulate. At this stage it was purely authentic. I had few words left at this point.

Joe's lawyers performed well. Bob appeared strong and actually *for* Joe. In an interview afterwards, he spoke of Joe's innocence. It was refreshing, though way too late in the game. I return back to Greensville to pick up the marriage papers. Still, I'm unsure whether I am getting married. At this point I'm simply functioning, following the path of an unwritten script laid out in front of me and doing all I possibly can to stay clear in my actions.

It's Tuesday morning, one day before they intend to take Joe's life. While the day starts off slow for me, it's a busy morning at the death house. Joe calls promptly at 7:00 a.m. "Good morning, darlin'." Even now, he is a charmer. I would miss that. We talk for an hour. During our conversation Joe suddenly starts to whisper, "The guards, the death squad, are here and they're preparing for my death. I heard a dry run of my own execution." A big burly guard walks by his cell. Joe huffs in defense, ignoring his presence. "They want to kill me so badly, Lori."

Sister Helen is scheduled to arrive soon. A phone call from the prison confirms that the marriage is approved. "It has to be on Wednesday." They have purposely put it off to generate a media circus around an otherwise troubling day for international relations and humanity. Always trying to find the bright side of things, I convince myself it's actually better for us. I phone Bob West. He'll find someone to perform the ceremony. Our minds are now distracted from death and focused on life, even if life is an eight-hour marriage.

I need to phone Mary Bauer at the ACLU to see if she will file Joe's papers in court. He is still fighting—we cannot just give up. She will fax me the papers for filing, she says. I have enough time to take care of the marriage license and make some calls regarding the court filing for habeas on the sentencing issue.

Just before I jump into the shower Joe calls mid-morning and we speak just briefly. Just as I'm finished getting dressed, there's a knock on my door. It's Sister Helen. We open our arms and smile as we warmly embrace. I stare for a moment at her calm and reassuring face.

Sister Helen grabs some food to go before we leave at noon to obtain the marriage license. When we arrive at the courthouse, the half hour I'm here seems to pass in slow motion. Helen waits in the car for me. When I walk in, it's apparent they know who I am. They inform me to expect the media. At first, the women in the office offer me a cool greeting. My disposition soon forces a change in their judgment and they begin to warm up to me. I suppose they didn't know what to expect, this crazy woman marrying a death row inmate on the day of his execution. I watch as she types my marriage license, line by line, right before my eyes.

I leave with the necessary paper in hand and a bunch of household goods the women give to me, things they give to all new brides, including two small boxes of detergent.

Helen starts ribbing me. It's laughter that is much needed. "Lori, I'm not sure what you're going to do with that darn detergent, but we'll find a use for it."

Earlier this morning Joe told me he will lay across the steps if they don't let me in tomorrow.

My nerves are even more frayed than I realized. I reach for the man who has been the love of my life. I call Walter. I need his reassuring voice. When he doesn't answer I realize it's because he must be working. He is the only one who *knows* me, and can offer me the comfort I need now. Instead, I call Joe's sister, Sheila. Not for comfort, but to talk to her about Joe. I need to keep busy. She wants to visit Joe. *Why now?* Our relationship has been strained for some time now. My values challenge the fact that she let fear of disapproval guide her as she stood by silently during the past eleven years of her brother's fight for freedom. Now, she refuses to honor Joe's wish to be buried in Italy. As his only family member she would control what happens to his body. Joe is adamant about wanting to be buried among those who fought for and believe in him. His sister doesn't want this. *Marrying Joe would give me control over his body.* The Italians *want* him in Palermo and already have a spot for him, just in case. The Italian Parliament and the vast majority of Italy's citizens have been the strongest support Joe and I have received. We won't let them down. Neither will I let Joe down. Sheila and I argue a bit and I hang up. When Joe calls again at 9:00 p.m. he tells me his sister just left. I don't say a word. I know he needs that. We stay on the phone for two more hours talking about his writ and whatever else we can talk about to keep our minds busy.

I can't possibly be aware of what is going on around me, but on the steps of the U.S. Supreme Court, in the pouring rain, from 5:00 p.m. to 9:00 p.m. tonight stand strangers, holding a vigil for Joe. Perhaps they are strangers only because we do not know their names, but they are standing in solidarity with us. Though I don't know this now, soon I will find out that many powerful messages of love circulated on this day.

It's raining outside and there's a downpour in my heart.

Chapter 25

~Wednesday, July 23, 1997~

8:00 a.m. Joe calls.

"The SWAT force is here and two death squad guards are looming around. The guards are cold as ice. They asked what I want for my last meal and I told them, 'I forego my last meal to stand by all the hungry children in the world' The guard's response was, 'Can we release this to the media?'"

Ray and Jackson are two guards who are supportive of Joe. When they left last night they said, "We pray you get off." The psychologist said, "If you need anything, let me know." Joe said, "Thank you, but no. I'm sustained by the strength of the Lord."

Joe sees compassion and evilness in the same place. He says he's not mistreated by anyone. I have to question his definition of mistreatment. He's always standing up for the guards and has never said anything bad about any of them the entire time I've known him.

"It is the most evil thing to see people scurrying around to kill me." They want to kill me so badly, I can feel it," Joe says. Joe is tortured by the horror of what he sees around him. He also knows what to expect, having been forced to witness the preparation for his friend's death, who was killed just a few months ago just feet away from where Joe is being held.

I tell him I will be there soon. "Hang tight, Joe, just ignore them."

Easy for me to say.

In preparation for our visit I slip on the dress I bought in Cape Cod. I hadn't gone "wedding dress" shopping. This dress is sleeveless, patterned with a black background and small flowers scattered on it, it falls to my ankles. It will have to do.

Sister Helen is with me and Russ Ford, the minister, is waiting for us in the lobby. We talk about the ceremony.

"They told me you cannot touch one another, no holding hands or kissing", he says. Immediately, Russ and Helen figure a way to officiate at the ceremony, beyond the mere reading of words. After we converse a bit, I'm told I have to be searched. I expect to be searched the same way I have been the past few days. But they have something else in mind. They escort me to a different building. I am told to step into a separate room. This is highly unusual so it begs the question—why?

"You need to be strip searched. Take off all of your clothes and bend over and touch the floor," the female guard says. There are two female guards now standing behind me. They must have noticed the expression of disbelief on my face. "May I speak to Sister Prejean?" I ask. "Make it brief," the heavyset guard replies.

"Helen, what do I do? They want to strip-search me? This is insane, they know I am not a security concern."

"Lori, the inmates go through this all the time. Joe has had to endure the same. Nothing can take away your dignity. Just do it. It's okay. Remember, they're just trying to intimidate you," Helen whispers to me. She is right.

I walk back to the guards and do as I must to see Joseph. He is what matters now, not me. I drop my clothes and stand naked on the cold cement floor before I bend over and show my ass to the guards. The "kiss-my-ass" motion filed by the attorneys now has a whole new meaning.

After the strip search they escort me back to Joe. When I enter the room I notice for the first time Joe's sullen face. The Department of Corrections, even on the day they plan to kill Joe, refuse to let us touch. Helen and Russ Ford are with me. They are determined to get by this ridiculous rule. Russ starts, "Let's all hold hands. This way the love between Joe and Lori will flow through our bodies to each other." Joe is standing opposite me. As I watch his face, a steady stream of tears drip from the corners of his tired eyes, mixing the joy of the moment with the torment of finality. I have never in my life witnessed anyone cry in this way. My heart is breaking. Russ has rings we managed to acquire in a hurry. He asks Joe to take the ring and hold it, to cup it in his hand and to put all of his energy into it. I watch as Joe kisses the ring that would fall gently on my finger as Russ places it on my left hand. I do the same with the ring I have for Joe and Sister Helen places it on Joe's ring finger. Joe and I exchange vows and we join in the Lord's Prayer. Even guard Givens joins in with us. The peace Joe and I feel at that moment is what we need to get through the next few hours of terror. We are not allowed to touch or hold hands. But Russ is ingenious. "Let's take a moment, Joe and Lori, and breathe the same air." We close our eyes and take a long breath. Russ makes sure we don't rush the moment.

"I smell flowers, like the flowers on your dress, Lori," Joe says. My heart softens to his words. It is all I can give Joe in his last few hours on earth. They have taken away everything else. They cannot, will not, take away his dignity.

After the ceremony I'm told I can visit with Joe. A fold-up metal chair is placed a few feet in front of Joe's cell. Most family members can get right in there with the condemned. But not me. We talk some, smile and try to act as normal as one can under the circumstances. We share a cigarette, though I don't smoke. It's our way of bonding. A guard watches our every move. To my immediate right is a tall, solidly built guard in dark clothing. At least one or two more are present to remind us what their bosses have in store for Joe. To the left of Joe's cell are two, maybe three cells. At the end of the hall, just a few feet away, is the door to the death chamber. I can hear noises coming from the room, people scurrying about. It's making me nervous but I try to ignore it. It's important to remain calm and assured. We have not given up the fight. Not yet.

The guards remind us of the time and tell us to wrap it up. I still am not thinking this is the last time I will see Joe. We're still hoping the courts will listen to a motion he has prepared. It's handed to me by one of the guards when I leave the building. I smile at Joe and with every fiber in my body and the strongest breath I could muster, I say, "I love you, Joseph."

"I love you too, Lori," Joe echoes back to me.

It's time to go. Before I do, Joe reminds me he has two documents for me. "Lori, I left a motion for you to file in the court, be sure to do it when you leave here, okay? The lawyers forgot to include this. It's good; I think they'll listen. I also wrote my last will and I left everything to you. I don't have much but we already discussed my wishes and I want you to have whatever it is I own. Be sure to keep it with you, honey."

Joe cannot hand it to me, the guards do. I turn to walk away, my head up high. I want to cry, but I would never give them the satisfaction. Never. As we leave through the front gates of the prison I suddenly notice the press is loitering everywhere. The DOC purposely delayed our marriage to ensure there'd be a media circus. No one else could have told them. It was a private decision. I have nothing to say to them, and don't want to talk, but Helen encourages me. "Just say something briefly." I inform them that I just married Joe O'Dell and then move on to the facts of the case. Helen takes me by the arm and gently nudges me away from the crowd and back to the car. I must file the document Joe has prepared.

I reach the courthouse around 4:00 p.m., frantically saying, "This is an emergency; it's for Joe O'Dell. They want to kill him, it's important the court sees this right away." The court clerk gently takes the form from my hands and stamps it. It's official. I have done what Joe has asked. Again, his life is in the court's hands. Or is it?

As we head back to the motel in Emporia I lift my cell phone from the dashboard and call Doug, Joe's lawyer. I want to know about the decision from the U.S. Supreme Court and the governor. As I listen to the news, I begin sobbing, unable to drive anymore. Helen tells me to pull over, she wants to drive.

I'm trying to get the words out, but they are mumbled, "Governor Allen denied Joe on everything. He won't grant clemency and he won't let him do the DNA test." I know now that there is one last hope—the courts. I think I may have to face the fact that Joe will die. Helen drives us back to the motel and makes sure I'm settled before she leaves to be with Joe. She can visit with him from 6:00–11:00 p.m.

I am on the phone with Joe when I hear that Helen has just arrived. She talks with the lawyers. Bob Smith and Andy Sebok are there for Joe. We're holding on to each other's words, refusing to say goodbye. We don't know how to act, we can only reach out for one another's love and support. While we're on the phone, Helen talks to the lawyers about the process; they want to know what will happen next.

At 7:28 p.m. the death squad lurks over Joe and forces a shot of ten milligrams of Valium into his shaved chest. Joe and I are on the phone. "Let's not say goodbye, Lori." And we don't. I'm still praying his life will be spared. There are too many issues, too many unanswered questions, too much doubt surrounding this case for them to kill him.

At 7:30 p.m. Helen and the lawyers are asked to leave the room while they "prepare" Joe for his death. He must take a shower in the shower that has been right across from his cell since he arrived. The same shower that Ronnie and Tuggle were forced into, right before their deaths. The same one Joe sat in front of just months ago and has stared at for days now.

At 8:00 p.m. Helen, Bob and Andy are allowed back into Joe's cell area. Joe has already stepped into the shower and dressed in the blue pants and short sleeved blue shirt. Joe and I are still talking—we don't want to hang up.

"Darlin', be strong for me, okay? You take good care of that little squirt for me (meaning Jennifer). I will love you through eternity, you know that. Thank you so much for all that you did for me. Vaya con dios." Joe hangs up now. It's 8:40 p.m. Only 20 minutes left before we need a miracle.

Bob and Andy walk into Joe's cell and with ashen faces reach for his hand and tell him it's been a privilege being on his team. They don't know that half the reason Joe is where he is at is because of the lawyers, their failure to file the right motion, to fight for their client and, most importantly, to believe in him. I know Joe is not thinking this, but I would be. Helen nudges through the lawyers and reaches for Joe's hand.

"Sister, they gave me a shot of Valium, I didn't have a choice; they say it's to open up the veins to make sure the needle goes in easier. I'm going to be with my mama. She has suffered so much, died shortly after they sentenced me to die. Take care of Lori. She is so precious, so innocent. She needs you now."

Helen later tells me that Joe kept talking about me and how I was the best thing that ever happened to him. "I'm okay, God and I can do this. But, hey, Sister, what is the name of the Catholic book that I helped change?" Joe asks.

"Joe, you helped change a very big book, the *Catholic Catechism*. I think when the Pope personally read what you went through, the torture they put you through in preparation for your death back in December, it helped him see the torture in the death penalty and that it could never be justified."

"I did that?" Joe is surprised and happy at the same time. Maybe his death will help others.

Helen remembers last night when Joe was smoking a cigarette, how he told her he used to weight 295 lbs. He is now just 192 lbs. He spoke about me and our marriage and the happiness it gives him. It doesn't matter that it will be annulled after I accomplish my goals. It won't be until 14 years later that I come to understand the concept of love and oneness in the universe.

Joe repeats to Helen, "Lori is so innocent. You guys belong together."

It was important that someone be with me and Joe knew Sister Helen would. He also spoke about John Nutter and how he slashed his wrists, and how he appreciated my dilemma about John.

He then spoke briefly about his sister Sheila and how he had to tell her, "Lori is my warrior, my love. I have to be with her at this time."

He then tells Helen, "I may have helped Lori in her faith in God. I used to read scripture to her." And he did. He asks Helen, "Would you like something to drink?" She takes a root beer soda. Hospitality at the death house. Civility among inhumanity.

"They are doing this to you," Helen tells Joe, "but they cannot touch your soul." She pauses. "Joe, you know the story of Christ; he was innocent."

"Yes," Joe says with a nod.

The night before, Joe confided in Helen about what he would say or do on this very day.

"If I raise my eyebrows, stand back, because I'm going to fight them all the way, let them know they are killing an innocent man. I won't go quietly. And when the warden comes in and reads the death warrant and asks if I understand, I'm going to say, "No, I don't understand how you can kill an innocent man. But I will also tell him I know you are just doing your job."

Helen reminds him, "Don't be so quick to let the warden off the hook. It legitimizes their actions; all of them, the prosecutors, Attorney General, warden and the governor. It helps ease the burden of killing a man, especially an innocent man. Whatever you decide to do, I will stand by you. Lord knows what I would do if they were trying to kill me."

Helen tells Joe that no one can take away his dignity. Joe talks about his legal battle. "I am a writ lawyer, Helen, and though it was a raggedy thing, I'm surprised they did not listen, the courts. I just cannot believe what the courts did to me. With all that evidence how can they not listen? How can they just rubber-stamp all the wrong things that happened at my trial? How can they just let an innocent man die without the truth ever being told? And Sister, how can they not do DNA testing on the sperm?"

Joe is still in shock that the system failed him. So am I. We are both hoping for a last minute miracle. He is still hoping the court will listen to his last motion, filed just yesterday.

They also talk about Mother Teresa's statement. Being a nun has its advantages. They don't dare question her or they may be judged and sent to hell. Helen was able to slip into her pocket something she felt Joseph needed to hear during these difficult moments. Yesterday, July 22, 1997, Mother Teresa delivered a letter to Governor Allen and Justice Scalia. Helen had written the message on a single page of a pocket-sized bible. She slips it to Joseph after reading these words to him:

> Governor Allen and Justice Scalia:
>
> I come before you today to appeal for the life of a man - Joseph Roger O'Dell. I do not know what he has done to be condemned to death. All I know is that he, too, is a child of God, created for greater things - to love and to be loved.
>
> I pray that Joseph is at peace with God; that he has said sorry to God and to whomever he has hurt. Let us not take away his life. Let us bring hope into his life and into all our lives. Jesus, who loves each one of us tenderly with mercy and compassion, works miracles of forgiveness.

To you, dear Joseph, I say: trust in God's tender love for you, and accept whatever God gives you and give whatever God takes with a big smile.

Let us pray.
God bless you.
Lee Teresa mc

Joseph looks at Helen with tears in his eyes. The love that was pouring in from around the world now included Mother Teresa. His strength is bolstered now by love, replacing the hatred that surrounded him from the Commonwealth, the victim's family and the death squad keepers. Mother Teresa's statement was one of her last public statements made before her own death on September 5, 1997.

For the last few minutes they are together Helen and Joe are holding hands, praying.

"Thanks, beautiful Sis," Joe says.

"I thank God for your life, for Lori in your life, and those who have no one and are in your position. Christ was here and love was the strongest force."

"I am not afraid," Joe says. "God took that from me." Joe nods and squeezes Helen's hands.

"Joseph, if it happens, you pray—for me. It was a privilege to be brought into your life."

"Thank you, Helen. Take care of Lori, my little darling. She has to learn to rebuke evil forces. She is pure and innocent like a flower." Joe smiles as he talks about me.

"Joe, the power of your love is a threat to them," Helen says. She shares this with me back at the motel.

The guard had the TV on so their words could be privately shared.

The clock is just five minutes shy of 9:00 p.m. The warden walks in front of Joe's cell to read him the death warrant. Helen grabs Joe's hands for strength. "I'll be with you, Joe. May Christ's love and strength be with you." Sister Helen kisses Joe on the lips, as a sense for me, she later tells me. "I love you, Joseph," she says. "I love you, too," Joe says. Joe then shouts out, "Look, I'm about to be Allenized." This means killed by Governor Allen.

Joe is taken from his cell and placed in handcuffs. Even now they have to be sure he won't cause any trouble. He walks calmly with Sister Helen behind him, straight to the execution chamber.

The warden tells Helen she can touch Joe when he is strapped on the gurney but to please don't make the prayer too long. Even now they are dictating rules. Joe walks into the room and lays down on the table. The guards quickly strap his arms and legs. When the guards strap in Joe's chest, they pull very tight. Joe gasps, lifting his head. "Hey, man, you're cutting off my wind." The irony of his statement falls on deaf ears.

The guard looks scared and nervously glances at the warden for direction. The warden doesn't care, they don't adjust it. Another way to get back at Joe O'Dell for daring to challenge his conviction, for bringing the Italians in to question their right to kill him, and Mother Teresa, and that darn Lori Urs who made our life hell.

"Sister, they got it so tight," Joe calls out to Helen.

"Can't you adjust the strap a bit to help him breathe?" she asks. One guard shakes his head. The other ignores Helen.

But that would be the humane thing to do and this is not a humane process.

"They won't change it, Joe. Try to take shallow breaths; it won't be long."

Joe is looking straight at Helen as she places her hand on his shoulder and says the final words he will ever hear, "Christ's love surrounds you, Joe, and Lori is around you and all the people who love you are around you. I'll take care of Lori."

"I know," Joe says as he smiles.

The guards make Helen move out into the witness room. There is a sign above the "viewing" window which says, *Witnesses must remain seated. Press in back two rows.* As if this is a movie theatre—instead of popcorn, add the pads and pencils. For now the window is covered with the curtain draping inside the death chamber. It is too morbid to actually show them killing Joe so they must wait until after they have inserted the needles and the saline solution is flowing into his veins.

It is so quiet Helen tells me later you can hear a pin drop. Everyone is watching the curtain. Helen is praying.

"Oh Christ, be near him now, help him, strengthen him." Helen is silently praying and hoping Joe can feel her strength, what strength she is now maintaining for him. Helen folds her hands in her lap and closes her eyes. She is thinking about me, back in the motel room, praying for me, too. The only sound she hears is the scribbling motion of a pen on the pad of a journalist seated behind her.

Suddenly, the curtain is drawn back. As they open the curtain Helen is facing Joe, directly at his feet. She cannot see his face. He is lying flat so she can only see his chin and a bit of his nose. She cannot see his eyes. She wants to look into his eyes so he can see love before he dies, not evil. Helen is looking into the room and sees Joe's arms are wrapped with elastic bandages to hold the IV in place so there is no chance of a mistake.

The death squad must use four solutions to take the last breath from Joseph. Solution number one, saline, is already flowing. It opens the veins. The next solution is sodium thiopental which will put Joe to sleep. The third is Pavulon—or pancuronium bromide—which paralyzes his muscles and stops his breathing, just in case he is not asleep and moves about violently. The last and final solution is potassium chloride, this will stop his heart. Behind Joe is a blue plastic curtain. It hangs with two holes in it, one larger than the other. In the one is the intravenous tubing meant to kill Joe. The other must be a one-way viewing area for the technician, to ensure the solutions are working to do their job on Joe O'Dell.

The guard slowly moves to pick up the microphone. He places it up to Joe's mouth. They always give the condemned the right to say their last words, hoping to ease whatever pain the victim's family is feeling.

"Do you have any last words?" the guard asks.

"Yes, I do." Joe's voice strong and calm.

"This is the happiest day of my life. I married my wife, Lori. Governor Allen, tonight you get to go home to your wife and little girl, but you are taking this from me. Governor, you are killing an innocent man. To Eddie Schartner (Helen's son), if you are here, I'm sorry that your mother was killed, but I didn't kill your mother and I hope you find out the truth. Lori, I will love you for all eternity."

"Is that all?" the warden asks, as if additional time may alter the results.

"Yes," Joe speaks his final word before they kill him.

Because the strap is so tight he cannot even draw one final deep breath. The machines do their work at the motion of a human hand, and with that, Helen opens her eyes after a final prayer to watch the doctor as he places the stethoscope on Joe's chest to make sure he is dead. The warden nods and announces, "Joseph Roger O'Dell died at 9:16 p.m."

I am not watching the clock. I know what 9:00 p.m. means to Joe. I don't really want to know. I have no one with me. I have not asked anyone to be with me. To prepare would mean I know the outcome and I didn't, still don't. Helen will be back by my side soon. I sit silently on my bed, praying for Joseph. And myself.

Outside the prison are a swarm of satellites, at least eight, to broadcast the outcome around the world. Especially to Italy, the Parliament members, the Pope and Mother Teresa. There are hosts of TV and radio affiliates, and scores of print journalists. They are anxiously waiting for a statement. It is reported that over 5 million people stayed up in Italy—their prayers and love reaching across the Atlantic—to watch what the courts and Governor Allen would do.

Helen would later tell me that Bob and Andy looked stricken, not sure of what to do. Having been through this before, Helen gently guides them. "Bob, make a statement to the press about Joe and the legal issues and about what happened to him in the courts."

Bob waits for the warden to announce to the press Joe's last words. He is stoic, unmoved by his own words. After announcing herself as Joe's spiritual advisor and my friend, Sister Helen speaks her mind. She always speaks her mind, in a gentle, but strong southern accent that comes across with authority.

"Lori Urs fought with all she had to get the courts and Governor Allen to do justice for Joe O'Dell. I say that I believe the killing of any human being, even the guilty, is morally wrong, but that the killing of Joseph O'Dell, a possibly innocent man, without allowing him DNA testing is doubly heinous. I point out the great contrast: that here in Virginia, Joe's killing is just one more state killing that people scarcely notice, while in Italy and the European Parliament and even for Pope John Paul II, Joe's killing has provoked outrage and resistance. I end by thanking the Italian people for their prayers for Joe and the ten thousand faxes and phone calls to Governor Allen on Joe's behalf." Helen turns away from the media and walks toward the car. She doesn't linger.

Not long after Joe is executed Helen comes walking into my motel room. I have not cried, nor talked to anyone. I am sitting on my bed when she walks in. I can tell by the look on her face that the courts didn't listen. She lovingly looks at me with compassion. Seeing her is the moment I grant myself permission to release all that's been bottled up for so long. The tears begin to flow. I want to know what happened so I immediately put aside my feelings and ask, "Please Helen, tell me what happened. I want to know everything."

Her words are comforting, while I'm still unaware of what this new reality means for me, I listen intently as she describes Joe's last moments. She assures me that Joe died with dignity and shouted to the world, "This is the happiest day of my life." I am deeply satisfied when I hear this. Like Doug Curtis says, when you are faced with such incredible injustice and can't do a thing about it, you revert to the "kiss my ass" mode.

Helen continues to comfort me. "Lori, you left no stone unturned. You did everything in your power to stop this injustice, at all costs, and you resisted the errors of society with every fiber of your being. You did everything humanly possible. Joe is resting now."

And I know he is.

Chapter 26

~Planning an International Funeral~

The phone is ringing off the hook, but I can talk to no one. I have retreated into my own little world. I know with the support of Helen I can get through this. I must talk with Luciano and find out what to do next. This was the worst-case scenario that I refused to talk about because it meant it was a possibility. Now, it's my reality.

"Lori, they are transferring Joe's body to the funeral home in Norfolk, Virginia," Luciano gently tells me. The name of the funeral home is Cox. The Italian consulate is in Norfolk and he will help us with all the arrangements."

The next morning Helen and I drive to Norfolk. We have an appointment with Vito Piraino, the Italian Consulate. Luciano Neri and Rino Piscitello are leading the way. As we enter the office Piraino extends his hand to greet me. I thank him for all he is doing for Joe. It was a struggle to get permission to move Joseph O'Dell's body and transport him to Palermo, Italy, where he will be buried. The governor's aide had never handled a situation like this. Piraino was strong. "Should I expect a problem?" he asked. "I don't think you want an international incident over this, fighting over the body of Joseph O'Dell." He picks up a paper from his desk with a wide grin on his face. "This piece of paper is what will allow you to take Joe overseas. It grants you official permission to do so." He shares all the memos, letters and faxes sent from and to his office to ensure the wish of Joseph O'Dell and the Italian Parliament is honored.

This is the first time in U.S. history that the body of a death row inmate will be flown to a foreign country for burial, in a cemetery of the saints, reserved for dignitaries. This has the officials in Virginia confused. They intelligently agree not to fight this one.

Luciano retrieves the document. Piraino instructs him to keep it with him at all times. "You will need it when you depart the United States and when you arrive in Italy."

"I will guard it with my life," Luciano says. We all smile.

The Parliament and I just checked off one in our favor. My marriage to Joe has allowed me to take control of his body and to honor his last wishes. The people of Italy are waiting to welcome Joe. It's a victory for him, even if he's not here to see it.

I still need to pick out the casket and Joe's clothing for his burial, so Helen and I leave for the Cox funeral home. When we arrive we are greeted by the director.

"I am sorry for your loss," he says softly.

He leads me to the room where I must choose my *husband's* casket. The sound of this is strange to me, but I don't object. I am operating in pure survival mode. The Italian Parliament has graciously offered to pay for all of Joe's funeral costs. I'm instructed to pick out his casket among the many in front of me. I have never done this before. I want the best for Joe. I choose the classic bronze casket with white velvet interior. I want Joe to be comfortable. I am then moved over to where the clothes are and asked to select something for Joe. "Helen, how about this, do you think this would look good on Joe?" I choose a white shirt, blue paisley tie and a blue suit. I am instructed to wait while they dress him. Suddenly the moment I most dread is right before my eyes. I try to steady myself as we walk toward the casket. My eyes are filled with tears, but I'm not crying.

There he is. Laid carefully on a table before me is the body of

Joseph Roger O'Dell III. In conflict with my emotions there is an element of surprise that catches me off guard. He looks at peace, and in a strange way, better than he did those last torturous hours of his death. I kiss him and tell him not to worry, we are taking him to Italy. I will continue to fight to expose the truth. "Don't worry Joe, I promise to prove they killed an innocent man."

The funeral director wants to seal the casket. I am adamant it remain unsealed until we get to Palermo. Luciano is by my side. His presence is of enormous comfort to me. Without him, none of this would have been possible. He puts his arm around me. "It's alright, Lori. It will be okay." Reluctantly, the funeral director agrees and as he turns the key at the base of the casket, a metal covering is rolled over its length. He hands the key to Luciano, who is now responsible for its safekeeping. Luciano says, "Let's go, it's time to eat." What else but a wonderful Italian restaurant, where I am told I can get back some strength. I need to eat now.

To enter Rome I need a passport. I had not anticipated this so I'm unprepared. This necessitates a trip to Cape Cod, where my passport is safely tucked away. Helen agrees to join me on this road trip. The thought of her presence comforts me.

On our way to the Cape we stop in New Jersey to retrieve my photographs of Italy. I make a quick diversion to Walter's house. I want them to meet. Helen is quiet when we pull up to the mansion in which he lives. Walter graciously greets me with a warm hug and extends his hand to Helen. "It's so nice to meet you, Sister Helen. Thank you for being there for Lori." He brings us into the kitchen and offers us something to eat and drink. Walter is supportive and kind. Helen immediately likes him. I know in this room are two people who love and support me. We depart in time to make it to the Cape before dark, taking Walter's wishes with us for a safe trip to Italy.

Back on the road at 2:00 p.m., we're accompanied by the noise of a cell phone that won't stop ringing. The *Boston Globe*, the *Boston*

Herald and other newspapers are trying to reach me. The one phone call I did not expect was from Nina Bernstein at the Schiller Institute in Washington, D.C. "Lori, I wanted you to know that Mother Teresa gave a statement to the press about killing Joseph. It was addressed to Governor Allen." She also has a statement from Mother Teresa to me.

This is too important to get the words wrong. I pull over to the shoulder of the highway. Nina plays a tape of Mother Teresa asking to spare Joe's life. I am stunned. It ignites tears, though I thought I ran out of those by now. I'm overwhelmed by the sound of the sweetest voice I have ever heard. Helen takes the phone from me, offering me a moment to recover. Nina continues, "Lori, Mother Teresa sent an invitation for you to be received in Calcutta, *to stay with her*." I'm deeply humbled and honored by her invitation. But I know I cannot go now. *Is this all really happening?* It all seems so surreal.

When we get off the phone I remember I have work to do. A phone call to Doug reminds him to immediately write a letter to preserve the evidence. Doug tells me Frank Green is trying to get access to the evidence. I remind him, "No, it's mine!"

"Don't worry, Lori. I'll call Pat Schwarzschild to see if they will help us."

Just about this time I am feeling kind of funny. As I look down at the cloth car seat I see it is red. This is not the time for this. Helen and I are thinking fast. We pull over behind a building of a parking lot, near some woods. Seeing a puddle on the ground I suddenly realize I will get some use out of the detergent that was given to me as a wedding gift. I use it to clean the seat. Helen and I are hysterically laughing at this point.

Just before we had stopped, and while talking with Doug Curtis, Doug is laughing about all I have done with Helen and our current road trip.

"You two remind me of *Thelma and Louise*," Doug jokes. It was uncanny, for not long before this, Helen had mentioned the same thing.

From that moment we take on the personas of Thelma and Louise, Helen referring to me as "Thelma", and I call her "Louise". The names stick, to this very day.

Back on the road I phone the *Boston Herald* for an interview. I have learned by now that one never knows how the media will spin things. I can only hope the article is well written. Doug and I reconnect to discuss the pending issues. I had inquired about the possibility of a wrongful death lawsuit.

But what is most pressing is something far more important—I need to get access to the evidence. Before Joe's death I had strategized with the law firm of Miller, Cassidy, Larroca & Lewin in an attempt to perform posthumous DNA testing. I meant it when I told Governor Allen I would prove Joe's innocence, even *after* his death. The strategy would entail going after the evidence in two ways. We would recruit the Roman Catholic Diocese to file a motion to acquire the evidence, stating it was in the "public interest" to know whether the Commonwealth executed an innocent man. And I would file one as a family member to retrieve what is rightfully mine. It was brilliant. At least I thought so. *When I return from Italy I will file the motion in the Circuit Court of Virginia Beach.* Right now, I have a funeral to plan.

As we drive it starts raining, and we have three more hours before we reach Cape Cod.

John Nutter calls me at 10:00 p.m. I don't tell him where I am. I don't wish to discuss what happened or risk setting him off when he learns of the marriage. I need to keep him at bay.

Helen is out of sleeping pills and Stop and Shop is closed. As a result I will have to try to get some sleep on my own. It won't be easy. When we finally arrive at the house, I send Helen to the downstairs guest bedroom and climb the stairs to my own bed. When I think I have finally dozed off to sleep I am awakened by a horrid nightmare. My father is in a bathtub. An evil figure with no face is holding me up, violating me. I fall asleep again, only to awaken to another nightmare.

They are trying to execute Walter when I scream, "No, he's a doctor, don't kill him!"

It's Saturday now and I am up at 7:15 a.m. Nina told me yesterday she would be calling today. Mother Teresa wants to speak with me personally. Upon hearing this Helen had advised me to buy a tape recorder to record our conversation. It was worth a brief stop on the way home. I wanted this to last forever. It would be inspiration for me. I'm told Mother Teresa is quite ill. She's on oxygen, clinging to the last days of her own life. Even nearing death, Mother Teresa reaches out to others in love. The phone rings while Helen sits on the floor of my bedroom not far from me. Nina tells me Mother has gone to the chapel to pray. After three or four more attempts Nina hooks us up with a three-way call from the Schiller Institute. The call comes in at 10:40 a.m.

"It's Mother Teresa, Lori. She wants to speak with you."

Not knowing what to say and being struck by the moment I start rambling on. I'm so used to trying to get all the facts in about Joe's case that I don't realize this is different.

"Thank you for calling and for your support of Joseph. He was touched by your intervention," I continue rambling. Though she is ill, she has the strength and presence to quiet me.

"Shhhh!" she says. "Listen."

Mother Teresa tells me that she prayed for Joe. "He is with God and at peace now." During the five-minute phone call she broke once. To speak with me required her to go off her oxygen. Quietly, we say goodbye.

Sister Helen tells me she knows of no one who has ever received a phone call from Mother Teresa, straight from Calcutta, India. I am deeply honored.

After our phone call I rush to my safe deposit box at the bank to retrieve my passport, and next to the post office to get Joe's package from Mecklenburg prison. I'm also expecting Joe's photo, the one I left at the hotel. I hoped to bring it to Italy for the funeral.

As I step inside the house, the telephone is ringing. It's my friend Lorrie from Richboro, Pennsylvania. She is taking care of Jennifer while I'm getting ready to leave for Italy. She sounds upset.

"Lori, There's a radio show that is trashing you now. You need to defend yourself. Jen called in to tell them, 'You have no idea what you're talking about. How dare you speak about my mother that way (they had said I was mentally ill)! You don't even know the facts of the case. Did you know that the blood on his jacket did not match the victim's, that he was seen in a fight across town and that was his alibi, and that he left one half hour later than the victim from the club and I can go on and on, but I won't'".

The radio hosts asks Jennifer about paternity and Jen didn't know what that meant but came back with, "She gave him his last dying wish. That was very noble of her."

He asked what her dad felt about it and Jen said he thought it was very noble of her too!

What a tower of strength she is. She will face a lot when she returns to school and to her soccer team. She will need to stay strong. Jen would later tell me it was "fun" to call the show.

Helen would normally never give in to such trash from a radio show, but when she hears Jennifer had called in, she picks up the phone to do the same. First she calls Jen, and when they finish talking Helen turns to me, "That's one great girl you have there, I have a lot of respect for her." Her next call is to the radio station.

"This is Sister Helen Prejean."

"Oh, come on, we're sure this is a prank," the announcer says. Just as he said to Jennifer.

"No, this is Sister Helen Prejean. You just got off the phone with Lori Urs' daughter and what she says is correct," Helen says. "You don't know Lori, what she did was very noble. You have no right to speak about her that way."

She went on about the evidence a bit and how they did Joe wrong.

"Lori has integrity. I know the battle of Joe O'Dell and he was innocent."

I'm sure the show's listeners did not know what to think at this point. Nor did I care. Though I did not care about it as it relates to me, I did care about the defamation for the sake of my family. I make it a point to do a TV show when I return so they know who I am and what I am all about. My reputation is on the line now. At the moment I have no time for them. I refocus my limited energies back on Joe's funeral.

Knowing we have little time while on the way to Rome, Helen and I prepare our press statements and fax them to Luciano. The *Boston Globe* arrives at my home in the afternoon and for an hour and a half we talk about Joe's case. The journalist appears to be impressed with me. I am not sure what she expected.

"You are so sweet, articulate and very smart," she says to me. I pray she writes a fair article.

Shortly after the reporter leaves, there's a knock on the front door. Fed Ex is delivering a small package from Joe. Inside it are the last of his belongings.

While in town and in need of strength through spiritual connection, I decide to visit my church. The Chatham United Methodist Church is just a two-minute walk from my house. The service is at 10:00 a.m. Helen joins me. Thom Gallen, our minister and my friend, introduces her to the congregation. He addresses Joe's case as one the church has been following, thanks Sister Helen for her work, and then me for mine. Thom's sermons usually serve to inspire the audience. Today was no different.

When we return home we spend the day preparing for our trip overseas. The phone is still ringing off the hook. Helen is screening the press.

The next morning we are up early, run out for a quick breakfast and the *Boston Globe* simultaneously. The headline, "Love Conquers

Death Row", takes me by surprise, but as I read on I'm pleased. "After the execution she still believes." It was tastefully done, though I regretted not allowing the reporter to take our (Sister Helen and I) photo. Anything would be better than my picture at the death house after the wedding!

My mind is on what lies ahead of me when suddenly I receive a strange phone call. It's Cheryl Murden, Joe's longtime girlfriend and fiancée. She has been leaving mean-spirited messages on my answering machine. Until now I have ignored them.

"Joe and I really loved each other, for the past three years I have all of our tapes." On one of her messages she was crying hysterically. Helen helped screen her calls. Finally, I take her last call.

"I need to see Joe. Where is his body, Lori?" I do not need drama now. I politely hang up. She calls back again. This time Helen hangs up.

As if it's not enough that Joe has been executed, now the media is sensationalizing the battle I'm having with Sheila, Joe's sister. It's so difficult to understand all this as she's never been involved in Joe's fight for freedom. Now she wants to keep him in the United States against his very own wishes. She does, however, release a statement that it's all okay and says, "Lori is courageous." I make an attempt to phone her to help ease the tension. Her daughter hangs up on me. Fortunately, Joe and I knew my legal status as his wife would trump any rights she would have to claim his body.

Tonight MSNBC will be talking about Joe's execution. Doug, Paul, Eric from *Nations Magazine* (produced by World Outreach International) and Ann Coulter from *Human Interest* are discussing the case. Sister Helen joins in by phone. The show is entirely in Joe's favor, revealing the insanity of this case and how it undermines the death penalty. Ann Coulter comes across as a flake and it shows. She is unaware of the facts. While Doug should have briefly refuted the inaccuracies, he focuses on the DNA. Sister Helen gives me validity when the commentator says, "Lori Urs says this is (Joe's death) a symbol of injustice in America. Is that true?"

"Absolutely," Helen says. She goes on to say how my passion drew her in.

"Lori says she will write a book and do a movie. Will you help her?"

Helen replies again, "Absolutely."

I couldn't listen to the facts being aired incorrectly so I call in. Amazingly, I get through as a speaker. Later, Walter would tell me that I sounded a bit nervous at first but that I got right into it. I recited the facts of the case cold.

"The prosecutor's theory and contention was that Joe raped and killed Helen Schartner and that rape was the aggravating factor, not the beating. In 1985 (pre-DNA testing) serological testing revealed the sperm was a PGM 1. Their expert theorized there was a mixture, but later their own expert said it could not be determined who the donor was. I had spoken to scientific experts all over the country who agreed. They said DNA would be definitive and would prove he was innocent."

At the end of my recitation the female commentator asks, "Why did you marry him?"

I was not ready to answer that question. Perhaps I should have shared it with the world to avoid unwarranted criticism, but it was the only privacy I had left at the time. Plus, I didn't want anything to interfere with my ability to gain access to the evidence for posthumous DNA testing. I told her it was a personal decision. "I think we need to focus on the real issue here and that is Joe's innocence." That's when I went right into the facts.

Walter phoned to compliment me on a job well done, discussing my focus and contrasting it with Coulter's lack of knowledge and "ditzy" comments. Walter also tells me I'm on the front page of the *Virginian-Pilot*, and an inside page. But "it wasn't bad." I can tell he's proud of me for what I stood up for.

"You know Lori, I am for capital punishment to protect society, but if even one innocent person dies then we shouldn't have it," Walter says.

He and Helen speak briefly. I can tell she likes him a lot.

"What a kind and wonderful man. Too bad y'all couldn't get back together." Helen wanted someone for me. Especially now.

I speak briefly about the marriage to Joe with Walter. "I had to tell Jen," he says.

"Thanks, Walter. It helps in legal matters, his burial and a wrongful death suit." He also knows it was Joe's dying wish.

Jennifer and Walter are my true supporters. I have their approval and that's all I need. The fact that Joe is dead is all the more reason I must continue to speak out, at universities, and radio and TV shows around the world. I need to expose the truth. It's finally clear why Joe and I were joined—the universe brought us together to fight this injustice and bring it to the world's attention.

On Monday, July 27, Helen and I leave early for the airport to fly to Newark. We pack lightly, taking only what we must. Last night John Nutter telephoned, asking to see me. I didn't allow him to come to my home, or to meet Helen. I offered to meet him down the street at the beach for a few minutes. He was clearly upset again. I tried to console him. When he started to cry I shut down. "John, I need a friend now, don't push me," I told him. He's definitely a walking time bomb. It's a delicate dance that I'm confronted with.

Prior to getting on the plane I have some last minute details to attend to. And I reflect on how April through June were bad months for Joe and me. It was only in July that we pulled it all together in a last effort for justice.

I remember the press obtaining personal information from my divorce files in the courthouse and remind myself to call them and instruct them that they are not to give out this information again. It was sealed through a court order for privacy. They were not paying attention when Frank Green went through my files looking for anything sensational. He didn't care what was personal and what was not. Most of what he printed was sealed by court order. It was not public information. The clerks failed to protect my privacy. They should know better when reporters come snooping around.

An attendant at the Cox funeral home answers when I phone them to remind them that no one but the Parliamentarians are allowed to see Joe. I alert them to Sheryl Murden.

"She was Joe's fiancée for many years," I tell them. "But I don't want a circus. She is not allowed in."

"Don't worry, Lori, no one can see him," the funeral director tells me.

"Oh, and please, do not tell the press where he is. I don't want them around either," I said.

****

In Newark we take a connecting flight to Norfolk. The flight is a journey of despair. This is the event I dreaded most in my life, never thinking it would come true. With Sister Helen by my side I am strengthened, but I am not strong. I am in my own cocoon, going through the motions yet still raw from the trauma. I haven't listened to the radio or TV, nor read any papers but one. I'm sheltered from the world, and I thank God.

When we arrive in Norfolk Luciano and Rino come for us. Luciano escorts us to the Consul of Italy to meet with Vito Piraino.

He gently places some papers in my hand. "These are the papers for Joe's release from this country." While at his office, Mayor Orlando calls and we discuss the inscription on Joe's grave.

Joseph Roger O'Dell, beloved husband of Lori Urs-O'Dell.

Honorary Citizen of Palermo
Killed by Virginia in the USA in a merciless and brutal justice system
September 20, 1941 - July 23, 1997

I approve it. It's their show now.

Back at the funeral home I learn that because the casket weighs over 500 lbs, it can't fly under the belly of the plane in Norfolk. It has to be transported to New York for its final destination in Italy.

"Here is the key to the casket, Lori. No one can open it but you."

I am now ready to see Joseph. The funeral director leads me into a room. There is a casket there and I know Joe must be in it, but still I don't want to believe it.

The director opens the coffin. As I lean toward the side of it I don't see death. I see a beautiful face. Within seconds tears trail down my cheeks, threatening to fall into the casket. Having asked Helen, Luciano and Rino if I could see him alone at first, I'm happy for this private moment.

Slowly I bend over to kiss his cheek. I don't feel the stoned coldness of his face but the warmth of his love.

"Joseph, I promise to prove your innocence. I won't give up." I talk to him as if he can hear me.

I tell him what a tremendous sacrifice he was and how he had not died in vain. "I will miss you," I whisper to him.

I take my hands and cup his face, stroking his hair as if he were alive. In all the nearly four years of my fight to save him, I never had the chance to have a normal meeting with him. I wanted something, anything, to be normal. I waited, in my mind, hoping he would open his eyes.

His hands are cold and still, but his face, to me, is soft, tender and strong. Joseph is finally at peace. It shows on his face. The torture is not transparent anymore, like the last time I saw him in the death house.

Lord have mercy on the souls of those who murdered him.

I stay with Joseph for half an hour. The Italian Parliamentarians and Helen are now in the room with me. "We must take Joseph now," the director says leading me away from him. They need to drive him to New York. As we move away I glance over at Luciano. He has tears in his eyes. The director gives everyone else a moment with Joe before we leave. Luciano, Rino and Helen stand beside him. Quietly, silently, they pray for him. However odd it seems, it is a moment I will never see again. It seems important to snap a picture of Joe and his friends. In a strange way it feels appropriate. It is the only moment I have had with Joe, where I can see him amongst friends. *Capture its beauty before it escapes*, I thought. I *wanted* photos of Joe. And though Helen tried to talk me out of it, I didn't expect her to understand. No one could ever possibly understand. I never had pictures of Joe, and I was not going to let them take him away without taking them now. This memory would not be taken from me, however awful it is.

"Vaya con dios," I whisper as I walk away.

The key in my hand will allow me to open the casket one last time before Joe is buried. Somehow the director recognized my need for control, when all else has been totally out of my control. As he closes the top of the coffin over Joseph's body it sends my body into its own shutdown as I collapse on the chair. It's as if I were waiting for Joe to sit up and be just fine. Sister Helen embraces me and we leave.

Luciano, Rino and Helen want us all to go to dinner, but the thought of wanting to be alone is pervasive. I politely decline and retreat to my hotel room. Tomorrow will be a hard day, with long travel and enormous stress.

Nina is already preparing a vigil for us at the airport prior to our departure for Rome in the morning.

I know I cannot sleep so I take another sleeping pill and crawl into bed. Just as soon as I place the sheets to my neck Helen walks in.

"Luciano wants to see you," she says.

"Sure," I manage to respond. Just then Luciano walks in and offers me a hug. He also is my strength at this time. I trust him.

It's Tuesday, July 27, 1997.

I'm up early and working on my press statement while waiting to speak with Nina about the vigil at the airport. Doug plans on doing an interview with CNN's *Burden of Proof*. I leave the hotel with my closest friends now. Vito Piraino joins us. We have a connecting flight in Newark. Before we arrive I touch base with the lawyers about the motion to preserve the evidence. The lawyers are under the impression that the prosecutors will agree to release it. I'm amazed at how naive they are. Have they not learned anything yet? When we arrive at the Norfolk airport, Nina is waiting for us. So, too, is Father Tom and another priest, as well as a friend of Joe's, and strangers I do not know. CBS Channel 3 and other media are there for the vigil. We form a circle and join hands as we pray. This is for Joe—an American vigil on American soil before we fly him to the country that fought so hard by our side to save him. We close with the Lord's Prayer. I later learn that the Father who offered me his blessing wrote a letter to Vito Piraino in support of Joseph. He leans over to me and whispers, "What you did was beautiful, Lori." I am touched by this. Nina offers Helen and I a white carnation and the Consulate and Rino speak to CBS. It is my turn. *Can I do this?* Yes. I must.

"My county has failed Joseph and I, and all the people around the world. I will take Joseph to the soil of a country that has compassion and cares about the truth, but I am saddened by this." After a few more sentences, quiet in voice but strong in character, I turn to get onto the plane. I am reflecting on this as I sit by the window of the plane, bright sunlight shining on me. It's as if the spotlight is on Joe now.

At the airport, Helen and I are side by side on the pay telephones bolted against the wall. We're calling whoever we can think of to get a 501(3)C organization to request the evidence. Prior to Joe's execution,

I had debated with the lawyers on how I could possibly get the evidence after Joe was executed. I wanted to prove the Commonwealth killed an innocent man. We came up with a couple of angles. One of them was being placed in the position of a family member, but the other was to file a petition from a public interest group under the "public interest" aspect of the law. Earlier in the day I had called "James" at the Virginia Beach Circuit Court. He offered me the Virginian code on evidence handling. He said I couldn't claim the evidence. After speaking with Clive Stafford Smith I learn that the clerk is wrong. Indeed it is my property. *I can and will claim it.* Immediately, I phone Doug and instruct him to please write a letter to the court and inform them I wish to claim Joseph's belongings. I need to remind myself to do the same with the cops concerning Joe's car. I will ask Doug if he can do this for me tomorrow.

Last night I was asked to sign the funeral expenses form regarding Joe's burial. I scanned the document that was placed in front of me and was caught by surprise.

"I can't pay for this, I can't sign this," I exclaim.

"Don't worry, Lori, we're going to pay for it all," the Parliamentarians assured me. Since the bill is for approximately $18,000, I'm grateful for the Italian Parliament's generous gesture.

At 6:30 p.m. I sit in an Italian Air Force plane arranged by the Parliament. I am with Luciano, Rino and Sister Helen. Joseph is beneath me. The plane takes off at seven that evening and we arrive in Italy the next day at two in the afternoon.

The cocoon that has protected me from outside stimuli still exists. I'm pretty sure no one knows Joe is here, and not many, if any, know I am here too, nor Sister Helen. I am grateful for the anonymity. Helen is insisting I take a sleeping pill to rest. She knows I will need my strength. After I pop two I am still awake, though I am feeling a bit groggy. The daze is no different than the daze I have been in for days now.

I didn't know that Helen had faxed Monsignor Caccia at the Vatican to ask if he would greet us when we arrive. She knew how important a person he was in my struggle for Joseph. I knew he was away but would be returning on the 29th. I also knew he would greet us if he was back in Rome. When the plane lands, and as we are departing, there is a bit of commotion.

"Quick, the Pope will receive you, we must hurry to be on time." A dark sedan swings around the corner to pick us up. The driver rushes us to the Vatican to ensure our prompt arrival. Helen and I scurry from the car to the doors of the Vatican where we are greeted by Monsignor Caccia. I sigh when I first see him. It was *so* good to see him, even under these circumstances, to be in his gracious presence. His support strengthens me. We stop briefly to take pictures where the Pope had delivered Mass that very morning. We are rushing through the halls to see the Pope. As we run Helen says to me, "I can't meet the Pope in pants, I need to change." We duck into a room just outside the one we are to be received in. Helen changes in two minutes flat. In her hurry she rips the cross off her neck and breaks the chain. A quick repair makes it barely noticeable.

Here I am, suddenly sitting in a formal, yet not so elaborate room, waiting for Pope John Paul II. Seated beside me is Helen. My feet dangle inches from the floor in a chair that seems to hold me like Alice in Wonderland. Is this a fairy tale? I'm only vaguely aware of my surroundings. Luciano and Rino are waiting out in the hallway.

When a Vatican official announces the Pope's arrival, Helen and I stand and face the door. Meeting the Pope doesn't shock my senses; I am still functioning rather blindly after the horror of what I witnessed. Soon, when he stands before me, that will change.

I look up and there he is. Pope John Paul II is being aided into the room. He walks straight toward me, commanding my attention. He is wearing a white soutane. On his head is a white skullcap. I see him, true, but it's what I feel that is so pronounced and what will last a lifetime. Feeling his presence before me is a man much grander than life. Slowly, he walks toward me, almost hobbling. Though appearing frail in stature, I see a man with strength and holiness. His voice is quiet, slow, but deliberate. He reaches for my hand. I gently place it in his.

"I prayed for Joseph," the Pope says. The fact that he even knows Joe's name is bewildering. I know that his country has stood strong behind our battle, and he stands behind his country. He blesses me, touching my forehead, and then blesses me again on the same spot. I am here, yet unaware of the high significance of this moment until days later. I'm still blanketed in my cocoon.

"I married Joe in his last hours," I softly tell him. I sense he is touched by the gesture. There are few words exchanged. His presence is enough.

Not believing in the reality of the moment my words speak volumes, "Could you do that again?" He blesses me again and this time kisses my forehead. Afterwards, Helen, as she insists I call her—"forget the Sister part" she told me long ago, tells me that everything on me at this time is blessed. Her words fill me with contentment.

Sister Helen says to the Pope, "I was with Joseph his last hours. Thank you so much for your voice."

We wait for him to be escorted out of the room, signaling us to slowly exit behind him. In our hands is a white box with a gold etched symbol of the Vatican on it. Inside is a rosary gift from the Holy Father himself.

Luciano and Rino stand ready to transport us to the Parliament, each reaching for our arm, guiding us to our next destination. We haven't left the Vatican grounds before the Vatican press secretary starts typing a statement for immediate release. This validates the Pope's support and helps buttress the Italian campaign that mobilized all of Italy. When we arrive at the Parliament, the two girls in Joe's campaign office print out the Vatican's press release. We were still looking to finalize our own, the girls typing hard and fast for me. I remember them as the same two who assisted us in January, when we were first campaigning in Italy to save Joe. Now they are helping to make history, again.

I take a moment and call Walter.

"Walt," I said. "Guess what, I just met the Pope, please tell Jennifer for me."

"That's cool," he replies. And I knew I still loved him.

I also squeeze in a call to the lawyers and fax the statement that I prepared responding to Governor Allen's refusal of DNA. I need to address it at a press conference.

"Lori, there are some people who want to see you," Luciano tells me.

The Parliament members are ready to receive me. As I pass through the hallways of the Parliament I approach the room in which my friends have gathered to show their solidarity. Before we walk through the door to the room I am greeted by Rosa and her son Michelle. Having been one of the main leaders of the Parliament's support for Joseph, she knows my pain all too well. She and her son corresponded with Joseph prior to his death. Rosa and I embrace, holding tight to each other for a long time, knowing we're not here celebrating Joe's freedom as we had planned, but his burial in the ground of a united country. When we release our embrace I turn and feel the arms of her son wrapped around me. Helen later mentions she was very touched by the love and authentic welcome I received.

Stepping into the room, I see before me a huge gathering of many of the most influential and key supporters from the Italian Parliament. Our battle, Joseph O'Dell's and mine, became theirs in the most incredible display of compassion and solidarity I have ever known. I am guided to the only empty chair amongst 20, set in a large, but intimate circle around the room. The formality of the meeting is evident the moment I walk into the room. The Parliamentarians speak first. Rosa takes the floor and then Vice President of the Senate Mancino speaks to me.

"The President wanted to be here but he is otherwise detained," Mancino says.

"Thank you, I am very grateful for all that's been done for Joseph," I reply. Mancino discusses the Parliament's efforts and expresses his sorrow about Joe's death.

One of the girls stands to address me. She was largely responsible for so many of the signatures that circulated to Virginia on Joe's behalf. Though we lost the battle for justice, we have won in uniting millions of people around the world for one cause: for humanity and for truth. Our closeness is obvious to everyone in the room. Our hearts are heavy as they offer their compassion and their sorrow for our loss. I am grateful for their love.

It's my turn. I rise to address my Italian friends.

"Thank you so much for all you have done. It would not have been possible for me to have gone through this without your support," I say, speaking from my heart.

"Lori, I ask for your thoughts and permission: Would it be okay to put together a book of all the letters Joe had written to everyone?" Rosa asks.

"That would be fine," I reply, with some hesitation, not knowing what was in the letters.

My grief cannot be private. It's a very public affair. In a way, I recognize this is good for me, holding me together and keeping me strong.

Our time is limited. "We must leave," Luciano says as he hurries me out. I hug and kiss my friends goodbye, taking with me a moment that will forever be unforgettable. We leave the Parliament for an evening flight to Palermo. Luciano warns me there will be a journalist at the airport waiting to interview me. I notice him as we approach and take our seats. I'm peppered with questions before he moves on to Sister Helen. I don't recall what was asked or how I responded. As

I walk to the plane, journalists start swarming around me. When I board, I notice the same all around me. Many journalists are scattered in the seats of this flight. At least three or four attempt to speak to me before they are fanned off by Rino and another member of the Parliament. "She doesn't wish to speak now, please allow her some privacy." Rai TV asks my permission to be filmed. I reluctantly agree. They also film the gorgeous scenery of the mountains in Palermo as we are landing.

With my face pressed against the window of the small plane, I notice a roped off area when we begin to land. The media and so many local citizens are here to greet me. The enormity of our welcome stuns me. Officials immediately surround the plane. Police cars are everywhere. Small blue cars with a single light on top of them represent Italian security. As I walk off the plane, comforted that Joseph is traveling below me in the belly of the plane, I am surrounded by officials pulling me toward a Mercedes sedan. Luciano redirects me. "No, the media is waiting, you *must* acknowledge them."

I break away from the officials, walking toward the reporters. I wave to the people in the roped-off area and blow them a kiss. I thank the crowd for their presence. They respond with a cheer. Photographers capture the moment.

I was watching intently, asking at all times, "Where is Joe?"

A navy blue Mercedes van is parked alongside the plane. The driver is wearing a dark suit, white shirt and tie. Dark glasses cover his eyes. Four men, dressed in black suits, white shirts and dark ties, are standing at attention by the van. They wear black hats, adorned with a gold band, and white gloves. Sun visors shade their eyes from the bright sun. They are waiting for the casket to be unloaded from the plane. The Italians are ready to receive Joseph on their soil. The formality of the process is extraordinary. I watch them carry Joe into the car, amazed at the honor they are displaying for him. After Joseph is carefully placed inside the van a rather large arrangement of flowers, wrapped with a red and yellow bow with the town's name, Palermo, proudly welcomes him. By now the men are all standing with hats removed, out of respect.

Helen and I are escorted to an office at the airport to discuss Joe's burial. The casket size is a problem they say.

"We have rules in Italy that must be followed."

The casket will not fit in the plot chosen in the cemetery. Helen smiles, even laughs a bit, amused by this conversation.

"Joseph, are you watching all this? I know you're smiling down on us," she says.

"Yes, even in death, Joe creates a controversy," I respond.

I was learning that Joe has to be buried in a wooden casket. The casket needs for oxygen to enter it. This is Italian law.

"No way," I reply. "I chose the bronze casket so he will be sealed and protected. I don't want any bugs to get to him."

After a half hour of discussion the funeral director informs me the wooden casket has a metal seal inside so Joe will be protected. I think at this point they would tell me anything just to calm me down. I finally agree.

"Lori, we ask that you first see the cemetery so you can let us know if the place we chose is a choice you would honor." I am stunned by their graciousness. With all they have done for Joseph, they are now concerned about my opinion, my feelings.

Of course, Mayor Orlando was there to greet me at the airport. Three cars escort us to the cemetery. One car is in front of us, the mayor, Sister Helen and I are in the middle car, and a police car is in back of us. Inside the car, and on both sides of the doors, I notice what appears to be guns. They look like machine guns. I have to ask the obvious question. The reply to my question reminds me of the danger the mayor is in on a daily basis. Because of his initiative and pledge to fight the Mafia, he is a constant target. Therefore, he must travel in a bulletproof, bombproof, and bazooka-proof vehicle, and is accompanied by four armed bodyguards at all times. The sirens of the police cars ring through the streets, letting everyone know we are traveling through and to move aside. I feel like I'm in the middle of a president's motorcade.

As we arrive at the cemetery there are townspeople along the walkways and driveway leading to the church. I take in the surroundings and notice the church is simple yet elegant. Perched on a hill, it overlooks the beautiful mountains of Palermo. I know Joseph would have loved this spot. He will be buried in front of the steps of the church, leading out to the cemetery. It is obviously a great honor. I offer my approval of the church and burial site and we further discuss the plans. Afterwards, we are transported to a hotel where we polish our press statement and get much needed rest.

The hotel is lovely. As Helen and I walk in, we're greeted warmly. Our bags are taken to a suite, two separate but adjoining rooms. The decor of the suite exudes elegance. We are in awe of its beauty. I could tell that Helen is noticing the strong relationship I have built with the Italians and sense her wonder about it all.

Meanwhile, Elizabeth, Mayor Orlando's secretary, has the tapes (disks) and statements. She is preparing the press package. The plush, king-sized bed welcomes me as I pass out from exhaustion.

The following morning I rise early. Unlike any other morning in my life I'm getting ready for the funeral of a man I married just five days ago. I slip on a navy blue dress which flows just below my knees and wait for Mayor Orlando to pick me up at 8:00 a.m. He is bringing me to Joseph so we can visit right before the service they have arranged for him. As we arrive at the church and its adjoining cemetery, I'm taken aback by the amount of press there. And I see hundreds of people in the streets. They are gathered near the square, as close as they can get to the church. I'm told the service will be broadcast by speaker at the town square and throughout Italy. When asked, what do you have to say to the Commonwealth of Virginia, I reply, "Nothing."

The guards accompanying me have to push their way through the intense crowd. Bodyguards surround the mayor and me as we climb the steps to the church while Joseph is carried in by several men. On our way into the church we are saluted by two guards in white hats and gloves, and blue uniforms.

They carry Joseph to a separate building while I am greeted by the brothers of the church. Soon, I walk over to the building where Joseph is resting. The room is small, allowing my eyes to fixate on the casket before me. Two beautiful floral arrangements have been placed on top of his casket, one from the citizens and the other from the Parliament. In front of me, laid out in a folded square, are two flags—one in the colors of the Italian flag, the other red, white and blue.

"Which one do you want at his funeral, Lori, or do you want both?"

"Just the Italian flag will do," I reply. My disappointment in my own country is obvious to my friends.

They nod with approval.

"Can I please have a few moments alone with Joseph?" I ask.

"Of course. When you are done, just open the door. If you need Sister Helen, just knock on the tall wooden door," one my friends says.

Alone, I open the casket with the key given to me back in Virginia. I lift the top of the casket to see Joe's face for the last time. I do not cry. I fight back my tears. I pray for Joseph, then say what I have been telling him for years.

"I promise to clear your name, Joe, and stay strong to fight." Without closing the casket, I then open the door and signal for the mayor, Sister Helen and Luciano to come in. They walk toward me and I share Joseph with them. The mayor has tears in his eyes, as does Luciano. They pray while I stand silent.

Witnessing the sadness brought to the faces of my friends I break my own vow not to cry and suddenly tears start to flow from my eyes.

"Don't cry Lori, Joseph would want you to be strong," the Mayor says.

We leave the room and they proceed to show me two wooden caskets. One has a symbol of Jesus on the cross—it was more beautiful. I chose the box Joseph would be buried in.

"Please," I ask. "I want the pillow he laid his head on and the blanket that has covered him to be with him."

"Whatever you want," the mayor replies.

They are waiting for us now. As we walk into the church I notice the small sanctuary is filled to capacity, flowing with more people onto the steps, urgently trying to hear what's going on inside.

As I step inside, immediately the lovely and warm Italians are greeting me, shaking my hand and expressing their sorrow. I'm seated in the front row next to Sister Helen. Mayor Orlando is on my left. Luciano is seated on the other side of the mayor. Franco and Rino are seated behind me.

I watch as they, the brothers of the church, in their brown robes, carry Joe down the aisle to the front of the room.

I walk to the casket and drape my arm over it, as if hugging him. Sister Helen stands right by my side. They all know I need her strength. Men in uniform surround the casket, standing at attention.

The service that I prayed and hoped would never happen, now begins. I wanted Joseph to be greeted by this Italian town in a much different way. A stranger passes by and offers me a fan.

The service, of course, is in Italian. Helen helps me to understand what little she can. When we can, we join in in English.

Standing by the casket are four honor guards. I listen to the priest. Helen whispers to me, "They are talking about Jesus and how he, too, was innocent, also executed by the state." The Mass lasts approximately half-hour. The final part of this ceremonial type funeral has the priest sprinkling holy water on the casket. The choir breaks out in song. I watch as one by one, men, women and children walk up to the casket and lay flowers for Joseph. For us all. Amnesty International

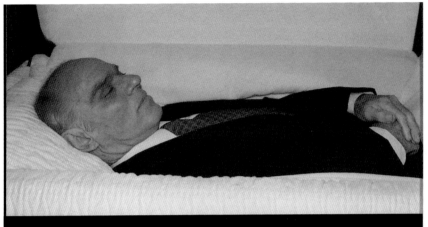

Joseph Roger O'Dell III at the Cox Funeral Home in Virginia.

Lori Urs, Sister Helen Prejean
and Pope John Paul II.

Arrival in
Palermo, Italy
for the funeral
of Joseph O'Dell.
Lori Urs greeting
the press with
Sister Helen
Prejean and
Luciano Neri.

Preparing to receive the body of Joseph O'Dell in Palermo, Italy.

Members of the church make their way through the crowd carrying Joe O'Dell.

Franco Danieli, Sister Helen Prejean, Lori Urs, Mayor Leoluca Orlando and Luciano Neri in a moment of prayer for Joe O'Dell.

Luciano Neri, Major Leoluca Orlando, Lori Urs, Sister Helen Prejean, Rino Plscitello and Senator Mario Occhipinti in a private moment before the funeral.

Sister Helen Prejean with
Lori Urs- a private moment
at the funeral.

Sister Helen Prejean,
Lori Urs and Mayor
Leoluca Orlando at the
funeral in Palermo.

Transporting Joe
O'Dell outside the
church for burial.

Mayor Leoluca Orlando explaining to Lori Urs
the procedure for burial .

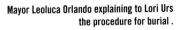

Preparing to lower the
body of Joseph O'Dell into
Italian soil. Palermo, Italy.

Traditional burial in
Italy- Joseph O'Dell.

Lori Urs responding to
the crowd's applause to
celebrate the life of Joseph
O'Dell.

Lori Urs kneeling over the
grave of Joseph O'Dell.
Palermo, Italy.

drapes yellow ones alongside the others. It is refreshing to see living, beautiful flowers surrounding Joseph. When the service is over, several men walk to the front of the church and lift the casket for the walk down the aisle and to the front step, where Joseph will be laid to rest. I follow right behind them, the Parliament members, my friends, and Helen right by my side. People are reaching out to touch the casket.

We depart from the front of the church. Everyone else departs from the side. Perched on the steps of the church we stand, surrounded by those who love Joseph, watching as they prepare for his burial. The press are too numerous to count, standing behind a rope with hundreds of citizens circling them. As I gaze up beyond them, I notice the beautiful mountains in the background. I kiss my hand and place it on top of the casket. Later, I learn this is the photograph that would circulate around the world.

I am standing inches from the grave. My hand clutches the Pope's rosary that is draped around my neck. Standing next to me with her arm around my waist is Helen. The mayor is on the other side of me, and surrounding us are Italian Parliament dignitaries and the ever-present secret service agents.

It is a tradition in Italy to celebrate death by honoring life. I am caught by surprise when the reaction to his burial is far from what I had expected. As the men who are placing tan straps under the belly of the casket are getting ready to lower Joseph into the ground, my heart sinks at first as I remain steady on my feet. Suddenly, my sorrow turns to jubilance as the crowd breaks the silence with a load roar of clapping in celebration of Joe's life. With that I raise my fist high in the air and join in the celebration. A smile replaces the solemn look on my face.

I had earlier spoken with clarity when I offered the following words upon our arrival in Italy:

I am privileged and honored to be welcomed with so much warmth and love. My presence, I hope, symbolizes the grave injustice in the intentional killing of Joseph O'Dell, who, as you are aware, became my husband in his final hours. I am here to stand in love for Joseph and to share in your honor of him, to preserve his struggle for justice. As I walk upon the soil of a country that embraces justice with a passion that is an example to the world, I am saddened that the country that Joseph and I once had faith and love for, is a country that failed to protect an innocent man from execution.

But, we must not stop this battle. Joseph's death must never be an event in a politician's career or a sensational story for the press. Joseph's death is a symbol of injustice, particularly the egregious nature of the application of the death penalty in the United States.

I call upon the world to join me in protest, to unite for Joseph and all the other Josephs in America and around the world. The United States, Virginia and Governor Allen need to be held accountable for their actions. They can no longer be insulated as a result of their power and their abuse of that power. The world can now send a message, a strong message, that we will not tolerate injustice. I ask that we boycott Virginia and their representatives who feel they can freely travel the world unaccountable for their actions.
No, this cannot happen.

As people who care about justice, whether you are in favor or opposed to the death penalty, Joseph's case, the execution of a man who begged for DNA tests, who begged for the truth to be printed about the evidence, and who died with such dignity and calmness in the face of such evil and injustice, must be a symbol to the world. I ask that when any diplomats from the U.S. visit your countries that you speak of Joseph O'Dell's case and the incredible injustice he illustrates concerning the inequities of the death penalty. We must urge officials to abolish the death penalty. Apart from the issue of whether it is morally right or wrong, we all would agree that we cannot tolerate the execution of innocent persons. I call upon the business leaders and consumers of the world to boycott Virginian products and to let them know why you are boycotting. For individuals who wish to travel to Virginia, choose a state that is more beautiful, a state that hasn't become the symbol of death in America, and let the governor know that you chose not to visit because he killed Joe and refused to honor his campaigning words "Without truth, there is no justice." Write or call Governor Allen.

Second, I ask the world to please contribute to the Joseph Roger O'Dell defense fund. Its purpose is to reveal the truth concerning the death penalty system as used by politicians, and to pursue the investigation and all avenues which will lead to proving Joseph's innocence to the world. Next, the funds will be used to bring out other cases of injustices like Joseph O'Dell's. We can give those people a voice, a chance to live, and expose the system for what is truly is. I thank you all for receiving Joseph with love and respect and I am confident you will honor his name forever.

After Joseph is lowered into the ground, the stone that was etched for him, with my approval, is laid to rest on top of him. Its message preserves what this long battle has meant to all of us.

Joseph Roger O'Dell, beloved husband of Lori Urs-O'Dell.
Honorary Citizen of Palermo
Killed by Virginia in the USA in a merciless and brutal justice system.
September 20, 1941 - July 23, 1997

Arms are waving and people are yelling things I cannot hear as the bodyguards lead our way from the service. Parting the crowd, bodyguards lead us to the limousine waiting for us. I am ready to rest, welcoming the ride back to the hotel. Helen and I will need to prepare for our return back to the United States. As we are packing, I am noticing the beautiful flower arrangements in each of our room. The vases are so beautiful I want to take them home with us.

"Helen, look at these vases, they are absolutely beautiful. How on earth do you suppose we are to get these home?" Helen is laughing and we instantly struggle over the correct pronunciation of the word. Is it vase, or it is *vase?*

After some thought we realize they are not to be taken home, they are the property of the hotel. We cannot stop laughing. The music of laughter is uplifting to me, and exactly what I need to alleviate my grieving ailment.

The flag from Joe's casket was taken by one of the Parliamentarians, with a promise to return it to me before I leave Italy. It was such a symbol for me, for Joseph. Regrettably, I would never actually receive it, but I always wondered, where is it and who has it? Somehow I always felt it was safely tucked away in honor of Joseph and his moment in history that united people around the world.

On our last evening in Italy, Luciano, Helen and I eat at a Brazilian cafe, outside on a warm, quiet evening. Because I have constantly been surrounded by people and confusion, I'm grateful for the peaceful company of just Helen and Luciano. The one thing I look forward to is seeing my darling daughter. Jennifer is my life now, along with a future of inspiring people to speak and live by the truth. I think about initiating a new international movement after encouragement from my Italian and American friends. Mayor Orlando has asked me to come back in October for an international convention. I will visit at his home and meet his wife and two daughters. The professor at the law school at which I spoke several months ago, requests that I speak about human rights in November or December.

"I will try to make these two things come together in October," the mayor tells me before I leave Italy. And he gives me the photographs of the entire funeral. Though it's a painful reminder of Joe's death, they will provide me with the memories I need of his burial. It also gives me contentment to know he is among those whom he loved. It also sets me free; I know where he's resting, and now I can move on. Where he is now is in stark contrast to what the Commonwealth had in mind for him back in Virginia. They would have preferred to bury their ugly secret quietly. I still have much to do back home.

Rino travels with Helen and I from Palermo to Rome and to the

Sant'Angelo Hotel for our last evening in Italy. After he drops us off, and on his way home, he reaches out to me with a phone call from the car, describing nostalgia of me.

"Massimo and so many others, Lori, send their greetings," Luciano tells me on my last night in Italy.

"Luciano, thank you for all you have done. I am so grateful to you and all the wonderful people that took Joe into their hearts. None of this could have happened without your love and support. I know this. And so does Joe."

I am flying back to the United States. And though I just went through the motions of the funeral, I'm still unaware of my grief and the real loss of Joseph. As I sit beside Helen on the plane I am comforted. I pray for the strength and courage I will need to go on.

I gaze out the plane's window. Like snow-capped mountaintops the clouds are magnificent in their display. It's as though the clouds and my mind are one, not having emerged yet from the state of mind I've been in for the past several weeks. The mind is wondrous in its ability to protect the human spirit. I know that having watched a man slowly prepare for his unjust death, has shaped my life in so many ways.

Don't be fooled. I am not done. I still have work to do. When I arrive home, I will regain my focus and move forward with my plans to prove Joe's innocence. Guess what, Alberi and the Commonwealth of Virginia. I'm back!

THE END

Epilogue

My desire to learn the hidden truth never died with the execution of Joseph O'Dell.

During my intense struggle to find answers to the myriad questions that arose during my investigation, and to acquire justice in the courts, I worked with some of this country's foremost experts regarding the death penalty. During the Italian campaign to save Joe O'Dell I was asked by dignitaries in Italy to initiate and direct an international organization against the death penalty. It is for these reasons that I felt there was a chance to demonstrate for the first time in the United States that an innocent man was wrongly executed. I wanted to turn Joe's unjust death into a benefit by preventing what happened to him from happening to others. What I discovered was a system that was not only fallible, but often depended largely upon the players in the game. This was a much greater social cause than my own concern about what people may have thought of my decision to marry a person who was scheduled to die. Immediately upon my return from Italy, I worked with lawyers to obtain the trial evidence in an attempt to effectuate a major shift in the criminal justice system.

The Roman Catholic Diocese filed a petition to gain access to the evidence "in the public interest" while I also filed a motion to get the evidence as "a member of the family". I know that my decision to marry Joe was critical in assisting the Italian Parliament and the citizens of Italy who stood in solidarity with us to bring Joe to their country—as both a sign of their compassion for him, and as a symbol of injustice in America. The Commonwealth of Virginia opposed all efforts to obtain the evidence and even said: "If the DNA test proved Joe O'Dell's innocence, it would be shouted from the rooftops!" And why not, we all thought. But the judge finally ordered the evidence that could definitively prove Joe's innocence be destroyed. It was incinerated with the truth. Not long afterwards, I filed for, and obtained, an annulment of the marriage on the grounds that it was entered into for the purpose of a social cause.

Subsequent to Joe's burial in Palermo, Italy, the Italian Parliament, in October 1998, asked me to speak on behalf of the United States at the 50th anniversary of the Declaration of Human Rights. After consulting with our countries' leading experts, the American Bar Association and death penalty lawyers, I convened the internationally held conference in Florence, Italy.

While I was writing this book, I had planned to contact Albert Alberi, who had become a judge, hoping to confront him regarding all the evidence I had unearthed. But I learned he had died years earlier at the age of 64.

Prosecutor Stephen Test is currently a partner at the law firm Williams Mullen in Virginia Beach.

Governor George Allen, who condemned Joe to death, went on to become a senator for the Commonwealth of Virginia. In 2006 he lost his bid for re-election and in 2012 the votes of Virginia again rejected his candidacy for Senate.

Joe Moore, the man who found Helen Schartner's body, was found dead in an alley. The police publicly asked for information concerning what I presume was a suspicious death.

Several years after Joe O'Dell's death, Steve Watson wrote to Sister Helen Prejean to say that he tried to do the right thing and that he, ultimately, felt responsible for Joe's execution.

Richard Reyna continues to investigate death penalty cases. We still remain good friends and carry a special bond as a result of our work together.

Sister Helen Prejean remains an active anti-death penalty advocate and we, too, are still dear friends as a result of our joint effort to save Joe O'Dell's life and the special part she played during my fight for the truth.

Attorney Robert Smith left the law firm of Paul, Weiss, Rifkind, Wharton & Garrison. He is still practicing law in New York.

John Nutter remained obsessed with me, and while I felt it necessary to maintain his goodwill in order to preserve our chance to save Joe's life, it later became what any victim of domestic violence will tell you: an attempt to not agitate him for fear of what he might do. The restraining order I obtained in 1998 was, of course, just a piece of paper, and because I refused his advances, he set out to hurt me in the worst way possible. My daughter and I were the victims of a home invasion at gunpoint that left us in a three-day hostage situation, fighting for our own survival. The hostage negotiation team, Chatham Police Department, and many other law enforcement agencies, were responsible for saving our lives. Subsequently, I was criticized by some regarding my decision to escape to get help for us, leaving Jennifer behind. The hostage negotiators informed us that had I not done so, we would both have surely been killed. But certain members of the press used this tragic situation to release my underage daughter's name and attempted to blame me for the horrific event. No victim is ever to blame for the violent actions of an evil or insane person. These are ignorant, intolerant and fear-based reactions. John Nutter was criminally prosecuted and is now serving 45 years in the state penitentiary for his crimes.

Sadly, Walter passed away quite suddenly in late 2012, before this book was completed. His support and belief that my actions at the end of Joe's case were "noble" served to offset those who voiced criticism and strong opposition, which naturally accompanies such challenges.

Jennifer graduated college with a double major, obtained her J.D. and then a Masters degree in sports management. She currently works in her dream job. Her father was able to see his only daughter grow up to be a beautiful, talented, kind, fun-loving, and ambitious young woman. Jennifer was a major force in my ability to do the work I did, often enduring long and difficult separations.

As for me, I returned to law school and graduated in the year 2000. While a student at Rutgers School of Law, I founded and directed The Innocence Project for Justice. At graduation I was presented with the Emil Jarmel Award for the student with the greatest interest and proficiency in public interest law. This honor was presented to me by Barry Scheck, who was the keynote speaker at graduation. After graduation I worked as an Assistant Deputy Public Defender in the adult felony division of the Newark Public Defender's office. I furthered my legal career in Colorado, which included a real estate development project.

Currently, I am a member of the New York, New Jersey and Colorado bar, and a licensed CPA in three states.

If I could share with you the most important lesson this case has taught me, it would be to never give up on what you believe in. Those that criticize or judge you are to be ignored in favor of supporters. Welcome and appreciate your challenges, as they make you the person you are destined to be.

While I was unable to save Joe, I was successful in bringing this injustice to the world's attention and uniting in solidarity a country that had no reason to care. Thus, when you think you are standing alone against the world, keep moving forward, stay focused and determined, and eventually the world will join you.

Author's Note

I started writing this book shortly after the execution of Joseph O'Dell in 1997. At the time, I was completing my law school education, founded and directed the Innocence Project at the Rutgers School of Law, and started a career in public interest law.

Many years ago, Barry Scheck (founder of the Innocence Project in New York) and I discussed what we felt would become the inevitable decline of wrongful convictions with the advent and use of DNA testing. I had hoped that what happened to Joe O'Dell would not happen to others, or at least in sharp decline. Since the O'Dell case, and over the past several years, I have seen an increase in the amount of wrongful convictions, at least those identified, recorded and accounted for. This greatly disturbed me. My hope is that this book, a rare opportunity to witness the criminal justice system in its true form, will effectuate change in the system.

I am not claiming that all cases are litigated in the same fashion as this one. In fact, I believe the majority are not. But there is no room for the kind of lawyering I saw in the O'Dell case. And I am convinced the same disturbing occurrences still exist today; intimidation of witnesses, suppression of evidence, use of jailhouse snitches, prosecutorial misconduct, mischaracterizations (both orally and in writing) to the court and manipulation of the media.

I was in a unique position in that I was able to watch the Commonwealth of Virginia engage in what I felt were unscrupulous acts in the continued pursuit of standing by their conviction. Rarely would anyone be in a position to challenge such a strong stance. But I could and did, in large part because I knew the truth. Political careers were also a strong influence in this case. This too needs reform.

Joe O'Dell was silenced by the government—permanently silenced when the Commonwealth put him to death, despite an international campaign to save his life, and to perform DNA testing. The Commonwealth could debate Joe's guilt or innocence all day long, but their refusal to perform DNA testing sparked public outrage. This would have offered the truth, one way or another. It is unfathomable that the Commonwealth of Virginia denied Joe O'Dell DNA tests, despite the fact that the Italian and European Parliaments, in an unprecedented action, officially voiced their opposition to his execution, and failure to conduct DNA testing. Millions of supporters wanted justice. To think the government demonstrated such signs of arrogance, and power, in ignoring the pleas of well-intentioned dignitaries, causes me concern. It should you too.

Joe O'Dell's case shines a light on the injustice he endured throughout the court system, and by the lawyers. It is an example of what we, the people, don't want from our public officials.

It was Italy that marked this case in history, demonstrating compassion and international solidarity.

EXHIBIT I

SEROLOGICAL GRAPH DEPICTING RESULTS OF BLOOD TESTS AT TRIAL

SEROLOGICAL ENZYME GRAPH
Re: COMMONWEALTH -v- JOSEPH ROGER O'DELL
O'DELL -v- COMMONWEALTH
O'DELL -v- THOMPSON

	EsD 1	PGM2-1	EAPBA	GLO2-1	ADA 1	PepA 1	AK 1	Hp2-1	Gc2-1	Tf C	
SHIRT	EsD 1	PGM2-1	EAPBA	GLO2-1	ADA 1	PepA 1	AK 1	Hp2-1	Gc2-1	Tf C	DNA TESTED EXCLUSION
JACKET	EsD 1	PGM2-1	EAPBA	GLO2-1	ADA1	PepA 1	AK 1	Hp2-1	Gc 2-1	Tf C	DNA TESTED INCONCLUSIVE
BLUE JEANS	EsD 1	PGM2-1		GLO2-1	ADA1	PepA 1	AK 1	Hp2-1	Gc 2-1	Tf C	
TAN JACKET	EsD 1				ADA1		AK 1			Tf C	
COAT	EsD 1				ADA1	PepA 1	AK 1				
BLOUSE	EsD 1					PepA 1	AK 1				
BRA	EsD 1				ADA 1	PepA 1	AK 1				
UNDERPANTS							AK 1				
RT. FRONT SEAT							AK 1				
CARPET	EsD 1	PGM2-1		GLO2-1	ADA 1	PepA 1	AK 1	Hp2-1		Tf CB	EXCLUSION
RT.FR. SEAT BACK					ADA 1		AK 1		Gc 2-1	Tf C	
SARDINE CAN				GLO2-1							
CELLO. FOIL WRAP										Tf C	
RED CLOTH	EsD 1				ADA 1		AK 1				
PAPERBAG					ADA 1		AK 1			Tf C	
BK. SEAT COVER	EsD 1	PGM2-1		GLO2-1	ADA 1		AK 1	Hp2-1	Gc2-1	Tf C	
SEAT COVER		PGM2	EAPBA	GLO2-1	ADA 1		AK 1	Hp2-1		Tf C	
SEAT BK. COVER							AK 1	Hp2-1	Gc2-1	Tf C	
FLOOR MAT	EsD 1			GLO2-1	ADA 1		AK 1				

NOTE: All ENZYMES match the Shirt and Carpet Exclusion, and the Jacket inconclusive. There are no mismatches.

EXHIBIT II
AFFIDAVIT OF STEVEN WATSON

State of West Virginia

County of Randolph

Affidavit of Steven Watson

BEFORE ME, the undersigned authority on this 11th day of October, 1996 personally appeared Steven Lee Watson, first duly sworn on his oath, hereby deposed and said as follows:

My name is Steven Lee Watson. I am 38 years of age and I currently live in Elkins, West Virginia with my wife, Charlotte, and family.

I am the same Steven Lee Watson who testified in the trial of Joseph Roger O'Dell during the month of August 1986 in Virginia Beach, Virginia. My testimony pertained to several "conversations" that I had with Mr. O'Dell during a period of time that we were both detained at the Virginia Beach Correctional Center in the 3A Medical Block. I am also the same Steven Lee Watson who provided a sworn affidavit on April 6, 1995 to members of Mr. O'Dell's defense team. In this affidavit I mentioned in greater detail the same "conversations" with Mr. O'Dell.

Since my testimony in Virginia Beach, I have been troubled about things that I said that are untrue but I have been afraid to come forward for fear of being charged and prosecuted for perjury. I can no longer live with the fact that Mr. O'Dell may die because of innocent statements made to me; statements that I later changed and passed on to Virginia Beach prosecutors in hopes that they would help me with charges that I had pending in West Virginia.

In February 25, 1985, my wife (Carolyn Watson) and I were arrested in Virginia Beach on a fugitive warrant out of West Virginia. We were both placed in the Virginia Beach Correctional Center. ON February 28, 1985 I was transferred to the 3A Medical Block Section of the jail where I was to receive treatment for a heart condition and complications with my hearing. This is when I first saw Mr. O'Dell but we did not say much to each other.

On March 1, 1985 Mr. O'Dell and I began to talk to each other. I recall telling Mr. O'Dell that I had been arrested on a fugitive warrant out of West Virginia and that I was charged with attempted murder, arson and several burglaries. Mr. O'Dell talked like he knew a lot about the law and after going over the charges against me, Mr. O'Dell told me that I would probably get a life sentence. Mr. O'Dell told me that if the prosecutors offered me a plea bargain, that I should take it. The truth is that I got so scared that I even thought about trying to escape but realized that this was not possible. I was in a terrible state of mind and was looking for a way to keep from being transferred back to West Virginia.

I asked Mr. O'Dell what he was in for and he told me in his words "they got me for strangling a woman and dumping her body." Mr. O'Dell told me that he had been to the County Line Lounge and described the Lounge as a place where one can drink and dance and have a good time. Mr. O'Dell told me that it was a nice place to meet women, buy them drinks and just have a good time.

1

Affidavit of Steven Watson

On the following day, March 2, 1985, I decided to create a story based on what Mr. O'Dell told me the previous night. I decided to tell the Virginia Beach prosecutors, in a letter that I wrote to Mr. Alberi, that Mr. O'Dell confessed to me that he killed the woman. I was hoping that the Virginia Beach prosecutor would want to keep me in Virginia Beach and not allow me to be extradited to West Virginia. I tried to make contact with the prosecutors through the jail deputies but I had no luck. On March 4, 1985 my wife and I were transported back to West Virginia by a state trooper by the name of John Reid and Deputy Paul Brady.

After arriving in West Virginia I continued my efforts to reach Mr. Alberi. I still had hopes that the prosecutors would help me with the charges in West Virginia if, in return, I would say that Mr. O'Dell told me that he killed the woman in Virginia Beach. I remember telling Mr. Alberi, either in a telephone conversation or in a letter, that I would not be able to testify for him if I was still in jail in West Virginia. I remember Mr. Alberi telling me that there was nothing that he could do for me. I later pled guilty to the several charges against me and received a three year probated sentence and the charges against my wife were dismissed. I thought about Mr. O'Dell and how scared he had gotten me. I soon forgot all about Mr. O'Dell and the story that I made up because my problems were over and things turned out good for me.

Several months later my wife and I returned to live and work in Virginia Beach. I began to work as a cab driver. During the month of August, 1985, Mr. Alberi called the home of Odessa Stancill (my mother-in-law) in Virginia Beach looking for me. I was visiting at the time of the call and spoke with Mr. Alberi. Mr. Alberi told me that he wanted me to testify in the trial of Mr. O'Dell. Mr. Alberi wanted me to testify about the "conversation" that I supposedly had with Mr. O'Dell during the time that we were together in the 3A medical block.

It was a nightmare all over again! The prosecution wanted me to testify about a story that I made up and I was afraid that if I told them that this was not true, they would arrest me and charge me with making a false statement. I decided that it would be best if I just didn't testify so I told Mr. Alberi that I did not want to testify. Mr. Alberi sounded angry when he told me that he would get a subpoena and force me to testify. At this point I really didn't know what to do so in my mind, I decided that if the police charged Mr. O'Dell with this crime, then he must have done it. I thought that there was probably enough evidence against him and my testimony would make very little difference.

Prior to testifying, I met with Mr. Alberi, Mr. Test and other prosecutors in their office and I was coached on how to answer their questions. People were asking me questions and telling me things and all that I kept thinking about was getting my testimony over with as quickly as possible.

2

Affidavit of Steven Watson

I want to make it clear. Mr. O'Dell never told me that he killed the woman. I changed the words around in hopes that it would help me with the criminal charges in West Virginia. I'm sorry that my false testimony has caused so many problems for Mr. O'Dell.

Further, affiant sayeth not.

Steven Lee Watson
Steven Lee Watson

Sworn to and subscribed before me on this 11th day of October, 1996.

Kimberly S Barlet
Notary Public

My commission expires on _August 31, 2003_

EXHIBIT II (CONTINUED)
APPENDIX TO PETITION FOR A WRIT OF CERTIORARI, VOLUME II
UNITED STATES SUPREME COURT
OCTOBER TERM, 1996
PAGE 246A

NEWS · Oct. 23, 1996

Steven Watson's letter recanting testimony against Joseph O'Dell

October 12, 1996

Paul, Weiss, Rifkind, Wharton and Garrison
1285 Avenue of the Americas
New York, New York 10019

Dear Mr. Smith:

I am writing to you because I want to help in the case of Joseph O'Dell. I testified at his trial in 1986. At his trial I said things which were not true about how Mr. O'Dell confessed to killing the woman in Virginia Beach. I need to make it clear to you and everybody else that Mr. O'Dell never confessed to me. I said the things that I did in order to help myself because I was afraid of facing a life sentence on my charges at the time I was in prison with him. I was never offered a deal in exchange for my testimony, although I tried hard to negotiate one. I believe that if the prosecutors would have investigated some of the statements that I made to them they would have immediately known that my statements were not true.

What I did was wrong and I want to help you in whatever way that I can to keep Mr. O'Dell from being executed for something he did not do. I feel very badly about the problems I have caused Mr. O'Dell and could not live with myself if anything ever happened to him. I have been afraid of being charged with perjury and that is why I never came forward until now. I must clear my conscience and tell the truth about what really happened and I am prepared to face the consequences. Please let me know how I can help you and whoever else is working on his case. I will help in any way I can to protect this terrible problem.

Thank you.

Sincerely,
Steven Lee Watson

RETURN TO CURRENT NEWS OR PAST NEWS

EXHIBIT III
OFFICIAL DOCUMENT FROM THE DEPARTMENT OF CORRECTIONS DENYING LEGITIMACY OF "MARRIAGE"

Mecklenburg Correctional Center
Boydton, VA 23917

M E M O R A N D U M

TO: J. O'DELL, 80330

FR: MR. NETHERLAND, WARDEN

DATE: 2/9/96

SUBJ: REQUEST FOR A CONTACT VISIT

Your request for a Contact Visit to take place on March 8, 1996
is disapproved based on the criteria identified in IOP 822.3.
Inmates who are assigned to Death Row may only have a contact
visit with their immediate family. You submitted a marriage
certificate of a Cherokee Indian Marriage that occurred on 12/11/94
to verify that you are married to a Ms. Lori Urs (the individual
that you are requesting to have present during the contact visit)

Our records indicate that you were confined at Mecklenburg Correctional
Center on 12/11/94. Per DOP/IOP 859, the intended spouse will
appear at the jurisdictional court to provide information for a
marriage license. The Clerk's office located in the Mecklenburg
County Court House has verified that a marriage license was
not issued to Ms. Lori Urs and that no such marriage has
been recorded in Mecklenburg County, Boydton, Virginia. If you
can provide information that this marriage has been recorded
in a court of law, then your request for a contact visit may be
re-considered. I encourage you to speak to your assigned counselor
regarding any future requests.

CC: Mr. Hester, AWP.
       Ms. Royster, Operations Officer
       Mr. Gayles, Counselor
       file

EXHIBIT IV
AFFIDAVIT OF INSURANCE INVESTIGATOR WILLIAM HONBARGER

State of Virginia

City of Norfolk

AFFIDAVIT

BEFORE ME, the undersigned authority on the 25th day of July, 1995, personally appeared William Honbarger, known to be being by me who first duly sworn on his oath deposed and said as follows:

My name is William Honbarger, I am 74 years of age and I currently live in Norfolk, Virginia with my wife.

I am the same William Honbarger who investigated (for the Travelers Insurance Company) the murder of Helen Schratner, who was last seen at the County Line Lounge in the Executive Inn in Virginia Beach. I am responsible for the investigation of the victims activity at the County Line on the evening of February 5, 1985, her body discovered on February 6, 1985 in the field behind the After Midnight Club.

I was employed by the Travelers Insurance Company to defend the Executive Inn against a lawsuit by the victims family for negligence arising from the establishment. During my investigation I interviewed several people who worked at the County Line and others who would have any knowledge about either the victim (Helen Schratner) or Joseph O'Dell, the suspect. After a complete investigation I found nothing to link the two persons together. I do recall that the investigation revealed that either the victim, someone who was in her party that evening or someone connected with the victim had a room at the Executive Inn the evening she was murdered. During my investigation I had occasion to speak with Virginia Bullard, the manger of the establishment, and I recall that she showed me the reservation; although I saw a record of the check-in, I do not recall the name or the time involved. I do remember that the room was on the southside of the motel and that the victims car was found on the southside of the motel. This seemed to be of importance during the investigation. The room 203 seems to ring a bell, although I cannot be sure that was the room.

During the investigation the police were apparently informed of the rooms at the motel and they concentrated their efforts on that one or two rooms in the motel. I do not recall how they knew about the room, just that they did and they concentrated on that one or two rooms in the motel.

I spent several days observing the trial and it was my gut feeling that Joseph O'Dell was an innocent man.

Further affiant sayeth not. Executed this 19th day to July, 1995.

William Honbarger
William Honbarger

25th
SWORN TO AND SUBSCRIBED BEFORE ME on this 19th day of July, 1995 to certify which witness my hand and seal of office.

Notary
Notary Public

EXHIBIT V
AFFIDAVIT OF JUROR CAROL KELLY

State of Virginia

City of Virginia Beach

AFFIDAVIT OF CAROL KELLY

Carol Kelly, being first duly sworn, hereby deposes and says as follows:

1.   My name is Carol Kelly and I live at 2573 Elon Drive, Virginia Beach, Virginia.

2.   I am the same Carol Kelly that served as a juror, in 1986, in the capital murder trial of the Commonwealth of Virginia vs. Joseph O'Dell III.

3.   The blood evidence was the main factor for ~~me~~ CK in reaching a decision on Mr. O'Dell's guilt.

4.   Because I was a registered nurse, I explained to the other jurors the significance of the blood test evidence. For this purpose, I drew on my professional knowledge of blood testing rather than just the testimony given at trial. I believed that my professional understanding of blood testing was correct, even if it was different from testimony at the trial.

5.   At the time of Mr. O'Dell's trial, I knew that the serology method of testing was considered to be more definitive than previous methods for limiting the number of people who might have been the source of the blood. It was my misimpression at that time that the kind of blood evidence presented at the trial was similar to fingerprinting in that no two people could have the same genetic markers on the serology tests. That is how I explained the test results to other members of the jury when, as a nurse, I attempted to help them understand the complicated blood evidence. I told the other jurors that the blood

evidence presented by the prosecution at the trial was a form of genetic chromosome typing and that no two people could have the same result on those tests.

6.   Years later, when DNA testing became popular, I believed that the blood evidence we had reviewed at Mr. O'Dell's trial must have been DNA test evidence.

7.   I learned very recently that the blood test results we reviewed at Mr. O'Dell's trial did not come from DNA testing or from any other form of testing that could uniquely identify a blood sample as coming from a particular person.

8.   Although I believed at the time of the trial that my explanation to the other jurors about the blood evidence was accurate, I realize in retrospect that ~~the way it was~~ ~~presented at trial was misleading~~ could have ~~the way it was~~ and that I inadvertently misled other members of the jury when I gave them extraneous information about blood testing.

9.   I learned recently that DNA testing was performed on Mr. O'Dell's shirt and jacket after the trial, and that the DNA test showed an exclusion on the shirt and an inconclusive result on the jacket. If I had had the results of such DNA tests at the time of trial, it would have created a reasonable doubt in my mind about Mr. O'Dell's guilt.

10.   In addition, I was informed recently that there was evidence, not presented at trial, that might have further raised a reasonable doubt about Mr. O'Dell's guilt. This evidence included a police report of the fight Mr. O'Dell testified about, which explained how he got blood on his clothes, a U.S. Navy Shore Patrol arrest report concerning the ~~would have substantiated his alibi~~ at the crime scene, fight and soil samples that were taken by the police but never introduced at the trial.

11.   It is only within the last year or so that I have been willing to disclose this information. If I had been approached earlier, I would not have disclosed this information to

anyone because I felt quite uncomfortable talking about the case because of my duty as a

juror. I would not have been willing to talk with anyone in any detail concerning this or

other factors related to the trial or deliberations.

Further, affiant sayeth not.

Carol Kelly
Carol Kelly
084-58-4932

Sworn to and subscribed before me on this 24th day

of July, 1996.

Notary Public
Rose m Nelson

My commission expires 1-31-98

About the Author

Lori St John graduated from the University of Connecticut and the Rutgers School of Law in Newark, New Jersey. For over a decade she practiced as a Certified Public Accountant. Volunteer work led her to seek a career in law where she first studied at the New England School of Law. A law journal member of the *New England Journal on Criminal and Civil Confinement*, she published *"Commonwealth of Virginia v. O'Dell: Truth and Justice or Confuse the Courts, the DNA Controversy"*, 25 NEW ENG. J. ON CRIM. & CIV. CONFINEMENT 311 (1999), which earned her the distinguished Scholar's Paper Award at the Annual Academic Convocation at the Suffolk University Law School Lawyers' Guild. While a student at the Rutgers School of Law she founded and directed the Innocence Project for Justice, as part of the Constitutional Litigation Clinic. At graduation she received the Eli Jarmel Memorial Prize, a Public Interest Award for "the student demonstrating the greatest interest and proficiency in public interest law". After graduation she continued to teach at the law school while practicing as an Associate Deputy Public Defender for the Adult Felony Division of the Essex County Public Defender's Office in Newark, New Jersey. She furthered her practice in Colorado where she litigated criminal cases in the adult felony court while also engaging in post-conviction appellate work for the Alternate Defense

Counsel for the State of Colorado. While a resident in Colorado she served as a committee member of the Colorado Innocence Project. Her entrepreneurial spirit led her to successfully engage in a mountain community real estate development project, creating a planned urban development outside of Denver. She currently resides in Florida and is an international speaker and educator.

Acknowledgments

In some regards this is the hardest page to write for there are so many people who have contributed to my story in one way or another. If I fail to include your name, rest assured it has more to do with the passage of time, and its ugly partner called age, than anything else. I have attempted to research the whereabouts, or current status, of many of those who helped me. Sadly, I learned of the passing of at least two people. My apologies if I got any information wrong.

First and foremost, I wish to thank my darling daughter Jennifer who has always been, and still is, my number one supporter. Miraculously, at age twelve, you knew the facts of the case better than anyone, besides your mother. Your strength and fortitude kept me solid on the journey and allowed me the time I needed to work on an issue so important. You were also incredibly grounded, which allowed me to plunge head first into the hardest, yet most rewarding work, I have ever known. Thank you, Jennifer, for your unwavering support and enduring what I know was a tough road alongside your mother. I could not have done this without you.

Walter, I know you have a bird's-eye view now. I could not have accomplished all I did without all you did for me. Your strength often came when the adversity I faced was at its peak. Thank you for standing by me and for the strength you always had in your own convictions.

Richard Reyna. For joining me as I forged blindly ahead into the unknown area of crime investigation. Your genuine care and concern for people who have felt the harsh whip of the justice system was refreshing and encouraging. Our journeys in Virginia will always remain memorable moments in my life.

Sister Helen Prejean. For stepping up and taking on my battle for Joe. Your gentle presence and quiet, and sometimes not so quiet, strength kept me moving in the last days of my journey. Your loving friendship is deeply valued by me.

Luciano Neri, Franco Danieli, Mario Occhipinti, Calogero (Rino) Piscitello, Giuseppe Scozzari, Rosa Jervalino Russo and her son Michelle. For your unwavering stance against the injustice in Joe's case and for your united efforts in bringing the Italian National Campaign to Save Joseph O'Dell to fruition. You, your staff and so many other Italian Parliament members were instrumental in giving a voice to Joseph O'Dell. And while it was a voice for one, it stood for the voice of many. I remain grateful for your open arms, warm hearts, and the love you demonstrated while making a difference for humanity. Also, for the Italian Parliament's official declaration to halt the execution.

Italy's Ambassador-His Excellency Signor Luigi Amaduzzi. Thank you for your support and for receiving me at the Parliament with a message from the president.

President Oscar Luigi Scalfaro. Sadly, I learned the late president passed in January 2012. I am grateful that he embraced my cause. For voicing the Republic of Italy's strong opposition to the execution of Joseph O'Dell, and for interceding for Joe by reaching out to President Clinton and the governor of Virginia. Italy's current president, Giorgio Napolitani, refers to Scalfaro as a "leading figure of the democratic political life in the various decades of the republic, a perfect example of coherence and moral integrity".

Speaker and President of the Senate (the most senior office of state after the presidency), Nicola Mancino. For a series of efforts you made on behalf of Joseph O'Dell, including writing a letter to Vice President Al Gore protesting the execution and receiving me in Italy.

Romano Prodi, Prime Minister of Foreign Affairs. For your support. I thoroughly enjoyed our brief time on the Italian national talk show.

Luciano Violante, President of the Camera dei Deputati (Chamber of Deputies) of the Italian Parliament. For your support of Joseph O'Dell. Wikipedia describes Violate as a "man who is particularly interested in questions of justice, the struggle against the Mafia and institutional reform".

Mayor Leoluca Orlando. You hold a very special place in my heart. For the honorary citizenship you gave to Joe; for your key role in the official declaration by the European Parliament; for your personal visit at the governor's office in Virginia and for all you did to transport Joseph to Italy for burial in Palermo. For your compassion and strength.

Piraino, member of the Italian Consulate in Virginia. For your staunch efforts in accomplishing a historical event by arranging for the international transport of Joe O'Dell's body from Virginia to Palermo, Italy.

Former Presidents of Todi, Milan, Perugia, Florence, Umbria, Milan, Rome, including President Chiti from the Region of Tuscany. For your voices, letters to Governor Allen and the President of the United States; for your kind reception in Italy and for the tokens of friendship and solidarity.

At the Vatican:

Monsignor Caccia. For your gentle nature, kindness and receiving me at the Vatican. You have etched an indelible impression on me to this day. Thank you for arranging my personal visit with Pope John Paul II, and for caring.

In memory of Father Gino Concetti. For your dedication and support of Joseph O'Dell and I during our campaign and for the coverage you gave him in the Vatican newspaper. You still bring a smile to my face.

Joaquin Navarro-Valls, Papal spokesman. For your outspoken words reflecting the support of the Pope for Joseph O'Dell.

Pope John Paul II. No words could ever describe the gratitude and respect I have for the late Pope John Paul II. Few people touched my life the way he did I was honored by his voice, his presence and the gift he bestowed upon me.

In Assisi:

Father Julius. For your message to save Joseph O'Dell and for receiving me in Assisi.

Father Nicola. For the wonderful tour and support of me while visiting in Assisi.

Worldwide:

Mother Teresa. She passed shortly after we spoke in Cape Cod. For her voice, her constant love for humanity and her messages to the president of U.S., Governor Allen, Joe's supporters and me. For her invitation to stay with her in Calcutta.

The European Parliament, representing countries such as Sweden, Belgium, France, Germany, and Spain. For the official declaration to save Joseph O'Dell and to perform DNA testing.

Reporters, Newspapers, TV and radio talk show hosts:

Joe Jackson. For your integrity. You are one of the most honest and fair-minded reporters I have come to know. Your strong convictions made a difference through your expressive voice at the *Virginian-Pilot*. Thank you for taking up the battle in trying to print the truth about the evidence in Joe's case, and for standing up to the newspaper when Alberi threatened to sue if the newspaper printed your story.

Giorgio Morelli. For your tenacity. You pushed Joe's story into the Italian media mainstream as much as you possible could. Your constant commitment was evident from the onset of the campaign.

Radio and TV talk shows: Rai Italia Radio, *Democracy Now*, Rai Italia 1, 2, and 3, *Maurizio Costanzo Show*, *Dinatello Raffi Show* and other radio shows that are too numerous to list.

Editors of the following newspapers: In Italy: For the constant and generous coverage you gave Joe. *Corriere Della Sera, La Stampa, la Repubblica* (Editor Vittorio Zucconi), *il manifesto, Il Messaggero, il Giornale, La Sicilia, Gionale Di Sicilia, il Mattino, Liberazione, il Mediterraneo, l'Unita, ItaliaOggi, il Popolo*. In Germany: *Frankfurter Rundschau; Tageszeitung*. American Press: *New York Times, Washington Post, Philadelphia Inquirer, Los Angeles Times*. And too many others to include.

Rick Smolan and staff from the *24 Hours in Cyberspace* project. For including Joseph O'Dell in the largest one-day, online, unprecedented, global event.

Nina Bernstein, who was largely responsible for circulating messages from Mother Teresa to President Bill Clinton, Governor George Allen, Joe O'Dell, his supporters and finally to me, connecting us in conversation before she passed in September 1997. For one of the most memorable events of my life.

Supporters:
National Law Society in Italy; President of the University of Italian Jewish Communities; Tullia Zevi; International Aquarian Movement for the Conscious; the more than 10,000 Italians and foreign citizens who faxed Governor George Allen to halt the execution; the estimated 5 million supporters in Italy who stayed up all night to watch the execution; the demonstrators on the U.S. Supreme Court steps in the pouring rain; the Franciscans in Assisi; the website supporters from Ireland, Denmark, United Kingdom, Australia, Switzerland, Canada, Spain, Netherlands, Holland, Brazil, and several other countries; Percy Ross, the Columnist.

Attorneys:
Clive Stafford Smith, Steve Rosenfield, David Bruck, George Kendall, John Blume, The American Civil Liberties Union (ACLU), Doug Curtis and Paul Enzina from the law firm Miller, Cassidy, Larocca & Lewin. For all your hard work and dedication to justice. Steve Rosenfield, for your detailed review of my manuscript for legal citations; for your assistance in the civil rights action on behalf of Joe O'Dell; and for helping with Steve Watson, the jailhouse snitch, when the Attorney General's office threatened him with perjury charges. You are a stand-up man with great integrity.

Richard Dieter, Death Penalty Information Center. For your support and wealth of information regarding the death penalty in America.

Scientific Experts: Barry Scheck. For your support of Joseph O'Dell's right to DNA testing and your exhaustive efforts in fighting for the rights of the innocent, while advancing new laws and public awareness of wrongful convictions; Michael Baden. For your *pro bono* post-conviction review of evidence in the O'Dell case; Diane Lavett, Joe O'Dell's scientific expert. For your conviction and attempt to bring justice to the courts of Virginia.

Michael Radelet, author and educator. For your support of Joe O'Dell.

Key witnesses/affiants:

Trooper John Reid. For your honesty, integrity, and your affidavit concerning the jailhouse snitch, Steve Watson.

In memory of William Honbarger. For your honesty, integrity and for the affidavit regarding the room at the Executive Inn, and your belief in Joe O'Dell's innocence.

My friends: Marie Gallagher for your constant love and support during my journey. When others wondered what the hell I was doing, you always knew I had a purpose and a mission. Danielle Velasquez, for your sweet character and constant belief in me, always shining a light on the blessings in life. Thom Gallen for your constant ear and friendship from the time you learned of this case to today. Doug Fields and Gail Port for your belief in me and the cause. Debbie Matthews, who heard about this case for years as I wrote it.

Dr. John F. Demartini, my loving partner. Your guidance and support has been instrumental in advancing my goal to ensure my mission reaches its destination. You inspire me, and your love is an ever present omnipotent source of all that I have come to learn through my journey. Your work, through the Demartini Institute, was in my heart even before I met you, and is what ultimately drew us together. Thank you for being you.

My editor, Ann Kempner Fisher, who was masterful at retaining my voice and who skillfully edited this book with unmatched expertise. You never lost sight of my mission and was able to stand in my shoes as you went through the journey with me, page by page.

My graphic designer, Marc Cohen, from www.mjcdesign.com. You are genius at your work. Thank you for believing in my story enough to take on an unknown author.

My proofreader, Hilary Westwood, whose precision and attention to detail is greatly appreciated, especially at the very end when I could not truly read it yet another time.

And finally, to Joseph O'Dell. For teaching me so much about humanity, and for believing in my capabilities as we fought to obtain justice. Your cause, the truth, became my mission.